CONCENTRATION, MERGERS, AND PUBLIC POLICY

CONCENTRATION, MERGERS, AND PUBLIC POLICY

YALE BROZEN

with the assistance of
George Bittlingmayer

Studies of the Modern Corporation
Graduate School of Business
Columbia University

MACMILLAN PUBLISHING CO., INC.
NEW YORK

Collier Macmillan Publishers
LONDON

Macmillan Publishing Co., Inc.
866 Third Avenue, New York, N.Y. 10022

Collier Macmillan Canada, Inc.

Library of Congress Catalog Card Number: 82–70080

Printed in the United States of America

printing number

1 2 3 4 5 6 7 8 9 10

Library of Congress Cataloging in Publication Data

Brozen, Yale
  Concentration, mergers, and public policy.

  Includes index.
  1. Industrial concentration.   2. Industrial
concentration––United States.   3. Trusts, Industrial––
United States.   4. Industry and state––United States.
I. Title.
HD2757.B76   1982   338.8'0973   82-70080
ISBN 0-02-904270-4   AACR2

STUDIES OF THE MODERN CORPORATION
Graduate School of Business, Columbia University

The Program for Studies of the Modern Corporation is devoted to the advancement and dissemination of knowledge about the corporation. Its publications are designed to stimulate inquiry, research, criticism, and reflection. They fall into three categories: works by outstanding businessmen, scholars, and professional men from a variety of backgrounds and academic disciplines; annotated and edited selections of business literature; and business classics that merit republication. The studies are supported by outside grants from private business, professional, and philanthropic institutions interested in the program's objectives.

RICHARD EELLS
Director

Contents

List of Tables   xiii

List of Figures   xix

Preface   xxi

INTRODUCTION   1

The Attention Paid to Concentration
Concentration Policy
Foreign Attitudes Toward Size and Concentration
Pre-1930 Attitudes in the United States
The Attitude Shift During the Great Depression
Revision in the 1970s
Collusion the Proper Target of Antitrust, Not
    Concentration
Do Concentration-Profit Correlations Demonstrate
    Rampant Collusion in Concentrated Industries?
Why Some Industries Are Concentrated
Misdirection in Current Antitrust Endeavors

CHAPTER 1   *Concentration in American Industry*   19

Clashing Views on Concentration and Competition
How Concentrated Is American Industry?
Industry and Aggregate Concentration Trends
Innovation and the Concentration Cycle

CONTENTS

The Number of Firms in the Concentration-Profit
    Cycle
Concentration of Diffused Industries
National Concentration Without Market
    Concentration
Conclusion

CHAPTER 2 *Measurement and Significance of
                Concentration*   46

Concentration Measurement by the Bureau of the
    Census
Census Concentration and Market Concentration

CHAPTER 3 *Benefits of Concentration*   56

The Primary Reason for Concentration
The Benefits to Wage Earners from Concentration
Concentration, Productivity, and Prices
Relative Productivity of Leading Firms
Concentration and Inflation
Concentration and International Competitiveness
The Effect of Learning
The Size of Firms and the Cost of Capital
Concentration, Firm Size, and Innovation
Conclusion

CHAPTER 4 *Determinants of Concentration*   91

Mergers, Entrenchment, and Inertia
The Centripetal Tendency of Concentration Ratios
The Effect of Competition on Concentration
The Shifting Equilibrium Structure and
    Competition
The Effect of Intra-Industry Profitability on
    Concentration
The Effect of High Industry Profitability on
    Concentration
Capital Intensity and Concentration
Wage Rates and Concentration

Contents

The Influence of Entry Barriers on Concentration
The Influence of the Postwar Revolution in
    Distribution on Concentration
Conclusion
Appendix: Risk and Concentration

CHAPTER 5   *Assumptions of the Concentration-
              Collusion Doctrine*   130

Two Crucial Assumptions: Cooperation and Entry
    Barriers
The Contribution of Oligopoly Theory
The Extension of Oligopoly Models to Actual
    Markets
How Many Firms Does It Take to Produce the
    Competitive Price?
Evidence of Competitive Behavior and the
    Interpretation of the Concentration-Collusion
    Doctrine
Conclusion

CHAPTER 6   *The Likelihood of Tacit Commercial
              Conspiracy*   147

The Economics of Explicit Collusion
Potential Competition and Entry Barriers
American Price-Fixing Conspiracies
Evidence from Abroad
The Economics of Tacit Collusion
Alleged Instances of Tacit Collusion
Conclusion

CHAPTER 7   *Do Leading Firms in Concentrated
              Industries Possess Market Power?*   186

The Administered Price Hypothesis
Concentration and Profits
Concentration and Productivity
The Profitability of Monopolizing by Dominant
    Firms

CONTENTS

The Perishability of Market Shares of Dominant
    Firms
Conclusion

CHAPTER 8   *Are U.S. Manufacturing Markets*
                Monopolized?   225

The Structural Test for Monopoly
A Dynamic Test for Monopolization
What the Data Show
Has American Manufacturing Grown Less
    Competitive?
Conclusion

CHAPTER 9   *Does Advertising Create Business*
                Power?   246

The New Economics of Advertising
Origin of the Entry Barrier View of Advertising
Advertising and Profits
Advertising and Entry
Advertising and Prices
Advertising and Concentration
Conclusion

CHAPTER 10   *An Empirical Test of Oligopoly*
                 Theories   277

Market Share Trends Postulated by Oligopoly
    Theory
Replication of the Shepherd-Kamerschen Tests
Regression Accounts for the Average Changes in
    Concentration
The Expanding Number of Firms Test
Conclusion

CHAPTER 11   *Aggregate Concentration: A*
                 Phenomenon in Search of Significance   309

Is Aggregate Concentration Increasing?
Some Causes of the Aggregate Manufacturing
    Concentration Trend

Contents

How Powerful Is One of the Top 200?
Bigness and Political Power
Conclusion

CHAPTER 12 *Mergers and Conglomerate Power*   330

Potential Predatory Pricing
Potential Reciprocity
Entrenchment and Potential Mutual Forbearance
Decline in Number of Potential Entrants
Mergers Increase Entry
Conclusion

CHAPTER 13 *Conglomerate Mergers and Efficiency*   350

Evidence Showing Mergers Improved Efficiency
Other Evidence of Conglomerate Efficiency
Sources of Conglomerate Efficiency
Conclusion

CHAPTER 14 *Policies Toward Concentration: An
            International Comparison*   359

U.S. Policy
European Community Policy
National Policies
Policy and Concentration
The Aims of U.S. Industrial Policy

CHAPTER 15 *Second Thoughts of Deconcentration
            Advocates*   386

Turner and Kaysen
Members of the Task Force on Antitrust Policy
Schwartzman, Weiss, and Simons
Stigler
Conclusion

CHAPTER 16 *Public Policy and Concentration*   395

Should Antitrust Aim at Reducing Concentration?
Should Horizontal Mergers Always Be Restrained?

Contents

Non-Horizontal Mergers and Aggregate
    Concentration
The Proper Focus of Antitrust Efforts

Index   409

About the Author   427

List of Tables

1-1	Cigarette Production Shares, 1910–80	20
1-2	Distribution of Manufacturers' Shipments by Four-Firm Concentration, 1935 and 1972	23
1-3	Four-Firm Concentration Ratios in Selected Industries, 1935–72	24
1-4	Rate of Return in Leading Firm and Industry Output in Three Industries and Pharmaceutical Research Investment and Output	34
1-5	Regressions with Log NO the Dependent Variable	37
3-1	Declines in Market Share of Selected Turn-of-the-Century Combinations	58
3-2	1890–1905 Consolidations with Large Market Shares Failing Within a Few Years after Their Formation	59
3-3	Production Worker Wage Rates in the Leading Four Firms and in Other Firms in Manufacturing Industries Categorized by Concentration in 1963	61
3-4	Wage Rates of Production Workers in Manufacturing Industries Categorized by Concentration, 1967 and 1972	64
3-5	Average Annual Productivity Growth and Price Change by Degree of Change in Industry Concentration	68

3-6	Indexes of Passenger Car List Prices and Market Shares, 1947–56	71
3-7	Ratios of Value-Added per Production Worker-Hour in Leading Four Firms to Second Four Firms by Concentration Quintile, 1972	73
3-8	Average Annual Percentage Price Change by Concentration Quartile, 1958–73	76
3-9	Annual Rate of Productivity Growth in Selected Countries, 1960–73 and 1973–79	77
3-10	Size of 100 Leading Foreign Industrial Firms Relative to 100 Leading U.S. Industrial Firms by Groups, 1965, 1977, 1980	78
3-11	Regressions of Profitability and Profitability Differences in First- and Second-Tier Firms, 1971	81
3-12	Estimates of Risk (Measured by Beta) by Firm Size, 1926–75	83
4-1	Percentage of Industries with Rising, Stable, or Declining Concentration by Concentration Level, 1947–72 and 1958–72	93
4-2	Industry and Product Group Concentration Ratios in "Highly Concentrated" Industries, 1963 and 1972	94
4-3	Rates of Return on Book Net Worth in Leading Firms (1936–40) and Four-Firm Concentration Ratios (1935, 1947) in Selected Industries	103
4-4	Total Ingot Production: U.S. Steel Corporation and Other Steel Producing Companies	108
4-5	Average Concentration Ratios and Wage Rates in Industry Quintiles Ranked by Depreciable Assets per Employee, 1972	110
4-6	Changes in Value-Added, Employment, and Number of Establishments for Several Low-Wage Industries by Type of Operation: 1947–54, 1954–58	112
4-7	Net Entry by Concentration Quintiles, 1947–72 and 1967–72	116
6-1	Sales of Leading Cigarette Brands, 1930–39	178

List of Tables

7-1   Bureau of Labor Statistics Price Indexes for Tranquilizers and National Bureau of Economic Research Price Indexes Based on Transaction Prices, 1957–66   190

7-2A   Profitability Trends in Selected High-Concentration Industries, 1953–57 to 1962–66   195

7-2B   Movement of Averages of Industry Profit Rates Within Concentration Deciles for 42 Selected Industries, 1936–40 to 1953–57   196

7-2C   Movement of Average Accounting Rate of Return on Net Worth for 19 Selected Concentrated Industries Classified by Barriers to Entry, 1950–60 to 1961–66   196

7-3   Average of Industry Profit Rates within Concentration Deciles, 1936–40   198

7-4   Rates of Return, Standard Deviations of Rates of Return, and Concentration-Return Correlations for 141 Manufacturing Industries, 1947–68   199

7-5   Regressions Measuring the Influence of Several Variables on Profitability   200

7-6   Predicted (1910) and Actual Rates of Return of Leading "Dominant" Firms   210

7-7   Predicted (1935) and Actual Rates of Return of "Dominant" Firms   213

8-1   Return on Net Worth in Leading Manufacturing Corporations and Rank by Industry Group, 1948 and 1956   232

8-2   Return on Net Worth in Leading Manufacturing Corporations and Rank by Industry Group, 1966 and 1979   234

8-3   Intertemporal Correlations of Rates of Return for Concentrated, Unconcentrated, and Ambiguous Industries, 1919–28, 1947–57, and 1958–68   236

8-4   Profit Rate in Major Manufacturing Industries, 1850–60   240

8-5	Profit Rate in Major Manufacturing Industries, 1860–70	241
9-1	Profit Rates and Advertising Intensity	256
9-2	Average Intertemporal Correlations of Profit Rates for Restricted Values of the Bias Indicator (BI)	260
9-3	Regressions Explaining Changes in Market Structures, 1952–70	264
9-4	Regressions of Industry Advertising-to-Sales Ratios on Concentration Ratios, 1963	268
9-5	Investment and Payroll per Dollar of Shipments in Industries Ranked by Concentration Ratios	271
9-6	Regressions with the Log of the Four-Firm Concentration Ratio the Dependent Variable	272
10-1	Industry, Product Group, and Value-Added Four-Firm Concentration Ratios, 1935–72, in Industries 75 Percent Concentrated or More at Some Point	280
10-2	Summary of Concentration Changes in High-Concentration Industries	288
10-3	Percentage of 163 Selected Four-Digit Industries Showing Rising, Stable, or Declining Concentration by Concentration Quartiles, 1947–72	292
10-4	Regression of Changes in Industry Concentration on 1947 Deviation of Concentration from the All-Industry Average	293
10-5	Average Actual and Predicted Concentration of Industries in Later Years That Were 75 Percent Concentrated or More in 1947 and Their 1947 Average	295
10-6	Concentrated Industries with Increasing Concentration and Number of Firms	297
10-7	Concentrated Industries with Decreasing Concentration and Number of Firms	298
11-1	Leading Nonfinancial Corporations' Shares of All Nonfinancial Corporate Assets	310

11-2   Shares of Manufacturing Value-Added and Ship-
        ments of the Largest Manufacturing Compa-
        nies of 1947 and of Each Census Year,
        1937–77   313

11-3   Assets/Sales Ratio for the Largest and for All Man-
        ufacturing Corporations, 1947–67   316

11-4   Shares of Manufacturing Employment and Earn-
        ings Provided by the Largest Manufacturing
        Companies, 1937–77   321

11-5   Import Quotas of Refineries as Percent of Daily
        Input of Petroleum   324

12-1   Corporation, Business Enterprise, and Entrepre-
        neurial Populations of the United States,
        1945–75   344

13-1   Comparisons of Value-Added and Wages per Em-
        ployee in Conglomerate Firms and Single-
        Industry Firms   353

13-2   Legal Costs per Million Dollars of Sales by Firm
        Size   355

14-1   The World's Leading Industrial Firms   362

14-2   Shares of World Iron and Steel Sales, 1962, 1972,
        and 1979   369

14-3   1962 Sales Rank and Percentage Increase in Sales,
        1962–78   377

14-4   Distribution of Sales of the World's Largest Firms,
        by Industry and Geographical Area, 1962–72   378

List of Figures

3-1   Price Fluctuations in Three Groups of Manufacturing Industries   66

12-1   Earnings of Stockholders of Acquired Firms Relative to Average Stockholder Earnings in the Four Years Preceding Acquisition Announcement   337

12-2   Returns of Stockholders to Acquiring Firms   338

Preface

HAVING been brought up in a community of small business proprietors in a populist section of the Midwest, I began my studies in economics prejudiced against large corporations and chain store octopi. Inventor-entrepreneurs and founders of small firms were my heroes. The bureaucrat, whether in government or business, was simply a cowardly guardian of the status quo. Much of my early training in formal economics reinforced my prejudice against corporate giants.

Subsequent experience and research forced me to alter my views. Participation in antitrust cases, analyses of markets, examinations of data, study of industrial history, and my experiences as a consumer drove home the realization that I would pay a high price if arbitrary checks were imposed on the growth of business firms. For reasons that I had not before thoroughly examined, large firms attract buyers for their products, capital to finance their operations, and workers to the jobs they offer. I concluded that I was not willing to pay the price required to indulge what were, after all, only my prejudices.

Some of the reasoning and data that led me to recognize the cost of a wholesale business deconcentration program are assembled in this volume. I would not support programs to promote the growth of large enterprises, such as have been common in England, France, Japan, and many other countries, but neither would I endorse restraints, such as many of those already in place in the United States, in order to slow their growth.

This book is a partial report on a revolution in economics—in that part of the field called industrial organization—which is nearly complete in the professional journals. Unfortunately, the fruits of that revolution have not yet appeared in the textbooks used in economics courses. They have barely surfaced in the most recent antitrust law books. The revolution is beginning to make an impression on the policies of antitrust agencies and on judges' decisions. But the antitrust bar is still for the most part busily reaching for windfall gains and creating deadweight losses (costs that produce no benefits) on the basis of obsolete economic analysis.

A brief survey of the state of opinion among the scholars who have substantially increased our knowledge in this area will illustrate how far removed most antitrust policy has been from actual economic life. There is hardly a leading industrial organization economist who still takes seriously the notion that a few firms selling most of a product automatically conspire either tacitly or explicitly—a notion once widely accepted. Even less accepted today is the assertion that advertising is a barrier to entry. It was once widely believed that economies of scale create natural monopolies or oligopolies that must somehow be restrained—by regulation if not by antitrust. Today this notion is being questioned in quite fundamental ways and can claim virtually no adherents among the leaders of the field. Vertical integration and vertical restraints are no longer regarded as paths to monopoly or as possessing a potential for lessening competition. Conglomerates were never taken as a threat by leading industrial organization economists. And the notion that reducing a price should ever be ruled an antitrust violation is regarded as an anticompetitive doctrine that should be discarded from the law.

Robert Bork, in *The Antitrust Paradox,* with the help of some of the insights of modern industrial organization theory, analyzed the unsatisfactory state of antitrust law from the point of view of a legal scholar. In many ways, this book parallels his endeavor from the point of view of an economist. By producing it, I hope that news of the revolution already nearly finished in the professional literature will be carried to those who do not follow the studies reported there.

In writing this book, I tried to avoid using the "priestly" language in which economists talk to each other. While that language shortcuts the need for much verbiage, it makes too much material inaccessible to the interested student with little training in economics. Generally, I have provided numerical data in tabular form as a substitute for correlation coefficients and regression equations, but that is not possible in all cases. Occasionally a multiple variable equation presents the data in a useful form. I have set such regression results down for those who find them intelligible.

The origin and writing of this work owes much to many people.

Professor Benjamin Rogge suggested the subject for a series of lectures at a Liberty Fund Conference at Wabash College, which he directed in July 1979. The audience for those lectures included philosophers, historians, sociologists, political scientists, and a few economists. It was there that the idea for a less technical discussion of the issues of bigness and concentration blossomed. Earle Birdzell, Robert Nitschke, and Brent Upson stimulated some of the earlier research and thinking, which went into the formulation of the conclusions expressed here; but they are not necessarily in agreement with every point. Professor Sam Peltzman, Katherine Hart, Marie Cavaleri, and Larry Siegel had an embarrassing penchant for finding inconsistencies and infelicities of expression.

James Ellert, Aldy Keene, and Mustafa Mohatarem assembled much of the data that are reported here or that were used to draw inferences and check conclusions. My debt to colleagues and to predecessors is obvious in the many citations. A special debt is owed to Marilyn Ashley, who struggled to transcribe handwritten materials into a legible typescript and orderly tables.

I am grateful to Chauncey G. Olinger, Jr., the Editorial Consultant to the Program for Studies of the Modern Corporation at the Graduate School of Business of Columbia University, who edited the manuscript and translated the "economese" that did creep into the text—despite my good intentions—into English. George Bittlingmayer did much of the literature search, suggested data sources, wrote some sections of this book, and rewrote other sections. His work is so intertwined with my own that he should be called a co-author, but he declined.

Financial support was provided by the General Electric Foundation, the Kaiser Aluminum Company, the Business Roundtable, the American Enterprise Institute for Public Policy Research, and the Graduate School of Business at the University of Chicago. Any inaccuracies or illogic may be blamed on the stubbornness with which I cling to my errors.

CONCENTRATION, MERGERS, AND PUBLIC POLICY

Introduction

B IG Business perennially concerns the Congress and offers a conveniently large target for congressional darts.[1] Will Big Business take over all economic activity? Yes, if you choose to believe the recurring horror tale told by witnesses at committee hearings and echoed in Federal Trade Commission (FTC) staff reports. They follow the tradition of the 1932 Berle and Means book, *The Modern Corporation and Private Property*. It painted trends, which, if continued, the book said, would result in all nonfinancial business assets being owned by 200 corporations by 1969. The FTC added, in its 1948 report on mergers: "No great stretch of the imagination is required to foresee that if nothing is done to check the growth in concentration . . . the giant corporations will ultimately take over the country."[2]

The Attention Paid to Concentration

The Temporary National Economic Committee, created by the Congress in 1938, produced a shelf of reports and monographs on Big Business. Aggregate and industrial concentration occupied lead roles in those reports. The committee recommended doing something about industrial concentration.[3] Postwar congressional hearings produced more volumes on the subject, despite the 1950

1

enactment of the Celler-Kefauver Amendment to the Clayton Act, the aim of which was to nip incipient concentration by horizontal merger in the bud.[4]

The industries on which these acres of print focus are those in which the four largest firms produce more than 50 or 70 percent of domestic output. (Four is the magic number since the Bureau of the Census does not disclose data for any smaller number.) The largest firms in "concentrated" industries are frequently viewed with a suspicious eye for no reason other than their unusual size and apparent success. The impression emerges that producing more is bad. That is, after all, what makes a firm dominant or, at least, an oligopolist. To produce less, then, must be good. But then why are we concerned about our slowing growth and limping productivity?

Some fear that leading firms in concentrated industries control output and prices in ways adverse to the interest of consumers and the nation. To prevent this, a White House task force proposed legislation to limit any one firm's share of an industry's domestic output. Bills introduced in the Congress from time to time would break up firms with industry shares exceeding 15 percent where the four-firm share exceeds 50 or 70 percent. This would put a ceiling on the amount of any one product produced by a business. Those who might price a product attractive enough to sell more than the ceiling amount would have to refrain from doing that. Other bills would forbid acquisitions by large firms and make antitrust laws more stringent, all in the name of preventing these feared adverse effects.[5]

Although such proposals have received support, this support materializes largely in disregard of the relevant facts. Do large corporations in centralized industries have the power attributed to them? Are big enterprises less productive and competitive than the smaller concerns that might replace them? Would a lack of large domestic companies in some industries mean that we would find ourselves out-competed by foreign firms for markets at home and abroad? Is the traditional hostility of American government toward large-scale business compatible with solutions to the problems of productivity growth and the efficient use of resources? And finally, can we even answer these questions by any means other than allowing markets to provide the experiments necessary to identify the appropriate sizes of firms in various industries?

Concentration Policy

Despite a long history of study and debate about the role of the large corporation, the effects of "dominant" firms, and the consequences of industrial concentration, vigorous advocacy continues for various diverging public policy prescriptions. Depending on to whom one listens, we would be best served by a policy of (1) dissolving large corporations with sizeable assets or market shares ("bust-'em up"),[6] (2) restricting mergers, (3) letting the market determine business size,[7] or (4) deliberately promoting growth in firm size.[8] With growing international and inter-product competition and the loss of leading positions in many world markets to foreign firms, much of the discussion of the market power of U.S. companies seems quaint. Yet the Congress continues to devote extensive hearings to the subject.

Debate in the United States focuses on the first three policies. Existing legislation restricts mergers and cooperation among firms, often going to absurd lengths. An antitrust case was brought against the automobile manufacturers, for example, for exchanging research and technical information to assist each other in the development of smog-control devices. As a consequence, the cooperation was ended. Each company was forced to bear the entire expense—a good deal of it redundant—of meeting emission standards. Merger and antitrust policies are not the only policies directed at firm size. Tax and subsidy policies favor small firms and restrain the growth of large firms. The expansion of banking firms is hobbled by such devices as restrictions on branching.

Antitrust has slowed the expansion of large firms by means other than just the prevention of mergers. The antitrust agencies threaten leading companies with antitrust action if they choose to serve more customers. Also, antitrust law is used to prohibit companies from doing certain kinds of business or competing for certain kinds of business.[9] In addition, the agencies impose heavy costs on large firms with antitrust demands and litigation. These consume resources that would otherwise be used to raise production and to expand capacity. The Federal Trade Commission, for example, served subpoenas on American Motors, Chrysler, Ford,

3

and General Motors demanding data and documents that would cost each from several million to 110 million dollars to assemble.[10] Similar burdens are being laid on IBM, on American Telephone & Telegraph, and on the eight leading oil refiners in current antitrust cases. The FTC forced Brown & Williamson, the third-ranking cigarette company, to spend $800,000 to provide documents concerning its advertising practices over the past fourteen years for no discernible reason other than staff inquisitiveness.[11]

Government agencies and the courts aim at reducing concentration or restraining its rise in some industries. They ignore it in others. Only in the regulated utility industries is concentration promoted (by preventing entry through the grant of exclusive franchises and refusing to grant certificates of public convenience and necessity to those desiring to enter these industries).[12]

Foreign Attitudes Toward Size and Concentration

Abroad, growth of large firms is encouraged.[13] The supporters of this approach argue that large firms compete more effectively in world markets. Increased firm size provides scope for superior management. More rapid innovation, higher wage rates, the efficiencies of large scale, and expansion of output and trade accompany growth in business size. The U.S. economy's once-rapid growth, especially around the turn of the century, and its high per capita income, they argue, were the consequences of the size of U.S. firms. Slower U.S. growth in recent years they attribute in part to the restrictions placed on the growth of U.S. firms or, at least, to the burdens laid on large concerns. They see growing idle capacity and a waste of capital in some industries because expanding firms are forced to build new plants instead of being allowed to acquire capacity by merger. They also see some U.S. corporations in leading positions in their industries going to such lengths as building additional capacity outside U.S. boundaries, rather than expanding at home, in order to avoid an antitrust attack based on their share of domestic production. Rather than permit this to happen in their own companies, they encourage expansion at home.

Japan, for example, gives special assistance to the formation of larger firms by merger and growth. Its leading corporations grow

4

increasingly large relative to the largest in the United States. A government-promoted merger in 1969, for example, created Nippon Steel, the world's largest steel firm. Its annual output surpasses U.S. Steel by millions of tons (31.2 million metric tons produced in 1978 versus 28.4 million metric tons by U.S. Steel).[14] The impressive Japanese economic miracle is associated with rapidly increasing relative firm size. Japanese corporations producing electrical equipment, machinery, ships, and motorcycles, as well as steel and automobile concerns, have surged to leading positions in the global market. Only one Japanese firm was listed among the world's fifty largest industrials in 1967. And it was number fifty. Now there are six (Table 14-1). Similarly, the German economic miracle is associated with a growth in the relative size of German firms. They now have seven listed among the world's fifty largest industrials—up from only two in 1967.

Other countries, noting the pre–World-War-I example of the United States and the post–World-War-II experience of Japan, have encouraged the growth of firm size and concentration in their own industries. Hoechst in Germany has become the world's largest chemical company, surpassing du Pont. Roche, in Switzerland, has become the largest pharmaceutical firm, surpassing Merck. The United Kingdom has encouraged mergers in its textile and automobile industries by government subsidies. France and Germany have assisted the growth of their leading computer manufacturers while the United States has hobbled IBM with a costly antitrust suit. The French government assisted the mergers that made Peugot-Citroen Europe's largest and the world's third largest automobile company with a one-billion franc loan.

Other countries encourage the growth of leading companies to global scale to make them effective competitors in foreign markets, especially markets in the United States, once the primary home of the largest corporations.[15] Professor F. M. Scherer, noting attitudes in other countries, remarks that

> Those who read extensively in both the American and European industrial organization literature cannot avoid being struck by the contrast in emphasis. American economists seldom get very excited about scale economies, while for the typical European industry analyst, the day begins and ends with an impassioned tract on the advantage of size. . . . Only big affluent nations . . . can afford to be callous about scale economies.[16]

Other governments deliberately promote growth in firm size not only to be competitive outside their national boundaries but also to meet the competition of foreign companies—particularly American companies—in their domestic markets. In many industries only the economies of scale and increased productivity brought about by size make it possible to compete domestically with the large foreign manufacturers who have overcome the handicaps of distance, tariffs, and cultural differences.[17]

Pre-1930 Attitudes in the United States

Economists who observed first-hand the industrial combinations formed around the turn of the century were not concerned about this growth in concentration. They were not alarmed about possible adverse consequences of very large market shares in the hands of *single* firms, much less in the hands of a few firms. They saw firms with 50 to 90 percent market shares lose their markets —many going into bankruptcy or reorganization—when they attempted to profit by raising prices above competitive market levels.[18] Those consolidations that reduced costs, increased efficiency, and improved their products prospered. They maintained their positions only if they made cost reduction and product improvement continuous activities.

Pre-1930 economists viewed the rise of the large corporation as a response to changes in technology, particularly in transportation, but also in communications and mass-production techniques. They saw the market (customers and competitors) controlling the large company. They saw small firms become large by offering superior products or lower prices. They saw the large corporation benefiting consumers by making lower-priced and improved products available.[19] They praised the installation of research departments and the systematization of innovation by large corporations as contributions to progress. With few exceptions the prevailing attitude came to verge on "the bigger the better."

The Attitude Shift During the Great Depression

During the Great Depression of the 1930s and the inflation of the 1940s and the early 1950s, a new group of economists arose seeking an explanation of these woes. They concluded that markets did not work and sought a reason. Misunderstanding the role of erratic money growth-rates coupled with recursive expectations, they attributed the failure of markets to maintain full employment in the 1930s to downward price rigidity. They blamed the postwar inflation on upward price flexibility and "unliquidated monopoly power" in concentrated industries. They *assumed* that concentration automatically led to collusion among leading firms or to interdependent pricing equivalent to tacit collusion. They assumed that these alleged conspiracies restrained output, raised prices to monopoly or near-monopoly levels, and kept them there in the face of falling demand in times of recession.

In their endeavor to blame market failure for the Great Depression, post-1930 economists not only ignored the perversity of monetary policy but also overlooked the role of government in preventing price and wage adjustments. President Hoover's appeal to the business community in 1930 to maintain wage rates (which, he argued, would maintain purchasing power) made wage adjustments unpatriotic. The Smoot-Hawley Tariff of 1930 drastically decreased competition from foreign producers (and decreased American exports as well as imports). The passage of the Davis-Bacon Act in 1931 introduced rigidities in the construction market. The Farm Board tried to prevent adjustments in agricultural prices. The National Industrial Recovery Act and the Agricultural Adjustment Act of 1933 installed wage and price floors. And the regulatory commissions went so far as to raise rates in the face of falling demand. These acts by government created price and wage rigidities that deepened and prolonged the Great Depression.

Revision in the 1970s

A revisionist group of economists is now gaining ground. Its analyses show that the woes originally attributed to industrial concentration in fact followed from inappropriate monetary and fiscal programs and from lags in the adjustment of expectations to unexpected changes in monetary policies. Also, the alleged perverse behavior of concentrated industry prices is now known to be an illusion created by the use of inaccurate and incomplete data.[20]

Many prominent modern economists and students of antitrust

who once favored a deconcentration policy no longer do so. Demonstrations of the faultiness of the investigations of prices, profits, and productivity, which had indicted concentration, changed their minds. Those whose views were based on studies done from 1935 to 1970 now know that those inquiries employed inaccurate data, used unrepresentative industry and firm samples, misinterpreted the statistical relationships found, applied inadequate methodology, classified industries subjectively, and misrepresented historical trends and associations. To some extent, the faultiness of those studies may be attributed to the researchers' preconceived opinions that concentration is anticompetitive. Since a large number of firms in an industry makes it competitive, according to the textbooks, anything else must be noncompetitive. This view became encrusted in the structure-conduct-performance paradigm. Structure was assumed to determine conduct, which determined performance. Only recently has it again dawned on analysts that the reverse causation operates, that is, that *performance and conduct determine structure*.[21]

These flawed statistical examinations and the loose theorizing that accompanied them supported the assumed equivalence of high concentration and collusion (at least tacit if not explicit). Their authors urged that large firms in concentrated industries be dissolved to eliminate collusion (shared monopoly). But the occurrence of effective collusion or interdependent pricing equivalent to effective collusion was assumed, not demonstrated. They failed to demonstrate that the slightly higher profits earned in leading firms in some concentrated industries (which was the main ground for the belief that collusion was rampant in concentrated industries) were a result of supracompetitive pricing (prices raised above the level that would prevail with many firms competing for business).[22] They neither examined nor suggested as a possibility the alternative hypothesis that superior profits could be earned by reducing costs and that large market shares could be earned by superior performance. Higher profits were assumed to be proof of inferior performance, that is, proof that prices were raised by firms in concentrated industries once these industries became concentrated.

Readers of the concentration literature should be astounded that the correlations of concentration and profitability were taken as proof of inferior performance. If a firm continually innovates and improves efficiency faster than its competitors, offering attractive products at competitive prices, would it not be expected that it would attract a large share of the customers in its markets and be more profitable? Would not the greater profitability of leading firms and their large sales share, then, be a demonstration of outstanding performance? How can these results be interpreted as indicators of collusive conduct and poor performance? Benjamin Fairless put it well in 1950:

> The size of any company depends, in the first instance, upon the product it intends to manufacture—upon the amount of money it is going to take to buy the plants, machines and tools that will be necessary to produce that product efficiently and competitively. From that point on, the growth of the company depends on its customers. If they like the product and want to buy more of it, the company will have to expand to meet their demands. If they don't like the product there is no way on earth that the company can force them to buy, no matter how big . . . it may be. That is why today's giant must be useful, helpful, and necessary or he simply goes out of business because he failed to serve his customers to their satisfaction and therefore failed to serve the public interest.
>
> . . . In industry or in sports, concentration is the result of competition. If the top teams in any baseball league don't win the highest percentage of games, how are they going to stay on top? And when the top companies in any industry win the highest percentage of the customers, they naturally are going to have the highest percentage of the business.[23]

Collusion the Proper Target of Antitrust, Not Concentration

Critics of the concentration-collusion doctrine suggest that antitrust laws should aim at *collusion,* not concentration. They point out that concentration and collusion are not associated in any predictable way. The critics contend that tacit collusion is unworkable and unlikely; when collusion occurs it will be express and actionable under present antitrust laws.[24] Therefore, no need exists for a mechanistic deconcentration program, such as that advocated by Professors Turner and Kaysen and by the Neal Task Force.

These critics also suggest that collusion occurs most frequently in *low-profit* industries. It occurs in low-profit industries, whether concentrated or unconcentrated, because profitable industries attract entry and cartels cannot survive in the face of entry. Recent empirical studies demonstrate that collusion is *negatively* related to profitability.[25] This destroys the major premise of most of the studies, which conclude that concentration produces results equivalent to those expected with explicitly collusive behavior. Even those who still adhere to a deconcentration policy now speak of concentration *facilitating* collusion, instead of automatically causing it. Also, these adherents now cite the necessity of entry barriers for collusion to succeed in elevating prices. The steady erosion of the concentration-collusion doctrine should lead us to a thorough reexamination of the now ancient calls for universal deconcentration and the perennial, reflexive opposition to any and every increase in centralization.

Do Concentration-Profit Correlations Demonstrate Rampant Collusion in Concentrated Industries?

The major finding in the pre-1970 studies was a positive relationship between concentration and profits. The authors *assumed* that the correlation constituted evidence that collusion elevated prices in highly concentrated industries. The profit measure usually used was the accounting rate of return on assets or equity of existing firms. This in itself made the studies suspect. Conventional balance sheets and income statements do not allow for (1) intangible capital, (2) inflation, (3) age of assets, or (4) write-offs of past investments in unsuccessful projects. Because the studies were confined to surviving firms, they neglected the capital investment of defunct firms. In risky industries, where many firms invest in unsuccessful projects and consequently disappear, this resulted in understating the total amount of capital needed to produce the observed profits. Hence, industry rates of return were overstated.

The higher profits believed to be prevalent in concentrated industries were attributed to successful collusion in those industries. Even if we ignore the problems raised by the use of accounting measures of profit, this has now been shown to be an invalid inference.

> *First,* accounting profits are positively related to concentration only in some years, not all years.

Second, if collusion were the source of excess profits, not only would large firms be more profitable in concentrated industries than in unconcentrated, but smaller firms in concentrated industries sheltered under the price umbrella of colluding major firms would be more profitable than the smaller firms in more atomistic industries. They are not. Also, the second largest firm tends to be less profitable than the largest in concentrated but not in dispersed industries. This indicates that the efficiencies of large size and superior performance are major reasons for high concentration.

Third, the *largest* firms in almost *all* industries are more productive than smaller firms in the same industries. Since leading firms constitute the bulk of a concentrated industry, average profit rates in such an industry will be above the average of all industries to the extent that higher profits accompany lower costs. This circumstance, and not concentration, caused the positive concentration-profit relationship in those years in which it occurred. Profits in concentrated industries were found to be a result of 20 percent *lower costs,* accompanied by 10 to 15 percent *lower prices,* than would prevail following the dissolution of the leading firms in concentrated industries.

Fourth, the concentration-profitability relationship weakened or disappeared when other causes were admitted into the design of regressions. The correlations that had been found were weak. They weakened further when some of the omitted variables explaining accounting measures of profitability were incorporated into profit-concentration regressions.[26]

Fifth, profitable concentrated industries (and profitable diffused industries) were shown to be profitable because of disequilibria. Unanticipated changes in demand or in cost had created the situation. These disequilibria were temporary. They disappeared as competition led to adjustments moving these industries toward long-run equilibria.

Why Some Industries Are Concentrated

Concentrated industries become concentrated (and some firms become and remain "dominant") because that is the road to greater efficiency and lower costs *in those* industries. A number of factors—accumulated experience in individual firms, economies of scale, superior management, decreases in the number of less-than-optimum size plants, and capital-intensive technology coupled with the lower cost of capital to large firms—produce the lower costs. Numerous other factors, ranging from the reduction of risk for firms and customers to greater investment in the training of workers, also decrease costs in large firms and enable large firms to provide better service to customers in some cases.

These factors account for the concentrated industries, which emerge from an earlier, diffused state. Other industries are born concentrated, based on a product innovation. Aluminum and rayon are premier examples. To the extent that the factors discussed above are at work, they may remain in a centralized state. But if they are very profitable and the pioneering firms fail to expand rapidly and provide a sufficient supply to depress price and drive profits down to the long-run equilibrium level, entry soon diffuses them.

The continuing existence of a dominant firm, or group of dominant firms—the persistence of dominance in the absence of governmentally granted franchises—is evidence of lower costs and better customer service in those firms than can be provided by new entrants or the expansion of small firms. It is evidence of competitive behavior that depresses prices to levels unattractive to entry or to the continuance of many small-scale operations.

The fact that leading firms with a large share of domestic production perform outstandingly in some industries should not be interpreted as meaning that all industries not yet as concentrated should be forced in the same direction. A policy of encouraging mergers or subsidizing the growth of large firms—the practice in many other countries—may be as unwarranted as a deconcentration policy. Economies of scale are not available in every industry, neither is it universally the case that management in a few firms is outstandingly superior to that of other firms in the same industry. Some industries produce more efficiently if concentrated, some if not concentrated. No magic formula applicable to all industries and all circumstances exists. We should not try to fit every industry to some Procrustean bed.

Misdirection in Current Antitrust Endeavors

The current attack on aggregate concentration and conglomerate mergers (S.#600 and S.#1246, 96th Congress) also rests on specious fears and biased data. Although aggregate concentration in manufacturing increased between 1947 and 1963, the 1947 level was a drop from the mid-1930s level. There is not a rising aggregate concentration trend in the largest fifty manufacturing

12

firms and only a slight trend in the largest 200 from the prewar years (see Table 11-2, colums 4 and 9). Furthermore, the share of nonfinancial corporate assets owned by the 200 largest nonfinancial corporations has been shrinking. From 49.2 percent in 1929, their share has declined to 39.1 percent in 1975. Professor Sylvester Petro, after examining trends in both aggregate and industry concentration, concluded that, "The . . . fear of an ever increasing concentration of economic power, reflected murkily in antitrust thinking, lacks a basis in either fact or theory."[27]

Conglomerate mergers have had little effect on aggregate concentration. Preventing such mergers would prevent the transfer of assets from poor to good management, decrease the rewards of successful entrepreneurs, decrease entry, hurt the efficiency of capital markets, and slow productivity growth. A slower rise in real wage rates and national income would result.

The restraints on large firm growth imposed by public policy in the United States probably have restrained productivity growth.[28] In contrast to U.S. policy, public policy in many other countries encourages large firm growth. There may be a causal relationship underlying the correlation between the more rapid expansion of large firms abroad in the postwar years (Table 3-10) and the more rapid rise of productivity in other industrial countries (Table 3-9), although other factors also play a role.[29] The endeavors aimed at maintaining diffused industrial structures in the United States have slowed the growth of firms with outstanding performance. These would otherwise have concentrated their industries, but they also would have brought improved productivity, lower prices, and higher average product quality to their industries.

The Antitrust Division and the Federal Trade Commission, in focusing their investigations on concentrated and increasingly concentrated industries and on dominant firms, are misallocating public resources.[30] If inflation is the issue, monetary and fiscal policy are the appropriate instruments. Price rises in concentrated industries and in industries with dominant firms have been more moderate than those in the less concentrated industries. (The most dramatic price rises in major consumer goods have been in food, housing, medical care, and primary energy, all of which are among our least concentrated industries.) If it is collusion that concerns them, conspiracy occurs as often in diffused as in concentrated industries. Some of the most effective price-propping arrangements occur where there are many small producers, such as dairy farmers, who have the votes to get legislative endorsement of their cartel arrangements. If it is efficiency in the allocation and use of resources that concerns them, they should note that the industries with rising concentration, industries already concentrated, and industries with dominant firms show higher productivity and more rapidly increasing productivity than the unconcentrated industries.

Public policy in the United States needs regearing. Restrictions on the growth of firm size need to be loosened. These restrictions prevent competitive behavior by our most efficient firms. At the same time, public policy should be directed at reducing the reporting and regulatory burdens on all firms (which would particularly benefit small firms)[31] and at removing entry barriers—almost all of which are imposed by government and administered by regulatory agencies and licensing authorities. The antitrust agencies should be devoting themselves to assisting in the removal of barriers to entry, as the Federal Trade Commission has done in ridding us of bans on advertising by optometrists and druggists, and to detecting and prosecuting the types of explicit collusion that restrain output.[32] In devoting investigatory and prosecutorial effort to persistently concentrated industries, increasingly concentrated industries, and dominant firms, the agencies selected exactly the wrong targets.[33] They are themselves restraining output and the growth of productivity. They are contributing to a deterioration of the competitive position of the United States in international markets.

Notes

1. The hostility to business, and especially to large corporations, is producing deleterious effects on capital formation in the United States and, as a consequence, on productivity growth. More capital has gone abroad to spread political risks than would have occurred in the absence of the growing use of business as a scapegoat by politicians eager to escape blame for some of the troubles, such as inflation, for which they are responsible. To see the effects of perceptions of political risks on the allocation of capital among jurisdictions, see Kenneth Lehn, Lee Benham, and Alexandra Benham, *Ideology and the Cost of Capital*, Working Paper No. 50 (Washington University, Nov. 1979).
2. U.S., Federal Trade Commission, THE MERGER MOVEMENT: A SUMMARY REPORT 68 (1948). For critical discussion of the report, see M. A. Adelman, *The Measurement of Industrial Concentration*, 33 REVIEW OF ECONOMICS AND STATISTICS 269 (Nov. 1951); and J. W. Markham, *Survey of the Evidence and Findings on Mergers*, in National Bureau of

Economic Research, Business Concentration and Price Policy
174–78 (1955).
3. U.S., Temporary National Economic Committee, Final Report and
Recommendations (1941). The recommendation was vaguely put, implying that concentration had gone too far and should be checked.
4. Robert H. Bork, The Antitrust Paradox: A Policy at War with
Itself 47–48 (1978).
5. Professor Richard Posner points out that these bills would produce the
adverse effects that they purportedly would remedy, in Antitrust Law:
An Economic Perspective 94 (1976). Also, see discussion preceding
note 13 in Chapter 4 of the events following the United Shoe Machinery
decision, and the text at note 6 in Chapter 2 discussing the cellophane
decision.
6. Phil C. Neal et al., *Report of the White House Task Force on Antitrust
Policy,* 2 Antitrust Law and Economics Review 1 (Winter 1968–
69); John Blair, Economic Concentration: Structure, Behavior,
and Public Policy (1972); and Carl Kaysen and Donald Turner, Antitrust Policy: An Economic and Legal Analysis (1959), exemplify
the "bust-'em-up" school.
7. John McGee, In Defense of Industrial Concentration (1971); Harold Demsetz, The Market-Concentration Doctrine (1973); Sam
Peltzman, *The Gains and Losses from Industrial Concentration,* 20
Journal of Law & Economics 229 (Oct. 1977); and George J. Stigler,
The Economies of Scale, 1 Journal of Law & Economics 54 (Oct.
1958), favor a market determination of concentration levels. Editorial, *A
New Worst in Antitrust,* 73 Fortune 111 (Apr. 1966), argues urgently
"for the action of the market . . . determining, through the rewards and
punishments of business risk, the evolutionary path of U.S. business."
Also, see Ralph G. M. Sultan, Pricing in the Electrical Oligopoly
(1974).
8. David E. Lilienthal, Big Business: A New Era (1953); Sumner
Slichter, *In Defense of Bigness in Business,* New York Times Magazine
(Aug. 14, 1957); and H. R. Seager, Introduction to Economics
(1905), favor the growth of large firms and, at least, the relaxation of
restrictions, such as anti-merger policy, on growth. Joseph Schumpeter,
Capitalism, Socialism, and Democracy (1942), is the best-known
economist advocating large firm size as a means of promoting technological progress and innovation.
9. Western Electric is forbidden to compete for the telephone equipment
business of companies other than American Telephone & Telegraph by
an antitrust decree. The Great Atlantic & Pacific Co. had to cease selling
to other firms as a result of the findings in an antitrust suit brought
against it. Morris Adelman, *Dirlam and Kahn on the A&P Case,* 61
Journal of Political Economy 436 (Oct. 1953). For more than half a
century the major meat packers have been restricted in the arenas in
which they are allowed to compete by an antitrust decree. General Motors operates its bus manufacturing business under a threat of reopening
an antitrust case to force it to set up a new bus manufacturer if its share
of monocoque, integral buses sold to common carriers, expands.
10. *Justices Reject 3 Auto Makers' FTC Challenge,* 59 Wall Street Journal (Nov. 6, 1979).
11. D. Pauly and K. Willenson, *Regulating the FTC,* Newsweek 104 (Oct.
15, 1979).
12. R. Koenker, *Optimal Scale and the Size Distribution of American Truck-*

ing Firms, 11 JOURNAL OF TRANSPORT ECONOMICS AND POLICY 54 (Jan. 1977). That this has been as inappropriate as the proposals for a deconcentration program is demonstrated by Harold Demsetz in *Why Regulate Utilities?*, 11 JOURNAL OF LAW & ECONOMICS 55 (Apr. 1968).

13. J. J. Servan-Schreiber, THE AMERICAN CHALLENGE (1968); D. L. Burn, THE ECONOMIC HISTORY OF STEELMAKING (1940); Great Britain, National Economic Development Office, FOCUS ON PHARMACEUTICALS 11–15 (1972). Also, see Chapter 13. A few dissenters are found on the staffs of Japan's Fair Trade Commission and Germany's Cartel Office.

14. How the mighty have fallen! U.S. Steel, the world's leading steel producer for nearly seven decades, now calls on Nippon Steel Corporation "to help it make some design changes on its largest blast furnace at its Gary, Indiana, steelworks" *Japanese Steel Firm to Help U.S. Steel at Gary Works*, CHICAGO TRIBUNE (Jan. 5, 1979).

15. For example, Andrew Malcolm, *Now Macmillan Wants Domtar*, NEW YORK TIMES 27 (Dec. 23, 1978), reporting on a proposed merger between two Canadian corporations, said, ". . . the resulting consolidation would create a Canadian corporate giant with combined sales in excess of $3.2 billion (Canadian) and with the capacity to compete strongly with American multinational counterparts."

16. F. M. Scherer, INDUSTRIAL MARKET STRUCTURE AND ECONOMIC PERFORMANCE 93 (1970).

17. See, for example, *Textiles: Europe Reels from the U.S. Onslought*, 3 FINANCIAL TIMES WORLD BUSINESS WEEKLY 8 (Feb. 4, 1980).

18. Arthur S. Dewing, CORPORATE PROMOTIONS AND REORGANIZATIONS (1914).

19. National Industrial Conference Board, MERGERS IN INDUSTRY (1929).

20. For a concise review of the "administered price" controversy, see W. Duncan Reekie, INDUSTRY, PRICES, AND MARKETS 61–64 (1979); also Betty Bock, *From Administered Pricing to Concentrated Market Pricing*, 12 CONFERENCE BOARD RECORD 20 (Feb. 1975).

21. Almarin Phillips, *Structure, Conduct, and Performance—and Performance, Conduct, and Structure?*, in J. W. Markham and G. F. Papanek (eds.), INDUSTRIAL ORGANIZATION & ECONOMIC DEVELOPMENT 26 (1970). J. W. Markham points out that "public policy as embodied in our antitrust laws, lacking a more firmly established basis, often proceeds on the rule that since oligopoly is *different* from atomistic competition, it is inherently *anti*-competitive," Foreword to Sultan *supra* note 7, at v.

22. Professor Leonard Weiss, *The Structure-Conduct-Performance Paradigm and Antitrust*, 127 UNIVERSITY OF PENNSYLVANIA LAW REVIEW 1104 (Apr. 1979), attempts to show a relationship between concentration and prices by use of examples drawn from studies such as the analysis of municipal bond prices by Professor Reuben Kessel. The Kessel study is deficient in its lack of recognition of the variation of quality within the discrete measures of quality used, and the consequent effect on both yield and number of bidders. As a result, it attributes lower yield to an increase in number of bidders when both the larger number of bidders and lower yield are a consequence of higher quality within each rank. Also, the Kessel study mis-specifies the relationship between size of issue and yield. Kessel uses a linear relationship, which underestimates the yield difference between small issues and medium-size issues and grossly overestimates the yield difference between middle- and large-size issues. Since very large issues require large consortia, there

tend to be few bidders for large issues, and Kessel mistakenly projects low yields for the large issues. The combination of higher-than-projected yield for large issues and small number of bidders leads to mistaken conclusions by Kessel about the relationship between number of bidders and yields. I am indebted to Professor Michael Mussa for this analysis.

23. Address of Benjamin Fairless before the Baltimore Association of Commerce, April 1950. Cited in Roy A. Foulke, BEHIND THE SCENES OF BUSINESS 21 (1952).

24. U.S., Federal Trade Commission, Office of Policy Planning and Evaluation, 1976 Budget Overview, ATRR, no. 692 (Dec. 10, 1974). Robert Bork tells us that, "The difficulty of maintaining small-number cartels based upon detailed communication and agreement should make us dubious that concerted action without explicit collusion is likely to be at all common or successful." See Bork *supra* note 3, at 175.

25. A. Phillips, *An Econometric Study of Price-Fixing, Market Structure, and Performance in British Industry in the Early 1950's* in K. Cowling (ed.), MARKET STRUCTURE AND CORPORATE BEHAVIOR 177 (1972). Erickson, *Economics of Price Fixing*, 2 ANTITRUST LAW & ECONOMICS REVIEW 83 (Spring 1969); P. Asch and J. J. Seneca, *Is Collusion Profitable?*, 58 REVIEW OF ECONOMICS AND STATISTICS 1 (Feb. 1976). Professor Wesley J. Liebeler, discussing the latter study, concludes that ". . . this finding certainly does not lend support to the Market Concentration Doctrine and it is intuitively attractive if one is prepared to believe that the appetite for risk rises directly with desperation." *Market Power and Competitive Superiority in Concentrated Industries*, 25 UCLA LAW REVIEW 1238, n. 25 (Aug. 1978).

26. For example, W. S. Comanor and T. A. Wilson, *Advertising, Market Structure, and Performance*, 49 REVIEW OF ECONOMICS AND STATISTICS 423 (Nov. 1967). Their regression shows no effect of concentration on the profitability of consumer goods industries when a variable measuring the influence of omitted intangible capital on the computation of accounting rates of return is included.

27. Sylvester Petro, *The Growing Threat of Antitrust*, 66 FORTUNE 128 (Nov. 1962).

28. Steve Lustgarten, INDUSTRIAL CONCENTRATION, PRODUCTIVITY GROWTH, AND CONSUMER WELFARE (forthcoming).

29. Lennart Hjalmarsson, *Monopoly Welfare Gains and the Costs of Deconcentration* in A. P. Jacquemin and H. W. de Jong (eds.), WELFARE ASPECTS OF INDUSTRIAL MARKETS 217 (1977).

30. U.S., Federal Trade Commission, Bureau of Economics, THE BREWING INDUSTRY 64 (1978), points out that the Department of Justice suits dissolving and preventing concentration-increasing mergers in the beer industry caused a misallocation of capital as well as being a waste of public resources. Efficient brewers were prevented from acquiring the breweries of the less efficient. As a consequence, new breweries were built and little use was made of the capacity of old breweries whose owners left the industry. Excess capacity and idle capital were a consequence of forcing efficient brewers into expansion by internal growth instead of by acquisition and merger, the very consequence that is supposed to be the undesirable result of the monopolization of a formerly competitive industry. The study concludes that the brewing industry is more concentrated today than it would have been if the mergers that were prevented had been allowed.

31. The burden of legal costs (costs of a firm's legal department plus fees paid to outside counsel) decreases with the size of the firm. B. Peter Pashigian, *The Legal Costs of Firms: Some Initial Findings* 24–25 (preliminary draft, working paper, July 1978). Presumably legal costs are related to reporting and regulatory (including antitrust) burdens.
32. Donald Dewey shows that where entry is "free," collusion may increase output if it reduces risks. *Information, Entry, and Welfare: The Case for Collusion*, 69 AMERICAN ECONOMIC REVIEW 587 (Oct. 1979).
33. Y. Brozen, *The Attack on Concentration*, 29 THE FREEMAN 38 (Jan. 1979).

1

Concentration in American Industry

Few industries display such durable concentration as the cigarette industry. Its production has long been centralized in a few firms. Even in the days of "handmade," concentration was high. Four firms produced 80 percent of the output in 1880 before the 1881 entry of James B. Duke. He became the country's largest cigarette manufacturer by being the first to adopt cigarette-rolling machinery and to exploit this advantage. In 1890, Duke combined 91 percent of the country's capacity to form the American Tobacco Company. Its large share did not, however, entrench the company. It lost 10 percentage points of its market share to other firms in a few years. Acquiring more cigarette companies, it recovered to a 93 percent share in 1899. After slipping to a 76 percent share by 1903, American Tobacco then maintained its position, selling 80 percent of all cigarettes just before it was dissolved in 1911. Although it produced a multiplicity of brands, its dominance rested largely on one, Sweet Caporal, which attracted 50 percent of the total cigarette trade by 1898.

Despite the fragmentation of this dominant tobacco company by antitrust decree into three cigarette manufacturers (a new American Tobacco, Liggett & Myers, and P. Lorillard) plus thirteen other corporations, concentration far above average persisted. Inertia or entrenchment cannot explain this since leadership did not remain in the hands of the same firms. Reynolds, which produced no cigarettes when it began its independent existence in 1912, introduced Camel at a retail price of ten cents in 1913. The popular brands then sold at fifteen cents. By 1917, Camel had attracted 35 percent of all sales. By 1923, it had 45 percent despite American and Liggett & Myers bringing out Lucky Strike and Chesterfield as direct competitors of Camel. By 1925, the three brands had captured 82 percent of national sales.

Leading cigarette firms were dislodged by others, notably when Reynolds crashed into top position early in the century. Lorillard fell from a top rank to a less than 2 percent market share in the mid-1920s (see Table 1-1). It then recovered by 1930, after introducing its Old Gold brand, only to lose out again by the late 1930s to Philip Morris and Brown & Williamson. After American lost its top position to Reynolds, it then recovered by promoting its competitive Lucky Strike brand. Reynolds dropped from its 45 percent share of the market in 1923 to 22 percent in 1945. It

TABLE 1–1
Cigarette Production Shares
1910–80

Year	American Tobacco	Liggett & Myers	Lorillard	R. J. Reynolds	Brown & Williamson	Philip Morris	Four-Firm Concentration
			Percentage				
1910[a]	37.1	27.8	15.3	0	n.a.	< 0.05	80.2
1915	n.a.	n.a.	n.a.	13.5	n.a.	n.a.	n.a.
1920	n.a.	n.a.	n.a.	39.5	n.a.	n.a.	n.a.
1925	21.2	26.6	1.9	41.6	n.a.	0.5	91.3
1930	36.5	25.0	7.5	28.5	0.2	0.3	97.5
1935	22.9	26.6	3.8	28.2	9.6	3.3	87.3
1940	25.2	20.3	5.0	23.5	10.0	6.9	79.0
1945	29.5	20.6	5.4	21.7	7.8	9.6	81.4
1950	30.6	18.8	5.1	26.7	6.1	10.8	86.9
1955	32.0	16.1	6.0	25.4	10.9	8.6	84.4
1960	25.7	11.7	10.9	32.6	9.4	9.3	80.9
1965	26.3	8.3	9.0	32.4	13.1	10.5	82.3
1970	19.6	6.9	8.6	31.5	16.7	16.6	84.4
1975	14.2	4.6	8.8	31.9	16.3	24.0	86.4
1980	10.7	2.2	9.8	32.8	13.7	30.8	88.0

Sources: William H. Nicholls, PRICE POLICIES IN THE CIGARETTE INDUSTRY (1951), pp. 31, 62, 91, 159; Marlboro Country, BARRON'S 9 (Oct. 27, 1975); Tobacco, STANDARD & POOR'S INDUSTRY SURVEYS Jan. 10, 1980, p. T98.
Share of top-ranked firm is italicized.
[a] Output of plants turned over to the new American Tobacco, Liggett & Myers, and P. Lorillard by the 1911 decree dissolving American Tobacco Company.

regained its number one rank in 1960 but is now being pressed hard by Philip Morris. Despite the dissolution of American Tobacco in 1911, loss of market share (later regained) by the top-ranking three brands to the ten-cent brands in the 1930s (see Table 6-1), turnover among the top firms (American fell from first to fourth between 1955 and 1975) and displacement of two of the top four, the industry continues among our most concentrated (and among the most concentrated in other countries).

Clashing Views on Concentration and Competition

Although such durability of high concentration is uncommon, many economists follow the lead of John Kenneth Galbraith in viewing the American economy as oligopolistic in character, with many large firms that are well entrenched in their positions. Others, however, view it oppositely. Descriptions of concentration in American industry vary in much the same way as the difference between an optimist and a pessimist has proverbially been described. Looking at the same partially filled water glass, the optimist finds it "half-full," the pessimist "half-empty."

Some observers see the American economy "dominated by large firms and concentrated industries." One textbook designated *all* manufacturing industries as oligopolies. It labels those industries where the share of business going to the leading four firms ranges from 0 to 40 percent "loose oligopoly." Where the leading four-firm share ranges from 60 to 100 percent it labels them "tight oligopoly."[1]

Other observers see the American economy swept by "perennial gales of competition." New technologies introduced by firms competing to serve buyers with better and less expensive products and services cause "creative destruction." They see active competition creating progress and rising levels of living unachievable by pure competiton in which firms passively adapt to changing conditions. Firms engaging in "pure" or "perfect" competition adapt to existing cost and demand constraints without seeking to change those constraints. Active competitors, on the other hand, reduce costs, improve goods, invent new products, and inform buyers of the availability of products of which they would otherwise be ignorant. New industries created by active competition and by product rivalry among the many existing manufacturing industries generate more dynamism than several dozen firms competing inside the same industry.[2]

Active competition is sometimes derogatorily labeled "imperfect competition" or is considered "oligopolistic behavior" focused on differentiating product and on advertising to bar the entry of would-be competitors. Passive behavior is labeled "pure" or "perfect" competition. This semantic twist puts policy analysts who favor progress and admire the fruits of active competition into a position of opposing the "pure" and the "perfect" and favoring "oligopolies" and the "imperfect." It would be less misleading to rename oligopolistic and imperfect competition with a title that does not carry such dishonorific connotations as "oligopoly" and "imperfect." A less emotive and more accurate title for the behavior to which these labels are usually applied is *multidimensional competition*. As Professor Clair Wilcox noted in his Temporary National Economic Commission monograph, *Competition and Monopoly in American Industry* (1940):

> Perfect and pure competition, since they require commodity standardization [and static circumstances—no changes in tastes, resources, technology, and institutions], pertain to competition in price alone. Imperfect and monopolistic competition, since they permit product differentiation, pertain also to sellers' competition in quality, in service, in style, and in advertising and salesmanship. Competition in quality and in service may be quite as effective in giving the buyer more for his money as is competition in price.

How Concentrated Is American Industry?

While the pessimists bemoan the "dominance" of giant corporations and the "concentrated" state of American industry, the fact is that the United States manufactures most of its factory products in industries in which the largest firm turns out only a fraction of domestic output. The leading firm in the average U.S. manufacturing industry (average of 314 industries) produces 17 percent of its industry's output. In a few, the largest firm produces less than 2 percent of output. The range across industries for the leading firm's share of production goes from 1.1 to 68.7 percent.[3] Even this overstates actual market shares. These percentages take no account of imports, nor of production in shops rebuilding and repairing manufactured items, nor of production in retail shops

22

such as bakeries, delicatessens, restaurants, and cabinetmakers. Many of these manufacturers must also compete with homemade goods such as apparel and furniture.

Seventy-eight percent of all domestic factory output occurs in 374 industries whose leading four firms fabricate less than 60 percent of their industry's national product (see Table 1-2). Other sectors—agriculture, banking, retailing, construction, mining, insurance, services—are even less concentrated.[4] The major excep-

TABLE 1–2

Distribution of Manufacturers' Shipments by Four-Firm
Concentration, 1935 and 1972

Four-Firm Concentration Percentage	Share of Shipments[a]	
	1935[b]	1972
	Percentage	
0–9	16.6 (20)	5.4 (17)
10–19	13.5 (40)	16.4 (70)
20–29	17.0 (44)	20.0 (97)
30–39	14.5 (50)	14.8 (72)
40–49	10.6 (31)	10.9 (61)
50–59	6.9 (25)	10.7 (57)
60–69	7.6 (26)	9.1 (28)
70–79	2.8 (17)	4.1 (26)
80–89	9.2 (18)[c]	1.4 (11)
90–100	0.2 (4)[d]	7.2 (11)[e]
0–59	79.1 (210)	78.2 (374)
60–100	19.8 (65)	21.8 (76)
Weighted average concentration	37.0 (272)	40.2 (450)
Simple average concentration	40.2 (272)	39.1 (450)

Sources: U.S., Department of Commerce, Bureau of the Census, CENSUS OF MANUFACTURES, 1972, CONCENTRATION RATIOS IN MANUFACTURING, MC76 (SR) -2 (Oct. 1975), Table 5; National Resources Committee, THE STRUCTURE OF THE AMERICAN ECONOMY (June 1939) Table I at 265.

[a] Number of industries in each group is in parentheses. The Census has 451 manufacturing industries in its 1972 Standard Industrial Classification code, but it combined industries 3572 and 3579 in calculating concentration ratios for 1972.

[b] Does not add to 100 because of the omission of six industries whose concentration was not disclosed. The Bureau of the Census combined eighty-two textiles and their products industries into twenty-two for its concentration report.

[c] Industry 1003 included here but not in the calculation of average concentration in all manufacturing.

[d] Industries 624 and 1314 included in this group but not in the calculation of average concentration for all manufacturing for lack of precise four-firm concentration figure. The six industries omitted for lack of data probably belong in this group.

[e] For SIC 3661, telephone and telegraph apparatus, the 1970 figure of ninety-four was used since the Census Bureau did not disclose the figure for 1972.

Table 1-3

Four-Firm Concentration Ratios in Selected Industries, 1935–72

Industry	1935	1947	1954	1958	1963	1967	1972
2011—Meat packing	56 (n.a.)	47 (1,999)	40 (2,223)	34[a] (2,646)	31[a] (2,833)	26 (2,529)	20 (2,293)
2062—Cane sugar	69[b] (n.a.)	70[b] (17)	67[b] (16)	69[b] (16)	63 (16)	59 (22)	59 (22)
2063—Beet sugar	68 (n.a.)	68 (17)	66 (15)	64 (15)	66 (11)	66 (15)	66 (16)
2082—Malt beverages	11 (n.a.)	21 (404)	27 (203)	28 (211)	34 (171)	40 (125)	50 (108)
2311—Men's and boys' suits and coats	—	9 (1,761)	11 (1,255)	11 (1,275)	14 (1,031)	17 (904)	19 (721)
2514—Metal household furniture	—	26 (305)	16 (635)	14 (614)	13 (508)	14 (464)	13 (426)
2541—Wood partitions and fixtures	—	—	—	—	4 (1,588)	6 (1,463)	5 (1,475)
3312—Blast furnaces and steel mills	—	50[a] (n.a.)	55[a] (n.a.)	53[a] (148)	48[a] (161)	48[a] (200)	45[a] (241)
3334—Primary aluminum	100 (1)	100 (3)	100 (3)	D (6)	D (7)	D (10)	79 (12)
3573—Electronic computing equipment	—	—	—	—	—	66 (134)	51 (518)
3652—Phonograph records	—	79 (96)	70 (135)	76 (85)	69 (128)	58 (306)	48 (537)
3671—Electron tubes, receiving type	—	—	—	—	87 (30)	94 (28)	95 (21)
3741—Locomotives and parts	D (n.a.)	91 (33)	91 (25)	95 (25)	97 (23)	97 (26)	— (n.a.)

Source: Bureau of the Census, CONCENTRATION RATIOS IN MANUFACTURING (1975), Table 5.

Note: Figures in parentheses is number of firms with at least one establishment whose primary product is in the designated industry.

[a] Concentration measured by the proportion of domestic value-added produced by the four leading domestic firms. All other concentration ratios measured by shipments.

[b] Establishments in Hawaii and Alaska which are important producers are not included.

D = Datum withheld by the Bureau of Census to avoid disclosing operations of individual companies.

tions are communications industries (telephone service, network broadcasting, and postal service) and intercity air, rail, and bus passenger transportation.

Even passenger transportation is relatively unconcentrated if we regard air, rail, and bus simply as parts of the intercity passenger transportation industry instead of viewing each as selling in a separate market. They do compete with each other. The introduction of the jet airplane at the end of 1958 took 4 percentage points from the automobile share of intercity passenger business in the United States (90.4 percent in 1958, dropping to 86.1 in 1969), doubling the airline share. Earlier, the airline share grew at the expense of first-class railroad transportation, practically causing its demise. Railroad passenger service had already suffered from the competition of the automobile in the 1920s and 1930s.[5] Now the bus companies complain bitterly because the taxpayer subsidy of $3 to Amtrak for every $2 paid by rail passengers is hurting their business.

In the average U.S. manufacturing industry, the four leading firms together ship 39 percent (1972) of the industry's domestic output. That is, however, the center of a wide range of concentration ratios (CRs) for the 450 industries for which the Bureau of the Census provides data. In seventeen industries, the four leading firms fabricate less than 10 percent of their group's domestic output; in eleven the four leaders produce more than 90 percent (see Table 1-3 for examples). The range for the four-leading-firm share in each industry goes from 4 percent in lithographic commercial printing (industry number 2752 in the Standard Industrial Classification Code) to 96 percent in cellulosic man-made fibers (industry 2823).

Differing economic characteristics of each of the many industries cause this wide variation in concentration ratios. (Concentration ratios are variously measured as the ratio of shipments, or employment, or value-added of the four leading firms in an industry to the total shipments, employment or value-added of all domestic firms in the industry.) Professor Joe Bain found (as did F. L. Pryor in a later study) that industries that are concentrated in the United States are concentrated in other countries. Those with low concentration are also the same abroad as in the United States.[6] This suggests that *fundamental technological and economic forces determine industry structure.* The notion, proposed by some statisticians and economists, that historical accident, luck, or waves of merger mania produced the concentration levels found in various industries, does not stand up in the face of this and other evidence.[7]

Industry and Aggregate Concentration Trends

In 1935, concentration ratios in 10 percent of the 281 manufacturing industries documented by the Bureau of the Census ranged between 80 and 100 percent. By 1972, the proportion of manufacturing industries found in this range dropped to 5 percent. The drop occurred despite a finer subdivision of manufacturing in 1972 into 450 groups instead of 281 industries. If 1935's manufacturing had been packed in 450 groups instead of 281, the proportion falling in the 80 to 100 percent concentration range in 1935 would have been higher. (For trends in specific industries in which the share of the four leading firms sometimes exceeded 74 percent in the postwar period, see Table 10-1.)

The decline in the proportion of manufacturing activity occurring in the 80 to 100 percent concentrated industries was smaller than the decline in the fraction of industries falling in this range. Some of the concentrated industries, such as motor vehicles, grew relative to all manufacturing. Some small concentrated industries, such as bluing, were replaced by large industries, such as ready-to-eat cereals, which were not in the concentrated group in 1935. This accounts for the smaller decline in proportion of manufacturing activity than in proportion of four-digit industries in the 80 to 100 percent concentration range. In 1935, 10.6 percent of all domestically manufactured products was sold by firms in these industries. By 1972, the concentrated industry share of all manufacturing had dropped to 8.6 percent.

Alarms are frequently sounded about the aggregate concentration trend in the United States. The figure sometimes used to measure this trend is the share of nonfinancial corporate assets owned by the largest 200 nonfinancial corporations. That figure dropped with the increase in the number of corporations from 500,000 in 1933 to 2,000,000 in 1975. The share of nonfinancial corporation assets owned by the largest 200 fell from 54.8 percent in 1933, apparently a high-water mark, to 39.1 percent in 1975. (The largest nonfinancial corporation measured by book value of assets, American Telephone & Telegraph, was the biggest in both 1933 and 1975.)

Sometimes the issue is the share of the largest fifty or 100 or 200 manufacturing corporations. These shares are expressed in terms of all manufacturing corporation assets, sales, or value-added. For reasons outlined in Chapter 11, the asset share is misleading. The sales share of the largest fifty dropped from 28 percent in 1937 to 24 in 1972, while that for the largest 200 manufacturers (including the fifty) increased from 41 to 43 percent (Table 11-2).

These aggregate share figures are meaningless since there is no accusation that the major fifty—or 200—corporations exercise any market power by conspiring with each other. Their interests are often antithetical, which prevents their acting together. The motor vehicle manufacturers, for example, prefer low steel prices, while the steel companies prefer high prices. Steel companies, in fact, pressure the government to erect trade barriers to shut out foreign competitors in order to get higher prices. Conflicts arise even among large firms that are in the same industry. Among petroleum companies, some support policies aimed at breaking up foreign cartels in order to obtain cheap crude while others prefer that crude imports be limited. Only to the extent that the largest companies have, in the last decade, formed the Business Roundtable, have any acted together to protect their interests and their customers' interests when issues come up in the Congress. Even here, however, they remain divided on many issues. Many of the Big 200 have refused to join. Others have resigned in disagreements after joining. And some members are from companies not in the Big 200.

Innovation and the Concentration Cycle

An industry's concentration level at a particular time depends partly on the industry's origins and stage of development. Some start out highly concentrated, beginning with an innovation that a pioneering firm brings to market. With low profitability and slow growth, high concentration may persist for a long period. If production is very profitable and demand grows rapidly, new firms swarm into the industry, eventually diffusing it. Even with a patent on the pioneering firm's product, new producers frequently spring up, inventing their way around the patent. Sometimes they simply infringe on the patent, as Eli Whitney discovered after he began producing his cotton gin.

27

The process consisting of (1) innovation, (2) production by a single firm, (3) growing output, and (4) entry of additional firms is still in its beginning in some industries. Some will be honored with a four-digit number assignment in the Standard Industrial Classification Code (SICC) some time in the future when a sufficient number of firms appear. In others, the market will never grow large enough to support more than a few producers. These few may have to operate at a world-market scale to be efficient.

Locomotives

The locomotive market, for example, seems unlikely to grow enough to support more than a few efficient organizations even though American firms sell a substantial portion of their output abroad. The domestic industry consisted of only a few firms in the days of steam. It still is occupied by only a few firms, although it was revolutionized by the development of the diesel-electric locomotive in the 1930s when firms new to the industry entered. Steam locomotive manufacturers began producing diesel power, following the lead of others, but they never developed into efficient competitors and soon dropped out. Locomotives disappeared in 1972 from the SIC as a separate four-digit industry because so few factories producing locomotives and parts as their primary product were still in operation.

Computers

Technological evolution and rapid growth in the computer market has already begun the deconcentration of that industry despite its youth (see Table 1-3). Its leading firm, formerly a producer of card tabulators and sorters, which displaced the pioneering producer (Univac) in 1956, continues to maintain its position as a sales and technological leader in both the U.S. and foreign markets. IBM's $23 billion in sales in 1979—more than half produced in foreign markets—make it ten times the size of its nearest competitor, but its relative size is decreasing. It continues to expand rapidly by improving technology, lowering prices, and enlarging capacity, but the industry and the market are expanding even more rapidly and concentration is falling. It should be noted that for the last decade, IBM's expansion has been hampered by the diversion of resources to fending off an antitrust attack on its position as a leading firm. The government argues that IBM's large size gives it monopoly power. As in the case of United Shoe Machinery, which is discussed in Chapter 4, the Antitrust Division's attack could have been avoided had the firm held a price umbrella high enough and hesitated more in introducing new technology. In that event, its market position would have eroded even more rapidly than it has. Under laws designed to outlaw behavior that restrains output, IBM and others are being attacked for expanding it.

Aluminum

The primary aluminum industry sprang from a discovery which turned costly aluminum extracted in a few laboratories into a much less expensive industrial metal. Charles Hall made the initial discovery. He helped found a firm in 1888 that became an efficient manufacturer of the product.[8] For several decades after the founding of the Pittsburgh Reduction Company, the domestic market remained too small to support more than one efficient domestic producer.[9] As the market grew, this one firm added capacity and produced additional primary aluminum less expensively than it could be manufactured by a would-be entrant. It increased output rapidly enough to keep prices and returns from rising to levels that would attract additional firms. Only one attempt was made, that by a French firm whose effort was aborted by the outbreak of World War I.

Aluminum ingot made from scrap became important around 1914, when its output reached 16 percent of primary production. This grew to 56 percent by 1927. Aluminum imports in the form of finished goods and ingot grew, but they seldom rose above 20 percent of domestic use and then only in times of unusually high domestic demand or depressed foreign demand. A tariff helped minimize imports.

By 1940, market growth made room for more primary firms to operate at an efficient scale. Also, prospective profitability became attractive. Domestic use of aluminum had doubled between 1930 and 1940, growing as much as it had in the previous four decades. Alcoa earned a higher return in 1940 than it did in 1909, just before the last of its basic patents expired.

Aluminum use tripled between 1940 and 1950, and more than doubled again between 1950 and 1960. With that growth, new producers entered. R. J. Reynolds (now Reynolds Metals), a manufacturer of aluminum foil, entered the primary aluminum industry in 1941 with the aid of a loan from the Reconstruction Finance Corporation, a U.S. government agency.[10] Permanente Metals Corporation (now Kaiser Aluminum & Chemical) entered after World War II with the purchase of government-owned alumina and smelting plants that had been built by Alcoa during the war years to supply aluminum for aircraft. With the entry of a fourth and a fifth firm in the early 1950s, in part coaxed into the industry by guaranteed government purchases and special tax concessions, four-firm concentration dropped below 100 percent (see Table 1-3). The industry now has twelve firms. The four-firm industry concentration ratio dropped to 72 percent by 1976. (This figure overstates *market* concentration since the market for aluminum is global. Domestic primary producers compete with foreign producers in addition to competing with secondary aluminum producers.)

Rayon

The American rayon fiber industry (cellulosic man-made fibers) followed the path trod by the aluminum industry, but at a more rapid pace. As artificial silk, the industry had a large ready-made market waiting once it perfected its products. Textile manufacturers had already learned to use the artificial silk available from foreign sources. Where the first producer of aluminum had to create a market for the metal—slowly and painfully—by developing applications, fabricating methods, and a host of special alloys suitable for special uses, these problems were largely absent in the market for artificial silk.[11]

The General Artificial Silk Company began operation in 1901. It never expanded to what could be called a commercial scale (its bleak prospects kept it from obtaining the necessary financing) in its nine years of existence. The American market was largely supplied by imports. The Viscose Company erected the first commercial-scale plant in 1910 using patented processes acquired from General Artificial Silk. It was fabulously profitable, earning returns far beyond those achieved by Pittsburgh Reduction, and was the world's largest producer for more than twenty years. By 1914, its production almost equaled the amount being imported. It had expanded output from 0.36 million pounds in 1911 to 2.3 million in

30

1914. It continued its rapid expansion, to 8.3 million pounds in 1919, 24.8 million in 1924, and 268 million in 1945.

In 1918, Celanese Corporation was founded, beginning work on a different process. It entered the market on a commercial scale in 1925. Viscose was joined in 1920 by du Pont, Tubize Artificial Silk, and Industrial Fibre Corporation. Total rayon production by the domestic industry increased from 8 million pounds in 1920 to 123 million in 1929. Thirty firms entered the industry or announced plans to do so in this period. The actual number of active producers expanded from one at the beginning of 1920 to twenty by 1931. Viscose's share fell from 100 to 44 percent of output. The concentration ratio (measured by capacity) dropped from 100 in 1924 to 74 in 1931.

Entrants were attracted by the high returns earned in the 1920s when capacity was short of what an eager market wanted despite Viscose's rapid expansion. By contrast, aluminum, due to its high cost, had to fight its way into the market on the basis of the special qualities it could offer in some applications. Indeed, rayon yarn was eagerly sought by textile producers as a low-cost replacement for silk. By 1932, capacity and output increased to an amount that depressed prices to a level too low to keep higher-cost producers in the industry. The number of firms began declining despite continuing growth in total output, dropping to fourteen by 1947.[12] Two firms disappeared by merger in the early 1930s and others, all small firms, simply stopped operating. The concentration ratio rose from 74 percent in 1935 to 78 in 1947, although the Viscose share continued to drop, falling to 26 percent despite a continuing rise in its total output. By 1963, more high-cost producers left the industry, leaving only eight firms by that date.

Cotton Textiles

Cotton textiles provides an earlier example of rapid growth with many firms attracted by the profitability of investment in the industry. The U.S. cotton textile industry was founded in 1790 by John Slater, who had memorized English machine designs. (A factory producing cotton duck was started in 1788, but it did not use mechanically-powered machinery.) By 1800, four-firm concentration, measured by employment, declined to 90 percent with the entry of seven additional firms. Despite a tripling of employment in the four leading firms from 1800 to 1810, the concentration ratio fell to 25 percent with the entry of fifty-two additional firms. Only one of the four leaders of 1800 was still among the four leaders in 1810. The industry quadrupled in size between 1810 and 1820, 176 additional firms entering. Concentration fell to 13.5 percent. Concentration continued to decline, dropping to 10 percent by 1860 with the number of firms peaking at 1,240 in 1840. Despite three major consolidations in the 1890s, the 1899 concentration ratio was only 8.7 percent (measured by capitalization).

In the following years, two of the consolidations failed. By 1920, new leaders displaced the four leading companies of 1899. The fourth-ranking firm had acquired a successor to one of the failed consolidations. The second ranking 1920 firm had acquired the fourth ranked firm of 1899. Mergers of sixteen firms between 1913 and 1920 created the four 1920 leaders.

The 1920s were a period of decline in cotton textiles both in capital and number of firms. By 1930, two of the 1920 leaders were displaced. The capitalization of the four 1930 leaders was less than that of the 1920 leaders, yet concentration increased to 11.0 percent in 1930 and to 12.1 percent in 1937.[13]

We see again the cycle of innovation, high profitability, rapid entry, expansion of capacity and number of firms, maturation, and then a declining number of firms as growth slowed, profits narrowed, and the less efficient closed or were acquired, although this cycle was spread over a much longer period in cotton textiles than in rayon. The industry became much larger and concentration dropped to very much lower levels than in rayon before rising as the industry matured.

The Number of Firms in the Concentration-Profit Cycle

The pattern of firms flooding into an industry in its early profitable stage—sometimes extraordinarily profitable (see Table 1-4) —has been repeated many times. So has a subsequent period with inefficient firms dropping out or merging with others as profit margins narrowed with continuing growth of supply forcing prices down. Steamboating on the Ohio and the Mississippi, which grew rapidly from 1812 to maturity by the 1830s[14]; bicycle manufacture in the 1890s, which grew from twenty-seven establishments in 1890 to 312 in 1900 and then declined to 101 in 1905[15]; automobiles in the first three decades of the twentieth century; radio manufacture in the 1920s; refrigerators and home laundry machines in the 1930s and 1940s[16]; black and white television in the 1950s and color television set manufacture in the 1960s[17]; calculators in the 1970s; and pharmaceuticals in the postwar period[18] all exemplify the pattern.

The economist who sarcastically remarked that, "Some economists have carried Schumpeter's Olympian view that no monopoly lasts a thousand years to its illogical conclusion that any profits in excess of normal will . . . cause a horde of competitors to spring into action," simply failed to observe American industrial history. When Reynolds International Pen Company brought ball-point pens to the market in 1945, it was quickly followed by more than 100 firms in the next two years. When fish sticks were launched in late 1953, thirteen packers entered the profitable industry by the end of the year. The number climbed to fifty-five four months later.[19] Word processors were first developed in 1967 and brought to a stage of commercial applicability in 1974. The industry now has eighty firms competing to establish themselves. From cotton to rayon, bicycles to automobiles, and in dozens of other industries, "hordes of competitors" sprang into action when entry was attractive. As the receiver for Distillers Securities testified in 1900 before the Industrial Commission:

> I do not regard all of these industrial trusts as dangerous as some people do because I do not think it is possible for them to . . . hold up prices for any long period of time. . . . [T]hey may start a trust and buy up a hundred or two hundred distilleries or factories, . . . but the only way they can keep them in operation is by keeping the cost of production below where it can be kept by small concerns. The moment they reach out for more than a reasonable profit on the cost of production, that moment other plants will be created faster than any trust can buy them up.[20]

A careful econometric investigation by Professor Lester Telser has demonstrated that the more profitable an industry, the more firms enter or remain in the industry, other things remaining equal. Using 1963 data for 398 industries, he found that at any given level of concentration, the greater the industry's profitability, the greater the number of firms. Essentially, his finding indicates that *the association of greater profitability with greater concentration is the consequence of temporary disequilibria.*

TABLE 1-4

Rate of Return in Leading Firm and Industry
Output in Three Industries and
Pharmaceutical Research Investment and Output

Year	Aluminum Return[a] (Percentage)	Production[b] (000 tons)	Motor Vehicles Return[c] (Percentage)	Production[d] (000)	Rayon Return[e] (Percentage)	Production[f] (000,000 lbs)	Year	Pharmaceutical Research Return[g] (Percentage)	NCEs
1904	—	3.5	113.8	23	—	—	1950	—	34
5	—	5.3	92.0	25	—	—	1951	—	39
6	—	6.5	34.8	34	—	—	52	—	35
7	—	11.8	114.7	44	—	—	53	—	48
8	—	5.9	60.4	65	—	—	54	20.9	32
9	14.1	6.8	148.1	131	—	—	1955	19.8	42
1910	16.1	15.4	95.9	187	—	—	56	21.2	36
11	18.1	16.8	97.5	210	—	—	57	21.6	50
12	15.9	18.1	115.1	378	—	—	58	21.7	28
13	22.5	21.5	106.7	485	—	—	59	22.3	52
14	18.8	30.4	74.9	569	—	2.4	1960	21.8	44
1915	19.1	48.8	52.8	970	26.3	3.9	61	23.0	33
16	30.6	69.8	68.6	1,618	109.2	5.8	62	22.5	19
17	16.3	73.5	24.5	1,874	96.0	6.5	63	22.5	12
18	11.1	70.3	34.0	1,171	69.5	5.8	64	22.6	17
19	9.1	75.3	30.6	1,934	97.0	8.3	65	22.0	17
1920	9.8	77.0	43.9	2,227	64.2	10.1	66	20.6	12
21	(6.7)	32.8	29.9	1,616	44.6	15.0	67	19.4	17
22	2.1	48.2	41.8	2,544	51.2	24.1	68	17.6	10
23	10.0	77.7	25.8	4,034	43.5	34.9	69	15.8	7
24	8.9	92.8	22.6	3,603	26.6	36.3	1970	14.2	15
							71	11.8	13

1925	13.5	103.6	20.1	4,266	32.4
26	9.7	107.0	10.8	4,301	21.8
27	7.3	116.2	(5.0)	3,401	26.2
28	10.0	139.0	(12.2)	4,359	28.8
29	12.2	147.4	14.0	5,358	23.4
1930	5.8	139.0	8.0	3,356	8.1
31	2.7	108.1	(6.1)	2,390	4.4
32	(0.2)	69.4	(11.3)	1,371	2.4

72	51.0	12.5	6
73	62.7	11.9	12
74	75.5	11.3	16
1975	97.4	11.5	12
76	121.9	11.4	—
77	127.7	10.4	—
78	151.7	10.3	—
—	135.8	—	—

a After tax rate of return on Alcoa's estimated average investment. D. H. Wallace, MARKET CONTROL IN THE ALUMINUM INDUSTRY (1937) at 544.

b Total annual domestic production of primary and secondary aluminum ingot, id. at 572. No secondary is included before 1914.

c Ford Motor Co. after tax rate of return on average equity computed from data in Federal Trade Commission, REPORT ON MOTOR VEHICLE INDUSTRY (1940) at 634, 645.

d Total U.S. factory sales of motor vehicles. Id. at 22.

e Pretax rate of return on total investment of American Viscose Corporation adjusting capital to disallow certain capital items and adjusting income to eliminate certain expense charges. Federal Trade Commission, RELATIVE EFFICIENCY OF LARGE, MEDIUM-SIZED, AND SMALL BUSINESS (1941) at 92.

f Total domestic production. J. Markham, COMPETITION IN THE RAYON INDUSTRY (1952).

g M. Statman, DYNAMIC COMPETITION IN THE DRUG INDUSTRY: THE MOVEMENT OF THE COMPETITIVE EQUILIBRIUM (forthcoming). NCE stands for new chemical entities.

The argument that the higher profits of concentrated industries indicate collusion or market power is shown by Telser's work to be very hard to sustain. As our histories of several industries have shown, concentration is largely a result of innovation. The profits of concentrated industries attract entry, which decreases concentration and rates of return, unless leading firms continue to innovate more rapidly than others. So lower returns tend to be associated with lower levels of concentration. Telser, using a measure of profitability in 1963 as his dependent variable, found that the number of firms, holding other things constant, rises with increases in the level of profits.

> The behavior of the coefficient of log NO [the number of companies in the four-digit SIC census industry] is of considerable interest. A priori, this coefficient can be either positive or negative. . . . If negative, then this would mean that, given the share of the four leading companies, the larger . . . the total number of companies in the industry, the lower . . . the rate of return. This could be explained by saying that, given the concentration ratio, the more companies there are in the industry, the more competition and the lower . . . the rate of return. On the other hand, there is an equally plausible argument for a positive coefficient. Thus the higher . . . the rate of return, the more companies enter the industry attracted by the prospect of obtaining high profits. In fact, all of the coefficients of log NO are positive. Nor is this all. The coefficients tend to rise with concentration. One can argue that this finding means that the higher is the concentration ratio the greater is the inducement for a company to enter the industry, which assumes that the inducement to enter is measured by the size of the coefficient of log NO. This finding I interpret as being consistent with the positive coefficient of C [concentration] itself. Moreover, it provides a clue in favor of a positive association between concentration and rates of return over time. Above I argue that a positive association between C and the rate of return in the cross-section implies a similar relation for time series. In particular a fall in the concentration ratio should be accompanied by a fall in the rate of return as a result of the entry and success of companies in the more concentrated industries. Hence the finding of a positive association between rates of return and the number of companies in the cross-section supports my argument about what time series data will show.[21]

Douglas Webbink confirms Telser's expectation that more entry will occur in concentrated industries. Webbink found a positive correlation (0.26) between the percentage change in the number of firms in an industry from 1967 to 1972 (280 industries) and the industry's 1967 concentration ratio (also see Table 4-7).[22] This is a surprise since the barrier-to-entry literature argues that high concentration is a result of high barriers to entry. According to this view, the change in number of firms should be negatively related to concentration.

In Table 1-5, regressions in which the number of firms is the dependent variable are shown. They indicate that in 1972, given the size of an industry as measured by its total payroll, a 10 percent rise in profitability leads to a 6 to 7 percent rise in the number of firms, allowing for the influence of other factors. The more capital intensive an industry, the smaller the number of firms tends to be, a relationship that will be discussed in Chapter 3. And advertising, which has been called a barrier to entry, shows no significant influence on the number of firms.

Inasmuch as a smaller number of firms in an industry means

TABLE 1–5
Regressions With Log NO the Dependent Variable

Constant	CR	Log OH	Log GBV	Log INV	Log TPA	Log ADV	$\bar{r}^2$
			1972 N = 307				
4.50 (18.2)	−.042 (−21.9)	.704 (5.8)	−.525 (−6.7)	−.216 (−3.3)	.553 (6.2)	−0.13 (−0.4)	.775
2.20 (6.1)		.641 (3.3)	−.783 (−6.3)	−.448 (−4.3)	1.25 (9.3)	−.067 (−1.4)	.412
			1963 N = 318				
1.85 (4.0)	−.044 (21.9)	.375 (4.0)	−.433 (−5.8)	−.148 (−2.2)	.646 (7.0)	.045 (1.4)	.761
−1.44 (−2.1)		.363 (2.5)	−.812 (−6.9)	−.368 (−3.5)	1.43 (10.6)	−.013 (−0.2)	.395

Sources: U.S., Department of Commerce, Bureau of Economic Analysis, THE DETAILED INPUT-OUTPUT STRUCTURE OF THE U.S. ECONOMY: 1972 (1979); INPUT-OUTPUT STRUCTURE OF THE U.S. ECONOMY: 1963 (1969); U.S., Bureau of the Census, ANNUAL SURVEY OF MANUFACTURES 1976, INDUSTRY PROFILES, Part 7 (1979); CONCENTRATION RATIOS IN MANUFACTURING (1975); CENSUS OF MANUFACTURES, 1972 (1975).

CR = concentration ratio; NO = number of firms; GBV = gross book value of depreciable assets; INV = book value of inventories; TPA = total payroll (less payroll of central offices and auxiliaries in 1972); ADV = advertisng expenditures; OH = value-added minus TPA and minus ADV; figures in parentheses below coefficients are t-ratios; N = number of four-digit industries.

that the industry will tend to be more concentrated (the simple correlation of the concentration ratio with the number of firms in 1972 is minus .36 and with the log of the number of firms is minus .75), the factors that influence the number of firms influence the level of concentration. As portrayed in the regressions shown in Table 1-5, the smaller or more capital intensive an industry or the less profitable, the smaller the number of firms and, therefore, the more concentrated the industry.

For any given state of advertising technology, it appears that advertising has no influence or, at most, an insignificant influence on the number of firms in an industry. The regressions in Table 1-5 show that the important influences on the number of firms in an industry are the industry's profitability and its capital intensity. At any given level of concentration and industry size, the more profitable an industry, the larger the number of firms, while the more capital intensive an industry, the smaller the number of firms. Holding profitability, capital intensity, and size of industry constant, there is no relationship between advertising and number of firms, or at most a very weak relationship, which is a surprise. Larger investments in advertising might be expected to have the same influence as other varieties of capital intensity such as depreciable assets and inventories, but they seem not to.

Concentration of Diffused Industries

For every industry born with the founding of one or a few firms, others began their modern evolution from a base of dozens or hundreds of firms or from production in the home and in retail shops. Some became concentrated and continue in that state. Some became concentrated and then were deconcentrated as the efficiencies developed by superior management in a few firms were learned by many. Some never became concentrated. Industries illustrating these patterns range from sugar refining to meat packing to apparel.

In the last third of the nineteenth century, for example, concentration surged in the sugar refining industry. Increasing economies of centralized production, decreasing cost of transportation, superiority of management in a few firms, and competition among firms produced the trend. From 1867 to 1887, sugar output doubled. Yet the number of refineries in operation decreased from

60 to 23. Average plant capacity quintupled, rising from 200 to 1,000 barrels per day, with two thirds of the industry's capacity centralized in four refineries.

Centralization in sugar refining proceeded as far as it did because of a concomitant 60 percent decline in transportation cost. Decreasing transport costs played an important role in centralizing production in many industries where scale economies were significant. Where firms under superior management expanded and enlarged their share of their industries, output grew and prices fell. The margin over the cost of raw sugar in sugar refining, for example, fell by more than 40 percent from 1879 to 1887 (from 1.362 to 0.768 cents per pound in current dollars or from 1.362 to 0.808 cents in constant dollars).

The same general tendency prevailed in the years following World War II. Professor Steven Lustgarten reports that from 1947 to 1972, industries whose concentration increased more than 12 percentage points showed a 20.4 percentage points greater increase in total factor productivity, on average, and a 13.4 percentage point smaller rise in prices than industries whose concentration did not increase.[23]

The fall in transportation costs in the nineteenth century and the resulting rise in firm size and of concentration did not necessarily mean a decline in the number of competitors in local markets.[24] Professor Donald McCloskey warns us against accepting this easy conclusion. He points out that

> One cannot take the nation as the unit. Manufacturers in the 19th century did not compete over the whole nation, but over one locale. The sellers of hammers in Franklin County, Vermont in 1877 faced a few competitors (locally); the seller of hammers in Northeastern United States and Eastern Canada in 1977 also faced a few competitors (regionally). Those very improvements in transport and communication that made large enterprises possible also made possible national and international competition. The number of firms grew smaller, but at the same time their region of marketing grew larger. Is it obvious that monopoly power grew?[25]

A decline in number of firms and an increase in concentration not only did not necessarily mean a decline in the number of competitors; it often increased the number facing each other. A study by the FTC Bureau of Economics shows that the decline in the number of brewers from 400 after World War II to less than

100 was accompanied by an increase in the number of competitors in individual markets.[26] Professor Ambrose Winston, writing in 1924, graphically describes this sort of development in the nineteenth century.

> First, it should be understood that increased size in manufacturing organization is not the same thing as monopoly. The increase in size has resulted chiefly from improvements in transportation. When, one hundred years ago, it cost $249 to send a ton of iron from Philadelphia to Erie, the market for iron from any producing center was limited to a small radius. When a ton of iron can be sent from Pittsburgh to Vancouver for $18 the marketing radius is wide. The industrial unit was necessarily small when the market was narrow; it is large in an extensive marketing area. The change in size of factories and size of marketing areas does not mean a decrease in the number of producers within reach of the buyer. The twentieth-century consumer buys from a large factory selling across half a continent; his nineteenth-century ancestor bought from a little shop or mill which sent its product across half a county.
>
> *A Local Situation*
>
> In the small gristmill a family had few mills to choose from and paid the same price (or toll) to everyone. The millers could readily agree on prices without interference by officers of the law. In my Illinois village we were confronted when we bought meat, not by a beef trust, but by an entire consolidation of the beef industry in one person, namely, Joe C. We bought our beef from him or went without. Later Charley D. came in—we dealt not with a Big Five and two hundred independents described in the Federal Trade Commission report, but with a Big Two. The rich man of the region in a neighboring town had his meat sent in from a distance. This doubled the cost. With the one exception and occasional purchases in the winter of frozen beef from farmers by the "quarter," not one family in that region ever found relief from the power of our Beef Trust.
>
> Not only has the substitution of large for small producing units resulted in no weakening of competition; more than that, it is an obvious deduction, from facts known to all observers, even from the hackneyed commonplaces of recent industrial history, that, with and because of the growth of capitalism, competition has in our day become intense and swift and sure beyond all previous human experience.[27]

In the meat packing industry, concentration rose substantially in the late nineteenth and early twentieth century. Pioneering by Swift and imitation by a few firms of such innovations as assembly line methods (later made famous by Henry Ford in the auto industry) with complete utilization of all by-products brought this result. The leading firms became known for "using everything but the squeal." Also, their development of refrigerated packing houses, cold storage, the refrigerator car, and an efficient distribution system created enlarged markets for meat supplied from cheap sources of livestock. They grew large by innovating and by offering lower prices. Their industry grew concentrated, despite protective legislation in some states forbidding the importation of "foreign" meat, as a result of a few firms providing less expensive service to consumers. At the same time, ranchers in remote regions benefited from the improved market for their livestock.

Once the innovations of the "Big Five" (which became four with the merger of Armour and Morris in 1922) were imitated by other packers, deconcentration began. It accelerated with the spread of highways and the rise of trucking and mechanical refrigeration. Also, the increasing size of the market led to the growth of single species packers. The resulting economies of specialization without the loss of scale economies contributed to deconcentration. Not only did the innovative lead of the "Big Five" disappear; it passed to smaller firms, some of which have now grown large enough to displace members of the original "Big Five." Swift and Armour, once the giants of the industry processing 48 percent of total inspected slaughter in 1924, no longer hold that position. Cudahy dropped out of the leading four-firm group by 1955 after closing four meat plants and twenty-six wholesale branches, falling to seventh rank in size. Iowa Beef Processors, Hormel, and Oscar Mayer replaced Wilson and Armour in addition to Cudahy. The leading four-firm share of the market, which had declined to 56 percent in 1935, continued its slide to 20 percent in 1972 (see Table 1-2). The decline occurred in part because the old "Big Five" did not expand with the growth in the market and in part because the more innovative smaller firms captured all the growth and more.[28] The smaller firms led the way in building packing plants near livestock sources (taking advantage of the economies and flexibility of mechanically refrigerated trucking), in "breaking" carcasses for shipment, in reducing transportation costs, and in the use of lower cost labor outside large metropolitan areas to the disadvantage of the leading firms, which clung to their plants at central distribution points when that was no longer advantageous.

National Concentration Without Market Concentration

The spread of canals and railroads in the nineteenth century dramatically decreased transportation costs and widened markets. Local markets formerly served by a few local producers were invaded by more distant firms in those instances where economies of large-scale production were important and transport costs dropped enough to no longer offset the economies of centralization. While national concentration in many industries rose with those developments, concentration in local markets often declined. And local cartels, which endured as long as local markets were insulated by high transportation costs, crumbled before the onslaught of outsiders.

The growth in establishment size as the railroad network spread and transport costs fell was dramatic. Capital invested per manufacturing plant doubled between 1879 and 1899. It doubled again between 1899 and 1919. With the commitment of larger amounts of capital to single plants and the growing need to market over an enlarged territory (which could be invaded by others also benefiting from economies of scale and reduced transport costs) risks increased and the need to mitigate these risks grew. Multi-plant firms serving several regions developed, thus reducing risks by regional diversification. Despite this growth in national concentration, competition flourished and prices fell. More firms were meeting each other in each marketplace, each trying to enlarge its business to enhance its scale economies.

Professor Harold Vatter summarizes these developments in the following words:

> The large-volume plant and firm and the multi-plant firm could sell or buy in several regions, in the entire national economy, and in the rest of the world. Large production of commodities of uniform quality brought lower unit costs than was possible when the scale and techniques of production were constrained by more limited sales areas. This development worked in favor of bigness.
>
> "Bigness" is a relative term. What is here meant is bigness relative to plants and firms in the pre-Civil War decades. The giant firm as it evolved in the period under study was not necessarily bigger, in terms of its market share in a market defined in terms of a single product, than its predecessor who operated in a much smaller local or regional market segregated by a high transport cost barrier.[29]

Conclusion

Firms and industries in the dynamic American market do not stand still. Whether a high level of concentration persists in a newly founded industry depends on the growth rate of the market for the industry's product, on the attractiveness (profitability) of the industry to new entrants, and on other factors such as the economies of scale. If small firms—small relative to the size of the market—can operate as efficiently as large companies, the industry quickly diffuses. If they cannot, the industry remains concentrated, although not necessarily in the hands of its pioneering firms unless they are progressive in their technology, in their organizational structure and labor relations, and in other facets of their business.

A diffused industry may remain diffused if innovations are usable in small-scale operations and are speedily adopted by large numbers of those in the industry. If a few firms innovate quicker than others and imitation is slow, the industry may grow concentrated. But companies from outside the industry may displace the drones and deconcentrate the industry, particularly if the leaders themselves become slow in adapting to changing circumstances.

The relative performance of different businesses, as well as the technological and organizational possibilities, play a large role in determining an industry's structure. Empire builders may merge many businesses to form a "dominant" firm—that is, a company producing a very large share of an industry's output—but such firms do not persist in their leading position unless they perform well (see Tables 3-1 and 3-2). A pioneer may found an industry with a new product, but it does not occupy a dominant or leading role long if it does not continue to innovate and does not organize and operate itself efficiently. Competition is perennially at work preventing anyone from resting on his or her laurels.

Notes

1. W. G. Shepherd, THE ECONOMICS OF INDUSTRIAL ORGANIZATION 201 (1979). Shepherd adds that "industries below 20 percent concentration account for only 3 percent of manufacturing activity," after adjusting reported concentration. Census data show such industries account for

21.8 percent of value of shipments (Table 1-2). J. K. Galbraith asserts that "the dominant market of modern capitalism is not one made up of many sellers. . . . Rather it is a market of few sellers." *Monopoly and the Concentration of Economic Power* in H. Ellis, ed., A SURVEY OF CONTEMPORARY ECONOMICS (1948).

2. Joseph Schumpeter, CAPITALISM, SOCIALISM, AND DEMOCRACY (1942). Clare Griffin, *Testimony,* A STUDY OF THE ANTITRUST LAWS, SENATE HEARINGS 387 (Jun. 9, 1955), cited in Y. Brozen, THE COMPETITIVE ECONOMY vi (1975).

3. John E. Kwoka, Jr., *The Diversity of Firm Size Distribution in Manufacturing Industries,* INDUSTRIAL ORGANIZATION REVIEW (1979). The second largest firm in the average U.S. manufacturing industry in 1972 produced 10 percent of its industry's output.

4. Clair Wilcox, *On the Alleged Ubiquity of Monopoly,* 40 AMERICAN ECONOMIC REVIEW 67 (May 1950).

5. George Hilton, AMTRAK: THE NATIONAL RAILROAD PASSENGER CORPORATION (1980).

6. Joe S. Bain, INTERNATIONAL DIFFERENCES IN INDUSTRIAL STRUCTURE (1966); F. L. Pryor, *An International Comparison of Concentration Ratios,* 54 REVIEW OF ECONOMICS AND STATISTICS 130 (May 1972). Pryor concludes that "the data show that the average four-digit concentration ratios among *large* industrial nations are roughly the same. . . . The data show that the rank order of concentration ratios are roughly the same in all nations," at 138–39 (emphasis supplied). Also, see F. M. Scherer, A. Beckenstein, E. Kaufer, and R. D. Murphy, THE ECONOMICS OF MULTI-PLANT OPERATION: AN INTERNATIONAL COMPARISONS STUDY 218–19, 426–28 (1975).

7. F. M. Scherer, *Stochastic Determinants of Market Structure,* INDUSTRIAL MARKET STRUCTURE AND ECONOMIC PERFORMANCE 125 (1970), and the references given there.

8. It might be argued that Pittsburgh Reduction remained the sole manufacturer of primary aluminum in the United States until at least 1901 because of the Hall and Bradley patents. However, the Bradley patent was sold to Pittsburgh Reduction by its owners, who had engaged in aluminum production for two years. If the owners of the Bradley patent had been more efficient in aluminum production than Pittsburgh, their patent and Hall's would have been worth more to them than to Pittsburgh and the Bradley plant owners would have bought the Pittsburgh Reduction Company.

9. One other producer made primary aluminum for two years. "From 1891 to 1893 Alfred and Eugene Cowles, pioneers in aluminum alloys, also made pure aluminum by the Hall process; but they shifted to fabrication after losing a patent infringement suit filed by the Pittsburgh Reduction Company." Simon N. Whitney, ANTITRUST POLICIES: AMERICAN EXPERIENCE IN TWENTY INDUSTRIES, vol. 2 at 86 (1958.)

"Until 1938 there was only one alumina plant in the United States. One study estimated that in 1940 a 100,000-ton alumina plant would have costs 20% higher than a 500,000-ton plant. . . . The United States did not reach this level of consumption . . . until 1942." L. W. Weiss, ECONOMICS AND AMERICAN INDUSTRY 178 (1961).

10. One of the factors persuading R. J. Reynolds to enter the market was Alcoa's refusal to expand capacity even more than its planned $200,000,000 expansion begun in 1938, despite a request from Rey-

nolds. Alcoa was reluctant since an antitrust suit had been filed against it in 1937.

11. E. R. Corey, THE DEVELOPMENT OF MARKETS FOR NEW MATERIALS (1956).

12. Jesse Markham, COMPETITION IN THE RAYON INDUSTRY (1952).

13. W. L. Thorp and G. W. Knott, *The History of Concentration in Seven Industries* in Thorp and W. F. Crowder, THE STRUCTURE OF INDUSTRY 251 (1941).

14. E. F. Haites and J. Mak, *Steamboating on the Mississippi, 1810–1860: A Purely Competitive Industry,* 45 BUSINESS HISTORY REVIEW 52 (Spring 1971).

15. Nathan Rosenberg, *Technological Change in the Machine Tool Industry, 1840–1910,* 23 JOURNAL OF ECONOMIC HISTORY 434 (Dec. 1963); Arthur S. Dewing, *The American Bicycle Company,* CORPORATE PROMOTIONS AND REORGANIZATIONS 249 (1914). The first American bicycle was manufactured by the Weed Sewing Machine Co. in 1878. The sewing machine works were gradually transformed into a bicycle factory.

16. *Fight for Appliances,* BUSINESS WEEK 96 (Nov. 12, 1956); *Whirlpool Corp.,* FORBES 18 (Feb. 1, 1963).

17. *So Where Can the Profits Grow?* BUSINESS WEEK 144 (Mar. 9, 1957).

18. Meier Statman, DISEQUILIBRIUM AND GROWTH IN THE PHARMACEUTICAL INDUSTRY (forthcoming). The number of firms in the pharmaceutical preparations industry (2834) peaked at 1,128 in 1954. From 1954 to 1963, the number fell 2 percent per year, then accelerated to 3 percent per year from 1963 to 1972 as prospective profitability declined.

19. G. J. Church, *Fish Sticks,* 36 WALL STREET JOURNAL (Aug. 30, 1956).

20. U.S., Industrial Commission, PRELIMINARY REPORT OF THE INDUSTRIAL COMMISSION AND TESTIMONY 217 (1900).

21. Lester G. Telser, *Some Determinants of the Returns in Manufacturing Industries,* COMPETITION, COLLUSION, AND GAME THEORY 332–33 (1972).

22. Douglas W. Webbink, *Predicting 1972 Concentration Levels Using 1967 Concentration and Other Variables for 280 4-Digit Industries,* FTC WORKING PAPER 15 at 5 (Oct. 1979).

24. Fred Bateman and Thomas Weiss, *Market Structure Before the Age of Big Business: Concentration and Profit in Early Southern Manufacturing,* 49 BUSINESS HISTORY REVIEW 312 (Autumn 1975).

25. Don McCloskey, *Hunting the Unicorn: Some Doubts on the Rise of the Corporate Economy, Managerial Capitalism, Monopoly Capital, and the Like* 2 (presented at Economic History Conference, Harvard University, Sept. 1977).

26. Charles F. Kiethahn, THE BREWING INDUSTRY (Dec. 1978).

27. A. P. Winston, *The Chimera of Monopoly,* THE ATLANTIC MONTHLY (Nov. 1924), reprinted in 10 THE FREEMAN 39 (Sept. 1960).

28. In addition to the rise of new competitors, changes in concentration can be a result of declining markets as well as of growth in new markets. The effects of decline and growth on industry structure are illustrated by examples in Betty Bock, RESTRUCTURING PROPOSALS: MEASURING COMPETITION IN NUMERICAL GRIDS 25–26 (Jan. 1974). Also see P. G. Porter and H. C. Livesay, *Oligopoly in Small Manufacturing Industries,* 7 EXPLORATIONS IN ECONOMIC HISTORY 371 (1969–70).

29. H. G. Vatter, THE DRIVE TO INDUSTRIAL MATURITY: THE U.S. ECONOMY, 1860–1914 at 169 (1975).

2

Measurement and Significance of Concentration

The determination of *market* shares is a major issue in most antitrust cases. To measure market shares, market boundaries have to be drawn.[1] That frequently becomes a contentious matter, sometimes occupying months of hearings in antitrust trials. Does primary aluminum compete with secondary aluminum? In order to find Alcoa guilty of violating the antitrust laws, Judge Learned Hand had to find that Alcoa "controlled" the secondary aluminum market, despite the production of secondary aluminum by many suppliers, as well as that it had a "monopoly" of primary aluminum. But he never considered whether aluminum competes with galvanized sheet metal, copper, magnesium, zinc, tinplate, glass, tin, and other materials used for some of the same purposes as aluminum.

One of the first uses of aluminum was in decorative applications where it became a rival of silver foil. Early in the century it competed with copper for the electric power transmission market and won a large share of the business. An important use for aluminum developed in the 1920s making it a competitor of tin in the foil market. It succeeded in largely replacing tinfoil by the late 1920s. (Aluminum foil is still sometimes referred to as "tinfoil" by consumers.) In the 1940s, it invaded still other markets, even replacing wood and canvas in the construction of canoes. In the 1950s, it began replacing glass and tinplated steel in the beer container market. A study of the demand for aluminum by Professor Franklin Fisher demonstrated that it competes with steel in many applications. He found that each one percent reduction in the price of aluminum relative to the price of steel increased the quantity of aluminum demanded by 2 percent.[2]

In the cellophane case, in which the government accused the du Pont Company of obtaining a monopoly of cellophane by monopolizing the market for cellophane, the Court took a somewhat different stance. It ruled that the market consisted of flexible wrapping materials with which cellophane was interchangeable. As the quality of cellophane improved and its price decreased, it was substituted for other wrapping materials in an increasing number of applications just as aluminum was substituted for other materials as new alloys were developed and its relative price decreased.

The Court held that du Pont's 76 percent share of cellophane production did not constitute a monopoly, in contrast to Judge Hand's ruling in the aluminum case, since cellophane was only 18 percent of wrapping material. The decision has been criticized on the ground that if cellophane and other wrapping materials were substitutes, a decrease in the price of cellophane would cause decreases in the prices of the other materials—and it did not.[3] Chief Justice Warren's dissent argues that

> . . . from 1924 to 1932 du Pont dropped the price of plain cellophane 84% while the price of glassine remained constant. And during the period 1933–1946 the price for glassine and waxed paper actually increased in the face of a further 21% decline in the price of cellophane. If "shifts in business" due to "price sensitivity" had been substantial, glassine and waxed paper producers who wanted to stay in business would have been compelled by market forces to meet du Pont's price challenge. . . . That producers of glassine and waxed paper remained dominant in the flexible packaging materials market without meeting cellophane's tremendous price cuts convinces us that cellophane was not in effective competition with their products.[4]

The criticism and the dissent show a misunderstanding of the economic measure of substitutability. By "substitutes" we mean those things that have an appreciable cross-elasticity of demand. (The Court referred to the cross-elasticity between cellophane and other materials in its decision.) "Cross-elasticity" does not refer to a relationship between prices; rather it is a measure of the decrease in the *quantity* of an item purchased resulting from a decrease in the price of another item. If no decrease in the cost of production of a competitive wrapping material occurs, and if it is being sold at its long-run competitive-equilibrium price, then the decreasing price of cellophane should not be expected to affect the price of the alternative material. It would affect only the quantity sold. This was recognized in the Court's opinion. It pointed out the portions of the various wrapping material markets taken by cellophane. The majority opinion stated that

> . . . cellophane furnishes . . . 7% of wrappings for bakery products, 25% for candy, 32% for snacks, 35% for meats and poultry, 27% for crackers and biscuits, 47% for fresh produce, and 34% for frozen foods. Seventy-five to eighty percent of cigarettes are wrapped in cellophane.[5]

There is a paradoxical aspect to the Court's decision. If du Pont had succeeded in further reducing its cost and the price of cellophane and won a much larger share of the wrapping material market, the decision implies that the Court would have ruled that du Pont was a monopolist. Superior performance and competitive behavior resulting in the concentration of sales in the hands of a single firm have been taken by the courts as evidence of monopoly and of monopolizing (United Shoe Machinery and Alcoa, for example). In order to escape a finding of antitrust law violation, firms must restrain output—the behavior the antitrust laws sought to prevent. The acceptance of the market-concentration doctrine by the courts warns firms that they must not share so much of the gains from technological progress or superior management with their customers that they win a major share of something that can be defined as a market or line of commerce.

This is a perversion of the antitrust laws, but it is the doctrine that has been applied by the antitrust agencies.[6] It has been accepted by the courts as a basis for some decisions. As Professor Richard Posner remarks, "The thrust of monopolization law has been to encourage the charging of monopoly prices."[7]

Concentration Measurement by the Bureau of the Census

A major determinant of census concentration ratios is the set of compartments used for designating industries. The intercity trans-

48

portation market discussed earlier provides an example of this. Automobiles, buses, and trains compete with airlines and with each other for intercity passengers. The four leading bus companies have only a small share of this business. But the intercity bus industry, taken as a separate category, has a high concentration ratio. Similarly, metals are interchangeable in many uses and compete with each other. Gutters and downspouts made of aluminum, copper, or galvanized steel compete with each other. These materials serve this and many other markets interchangeably. But no concentration ratio is computed by the Bureau of Census for the metals industry. The industry is divided into blast furnaces and steel mills (3312), electrometallurgical products (3313), primary copper (3331), primary lead (3332), primary zinc (3333), primary aluminum (3334), primary nonferrous metals not elsewhere classified (3339), and secondary nonferrous metals (3341). This categorization raises industry concentration ratios substantially in the various metal industries relative to market concentration.

The increase in the number of manufacturing industries from 281 in 1935 to 450 in 1972, in itself, raised domestic concentration ratios. The more compartments among which establishments are divided, the fewer there will be in each. With fewer factories in any one category, those belonging to the four leading firms in each compartment (industry) will show a higher share. That is the major reason that the average concentration ratio in manufacturing industries in the United States shows no drop between 1935 and 1972 (see Table 1-2) despite the great growth in the size of the manufacturing sector of the economy and in the number of firms in manufacturing.

In general, the smaller the size of an "industry"—and industries will be smaller the narrower their definition as we saw above—the smaller the number of companies in each industry and the higher the concentration in each. If we take single products that sell in small volume and define those as "industries," concentration ratios will be very high. About $100 million worth of bromine is produced each year in the United States, for example. Defining this as an "industry," we find that there are only four firms in the industry and its four-firm concentration ratio is 100 percent. The same result would follow in such small industries as boron, columbium, tin, and magnesium. That is why the White House Antitrust Task Force in 1968 suggested that worries about any presumed need to deconcentrate be focused only on those "industries" that produce at least $500 million worth of product (equivalent to 1.3 billion in 1981 dollars). However, just as economies of scale dictate a small number of firms in small industries, they may also dictate a small number of firms in some very large industries, especially where the value of each unit of product is very high as it is in the aircraft, turbine, and locomotive industries.

Whether a concentration ratio measures anything economically meaningful depends on the correspondence between what is measured and what takes place in the market. The measure commonly used is total shipments from plants "assigned" to an industry by the Bureau of the Census. A plant's entire output is assigned to the industry whose products make up the plurality of total shipments from the plant. If a plant belonging to a leading firm produces trucks and refrigerators, and more than half the value of its shipments is trucks, all the plant's shipments are assigned to the motor vehicle industry. That firm will then show a higher share of motor vehicle industry shipments than its actual share. A higher industry concentration ratio will be a consequence if the firm is one of the four largest in the motor vehicle industry.[8]

The household vacuum cleaner industry (SIC 3635) provides an illustration of this problem. In 1963, the establishments belonging to the leading four firms in this industry shipped 81 percent of the product shipped by all establishments classed in industry 3635. But 13 percent of the product shipped by these establishments consisted of items other than vacuum cleaners. (That is, the Primary Product Specialization Ratio reported by the Bureau of the Census was 87 percent.) If all these non–vacuum-cleaner products were produced in the plants of the four leaders, then their share of vacuum cleaner shipments from plants classified in the industry was 78 percent, not 81 percent. However, 20 percent of all domestically produced vacuum cleaners in 1963 was produced in plants not classified in the vacuum cleaner industry, a fact reported in the form of a Coverage Ratio, which was 80 percent. The four leading firms, then, could be producing 78 percent of 80 percent of domestically produced vacuum cleaners, that is, 62 percent. The actual share furnished by the four leaders in 1963 was 64 percent, reported by Census as the "product" concentration ratio, 17 percentage points less than the reported 81 percent "industry" concentration ratio. (See Table 4-2 for comparisons of these two measures in "high" concentration industries.)

Census Concentration and Market Concentration

There are many other problems afflicting the commonly used industry concentration ratios.[9] The key argument on which advocates of deconcentration base their case, namely, that there is some relationship between market concentration and monopoly power, is already very much in doubt.[10] Professor George Stigler has pointed out that

> A concentrated industry need not be monopolistic. High elasticity of demand for the industry's product, or ease of entry by new firms, or the extent of independent rivalry among firms may make the concentrated industry . . . differ in, at most, trifling respects from a fully competitive industry.[11]

Compounding this problem is the question of how well an industry's concentration ratio portrays *market* concentration (even if all plants produce only one product and no industry's primary product is manufactured in plants not classified in its industry). As it turns out, concentration measures reported for some industries are high simply because of what is defined to be an industry, not because firms competing with the Big Two or the Big Four are few or small.

Industry definitions are generally based on technology or on inputs employed, not on markets. Separate concentration ratios are reported for beet and for cane sugar refiners, for example. But since beet and cane refiners compete with each other for the same customers, these ratios mean little in market terms. Their outputs are indistinguishable. In addition, glucose, dextrose, and fructose sugars are produced by the corn wet milling industry. Maple syrup and honey are produced by still two more industries. Artificial sweeteners are produced by still another industry. There is no concentration figure reported for the sweetener market. Although cane refiners compete with beet refiners and both compete with corn millers, maple sap boilers, beekeepers, and chemical firms, no account is taken of this in measuring concentration.

Firms in a single SIC industry may compete in many different markets. They may meet a different set of competitors from different SIC industries in each market. There are twelve firms in the primary aluminum industry. Its four-firm industry concentration ratio is reported as 72 percent in 1976. The top four aluminum producers shipped 95 percent of the aluminum going into flat-rolled sheet used to make beer cans. But beer is also canned in tinplate and bottled in glass. Aluminum's share of the beer container market is 42 percent and the top four share of the beer container market is 40 percent. Aluminum is also used to produce insulated electrical conductor. The top four producers sell 74 percent of the aluminum going into the electrical conductor market, but only 35 percent of the metal used for electrical conductor is aluminum; the rest is copper. So the Big Four have 74 percent of 35 percent, or 25 percent of the insulated conducted metal market.[12]

The Census Bureau itself, when transmitting concentration data to the Senate Subcommittee on Antitrust and Monopoly, warned the committee that the data did not measure the state of competition or of markets:

> In this system of classification the basis of grouping products is not whether they are competitive in the sense that the prospective purchaser can satisfy a need by selecting one or the other product. In some cases items in the same industries or commodity categories appeal to different needs and in others the same need can be satisfied by products in different categories. As an example of the latter condition paper products are often substituted for similar products made of metal, wood or glass. However, the paper products are typically classified in industries different from those producing the metal, wood or glass products. *No special purpose system designed primarily to measure market shares of large companies in particular industries or commodity areas is in existence . . .*[13]

A further difficulty is that industry concentration figures take account of only one source of product—current domestic production. The automobile production concentration figure is high, but it does not measure *market* concentration. It takes no account of imports, of cars offered from stocks manufactured in prior years, or of used cars. The 99+ percent domestic-production concentration figure reported for the automobile industry would drop to 78 percent if account were taken of imports, to 30 percent if account were taken of all automobiles sold in the United States in any given year whether new or used, and to 10 percent if it were recognized that new cars compete with the entire stock of existing automobiles.

Every repair and maintenance shop competes with the foreign and domestic producers of new cars. "A car could be driven forever if parts that wore out were replaced."[14] This became dramatically obvious in the early 1930s when new car and truck sales in the United States declined by 73 percent, yet registrations declined less than 6 percent and gasoline consumption less than 5 percent. The scrappage rate fell more than 80 percent. Maintenance of old vehicles was substituted for the purchase of new cars as maintenance costs fell relative to the price of packaged pre-maintenance in the form of new cars. Argentina in the 1950s provides an equally dramatic example of the competition of repair shops with auto manufacturers. The price of imported cars was forced up to $10,000 by duties and import fees. The maintenance industry boomed. There was no decline in the car population, but the preponderance of vehicles seen on the streets consisted of shiny fifteen- to thirty-year-old automobiles.

Professor George Stigler, in his introduction to *Business Concentration and Price Policy,* a volume reporting the proceedings of a conference on the topic held by the Universities-National Bureau Committee for Economic Research, tells us that

> Price theory has certain direct implications for this problem of defining industries that have not received adequate recognition in official practice . . . An industry should embrace the maximum geographical area and the maximum variety of productive activities in which there is strong long-run substitution. If buyers can shift on a large scale from product or area B to A, then the two should be combined. If producers can shift on a large scale from B to A, again they should be combined.
>
> One important application of the rule of high substitution is to international trade. If a commodity is on either an export or an import basis, its concentration should usually be measured for a market larger than the domestic area. If the commodity is on an export basis, foreign buyers have alternative sources of supply, which must be included in the "industry"; if it is on an import basis, domestic buyers have alternative domestic supply sources, which again should be combined with the foreign supply. In either case it is necessary to take account of the industry structure abroad.[15]

Professor Fred Weston has computed concentration ratios taking into account the suggestion of Professor Stigler with regard to foreign trade. Using 1963 data, he determined that 97 percent of the domestic output of locomotives and locomotives parts is produced by four firms and exports account for 11 percent of this output. Since the industry competes with foreign firms for customers, the market concentration ratio is in fact only 63 percent. The Census Bureau computed a 76 percent 1963 concentration ratio for the typewriter industry, but foreign suppliers provide 20 percent of the typewriters sold in the United States. The appropriate measure of typewriter market concentration is 53 percent.[16] The Budd Co. is the sole producer of rail passenger cars in the United States, but it regularly loses U.S. orders to foreign firms. It competes with Bombardier, Inc., and Hawker Siddeley, Ltd., of Canada, Nippon Shanyo and Kawasaki of Japan, a French firm (which won the contract for cars for the Atlanta subway), and an Italian firm (which won a Cleveland contract). In today's world economy, American products compete directly with foreign products at home and overseas, making domestic shipment ratios meaningless.

Notes

1. We are not concerned here with alternative measures of size-distribution of firms such as the Herfindahl index, the Gini coefficient, entropy, et cetera, but only with the census measures, which are defined by the share of output produced by some given number of leading firms. For discussions probing the choice of alternative measures, see M. O. Finkelstein and R. M. Friedberg, *The Application of an Entropy Theory of Concentration,* and G. J. Stigler, *Comment,* 76 YALE LAW JOURNAL 677, 718 (Mar. 1967); S. E. Boyle and C. Marfels, *Absolute and Relative Measures of Concentration Reconsidered,* 24 KYKLOS 753 (No. 4, 1971); L. Hannah and J. A. Kay, CONCENTRATION IN MODERN INDUSTRY: THEORY, MEASUREMENT AND THE U.K. EXPERIENCE (1977); John E. Kwoka, Jr., *Does the Choice of Concentration Ratio Really Matter?* FTC WORKING PAPER no. 17 (Oct. 1979); Eugene M. Singer, *Concentration Indexes,* ANTITRUST ECONOMICS 156 (1968).
2. Franklin Fisher, *The Demand for Aluminum Ingot in the United States,* A PRIORI INFORMATION AND TIME SERIES ANALYSIS (1961).
3. G. W. Stocking and W. F. Mueller, *The Cellophane Case and the New Competition,* 45 AMERICAN ECONOMIC REVIEW 54 (1955).
4. 351 U.S. 416–18 (1956).
5. *Id.* at 395.
6. Y. Brozen, *The Attack on Concentration,* 29 THE FREEMAN 38 (Jan. 1979); Robert Bork, THE ANTITRUST PARADOX (1978); Richard Posner, ANTITRUST LAW: AN ECONOMIC PERSPECTIVE (1976).
7. Posner *supra* n. 6, at 207.
8. Industry concentration measurement problems arising out of the multiproduct production of single plants are thoroughly analyzed by Betty Bock, in CONCENTRATION PATTERNS IN MANUFACTURING 25–28 (1969). One of the mysteries of the concentration studies done by economists is why they have so uniformly chosen to use industry concentration measures instead of the product concentration measures that have been

available since 1954. These come closer to fitting markets than industry measures. While the correlation between industry and product concentration measures is high, there are sometimes wide differences. For example, see *id*. at 27. In view of the conventional usage of industry concentration ratios and the large body of statistical analysis reported in this form in the literature, the same practice is followed here in order to maintain a basis for comparing results with those reported elsewhere.

9. Sanford Rose, *Bigness Is a Numbers Game*, FORTUNE (Nov. 1969). Reprinted in Y. Brozen, THE COMPETITIVE ECONOMY 102 (1975). Also, see E. M. Singer, *The Compilation of Census Concentration Data*, ANTITRUST ECONOMICS 156 (1968).

10. "Structure is little more than a check on conclusions drawn from behavior. It is simply too imprecise. Even with market boundaries quite clearly defined, the number of sellers and their distribution by size is compatible with a wide variety of results." M. A. Adelman, *World Oil and the Theory of Industrial Organization,* in J. W. Markham and G. F. Papanek, eds., ESSAYS IN HONOR OF EDWARD S. MASON 151 (1970).

    "[A]ctual patterns of market conduct cannot be fully enough measured to permit us to establish empirically a meaningful association either between market conduct and performance or between structure and market conduct." J. S. Bain, INDUSTRIAL ORGANIZATION 329 (1968). Also, see note 1, Chapter 8, *infra,* for additional references.

11. G. J. Stigler, CAPITAL AND RATES OF RETURN IN MANUFACTURING INDUSTRIES 67 (1963).

12. Kaiser Aluminum & Chemical Corporation, AT ISSUE: THE CONTROVERSY OVER CONCENTRATED INDUSTRIES 12 (1978).

13. U.S., Senate Subcommittee on Antitrust and Monopoly, CONCENTRATION IN AMERICAN INDUSTRY, 85th Congress, 1st session (1957) 752–53.

14. J. Scoville, BEHAVIOR OF THE AUTOMOBILE INDUSTRY IN DEPRESSION at 27 (1935).

15. George Stigler, BUSINESS CONCENTRATION AND PRICE POLICY 4–5 (1955).

16. Fred Weston, *Do Multinational Corporations Have Market Power to Overprice?* in Carl Madden, ed., THE CASE FOR THE MULTINATIONAL CORPORATION 25 (1977).

3

Benefits of Concentration

THE drafters of the Sherman Act recognized that the concentration of an industry, where it is economic, creates benefits for consumers. For this reason they outlawed "monopolizing" (efforts to create a "monopoly" not based on efficiency) but did not ban "monopoly." In the words of Senator Sherman, the act was to proscribe arrangements "designed, or which tend, to advance the cost to the consumer." Neither it nor the Federal Trade Commission Act was intended to fragment industry or to prevent occupancy of a major share of a market by a single firm.[1]

When Senator Hoar explained to the Senate the Judiciary Committee's final draft of the bill, he declared that a man who "got the whole business because nobody could do it as well as he could" would not be in violation of the Sherman Act.[2] Neither was the Act intended to penalize large corporations for their size alone. During the Senate debate, Senator Sherman praised corporations as "useful agencies" that had "enabled individuals to unite to undertake great enterprises only attempted in former times by powerful governments."[3]

The Primary Reason for Concentration

Concentration occurs and persists where that is the efficient structure for producing and distributing a product and for adapting to changing technical possibilities, shifting demand, and increasing regulatory requirements.

> . . . those industries that have remained highly concentrated for extensive time periods without government protection can have done so only because that structure serves customers better than any seemingly feasible alternative structure; competition brought about and has sustained such structures.[1]

Where centralization is not efficient, industries do not become concentrated. If artificially concentrated by industry-wide mergers without accompanying improvements in productivity, they soon cease to be concentrated.

Numerous combinations in the late nineteenth century amply demonstrate the fate of unprogressive (or simply less progressive) and inefficiently large firms. American Strawboard, organized in 1889 with 85 percent of its industry's capacity, fell to a one-third share by 1919 despite a shrinking market. International Paper consolidated sixteen paper mills in 1898 with two thirds of North America's newsprint capacity. By 1911, its share shrank to 30 percent. American Sugar Refining combined 95 percent of the nation's sugar refining capacity in 1892. Its share of the sugar market fell to 75 percent in 1894. Its fall continued to 49 percent in 1907 despite continued acquisition of sugar refining firms. It stopped further acquisitions at that time. Its share continued to shrink to 28 percent in 1917. Standard Oil's 88 percent share of oil refining operations in 1898 failed to entrench its position despite its efficiencies and pipelines. It fell to 67 percent in 1909. (In 1911, the company was broken into 34 separate firms by an antitrust decree.) The list goes on and on (see Tables 3-1 and 3-2). Size or large market share does not entrench a business. Inertia does not preserve a leading firm's position.

Concentration persists only where it brings efficiencies or is the consequence of superior management. Professor Sam Peltzman, using 1947–67 data, found that breaking up leading firms in those industries with greater than 50 percent concentration into sizes small enough to reduce concentration to less than 50 percent would increase costs in those industries by 20 percent and prices by 10 to 15 percent.[5] Professor Lustgarten arrived at similar conclusions using data through 1972.[6]

That concentration results in cost savings that benefit pur-

TABLE 3–1
Declines in Market Share of Selected
Turn-of-the-Century Combinations

Company	Early Share		Later Share	
	Percentage	Year	Percentage	Year
Standard Oil	88	1899	67	1909
American Sugar Refining	95	1892	75	1894
American Sugar Refining	—	—	49	1907
American Sugar Refining	—	—	28	1917
American Strawboard	85–90	1889	33	1919
National Starch Mfg. Co.	70	1890	45	1899
Glucose Sugar Refining Co.	85	1897	45	1901
International Paper	66	1898	30	1911
International Paper	—	—	14	1928
American Tin Plate Co.	95	1899	54	1912
American Writing Paper	75	1899	5	1952
American Tobacco[a]	93	1899	76	1903
American Can	90	1901	60	1903
U.S. Steel[b]	66	1901	33	1934
International Harvester[c]	85	1902	44	1922
International Harvester[c]	—	—	23	1948
American Smelting and Refining	85–95	1902	31	1937
Corn Products Refining	90	1906	59	1914

Source: Simon Whitney, Antitrust Policies (1958); George Stigler, Five Lectures on Economic Problems (1949).

[a] Share of cigarette sales.

[b] Share based on steel ingot castings. A weighted average of ten products gives U.S. Steel 57 percent of the market in 1901 declining to 47 percent in 1913. A. S. Dewing, Corporate Promotions and Reorganizations at 527 (1914).

[c] Under a 1918 antitrust consent decree, Harvester disposed of its Champion and Osborne lines of harvesting machinery in 1919. These accounted for less than 10 percent of its output of four major implements and a smaller share of all farm machinery. S. Whitney, 2 Antitrust Policies at 230 (1958).

chasers despite any enhancement of market power was found to be the case by J. H. Landon in his investigation of the newspaper industry. He found that an increase in concentration reduced the price of advertising as a consequence of economies of scale. For example, his work demonstrated that the merger of a 400,000 circulation newspaper with one of 100,000 in a two newspaper town reduced the milline advertising rate from $3.58 to $3.52.[7]

Even the Twentieth Century Fund Committee on Cartels and Monopoly, which favored disintegrating firms with large market shares and the imposition of limits on firm size, admitted that limits on size could impair productive efficiency. It pointed out that

Benefits of Concentration

There are instances in which large-scale organization has apparently brought with it a more persistent downward pressure upon costs and prices than would have resulted from the competitive efforts of small concerns. The rubber tire and automobile industries are cases in point.[8]

TABLE 3–2

1890–1905 Consolidations with Large Market Shares Failing Within a Few Years after Their Formation

1. American Bicycle
2. American Barrel & Package
3. American Cement
4. American Cotton Company
5. American Electric Heating
6. American Felt
7. American Fisheries
8. American Fork & Hoe
9. American Fruit Products
10. American Grass Twine
11. American Laundry Machinery
12. American Malting
13. American Saddlery & Harness
14. American Wood Working Machinery
15. American Wringer
16. Asphalt Company of America
17. Atlantic Rubber Shoe Co. of America
18. Booth, A. & Co.
19. Consolidated Railway Lighting & Equipment
20. Consolidated Railway Lighting & Refrigeration
21. Consolidated Rubber Tire
22. Continental Cotton Oil
23. Corn Products Co.
24. Development Co. of America
25. Distillers & Cattle Feeders
26. Distilling Co. of America
27. Electric Vehicle Co.
28. General Roofing
29. Glucose Sugar Refining Co.
30. Great Western Cereal
31. International Car Wheel
32. Mt. Vernon-Woodberry Cotton Duck
33. National Asphalt
34. National Cordage
35. National Glass
36. National Novelty
37. National Shear
38. National Starch
39. National Wallpaper
40. New England Yarn
41. Pope Manufacturing
42. Standard Rope & Twine
43. United Box Board & Paper
44. United Button Company
45. United Copper Company
46. United Zinc & Lead
47. U.S. Cotton Duck
48. U.S. Dyewood & Extract
49. U.S. Finishing
50. U.S. Leather
51. U.S. Reduction & Refining
52. U.S. Shipbuilding
53. U.S. Worsted

Rejuvenations

54. Allis Chalmers
55. American Colortype
56. American School Furniture
57. American Soda Fountain
58. Central Foundry
59. International Fire Engine
60. National Salt
61. U.S. Cast Iron Pipe
62. U.S. Flour Milling
63. U.S. Realty & Improvement

Note: These companies were classified as early failures by Shaw Livermore on the basis that creditors suffered a loss within a decade after formation. The ten "rejuvenations" are classified separately on the basis of "a successful existence . . . subsequent to changes in capital set-up." *The Success of Industrial Mergers,* 50 QUARTERLY OF ECONOMICS (1935) at 90. Copyright, John Wiley & Sons. Reprinted with permission of the publishers.

The Benefits to Wage Earners from Concentration

Concentration of sales in the hands of a few firms, where it occurs and persists, not only benefits consumers; it also benefits labor. In 1938, the U.S. Bureau of Labor Statistics was asked by the Temporary National Economic Committee to investigate the consequences of "bigness" in American industry to the earnings of workers. It reported, in 1940, that

> It is clear . . . that workers in the plants of big companies have higher earnings than those in small companies, in industries in which concentration of ownership centers control of a large share of the industry in a few companies. Differentials in earnings do not appear clearly in industries in which ownership is more diffused.
> . . . This difference was not a function of region, size of community, or size of establishment, and could not be explained by unionization.[9]

Professor Ralph Nelson, using 1954 data, found that ". . . in almost all industries (92 out of 102) higher . . . hourly earnings were recorded in the [four] leading firms than in the remainder of the industry, and in almost two thirds (65 of 102) the hourly earnings were ten percent or more above the remainder of the industry."[10] The 1963 census data show the top four firms in 409 industries on average paid wages 15 percent higher than the wages paid in other firms in their industries. This occurred in the typical industry in every concentration quintile. The leading firms in the more concentrated industries paid wage rates about one-sixth higher than other firms in their industries. Leading firms in the less concentrated industries paid wage rates about one-seventh higher (see Table 3-3).

When leading firms increase their share of an industry's output, where it is economic to do so, the average wage in their industry rises. This results from the fact that they pay higher wage rates than other firms in their industries. An increase in their proportion of employment raises the average wage in their industries. However, the relationship between the wage rates paid by leading firms in an industry and the rates paid by other firms in the same industry should not be understood to be *the reason* that higher wage rates prevail in concentrated industries. Suppose that wage rates

TABLE 3–3

Production Worker Wage Rates in the Leading Four Firms and in Other Firms in Manufacturing Industries Categorized by Concentration in 1963

Four-Firm Concentration Percentage	Number of Industries	Average Hourly Earnings		Average of Ratios of Wage Rates in Leading Firms to Wage Rates in Other Firms	Depreciable Assets per Employee
		Four Leading Firms	Other Firms		
80–100	21	$2.92	$2.51	1.17	$15,599
60–79	46	2.83	2.43	1.18	17,577
40–59	91	2.78	2.41	1.16	11,967
20–39	161	2.55	2.25	1.14	9,191
0–19	90	2.47	2.17	1.13	5,037
0–100	409	2.63	2.30	1.15	10,167

Source: U.S. Bureau of the Census, Concentration Ratios in Manufacturing Industry 1963, Part II (1967).

(1) $W_4 = 2.40 + .006\ CR_4$ $\bar{r}^2 = .041$
     (38.4) (4.30)

(2) $W_{other} = 2.14 + .004\ CR_4$ $\bar{r}^2 = .031$
       (42.6) (3.72)

(3) $W = 2.10 + .008\ CR_4$ $\bar{r}^2 = .108$
     (40.8) (7.08)

(4) $W = 2.03 + .005\ CR_4 + .02AE$ $\bar{r}^2 = .243$
     (42.3) (4.44)   (8.46)

W_4 = production worker average hourly earnings in leading four firms in each industry in 1963.
W_{other} = production worker average hourly earnings in firms other than the leading four in each industry.
W = production worker average hourly earnings in all firms in an industry.
CR_4 = four-firm industry concentration ratio in 1963.
AE = assets per employee in each industry in thousands of dollars.
t = ratios in parentheses below coefficients.

are simply higher in the firms that are absolutely larger, rather than larger relative to their industries. It is then conceivable that wage rates in concentrated industries could be lower than those in unconcentrated industries although the largest firms pay higher wage rates than smaller firms. The largest firms in more concentrated industries are not necessarily larger than the largest firms in less concentrated industries. The largest firm in hard surface floor covering (93 percent concentrated), for example, is much smaller than the largest firm in petroleum refining (27 percent concentrated, measured by four leading firm share of value-added).

The possibility that absolute size, and not level of concentration, is the prime cause of higher wage rates should not lead us to conclude that a policy of deconcentration would not lower wage rates. Suppose, for example, that the wage in the four leading firms in an 80 percent concentrated industry is $5.00 an hour, and that it is $4.00 in other firms in the same industry. Consequently, the industry average wage is $4.80. If the leaders had not been permitted to grow beyond the level at which they produced 40 percent of the industry's domestic output, the industry's wage average would be, let us say, $4.30 instead of $4.80 even if the leaders pay $5.00 an hour. (Without the growth in the leaders, however, it is unlikely that they would be paying as much as $5.00 an hour.) Let us suppose that the four leaders in some unconcentrated industry have a 40 percent market share, pay $5.50 an hour, other firms pay $5.00, and the industry average wage is $5.20 (a higher wage than that in the concentrated industry in this hypothetical example). Deconcentrating this industry to, let us say, the 20 percent level (or never letting concentration increase beyond the 20 percent level) would result in a decline in the industry average wage to $5.10.

We see then that even if wage rates were lower in the presently concentrated than in the presently diffused industries, any drive to deconcentrate would result in still lower wage rates. The restrictions on rises in concentration imposed by the antitrust agencies and those on the growth of leading firms imposed by the tax structure, the subsidies given to smaller firms, and the regulations restricting expansion are preventing a rise in productivity and wage rates.[11]

But in our economy, as we saw earlier, wage rates for production workers are in fact higher in concentrated than in dispersed industries. This conclusion also holds if we look at yearly earnings. In 109 industries that were 50 percent concentrated or more, production worker annual earnings averaged $5,463 in 1963. In 154 industries whose concentration was 25 to 49 percent, annual earnings averaged $4,793. In 135 less than 25 percent concentrated industries, annual earnings averaged $4,417. Workers in the most concentrated stratum enjoyed 24 percent higher annual earnings than those in the least concentrated.[12]

The 1972 Census of Manufactures data show an equally strong association between concentration and wage rates. A statistical analysis of the relationship between wage rates and concentration shows a 14 cent rise in hourly wage rates associated with each 10 point rise in concentration, on average (see Table 3-4). The wage rate in an industry with a 70 percent four-firm concentration ratio was 69 cents higher, on the average, than the rate in a 20 percent concentrated industry. Louis Phlips found a similar relationship between wage rates and concentration in Europe. "An increase of the concentration ratio from 10 to 60 leads to wage increases of 16 percent in Belgium, 27 percent in France and 43 percent in Italy."[13]

Since concentrated industries also tend to be capital intensive, using above average amounts of equipment and other capital with each worker, part of the higher wage in the average concentrated industry is the result of this factor and the need to attract and hold employees possessing the skills and responsibility required in operating larger amounts of equipment. To the extent that some less concentrated industries are also capital intensive or require high skill levels, they too may pay high wage rates. Analyzing the separate influences of concentration and capital intensity, it appears that 4 cents of the 14 cent rise in hourly wages associated with each 10 point rise in concentration is the consequence of the greater average capital intensity of the more concentrated industries (see regressions in Table 3-4).

Concentration, Productivity, and Prices

The higher wage rates paid production workers in concentrated industries have often been attributed to a sharing with workers of

TABLE 3–4
Wage Rates of Production Workers in Manufacturing Industries
Categorized by Concentration, 1967 and 1972

Four-Firm Concentration Percentage	1967		1972		1972	
	Hourly Wage Rates	Number of Industries	Hourly Wage Rates	Number of Four-Digit Industries	Depreciable Assets per Employee	Number of Industries
80–100	$3.17	23	$4.36	22	$25,316	19
60–79	3.02	55	4.42	54	30,061	44
40–59	2.89	85	3.93	118	20,392	99
20–39	2.66	166	3.52	169	17,220	160
0–19	2.61	77	3.57	87	10,386	87
0–100	2.92	406	3.79	450	18,291	409

Sources: U.S., Bureau of the Census, CONCENTRATION RATIOS IN MANUFACTURING (1975); ANNUAL SURVEY OF MANUFACTURES 1976, Part 7; INDUSTRY PROFILES (June 1978).

$$W_{1972} = 3.248 + .0138 CR_4 \qquad N = 409 \qquad \bar{r}^2 = 0.11$$
$$\phantom{W_{1972}} (39.6) \quad (7.48)$$

$$= 3.148 + .0102 CR_4 + .0152 AE \qquad N = 409 \qquad \bar{r}^2 = 0.23$$
$$(39.1) \quad (5.63) \qquad (8.29)$$

W_{1972} = average hourly earning of production workers in 1972 dollars.
CR_4 = four-firm concentration percentage in 1972.
AE = assets per employee in 1972 measured in thousands of dollars.
Figure in parenthesis below each coefficient in the regression equation is the t-value.

monopoly returns. Higher returns than would prevail if those industries were less oligopolistic are allegedly split between workers
and the firms. As we will show shortly, higher productivity makes
the higher wage rates possible rather than higher prices (and competition for workers capable of filling the high productivity jobs
enforces a higher wage). This can be demonstrated using data on
prices, productivity, and concentration.

Let us look first directly at the price experience in industries
where concentration was increased by consolidations early in the
century. Then let us compare this with the price movements in
industries where no consolidations occurred. The National Industrial Conference Board found that in twenty-six industries in
which important consolidations took place and in which price data
were available, prices *fell* by 13 percent from 1900 to 1913 and
then rose by 49 percent from 1913 to 1925. In twenty industries
in which no consolidations occurred, prices *rose* by 10 percent
from 1900 to 1913 and then rose by 96 percent from 1913 to 1925
(see Figure 3-1). The increased concentration brought about by
substantial horizontal mergers lowered prices relative to those in
industries where concentration was not increased by mergers.

Similar conclusions concerning the effect of increasing concentration were reached by Professor Steven Lustgarten for the period
1954 to 1972. In the twenty-two industries in which concentration
increased by more than 12 percentage points, prices rose 4.7 percentage points less than in sixty-two industries in which concentration decreased (see Table 3-5).

It may seem paradoxical that the largest firms in an industry
(and concentrated industries) have lower costs and prices despite
paying higher wage rates. There is a general principle at work in
profit-seeking organizations that produces this puzzling combination. In profit-seeking enterprises, there is a reward for improving
efficiency. The business that figures out how to do a job at lower
cost by better organizing its work, developing or choosing more
productive equipment, or driving toward a larger scale of operation
when it lowers cost to do so, rewards its owners and managers for
their improvements in efficiency. This provides a constant moti-
vation to improve productivity. The firms with relatively greater
success in decreasing costs quote lower prices to attract additional
business since they can increase profits by increasing their volume. They can profit at these lower prices by their greater efficiency. (In 1978, the Federal Trade Commission complained that

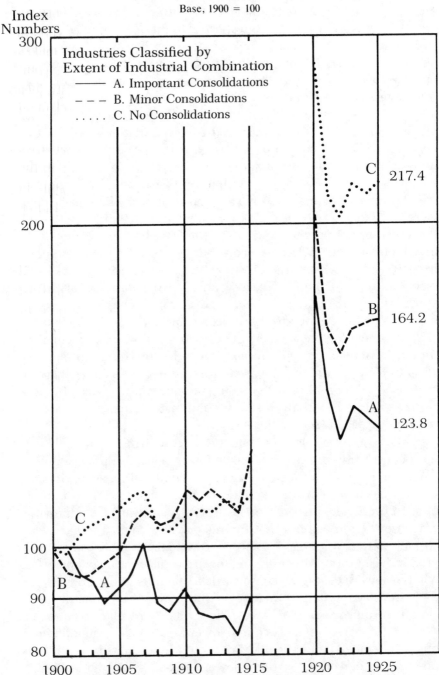

FIGURE 3–1

Price Fluctuations in Three Groups
of Manufacturing Industries

Base, 1900 = 100

Index
Numbers

Industries Classified by
Extent of Industrial Combination
———— A. Important Consolidations
– – – B. Minor Consolidations
. . . . . C. No Consolidations

300

C 217.4

200

B 164.2

A 123.8

C

100

B   A

90

80

1900   1905   1910   1915   1920   1925

Source: National Industrial Conference Board, MERGERS IN INDUSTRY: A STUDY
OF CERTAIN ECONOMIC ASPECTS OF INDUSTRIAL CONSOLIDATION (1929) at 146. Copyright by the Conference Board. Reprinted by permission of the publisher.

du Pont was becoming dominant in the titanium dioxide market by improving its technology, charging less than domestic and foreign competitors wished to charge, and expanding its capacity to take care of its growing volume of sales.)

Examples of the association of higher profits with lower prices abound. The experience of some turn-of-the-century consolidations, which found that their attempts to profit by raising prices instead decreased profits, provided a lesson well learned by American business men. In the 1920s, American business lore included the adage that the efficient firm producing an effective product increases its profits by selling at low prices. Henry Ford dramatized the precept by selling automobiles at low prices and becoming a billionaire. With his low prices, he dominated the automobile industry from 1911 through 1926.

National Steel applied the adage in the 1930s. Under the "code" installed in 1933 by the National Recovery Administration, steel producers were required to set minimum prices and file any changes ten days prior to their going into effect. The record of the filings shows that National Steel refused to follow several increases on sheet and strip steel and initiated several price cuts. It alone among all steel companies made profits in every year of the Great Depression. From 1930 through 1938, its pretax earnings on equity averaged 9.1 percent. That was the highest return among 11 leading steel companies, the next highest being Inland which averaged a 7.3 percent pretax return.[14] National's continuous strip mill and a new plant completed in 1929 made it a low-cost producer and made it profitable to follow a low-price policy. Other steel firms, which had to meet National Steel's prices to hold any business, were reluctant to produce at these prices. Enough business was left to National to keep its plant more fully and more profitably occupied than it would otherwise have been.

In this generation, examples of this sort are not well known since it has become general policy to meet such price changes. The usually quick response of competitors prevents the occurrence of such dramatic examples as that of Henry Ford and the Model T or the rise of Camel cigarettes.[15] But there are examples, nevertheless. In the 1960s, nonregulated Pacific Southwest Air (PSA) carried passengers by air between San Francisco and Los Angeles at half the price charged by competing interstate airlines regulated by the Civil Aeronautics Board (CAB). When it went

TABLE 3-5

Average Annual Productivity Growth and
Price Change by Degree of Change in Industry Concentration

Period	Percentage Point Change in Concentration						
	Concentration Decreases			Concentration Increases			All
	12 Percentage Points or More	Less than 12 Percentage Points or No Change	All Decreases	12 Percentage Points or Less	More than 12 Percentage Points	All Increases	
1947–72 Total Productivity	1.80	1.80	1.80	1.91	2.30	2.06	1.95
Number of Industries	19	41	60	48	29	77	137
1954–72 Total Productivity	2.67	1.84	2.02	1.95	2.71	2.12	2.08
Number of Industries	14	48	62	78	22	100	162
1947–72 Labor Productivity	2.77	2.81	2.80	2.66	3.23	2.88	2.84
Number of Industries	19	41	60	48	29	77	134
1954–72 Labor Productivity	3.67	2.69	2.91	3.02	3.81	3.19	3.08
Number of Industries	14	48	62	78	22	100	162
1947–72 Price Change	2.08	2.19	2.16	2.17	1.98	2.10	2.12
Number of Industries	19	41	60	48	29	77	137
1954–71 Price Change	1.55	2.16	2.02	2.08	1.84	2.02	2.02
Number of Industries	14	48	62	78	22	100	162

Source: Steven Lustgarten, INDUSTRIAL CONCENTRATION, PRODUCTIVITY GROWTH, AND CONSUMER WELFARE (1982). Copyright by the American Enterprise Institute. Reprinted by permission of the publisher.

public in 1963, its first yearly statement showed a 75 percent return on equity. As long as it stuck to the airline business, it continued to show high returns. With its low price, PSA dominated the Los Angeles-San Francisco airline market as Henry Ford once dominated the automobile market.

Even in the field of retailing, efficiency and low prices yield high returns. In 1970, independent druggists in the Pacific Coast states, where state regulation of pharmacies created entry barriers, earned only 4.0 percent profits on their sales despite the "blessing" of these barriers to entry. Those in East South Central (ESC) states, who lacked the protection given to Pacific Coast druggists, earned 6.5 percent. The theories applied in the studies of concentration and profits lead one to the conclusion that the higher profits of leading firms in concentrated industries are earned at the expense of consumers. On this view, the 60 percent higher profits of ESC druggists must arise from higher prescription prices than those charged by Pacific Coast druggists. We find, however, that prices in the Pacific Coast states were higher. The average prescription price charged by the druggists there, who earned only 4.0 percent on sales, was $4.80. The average prescription price charged by the ESC druggists, who made 6.5 percent, was $3.54.[16]

Carrefour, a French discount store chain, provides another example from the field of retailing of the high profits earned by low prices. Launching its first "hypermarket" in 1963 and selling at prices 10 to 15 percent lower than other retailers, it expanded to sixteen stores by 1970. *Business Week* reported that Carrefour netted 30.2 percent on invested capital in that year and that, "By this measure, Carrefour is Europe's most profitable company."

The higher profits (and growth in market share from 37.8 percent in 1946 to 50.8 in 1956) earned by General Motors in the automobile industry in the immediate postwar decade were apparently also gained by improvements in efficiency and a relatively slow rise in prices in this inflationary period. The profits of General Motors in the period 1947–56 averaged 25.4 percent on book equity; Ford's 14.8 percent, and Chrysler's 18.1 percent. Although the dominant-firm and market-concentration doctrines hypothesize that high profits are the result of high prices, General Motors prices consistently rose less rapidly than those of its competitors— just as Henry Ford's prices had done in the days when his firm earned extraordinary profits. As GM prices fell relative to its competitors, its profits improved relative to theirs. As shown in Table 3-6, General Motors' list price for four-door sedans advanced 122 percent between the model year 1941 and 1956, while Chrysler's price advanced 136 percent (and its market share declined from 22 to 16 percent between 1947 and 1956). The prices of the "independents" rose 143 percent (and their market share declined from 15 to 5 percent).

Although list prices are not necessarily transaction prices—the automobile firms frequently offer bonuses (discounts from list or rebates) to their dealers for meeting or exceeding sales quotas when sales slow or inventories of specific models become burdensome—sales campaigns such as we see today were infrequent before 1956. Thus the list price indexes for the period from 1947 to 1956 are closer than usual to representing the movement of transaction prices. The data indicate that General Motors' profits were earned by producing efficiently and minimizing its costs. This is a plausible inference from the association we see between its expanding market share and lower price increases.

As output at the more efficient, lower-price firms grows, they must attract more workers. They offer premium wage rates to attract employees from their less efficient competitors and from other industries.[17] As a consequence, we get the seemingly paradoxical result that successful profit seeking activity results in both higher wage rates and lower prices. Where these firms are successful, they grow into leading positions in their industries. Sometimes they grow large enough to make their industries concentrated. Professor John McGee, discussing research and development activities of firms, points out that

> . . . firms engaging in research, invention, and innovation not only find that it may pay, but that to the extent that they succeed, they will grow faster than those who do not. In time, their absolute and relative size will be affected by their relative success in these fields.[18]

Data assembled by Betty Bock and Jack Farkas substantiate the hypothesis that this is the process at work in generating higher wage rates in leading firms. Using 1963 Census of Manufactures data, they found that in 85 percent of the 345 industries they analyzed,

> . . . the top-four companies were at least 5% more productive than other companies in the same industry, while in only 5% of the indus-

TABLE 3-6

Indexes of Passenger Car List Prices and Market Shares, 1947–56

Model Year	General Motors		Ford		Chrysler		Independents	
	Index[a]	Market Share Percentage[b]	Index[a]	Market Share Percentage[b]	Index[a]	Market Share Percentage[b]	Index[a]	Market Share Percentage[b]
1947	150	42	151	21	153	22	160	15
1950	182	45	187	24	193	18 S	205	13
1953	207	45	209	25	229	20	228	10
1956	222	51	233	28	236	16	243	5

Source: Years selected from statement by Harlow H. Curtice on "The Development and Growth of General Motors," in A STUDY OF THE ANTITRUST LAWS, Hearings before Subcommittee on Antitrust and Monopoly, Senate Judiciary Committee, 84th Cong., 1st sess. 1955, Part 7, p. 3516; or Part 8, p. 4484.

[a] Index (1941 = 100).

[b] Market shares are measured by percentage of registrations of new passenger cars.

S The S symbol for Chrysler in 1950 denotes a strike, which affected its output.

tries were the top-four companies definitely less productive than others in the same industry. And in approximately one-fourth of the industries, the top-four companies accounted for at least 55% more shipments per production worker hour than the remaining companies in the same industry.[19]

Similar conclusions emerged using value of shipments per employee, value added by manufacture per employee, and value added per production worker hour.

Relative Productivity of Leading Firms

It has been argued that the measures used by Bock and Farkas —particularly value-added per employee and per production worker hour—reflect the monopoly power that firms in concentrated industries possess, which they use to set higher prices. This, it is said, is the reason for the higher dollar value-added per worker-hour in leading firms in concentrated industries. However, Bock and Farkas also found that shipments and value-added per employee were larger in the largest firms than in smaller firms in almost *all* industries, not just the concentrated industries. The higher prices charged by the top four would mean higher profit-margins and value-added for the other companies in the *same* industry, with which they were being compared, as well as for the top four, if it were higher prices that create higher value-added per employee. Concentrated industries show a superior record partly because the more productive leading firms are a larger portion of those industries. Also, concentrated industries became centralized in the first place because their leading firms are relatively more productive than leading firms in diffused industries (see Table 3-7).

Dr. Willard Mueller, head of the Bureau of Economics at the Federal Trade Commission, refused to accept the Bock and Farkas findings (that leading companies in nearly all industries are more productive than other firms in the same industry) on the grounds that these "spurious results" were a consequence of the fact that "often the smaller companies in a Census industry are actually in a different industry than the leading companies. . . . For this and other reasons, it is more relevant to . . . compare the productivity of the top four with the second four companies."[20]

TABLE 3–7

Ratios of Value-Added per Production Worker-Hour
in Leading Four Firms to Second Four Firms
by Concentration Quintile, 1972

Four-Firm Concentration Percentage	Number of Industries	Average of Ratios of Value-Added per Production Worker-Hour in Leading Four Firms to Second Four Firms
80–100	20	1.49
60–79	54	1.34
40–59	118	1.26
20–39	169	1.13
0–19	87	1.08
0–100	448	1.19

Source: U.S. Bureau of the Census, CONCENTRATION RATIOS IN MANUFACTURING (1975)

Making the comparison suggested by Mueller, the 1972 census data support Bock and Farkas and rebut Mueller. In the less than 20 percent concentrated industries, the top four firms show 8 percent greater value-added per worker hour than the second four, on average. The lead in productivity of the top four over the second four widens as we go up the concentration ladder, reaching 49 percent in the industries whose four-firm concentration ratio exceeds 79 percent (Table 3-7).

These findings strongly suggest that concentrated industries are concentrated because of the relatively greater efficiency attained by its leading firms. Breaking up the largest firms in concentrated industries would result in a much larger drop in output per worker hour than dissolving the leading firms in less centralized industries. Concentrated industries show a superior record not only because leading firms constitute a larger part of such industries, but also because leading firms in concentrated industries are much more efficient relative to other firms in their industries than is the case elsewhere.

That the higher wage in leading firms, and especially in concentrated industries, is the result of higher real productivity in these firms has been demonstrated by Professor Lester Telser. He found that the large firms in concentrated industries invest more in the training of their work force, that this makes their workers more productive, and that the higher wage is the consequence of the higher productivity resulting from this investment in human capital.[21]

73

Indirect corroboration of Professor Telser's finding and direct corroboration of the process causing increasing concentration and higher wage rates is provided by Professor Lustgarten. In a study of changes in output per worker-hour in 397 industries in the 1954–70 period, he found that productivity increased more rapidly in highly concentrated industries than in all other industries. (The annual increase in output per labor-hour was 5.1 percent in more than 75 percent concentrated industries; 4.3 percent in the 51 to 75 percent concentrated group; 4.0 percent in the 26 to 50 percent concentrated industries; and 3.5 percent in the less than 26 percent concentrated industries.)[22] Also wage rates increased more rapidly in concentrated than in unconcentrated industries, a finding established for an earlier period by Professor Bruce Allen.[23]

Another study by Professor Lustgarten compared industries that experienced marked increases in concentration with others in which concentration failed to increase. In this study, the relationship described above between increases in concentration and increases in productivity was confirmed in the data (Table 3-5). The industries with concentration increases of more than 12 percentage points showed a 21.9 percentage points greater gain in output per worker-hour from 1947 to 1972 than the industries in which concentration did not increase.

One reason for productivity increases with increasing concentration is the decrease in suboptimal capacity that occurs with the rise in concentration. Professor Leonard Weiss found

> . . . a systematic tendency for the suboptimal fringe to be smaller, the more concentrated the industry involved. This result was significant . . . and was also important. A 1.0 point increase in concentration led to a 0.95 point reduction in the percentage of shipments from suboptimal plants using Scherer's estimates and sample, a 0.61 point reduction using Pratten's estimates and sample, and a 0.83 point reduction using my own estimates and samples.[24]

The greater productivity of concentrated industries and the increases in productivity associated with increases in concentration are substantiated by these recent studies. This greater productivity rise and the employment growth in leading firms account for the higher wage rates found in concentrated industries and for increases in wage rates as industries become more concentrated.

Concentration and Inflation

Significant and sustained changes in the level of prices are primarily the result of monetary policy. To the extent that increases in productivity result in greater output, however, such increases can contribute to a decrease in the rate of inflation. As an empirical matter we do find that the more rapid increase in productivity in concentrated industries did not simply go into increasing profits and wage rates in these industries. It resulted in a contribution by concentrated industries to the moderation of inflation. From 1966 to 1973, prices in the 76 to 100 percent concentrated industries rose only half as rapidly as prices in all manufacturing (2.54 percent annual rise versus 5.05 percent). From 1958 to 1966, prices in our most concentrated manufacturing industries actually fell while those in less concentrated industries rose (see Table 3-8). These figures indicate that products in concentrated industries consumed proportionately fewer resources over time, allowing economic growth to be greater than would otherwise have been the case.

Concentration and International Competitiveness

The more moderate rise in prices and the greater increase in productivity in our more concentrated industries and in those with rising concentration have also served to strengthen the position of the United States in international markets. If firms in these industries had been broken up or had their expansion restrained even more than it was, the consequent costs and higher prices would have made their markets more vulnerable to import competition. It is notable that the shoe and textile industries and their unions, which have been vociferous in their demand for protection from imports, are among our less concentrated industries (32 and 36 percent concentrated respectively in 1972) and, also, among our lowest wage industries.[25]

The deterioration in our balance of payments and exchange rates in recent years, it should be emphasized, is primarily a consequence of large governmental deficits and an expansionary

TABLE 3–8
Average Annual Percentage Price Change
by Concentration Quartile, 1958–73

Four-Firm Concentration Percentage	1958–66		1966–73	
	Average Annual Percentage Price Change	Number of Industries	Average Annual Percentage Price Change	Number of Industries
76–100	−0.26	22	2.54	14
51–75	0.57	59	4.33	32
26–50	0.83	89	5.83	31
0–25	0.92	65	7.47	14
0–100	0.68	235	5.05	91

Sources: Steven Lustgarten, INDUSTRIAL CONCENTRATION AND INFLATION (1975) at 26; J. F. Weston and S. Lustgarten, Concentration and Wage-Price Changes in H. J. Goldschmid, H. M. Mann, and J. F. Weston (eds.), INDUSTRIAL CONCENTRATION: THE NEW LEARNING (1974) at 312.

monetary policy. But the effects of economic policy can usually be seen in a number of related areas simultaneously. One cannot help but be struck, when examining data for various countries, by the correlation between the higher rate of productivity rise in Germany, Japan, and other countries than in the United States (see Table 3-9); the more rapid growth in the size of their leading enterprises; and their positive balance of payments. The differences between the United States and other countries in public policy toward corporate size and mergers is equally marked. While other governments sponsored the growth of their largest firms and encouraged mergers contributing to the size of leading firms, the Antitrust Division's guidelines prohibited horizontal mergers among leading firms. Acquisitions by leading firms of smaller firms also is prohibited except in the case of failing firms or those with a less than one percent market share. Furthermore, even internal growth to a majority or near majority share of domestic production in any industry is frowned upon. In some instances, it is attacked by the antitrust agencies.[26] This inhibition on the growth of large firms does not exist abroad. Foreign firms are catching up to, and some have surpassed, U.S. firms in size (see Table 3-10 and Chapter 14) and productivity.

The impact of restrictions on firm growth in the United States and the consequences for the relative productivity of the United

Benefits of Concentration

TABLE 3–9
Annual Rate of Productivity Growth
in Selected Countries, 1960–73 and 1973–79

Country	1960–73		1973–79	
	Manufacturing	Private Sector	Manufacturing	Private Sector
United States	3.1	2.8	1.4	1.0
United Kingdom	4.0	3.8	0.5	0.5
Canada	4.6	4.4	2.2	1.0
Sweden	6.7	5.8	2.4	1.5[a]
Italy	7.2	6.6	3.7	2.6
Denmark	7.0	7.2	4.4	4.6
France	5.8	5 9	4.8	4.2
Netherlands	7.4	7.6	5.3	4.8[b]
West Germany	5.5	5.4	5.3	5.0
Belgium	7.0	6.1	6.0	4.4
Japan	10.3	9.9	6.9	3.8

Sources: International Comparison of Manufacturing Productivity and Labor Costs, NEWS, May 22, 1980, (Washington, D.C.: U.S. Dept. of Labor, Bureau of Labor Statistics); A. Neef and P. Capdevielle, *International Comparisons of Productivity and Labor Costs*, 103 MONTHLY LABOR REVIEW 32 (Dec. 1980); John A. Tatom, *The Productivity Problem*, 61 FEDERAL RESERVE BANK OF ST. LOUIS REVIEW 14 (Sept. 1979).
[a] 1973–78
[b] 1973–77

States were summarized by Professor Fred Weston in his testimony before a Senate committee in 1973.

Turning to international aspects, the United States had the advantage of the first common market in the 1880's when the transcontinental railroads were linked up and made the United States in fact one economic market. That larger economic market led to larger firms, but somewhat less concentration than in the small individual markets in Europe. The larger size of firms, the economies of scale and the higher productivity and growth represented a set of factors increasing the productivity of labor in the United States. This led to wage differentials between the United States and Western Europe and Japan.

Recent developments, including the encouragement of mergers by foreign governments, have resulted in increases in the size of foreign firms compared to those in the United States. The growth rates of the largest foreign firms during the past 5 years have been roughly double the growth rates of the largest U.S. firms. There has been roughly a 60 percent growth from 1966 through 1972 for the 100 largest U.S. firms versus 120 percent growth for the largest 100 foreign firms.

TABLE 3–10
Size of 100 Leading Foreign Industrial Firms Relative to 100 Leading U.S. Industrial Firms by Groups, 1965, 1977, 1980

Firm Group (by rank)	Ratio of Foreign Firms' to U.S. Firms' Sales by Rank		Foreign Firms' Total Assets Ratio to U.S. Firms' Total Assets	
	Ratio ($ billion)	Percentage	Ratio ($ billion)	Percentage
1965				
1–10	29/75	38	34/65	51
11–25	18/36	49	14/33	43
26–50	22/37	59	26/29	90
51–100	30/44	68	33/41	82
1–100	99/192	52	107/169	63
1977				
1–10	164/298	55	139/193	72
11–25	131/130	101	123/119	104
26–50	131/129	102	118/84	140
51–100	163/159	103	194/123	158
1–100	589/716	82	574–519	111
1980				
1–10	300/452	66	248/281	88
11–25	232/215	108	196/169	116
26–50	224/206	109	211/149	142
51–100	261/241	108	239/166	144
1–100	1017/1114	91	895/765	117

Source: FORTUNE, May-August 1966, 1978, and 1981. Cited from Fred Weston, *Do Multinational Corporations Have Market Power to Overprice?* in Carl H. Madden (ed.), THE CASE FOR THE MULTINATIONAL CORPORATION (1977) at 49.

During this same period of time the largest 100 foreign firms have risen from one-half the size of the corresponding group of U.S. firms to two-thirds their size. If the growth rate in assets of the top 100 foreign firms continues to exceed the growth rate of the large U.S. firms as during the last 5 years, in 4 years the top 100 foreign firms would exceed the total assets of the largest 100 U.S. firms.

The rough equilibrium between differential labor productivity and differential labor costs presupposed differences in the size of firms and economies of operation. That equilibrium was disturbed by the faster rate of growth of the Western European firms relative to the United States. This has been one of the factors causing the U.S. balance of payments problems. The proposal to deconcentrate U.S. industry would have further disequilibrating effects, aggravating our international financial problems. The proposed Industrial Reorganization Act would reduce efficiency in the U.S. economy at a time when we especially need more, not less, efficiency.[27]

Professor Weston's 1973 prediction that the growth of assets in large foreign firms could lead to the situation where "in 4 years the top 100 foreign firms would exceed the total assets of the largest 100 U.S. firms" has turned out to be remarkably accurate. By 1977, total assets of the largest 100 foreign industrial firms grew to where they exceeded the U.S. top industrials by 11 percent (Table 3-10). U.S. firms competing in world markets are slipping relative to their foreign competitors. The restraints placed on *domestic* concentration, on saving and the growth of capital, and on the uses for capital are dragging U.S. business down relative to that of other countries.

The impact of concentration on our sales abroad of manufactured goods has been measured by Professors Paugoulatos and Sorensen. After allowing for the influence of research and development, the tailoring of product and marketing services to the variety of needs in different countries, and the influences of economies of scale, they find that each 10-point increase in an industry's U.S. domestic concentration ratio is accompanied by an 0.8 point increase in that industry's exports as a percentage of OECD (Organization for Economic Cooperation and Development) countries' exports.[28] Inasmuch as the influence of economies of scale were allowed for separately, and economies of scale are possible and occur more fully in relatively more concentrated industries,[29] the influence of concentration alone is understated by the regression used to measure the separate effect of concentration on exports.[30]

The Effect of Learning

One of the factors leading to high concentration, which also plays a role in the more rapid advance of productivity in industries that are already concentrated, is the degree to which past experience or learning helps improve productivity. It has been found that the cost per unit of output in a firm is inversely related to the amount of experience the firm has accumulated in producing its product.[31] With a flat learning curve, a large amount of production experience does little to lower cost. With a downward sloping learning curve, the firm that has produced more product than others will have lower costs than those with less experience. If these lower costs and higher returns on additional investment lead it and other firms with the largest shares of the market to expand, their industry will become concentrated. Prices will be lower as a result of this low-cost expansion of supply than they would be if the industry remains unconcentrated.

Studies by Professors Paul McCracken and Thomas Moore, T. G. Sullivan, and Harold Demsetz provide confirmation for the progress curve effect in concentrated and in unconcentrated industries.[32] Examining the profitability of the largest and second largest firms in thirty-two industries, Professors McCracken and Moore found that "the second largest firm does unusually poorly in concentrated industries" as compared to the second largest firm in unconcentrated industries.[33] Marie Cavaleri, using sixty-nine three-digit industries and comparing returns in the largest firms with the next largest firms as grouped in each industry by the Internal Revenue Service, corroborated the McCracken-Moore finding (see Table 3-11). (Cavaleri corrected the accounting rate of return for the understatement of net worth caused by the omission of one form of intangible capital, advertising, by using the advertising to net worth ratio as a proxy for missing capital.) Evidently, the largest firms in concentrated industries realize cost benefits from their greater experience relative to the next largest firms and are able to earn higher profits because of their lower costs.[34] In less concentrated industries, greater experience does not bring such benefits and the largest firms do not enjoy lower costs than the next largest. This, of course, is one of the reasons that the diffused industries have remained unconcentrated or have become diffused if initially concentrated.

TABLE 3–11

Regressions of Profitability and Profitability Differences
in First- and Second-Tier Firms, 1971

Independent Variables	Dependent Variables					
	P_1		P_2		P_1-P_2	
c	8.77	6.62	13.97	12.73	−5.20	−5.08
	(5.45)	(4.09)	(7.06)	(6.82)	(−2.31)	(−2.37)
CR^2	1.97	1.45	−1.14	−1.42	3.11	3.07
	(2.73)	(2.12)	(−1.43)	(−1.79)	(3.08)	(3.21)
AD1		0.663				
		(3.47)				
AD2				0.383		
				(1.87)		
AD1−AD2						0.726
						(2.87)
R^2	0.10	0.24	0.03	0.08	0.12	0.22
F		6.25		1.88		6.25

Source: Marie Cavaleri, *Concentration Doctrine: Competition or Collusion?* (student paper, April 30, 1979).
t-value in parentheses.
c   =   constant
P_1 =   Ratio of before tax earnings of largest firms to net worth (in hundredths) in 69 industries as grouped in Internal Revenue Service Source Book.
P_2 =   Ratio of before tax earnings of second largest firms to net worth (in hundredths) in 69 industries as grouped in Internal Revenue Service Source Book.
CR^2 =   three-digit concentration ratio (average of four-digit concentration ratios weighted by value added) squared times 10^{-3}.
AD1 =   ratio of advertising by largest firms to net worth of those firms.
AD2 =   ratio of advertising by second largest firms to net worth of these firms.

The data in Table 3-7, using industries more finely subdivided (four-digit industries) than in the Internal Revenue Service data (which groups by three-digit categories), show productivity in the second four firms in concentrated industries is poorer relative to the first four than in less centralized industries. This is consistent both with the hypothesis that the progress curve is flatter in unconcentrated industries and with the hypothesis that the firm with superior management has lower costs, will compete and grow to a leading position, and will cause an increase in concentration in its industry.[35] Further confirmation for these hypotheses is provided in Sullivan's study, which finds that the leading firms in concentrated industries are more profitable than those in less concentrated industries and that market share growth was greater (from 1961 to 1968) in the more profitable firms.[36]

The progress curve effect is also confirmed by the finding that margins (the proportion of sales price that is not accounted for by direct labor and material costs) are larger in concentrated than in unconcentrated industries after accounting for the greater amount of tangible capital used per unit of product. However, the finding of large margins in concentrated industries is not an unambiguous confirmation since it could be a result of larger amounts of intangible capital per unit of product, of rental or royalty payments for the use of externally provided capital, or the use of greater amounts of externally provided services. The available margin-concentration studies have not taken these influences into account.[37]

The available evidence strongly suggests that concentration benefits the nation by increasing the accumulated experience and learning in large firms where these factors can increase productivity. The result is lower costs and larger output than would occur if accumulation of experience and learning were prevented by restraints on the allowable level of concentration.[38]

The Size of Firms and the Cost of Capital

Still another advantage of concentration and the resulting distribution of firm sizes is that the cost of raising capital is less to larger firms than the cost to smaller firms.[39] One of the sources of this economy of scale is the lower per-dollar cost of raising capital in placing large issues of securities. A Securities and Exchange Commission study of common stocks issued in 1971–72 found the direct cost of issuing and selling placements amounting to less than $1 million was 21 percent of the funds raised. For placements ranging from $5 to 10 million the cost dropped to 7 percent. Costs for issues of $100 to 500 million dropped further to 3 percent.[40] With lower flotation costs, more capital is made available to the firm for every dollar provided by investors.

When large firms raise capital, they can also offer investors lower risk as well as economizing on flotation costs. Investors prefer low- to high-risk securities for any given rate of return and

TABLE 3–12

Estimates of Risk (Measured by Beta) by Firm Size, 1926–75

Size Range Market Value of Equity	Estimates of Beta[a]				
	1926–35	*1936–45*	*1946–55*	*1956–65*	*1966–75*
0–$15,000,000	1.12 (384)	1.15 (467)	1.12 (371)	1.19 (168)	1.35 (73)
$15–$30,000,000	0.79 (87)	0.82 (120)	1.00 (194)	1.06 (170)	1.19 (143)
$30–$60,000,000	0.73 (69)	0.76 (77)	0.94 (163)	1.07 (206)	1.08 (234)
$60–$500,000,000	0.65 (112)	0.65 (116)	0.84 (238)	0.95 (457)	0.94 (692
$500,000,000 and larger	0.52 (12)	0.58 (10)	0.7 (29)	0.85 (126)	0.68 (272)

Source: G. B. Adesi, *The Sensitivity of Security Returns to Market Volatility,* presentation before Workshop in Economics and Econometrics, University of Chicago, May 30, 1980.

[a] Figure in parentheses is number of New York Stock Exchange listed firms used to make estimates.

willingly buy stocks and bonds with lower returns when the lower returns are offset by lower risks. The less risky operations of large firms, then, enable them to obtain lower cost capital and to produce at lower cost (see Table 3-12). According to one study, the average billion-dollar asset corporation borrowed at rates which average 0.34 percentage points less than the average $200 million corporation. In turn, the latter borrowed at rates averaging 0.74 percentage points less than $5 million concerns, reflecting the lower risk.[41]

Although the buyers of the bonds and stocks of large corporations receive a lower nominal or dollar return, before netting out the cost of risk and measuring the risk-adjusted return, buyers of the lower nominal yield securities receive a higher risk-adjusted return than would otherwise be available—a higher real return. The enlarged real return (income from investment plus the safety of the income) to providers of capital increases the rate of investment. From a Keynesian view of the economy, this enhances employment and total national income through the multiplier effect. From a neoclassical view, the larger volume of capital put in place raises productivity, real wages, and national income.

While it is sometimes argued that the reduction in risk in firms selling a larger part of the output of an industry comes from control of the market, studies of risk reduction find its source in other factors. When American Can was formed in 1901, it absorbed plants operating in many different parts of the country. (Although it aimed to monopolize the industry, it did not succeed in that endeavor. Its increase in can prices after its formation was quickly aborted by the entry of additional firms and expansion of independent firms.) "[T]here are important gains from geographic diversification. A multi-plant firm can meet extra demands for packers' cans (due to a large crop) by shipping in from another plant. . . . Also, company profits are not likely to be badly hurt by failure in any single crop."[42] Because American Can's geographic diversification provided offsetting risks (surplus crops in some areas causing high spot prices for cans in those areas while short crops in other areas caused low spot prices for cans), it was able not only to reduce its own risks but also to provide an insurance service to one-plant canners through its pricing structure for cans and can closing machinery.[43]

The reduction in risk arising out of the ability to use a plant, which would otherwise be idle, to serve that portion of the market where demand is strong is also exemplified by General Motors' BOP (Buick, Oldsmobile, and Pontiac) plants. When the demand is off in Buick markets but up in Oldsmobile or Pontiac markets, the capacity for producing Buicks, which would otherwise be idle, can instead be employed assembling Oldsmobiles or Pontiacs. Multi-product or multi-brand production may be equal in importance to geographic diversification in minimizing risk and maximizing efficiency. High concentration and large firm size is a means of producing this result.[44]

Concentration, Firm Size, and Innovation

Much of the economic literature on concentration also argues that greater incentives for innovation and for research and development exist in large firms and in concentrated industries. The National Science Foundation has pointed out that

> Although an estimated 11,000 firms perform research and development in the United States, a relatively small number undertake the majority of the effort. The 116 R&D performing companies with employment of greater than 25,000 reported R&D expenditures of $17 billion in 1975—73 percent of the U.S. industry total.[45]

While there is no clear-cut relationship between R&D spending and concentration,[46] it is the largest firms that perform most of our R&D.

Some studies also find a weak relationship between concentration and R&D spending or performance. Some analysts point out, however, that what relationship there is springs from outside causes. The same factors, which sometimes cause concentration, also sometimes cause higher R&D. They go on to show that the proportion of firms in any size class performing R&D increases with size, and that the relative scale of the R&D effort in firms performing research increases with size up to a point. Once a threshold size is passed, however, R&D spending in firms in most industries does not continue to increase disproportionately with size but only at most proportionately. Therefore, they conclude, once a critical concentration level is reached, further concentration could depress the amount of R&D in an industry.

None of these arguments is particularly relevant. What is desired of an industry is not an increase in resources used, which is the variable measured by R&D spending. Rather, what is desired is an efficient increase of output, whether of product or of innovations. Our goal is not more or less investment in R&D. Our goal is a greater production of innovations. The only objective measure encompassing innovation from all sources, whether from R&D in the industry or from other origins, is the rise in total factor productivity in an industry. This, then, is the preferred measure of performance. Professor Lustgarten, as described earlier, found that both output per worker-hour and total factor productivity rose more rapidly from 1947 to 1972 in those industries in which concentration increased and in the more concentrated industries.

Although relatively more rapid innovation and concentration occur together, it is uncertain which is cause and which is effect. Once again, performance may be determining structure.[47] Professor James McKie, looking at the performance consequences of industry structure, concludes that

> Technological innovation's . . . dependence upon structural variables remains obscure. The predicted relationship is inverse: more innovation is associated with higher concentration and barriers to entry. . . . [A]ll [the evidence] really shows is that atomistic industries do not seem to innovate rapidly while oligopolistic ones often do.[48]

Perhaps the findings of Pavitt and Wald best summarize the relationship between industrial structure and innovation. They concluded that large and small firms play complementary roles.

85

Large firms produce and apply innovations of the type requiring large scale R&D, production, or marketing. Small firms contribute more in specialized, sophisticated components and equipment. Sometimes they institute innovations passed up by large firms. We need all varieties of firm size and industry structure.[49]

Conclusion

The frequency of deconcentration recommendations by witnesses appearing before congressional committees would seem to indicate that centralization of business in a few firms is a common and persistent phenomenon with undesirable consequences. Yet fewer than one in twenty manufacturing industries are led by four firms whose domestic output is large enough, when combined, to constitute more than 80 percent of the total. Since their customers evidently prefer the products of these firms to those of their competitors, their workers prefer the jobs they offer, and investors willingly provide capital, there are clearly some advantages—whether universally praised or not—of concentration.

Notes

1. Layne E. Kruse, *Deconcentration and Section 5 of the Federal Trade Commission Act,* 46 George Washington Law Review (Jan. 1979).
2. Cited in Robert Bork, The Antitrust Paradox 20 (1978).
3. Cited in Whitney, Antitrust Policies, vol. 2 at 91 (1958).
4. H. Demsetz, The Trust Behind Antitrust 5 (March 1978). Also, see Bork *supra* 194.
5. Sam Peltzman, *The Gains and Losses from Industrial Concentration,* 20 Journal of Law & Economics 229 (Oct. 1977).
6. Steven Lustgarten, *Gains and Losses from Concentration: A Comment,* 22 Journal of Law & Economics 183 (Apr. 1978).
7. J. H. Landon, *The Relation of Market Concentration to Advertising Rates: The Newspaper Industry,* 16 Antitrust Bulletin 53 (Spring 1971).
8. G. W. Stocking and M. H. Watkins, Monopoly and Free Enterprise 541 (1951).
9. Isador Lubin, Letter of Transmittal, in Jacob Perlman, Hourly Earnings of Employees in Large and Small Enterprises xi (1940).
10. Ralph Nelson, Concentration in the Manufacturing Industries of the United States 87 (1963).
11. Charles T. Haworth and Carol Jean Reuther find that an industry's proportion of plants employing more than 1,000 production workers affects wage levels about two times the amount by which the concentration

ratio affects wage levels. *Industrial Concentration and Interindustry Wage Determination*, 60 REVIEW OF ECONOMICS AND STATISTICS 90–91 (Feb. 1978). However, Leonard Weiss finds that the percentage of shipments from plants below the minimum efficient scale in size drops by 0.86 percent for each percentage point rise in concentration. *Optimal Plant Size and the Extent of Suboptimal Capacity*, in F. Masson and D. Qualls, eds., ESSAYS ON INDUSTRIAL ORGANIZATION IN HONOR OF JOE S. BAIN 140 (1976).

12. Lester G. Telser, *Some Determinants of the Returns to Manufacturing Industries*, COMPETITION, COLLUSION, AND GAME THEORY 322 (1972).

13. L. Phlips, EFFECTS OF INDUSTRIAL CONCENTRATION 112 (1971).

14. U.S., Federal Trade Commission, RELATIVE EFFICIENCY OF LARGE, MEDIUM-SIZED, AND SMALL BUSINESS 78 (1941).

15. In the cigarette industry, for example, any price cut has been met very quickly since 1923. "During the 1917–23 period, both the list and net prices of the three leading brands were very frequently non-identical and often changed rank besides. . . . Since 1923, the major cigarette companies have followed a policy of virtual list-price identity." William Nicholls, PRICE POLICIES IN THE CIGARETTE INDUSTRY 55 (1951).

16. LILLY DIGEST 49 (1971).

17. L. Phlips found that the rate of growth of industry employment as well as industry concentration had a strong effect on wage rates. See *Supra* note 13, at 98.

18. John S. McGee, IN DEFENSE OF INDUSTRIAL CONCENTRATION 112 (1971).

19. Betty Bock and Jack Farkas, CONCENTRATION AND PRODUCTIVITY: SOME PRELIMINARY FINDINGS 23 (1969).

20. U.S., Federal Trade Commission, Bureau of Economics, *Competition, Efficiency, and Antitrust: Compatibilities and Inconsistencies*, ECONOMIC PAPERS, 1966–69 at 14 (1970).

21. See note 12 *Supra*. Also, Betty Bock, RESTRUCTURING PROPOSALS: MEASURING COMPETITION IN NUMERICAL GRIDS 57 (Jan. 1974) reports that the median concentration ratio in the thirty-five industries with the highest value added per employee in 1967 was 58 percent while that in the lowest thirty-five industries was 20 percent—a further confirmation of Professor Telser's conclusion.

22. Steven Lustgarten, INDUSTRIAL CONCENTRATION AND INFLATION, Table 3 at 31 (1976).

23. Bruce T. Allen, *Market Concentration and Wage Increases: U.S. Manufacturing. 1947–1964*, 21 INDUSTRIAL AND LABOR RELATIONS REVIEW 353 (1968).

24. Leonard Weiss, *The Structure-Conduct-Performance Paradigm and Antitrust* 21 (unpublished, presented at University of Pennsylvania antitrust conference, 1978). The studies referenced are F. M. Scherer, *The Determinants of Industry Plant Sizes in Six Nations*, 55 REVIEW OF ECONOMICS AND STATISTICS (May 1973); L. W. Weiss, *Optimal Plant Size and The Extent of Suboptimal Capacity* in Masson and Qualls *supra* note 11, at 123; C. F. Pratten, ECONOMIES OF SCALE IN MANUFACTURING INDUSTRIES (1971).

25. The steel industry is one of our highest-wage industries, paying 70 percent more per production worker hour than the average in all manufacturing. Its unions have been equally vociferous in their demands for protection. The industry is notable for its declining concentration and

slow productivity growth. From 1954 to 1972, its total factor productivity
rose by only 1.6 percent per year and its output per labor hour by only
2.5 percent. All declining concentration industries averaged 2.0 and 2.9
percent for total factor and labor producivity growth. Increasing concentration industries averaged 2.2 and 3.2 percent. Steel's wage increases
have outrun productivity increases by a far larger margin than any other
manufacturing industry. That, it seems, is the source of its troubles.

26. Brozen, *The Attack on Concentration,* 29 THE FREEMAN 38 (Jan. 1979).
27. U.S., Congress, Senate Subcommittee on Antitrust and Monopoly Hearings, THE INDUSTRIAL REORGANIZATION ACT, Part 1, 93rd Congress, 1st
session, March and May 1973 at 240.
28. E. Paugoulatos and R. Sorensen, *Domestic Market Structure and International Trade: An Empirical Analysis,* 16 QUARTERLY REVIEW OF ECO-
NOMICS AND BUSINESS 54 (1976). Inasmuch as the denominator rises
along with the numerator when measuring U.S. exports relative to total
OECD exports, the 0.8 point increase in percentage understates the
effect of concentration. If the U.S. were the sole exporter of some item,
an increase in exports resulting from an increase in concentration would
show no change in the U.S. percentage.
29. See discussion at note 24.
30. Paugalatos and Sorensen concluded that imports as a share of the domestic market rise with concentration in 38 import-competing three-
digit industries. Again, however, they employ a scale economy measure
in the same regression, which distorts the result. The influence of scale
economies on imports in their regression is negative. To the extent that
increased concentration is the consequence of, and allows, scale economies, the net effect of concentration may be to diminish imports despite
their finding to the contrary of the separate effect. See note 28 *supra,* at
53.
31. Boston Consulting Group. PERSPECTIVES ON EXPERIENCE (1968); Armen
Alchian, *Reliability of Progress Curves in Airframe Production,* 31
ECONOMETRICA 679 (Oct. 1963); Walter Y. Oi, *The Neoclassical Foundation of Progress Functions,* 77 ECONOMIC JOURNAL 579 (Sept. 1967);
L. Rapping, *Learning and World War II Production Functions,* 47 RE-
VIEW OF ECONOMICS & STATISTICS 81 (Feb. 1965).
32. In addition to the studies of McCracken, Moore, Sullivan, and Demsetz,
which are described later, D. K. Round, J. R. Carter, and R. Carlson
have found that concentration has resulted in greater efficiency in those
industries that have become concentrated in Australia, the United
States, and Sweden. D. K. Round, *Industry Structure, Market Rivalry,
and Public Policy: Some Australian Evidence,* 18 JOURNAL OF LAW &
ECONOMICS 273 (April 1975); J. R. Carter, *Collusion, Efficiency, and
Antitrust,* 21 JOURNAL OF LAW & ECONOMICS 435 (1978); R. Carlson,
*The Measurement of Efficiency: An Application to Swedish Manufactur-
ing Industries,* 74 SWEDISH JOURNAL OF ECONOMICS 468 (Dec. 1972).
33. Paul McCracken and Thomas Moore, Statement to the Subcommittee
on Antitrust and Monopoly, U.S. Senate (March 20, 1973), reprinted by
American Enterprise Institute as COMPETITION AND MARKET CONCEN-
TRATION IN THE AMERICAN ECONOMY (1974).
34. John E. Kwoka, in his MARKET SHARES, CONCENTRATION, AND COMPE-
TITION IN MANUFACTURING INDUSTRIES, Staff Report to the Federal
Trade Commission (1978), interprets the relationships he finds in his
regressions relating price-cost margins (contributions to advertising,

royalties, overhead, and profits) and market shares of the number 1, 2, 3, and 4 firms in each industry as the power of the two largest firms to extract monopoly or collusive returns when they have large market shares. The fact that there is a negative relationship with the market shares of number 3 and 4 firms indicates that the relationship is a learning curve phenomenon, not a market power phenomenon. See discussion following note 41 in Chapter 7.

35. The data displayed in Brozen, *Concentration and Structural and Market Disequilibria,* 16 ANTITRUST BULLETIN 246 (Summer 1971), support the hypothesis that where the largest firms in an industry show superior performance, they grow relative to their industry, do not restrain output to maintain supra-competitive prices, and concentration increases. Also, see Table 4-2.

36. T. G. Sullivan, *A Note on Market Power and Returns to Stockholders,* 59 REVIEW OF ECONOMICS AND STATISTICS 108 (1977). Sullivan misinterprets his regressions by reversing the causation. His explanations of his findings illustrate Professor Ronald Coase's observation that economists usually seek a monopoly explanation for business behavior that they do not understand. *Industrial Organization: A Proposal for Research* in V. Fuchs (ed.), POLICY ISSUES AND RESEARCH OPPORTUNITIES IN INDUSTRIAL ORGANIZATION 67 (1972).

37. However, see Telser *supra* note 12.

38. Professor Richard Posner has pointed out that restraints on concentration may also "have a serious disincentive effect. Firms may hold back from expanding sales to the point at which they would become subject to dissolution . . . even if they are more efficient than their competitors." *Oligopoly and the Antitrust Laws: A Suggested Approach.* 21 STANFORD LAW REVIEW 1595 (June 1969).

39. Roger Blair and Yoram Peles, *The Advantage of Size in the Capital Market: Empirical Evidence and Policy Implications* (working paper, Center for Study of American Business, Washington University, Dec. 1977). Also see D. J. Smyth, W. J. Boyes, and D. E. Peseau, SIZE, GROWTH, PROFITS, AND EXECUTIVE COMPENSATION IN THE LARGE CORPORATION (1975).

40. U.S., Securities and Exchange Commission, COSTS OF FLOTATION OF REGISTERED ISSUES, 1971–1972 at 9 (1974). With a lower risk in investing in a large firm, the security buyer will accept a lower return yet receive a higher risk-adjusted return. Also, see S. H. Archer and L. G. Faerber, *Firm Size and the Cost of Externally Secured Capital,* 21 JOURNAL OF FINANCE 69 (1966).

41. F. M. Scherer, A. Beckenstein, E. Kaufer, and R. D. Murphy, THE ECONOMICS OF MULTI-PLANT OPERATION 287 (1975).

42. See Whitney *supra* note 3, at 202.

43. David Flath, *U.S. v. American Can Company: Economic Analysis of an Antitrust Case* (dissertation, University of California, Los Angeles, 1977).

44. T. G. Sullivan finds that size of firm and concentration each contribute significantly to reducing risk (measured by β) and cost of capital. *The Cost of Capital and Market Power of Firms,* 60 REVIEW OF ECONOMICS AND STATISTICS, Table 1 at 213 (May 1978).

45. U.S., National Science Foundation, RESEARCH AND DEVELOPMENT IN INDUSTRY 1975 6 (Nov. 1977).

46. See M. I. Kamien and N. L. Schwartz, *Market Structure and Innova-*

tion: A Survey, 13 JOURNAL OF ECONOMIC LITERATURE 1 (1975), for a summary review of the rather unsatisfactory and contradictory literature assessing the relationship between concentration, R&D inputs, economies of scale in R&D, and inventive output primarily measured by number of patents. J. M. Vernon, MARKET STRUCTURE AND INDUSTRIAL PERFORMANCE: A REVIEW OF HISTORICAL FINDINGS (1972), provides a somewhat more elegantly categorized set of summaries of selected statistical studies with an overview of the arguments underlying opposing hypotheses. For a hard-headed and sensible view of the policy conclusions that can be drawn from the statistical relationships reported in various studies, see John S. McGee, *Concentration and "Progressiveness": Invention, Innovation,* IN DEFENSE OF INDUSTRIAL CONCENTRATION 96 (1971).

47. See quote in text at note 18.
48. J. W. McKie, *Market Structure and Function: Performance versus Behavior,* in J. W. Markham and G. F. Papanek (eds.), INDUSTRIAL ORGANIZATION AND DEVELOPMENT 7 (1970).
49. K. Pavitt and S. Wald, THE CONDITIONS FOR SUCCESS IN TECHNOLOGICAL INNOVATION (1971).

4

Determinants of Concentration[1]

THE turn of the century merger movement culminated with the formation of the world's first billion-dollar corporation. United States Steel, created in 1901 by consolidating twelve previous consolidations, became the symbol of Big Business in America. Because U.S. Steel has continued in its top-ranking position in the steel industry in the United States to this day, it also has become one of the grounds of the belief that current industry structure was largely determined by the 1898–1901 merger wave, which brought 20 percent of all manufacturing assets into the hands of a few hundred corporations.[2]

Mergers, Entrenchment, and Inertia

Those who attribute today's pattern of industrial concentration to the 1898–1901 mergers and to the minor merger wave of the 1920s believe that a dominant position, once achieved, persists by sheer inertia.[3] They assert that size carries advantages that entrench the market position of a firm. The belief that merger mania and inertia determine market structure persists despite much evidence to the contrary. For example, U.S. Steel's share of domestic production shrank from 66 percent in 1901 to 20 percent currently despite acquisition of additional producers (see also Tables 3-1 and

91

3-2). Professor W. G. Shepherd, one of those who share this view, asserts that

> . . . concentration is stable. Only a very few ratios change more than ten points during a ten-year period. Among industries with high concentration, the declines are relatively few and slight. Tight oligopoly, once formed, tends to persist.[4]

However, as Table 4-1 shows, in nearly three quarters of the industries in which concentration was greater than 74 percent (the industries often characterized as "tight oligopolies") in 1947, concentration decreased. Despite Shepherd's belief in the stability of leading four-firm market shares, decreases of more than ten points occurred in half of the group (see Table 10-1). Increases of more than ten points occurred in one sixth of the group. Even the identity of the four leading firms changed in 73 percent of these concentrated industries in the short span from 1947 to 1958.[5] If entrenchment or inertia determines the rank of a large firm in a concentrated industry, changes in the composition of the four leading concerns should have been rare.

An examination of shifts from 1963 to 1972 in the most highly concentrated industries (Table 4-2) reveals that the share of the four leading firms changed by more than ten points for a quarter of these "tight oligopolies." These data contradict Shepherd's belief that "only a very few ratios change more than 10 points during a ten-year period" in all industries. They also dispute his contention that "declines are relatively few and slight" in highly concentrated industries.

As one pair of authors put it, "The calm surface of average CR's conceals substantial undercurrents of change . . . [with] sharply contrasting patterns."[6] Mergers may centralize an industry, but concentration does not persist in the absence of conditions that make centralization an economic way to organize an industry. If leading firms fail to perform, they cease to be leading firms (see Tables 3-1 and 3-2). Performance, not inertia, determines industrial structure.

Of the 165 U.S. industries with sufficiently stable product and technology to require no change in definition from 1947 to 1972, nearly half (74) show concentration changes of 10 percentage points or more. Household laundry equipment concentration, for example, increased from 40 to 83 percent and beer concentration

TABLE 4-1

Percentage of Industries with Rising, Stable, or Declining Concentration by Concentration Level, 1947–72 and 1958–72

Concentration Percentage	Number of Industries[a]		More than 2 Percentage Points Increase in Concentration		Stable Concentration		More than 2 Percentage Points Decrease in Concentration	
	1947	1958	1947–72	1958–72	1947–72	1958–72	1947–72	1958–72
			Percentage		Percentage		Percentage	
0–24	58	69	71	62	14	29	15	9
25–49	53	69	42	39	25	38	34	23
50–74	33	50	24	32	15	26	61	42
75–100	21	16	24	25	5	19	71	56
	165	204						

Source: U.S. Bureau of the Census, CONCENTRATION RATIOS IN MANUFACTURING, MC72(SR)-2 (Oct. 1975).

[a] The industries selected are all those for which concentration data are available for 1947 and 1972 and for 1958 and 1972. Two 1947 industries were omitted in 1958 because 1958 data were not disclosed (3334, 3636).[7]

$C72_i - C47_i = 1.54 - .230 \ (C47_i - 39.4) \quad \bar{r}^2 = 0.181$
$ (1.73) \quad (-6.10)$

$C72_i$ = four-firm concentration in 1972 in industry i.
$C72_i$ = four-firm concentration in 1947 in industry i.
 t-value in parentheses below coefficient.

93

TABLE 4–2
Industry and Product Group Concentration Ratios in "Highly Concentrated" Industries, 1963 and 1972

SIC Number 1972	Industry[a]	Four-Firm Concentration Percentage Industry Shipments 1963	1972[b]	Four-Firm Concentration Percentage Primary Product 1963	1972[b]	Coverage Percentage 1972	Primary Product Specialization Percentage 1972
2043	Cereal preparations	86	90	82	84	84	77
2067	Chewing gum	90	87	86	84	88	90
2111	Cigarettes	80	84	D[d]	84	100	96
2296	Tire cord and fabric	79	84	71	81	97	91
2814 (1963)	Cyclic (coal tar) crudes	D	NA	95	92(28655)	NA	NA
2823	Cellulosic man-made fibers	82	96	79	84	D	D
2824	Organic fibers, noncellulosic	94	74	D	73	97	80
3031	Reclaimed rubber	93	78	73	74	55	96
3211	Flat glass	94	92	87	83	D	85
3275	Gypsum products	84	80	82	79	99	95
3331	Primary copper	85	74	NA	60	NA	NA
3332	Primary lead	D	88	D	D	NA	NA
3334	Primary aluminum	D	79	93	80	76	94
3463	Nonferrous forgings	84	71	56	NA	63	84
3492 (1963)	Safes and vaults	D	NA	D[e]	89(34991)	NA	NA
3511	Turbines & turbine generator sets	93	90	83	D	90	92

SIC	Product						
3624	Carbon & graphite products	83	80	82	79	98	95
3632	Household refrigerators and freezers	74	85	73	75	80–85	75–80
3633	Household laundry equipment	78	83	71	76	91	88
3635	Household vacuum cleaners	81	75	64	66	85	80
3636	Sewing machines	D	84	82	80	93	95–100
3641	Electric lamps	92	90	89	87	96	95
3661	Telephone and telegraph apparatus	92	D[c]	D	90	99	91
3671	Electron receiving tubes	85	95	83	82	94	83
3672	Cathode picture tubes	91	83	81	91	98	91
3692	Primary batteries	89	92	83	93	98	95
3711	Motor vehicles	NA[f]	93	NA	81(37285)	100	96
3723 (1963)	Aircraft propellers	D	NA	87	NA	NA	NA
3741 (1963)	Locomotives and parts	97	NA	92	83	NA	NA
3795	Tanks and tank components	NA	95	NA	83	77	95
3996	Hard surface floor coverings	87	91	85	90	99	88

Sources: U.S., Department of Commerce, Bureau of the Census, Census of Manufacturers, 1972, Special Report Series: Concentration Ratios in Manufacturing, MC 72 (R)-2 (1975).

[a] All industries 80 percent concentrated or more in either 1963 or 1972.

[b] Italicized figures indicate industries and product groups in which concentration increased between 1963 and 1972.

[c] 3661 was 94 percent concentrated in 1970.

[d] 2111 was 80 percent concentrated in 1958.

[e] 34991 was 87 percent concentrated in 1958.

[f] 3711 was 92 percent concentrated in 1967.

D = Datum withheld by the Bureau of Census to avoid disclosing operations of individual companies from 21 to 52 percent. (Beer concentration in Canada increased by 38 percentage points from 1948 to 1972 and in Great Britain the five leading beer firm share increased from 23 to 64 percent from 1958 to 1968.) On the other hand, meat packing declined from 47 to 20 percent and phonograph records from 79 to 48 percent. Concentration ratios moved in response to changing circumstances and competition. They shifted in the "tightly oligopolized" industries as well as in the less centralized.

The Centripetal Tendency of Concentration Ratios

If any one concept can be used to describe trends in industry structure, it is that there seems to be a centripetal tendency at work. Concentrated industries tend to become less concentrated, moving toward the average concentration ratio as in the aluminum and computer examples in Table 1-2. Dispersed industries tend to become more centralized also moving toward the central value of all concentration ratios as in the example of men's and boys' clothing in Table 1-2. The experiences of industries at various levels of concentration, shown in Table 4-1, fit this generalization. The changes in concentration demonstrate that the higher the level of concentration the smaller the incidence of increases and the greater the incidence of decreases. Among the most highly concentrated industries, concentration increased, from 1947 to 1972, in 24 percent and decreased in 71 percent. In the least concentrated group, concentration increased in 71 percent and decreased in only 15 percent. The comparable data for 204 industries with unchanged definitions from 1958 to 1972 show concentration increased in 25 percent of concentrated industries and decreased in 56 percent. In the least concentrated group, 62 percent increased and 9 percent decreased.

The same centripetal tendency manifested itself in an earlier period. Examining the 126 industries with unchanged definitions from 1935 to 1947, we find the same pattern. Although Section 7 of the Clayton Act was not an effective bar to mergers in this period, concentration decreased in 53 percent of the most concentrated industries. It increased in only 24 percent. In the next most concentrated stratum, the four leading firms' share decreased in 41 percent of the industries and increased in only 24 percent. Concentration decreased in only 20 percent of the least concentrated group and increased in 52 percent. Professor Walter Adams observes, of this period,

> . . . here indeed is an eloquent testimonial to the dynamism and competitiveness of the American economy. Here indeed is a graphic manifestation of the [competitive] forces in the economy—holding their own despite a public policy which left the highway to monopoly [horizontal mergers] unblocked and unguarded.[8]

That all industries did not uniformly experience increasing centralization would be a surprise to Karl Marx. That many concentrated industries became less concentrated would astonish him. He predicted that economies of scale and competitive behavior would result in single firms taking over all output in most industries. Friedrich Engels, in the 1890 edition of Marx's *Capital,* pointed to the formation of English and American trusts as evidence of the trend that Marx had expected. However, Professor Warren Nutter, examining trends from the turn of the century to the late 1930s found that the average concentration had probably not increased any further and may have decreased, as nearly as could be determined from the imprecise data available on market shares late in the nineteenth century.[9]

The shifts in the market shares of leading firms. which occurred behind the mask of stability in the average concentration ratio, demonstrate pervasive competition among firms within each of the industries. The fact that of the 452 industries of 1947 only 165 (plus three for which data were not available) had the same definition in 1972 indicates how dynamic and competitive American industries are. The major exceptions occur outside the manufacturing sector in industries in which governments have (a) granted exclusive franchises, as in the marketing of electricity, (b) barred entry without governmental permission, as in inter-city common-carrier trucking of nonagricultural freight, (c) set price floors above the market clearing level, as in milk marketing and railroad services, (d) established a monopoly for a government enterprise, as in the case of the U.S. Postal Service, or (e) differentially taxed various categories of firms, as in the crude oil production industry in which firms with large production are taxed more heavily than firms with less production (which are granted a depletion allowance). Within the manufacturing sector, the structure of the petroleum refining industry has been influenced by the subsidies provided small refiners by the oil import program from 1960 to 1973 and the entitlements program after 1973. Specifically, non-competitive "teapot refiners" were attracted into the industry and kept in business by the subsidy provided in the entitlements program, artificially boosting the number of firms in the market.

The Effect of Competition on Concentration

The fact that some industries become (or remain) concentrated in itself demonstrates the competitiveness of markets where the government does not intervene to stop competition. Professor Joe Bain observed that in some cases, a high

> . . . degree of seller concentration would emerge more or less automatically as a result of competition even if sellers were initially many and small. If there are important economies of the large-scale firm, so that to approach optimal scale a firm must supply a significant fraction of the market, atomistic competition among many firms will lead all to expand. This expansion will drive price down until only large-scale firms can survive, eliminating all but a few firms, and will thus "automatically" produce an oligopolistic or concentrated market structure.[10]

In the absence of competition, concentration may remain at low levels even when economies can be realized by centralization. If more efficient firms fail to expand output or to merge with others to acquire poorly managed assets or uneconomical small-scale operations, large numbers of high-cost firms can survive and more will join the industry as it grows. It has been estimated that 83 to 91 percent of the capacity acquired by merger between 1929 and 1958 in six major industries was of suboptimal scale.[11] For example, in the days of the Gunpowder Trade Association, whose members restricted output in order to maintain prices, fourteen new high explosives companies and eleven black powder producers entered the industry between 1903 and 1907. In 1907, when the Department of Justice filed a Sherman Act suit, there were fifty-three independent explosives manufacturers. Many were inefficient. They had entered the industry because prices were higher than the competitive level, and they managed to survive only because prices were held high.

With the ending of the Association's suppression of competition, output increased, prices dropped, and the number of producers began declining (despite the dissolution of du Pont into three companies in 1912). By 1913, the number fell to twenty-seven. By 1921, the number dropped to nineteen, a nearly two-thirds decline from the fifty-three that had operated under the price umbrella of the Gunpowder Trade Association. By 1935, the industry's leading four firms produced 82 percent of all product shipped.

British experience following the 1956 Restrictive Practices Act, which led to the abolition of cartels, shows similar results following the ending of restraints on competition. In 142 markets where price-fixing agreements were terminated, five-firm concentration levels rose 7 points (from 59.3 to 66.3 percent) between 1963 and 1968. In 127 markets that had not been cartelized by explicit agreement (using these as a control to measure the effect of general trends and influences), concentration rose 3 points (from 60.3 to 63.5 percent), a rise in the same time period that was smaller by a statistically significant 4 points.[12] Competition's appearance where it was previously restrained led to increasing relative concentration. *A change in conduct produced changes in structure.*

Not only is it the case that suppressing collusion can cause concentration to rise, but it is also true that suppressing competition can cause concentration to decline. In 1953, Judge Wyzanski ruled that United Shoe Machinery had monopolized the shoe machinery industry, although all its practices were "honestly industrial." He ordered, as a remedy, that United stop competing. These, of course, were not the literal words of the order. He ordered the cessation of "practices which without being predatory, abusive or coercive were in economic effect exclusionary." Since all successful competitive acts and practices are "exclusionary" in the sense that they divert business toward the firm and away from its rivals, he, in effect, ordered United to stop competing. The only basis for finding United guilty of monopolizing was its 85 percent share of the market for major machines. Since the decree, affirmed in 1954 by the Supreme Court, provided for a 1965 review by the Court, the only way for United to avoid further penalties on review was to stop being so competitive and allow its market share to dwindle.

As ordered by the Court, United stopped the provision of free repair service for its machines. Also, as ordered by the Court, it reduced the length of machine leases from their previous ten-year minimum. Since short-term leases carried higher yearly rentals than the long-term leases they replaced, annual rentals rose on the machines United leased to shoe manufacturers. Its accounting profits rose from a 7.2 percent return on book equity in the seven years preceding the decree to 11.5 percent in the seven years following. This increase in return is all the more astonishing in view of the large cost United incurred defending itself against treble damage claims by customers who had benefited from its low-price policy for long-term leases. While United's high prices for short-term leases following the decree resulted in short-term gains, they also invited entry. Fifty-six new competitors appeared in the nine years following the decree (eleven in the 1955–57 period, nineteen in 1958–60, and twenty-six in 1961–63). United's market share fell from 85 percent to 48 percent by 1963.[13]

We see then that behavior determines market structure, and not necessarily in the way we might at first believe. There were good reasons for the form that United's contracts assumed, reasons that were firmly grounded in efficiency considerations.[14] It should strike us as odd that new firms entered after restrictions were placed on United's exaction of "monopoly" prices when presumably they had always been free to compete with it. This illustrates that the competition we see between small, artificially restrained firms may prove to be less efficient than the competition between one large firm and its potential competitors waiting in the wings. The second sort of competition is in fact that which forces the level of concentration in each industry towards its equilibrium, or most efficient, level.

In the absence of constraints on competition, concentrated industries are concentrated because that is the efficient way to organize them. Unconcentrated industries are unconcentrated because that is the efficient way to organize them. As Professor Harold Demsetz pointed out,

> My own studies . . . indicate that the more *concentrated* the industry, the lower are the costs of large firms relative to the costs of medium and small firms in those industries; this difference in costs is substantial. The cost advantage diminishes to insignificance for very *unconcentrated* industries. I believe that is why one set of industries is and remains concentrated and the other does not. This suggests that where concentration is found, it is largely a consequence of the competitive process, and that such industry structures are derived from those techniques yielding low-cost production. Competition would have altered concentrated structures if there were no associ-

ated efficiencies; in fact, many industries remain unconcentrated or have become unconcentrated because no special efficiencies or entrepreneurial successes have called forth and maintained concentrated structures.[15]

Competition is constantly at work altering industry structures moving them toward their equilibria, which are, themselves, being moved by changing circumstances. A changing structural equilibrium results from changes in tastes, resources, technology, or institutional factors (such as tariffs and government regulations). Industrial structure is not arbitrary nor immutable. Rather it is the result of efforts by market participants to achieve their ends at least cost, and, as changes in a variety of industries demonstrate, is influenced by changing conditions.

The Shifting Equilibrium Structure and Competition

The beer industry provides another instance in which we can see that there is an equilibrium or efficient level of concentration peculiar to an industry at any given time and set of circumstances. In the beer industry, changing conditions and innovations shifted the efficient concentration level. Rising wage rates, an increasing proportion of sales in bottles and cans requiring large-scale filling equipment, declining barrel sales to bars and taverns, and a growing number of regulations (requiring larger legal and clerical staffs) imposed on breweries made small breweries increasingly costly to operate relative to large breweries. The equilibrium level of concentration shifted upward in the malt liquor industry because of this set of forces.[16] The number of breweries declined from 756 in 1934 to 94 in 1976. The average size of breweries increased more than tenfold. The four-firm concentration ratio rose from 11 percent in 1935 to 63 percent in 1977 as a consequence of these forces and the competition of large, efficient breweries.[17]

In such cases, where we find a high level of concentration appearing, we can very easily verify whether one or more of the leading firms is establishing monopoly control over output. If leading firms in concentrated industries attempt to restrain output in order to maintain or improve their profitability, routinely behaving as partial monopolists or colluding members of a partial cartel (shared monopoly), they will lose market share over time. Declining concentration will characterize centralized industries behaving as oligopoly theories predict. (This is not to say that declining concentration is by itself proof of oligopoly conduct by leading firms since other causes may be operating. Rapid growth in industry size, technological change favoring small-scale operation, decreasing regulation that reduces the size of the legal and clerical staffs required, or a fall in the cost of capital relative to the cost of labor or materials, all tend to decrease the optimum level of concentration. Also, as we have seen, if leading firms fail to maintain superior management teams and become less profitable than smaller firms, they lose market share to their smaller, more efficient competitors.) Professor Richard Posner has observed that

> . . . collusive practice involves cooperation between competing sellers (in the form of an agreement, express or tacit, limiting competition . . .) to raise the market price above the competitive level. The agreement generates monopoly profits, but it also induces other firms to expand their output of the product sold by the colluding sellers (or to begin making the product if they have not done so previously) in order to capture a share of the monopoly profits. The pure collusion practice thus carries the seeds of its own destruction.[18]

The Effect of Intra-Industry Profitability on Concentration

But as Table 4-3 shows, in those industries where the leaders were more profitable than other firms, the leaders *expanded* output. They won an increased market share, apparently on the basis of their efficiency and their ability to offer better bargains. Their behavior was the opposite of that hypothesized by the concentration-collusion or dominant firm doctrines. In the highly concentrated rayon industry, for example, where the leading firms were slightly more profitable (and efficient) than their competitors (if we can accept accounting rates of return within the industry as indicators at least of *relative* intra-industry profitability), the market share of the leading four firms *did not decline* as would be expected if they had restrained output to maintain higher than competitive prices. It even expanded by 4 percentage points between 1935 and 1947. Instead of holding a price umbrella, the leading firms aggressively competed to expand their sales.

TABLE 4–3

Rates of Return on Book Net Worth in Leading Firms (1936–40) and Four-Firm Concentration Ratios (1935, 1947) in Selected Industries

Industry	Rates of Return (1936–40) Percentage		Four-Firm Concentration Percentage	
	Four Leading Firms	Larger Number of Firms[a]	1935	1947[d]
Part I. Concentrated industries				
A. Rate of return of four leading firms greater than rate of return of other firms				
Cigarettes	15.0	14.4 (7)	89.7	90.4
Rayon	11.5	9.0 (8,9)	74.3	78.4
Cane sugar refining[c]	3.1	3.1 (7)	69.6	69.9
Beet sugar[c]	8.8	8.4 (7,8)	68.8	68.4
Liquor	15.2	13.4 (12,16)	51.2	74.6
B. Rate of return of four leading firms less than rate of return of other firms				
Tires and tubes	7.8	8.0 (10,11)	80.9	76.6
Metal cans	8.6	9.1 (5)	80.8	77.8
Farm machinery	8.9	9.1 (9,10)	72.4	49.8
Domestic laundry equipment	13.2	13.4 (10)	56.0	39.8
Meat	3.0	3.6 (13)	55.6	47
Part II. Unconcentrated industries				
A. Rate of return of four leading firms greater than rate of return of other firms				
Flavorings	44.3	41.5 (5,7)	47.7	57.9
Cigars	7.7	6.9 (8)	38.5	40.6
Shoes	8.1	7.5 (12,14)	26.0	27.0
Canned fruits and vegetables	8.1	7.5 (19)	23.1	28.9
Screw machine products	9.2	8.2 (5,8)	22.2	16.9
Confectionery	15.8	13.9 (9)	12.5	17.2
Malt liquors	18.8[b]	15.2 (31, 34)	11.8	13.4
B. Rate of return of four leading firms less than rate of return of other firms				
Steel	3.8	4.9 (26,30)	50.5	47.5
Petroleum	6.6	6.8 (33,36)	38.2	37.3
Printing-trades machinery	1.8	2.9 (8)	32.5	30.7
Cement	5.6	6.0 (14)	29.9	29.5
Leather tanning	0.5	2.1 (8)	22.5	26.5

Sources: Securities and Exchange Commission, SURVEY OF AMERICAN LISTED CORPORATIONS: DATA ON PROFITS AND OPERATIONS, 1936–1942 (1944); MOODY'S INDUSTRIALS (various dates); National Resources Committee, STRUCTURE OF THE

AMERICAN ECONOMY, 249–50 (1939); G. S. Stigler, CAPITAL AND RATES OF RETURN IN MANUFACTURING INDUSTRIES, 212–3 (1963); REPORT OF THE FEDERAL TRADE COMMISSION ON CHANGES IN CONCENTRATION IN MANUFACTURING, 1935 to 1947 and 1959, 138–47 (1954). The industries used in this table were all those for which data could be extracted from these sources.

a Number of firms shown in parentheses. Rates of return are for all firms with data available, including leading firms, weighted by net worth.

b This rate of return is for Anheuser-Busch. The other three leading firms were privately held and their data are not available.

c The 1935 and 1947 concentration ratios of the sugar refining industry (cane and beet) are 66.0 and 66.5 respectively.

d Concentration ratios that increased are italicized.

The same behavior apparently characterized the leading firms in other concentrated industries. Although we lack profitability data, rising market shares from 1935 to 1947 of leading firms in the concentrated breakfast cereal, chocolate, industrial gases, soap, gypsum, primary copper, files, safes, cork, and match industries (see Table 10-1) indicate competitive behavior by leaders in those industries. Similarly, competitive behavior seems to have characterized leading firms in highly concentrated industries in later periods. A rise in market shares of leading firms as measured by *industry* concentration occurred in half (eleven out of twenty-two) of all "highly" concentrated industries from 1963 to 1972 for which information is available (see Table 4-2). Measured by *product* concentration, a more relevant measure, more than half (thirteen out of twenty-five) increased their market shares. The centripetal movement from 1947 to 1972 that characterized the industries with unchanged census definitions (summarized in Table 4-1) appears to have been much weaker for the shorter period from 1963 to 1972 in the concentrated group.

Given the centripetal tendency expected by some observers, to what should we attribute the fact that as many as half the highly concentrated industries of 1963 became even more concentrated?[19] Expansion by leading firms in these industries indicates that they did not behave collusively, or price their products above competitive levels. It would have been very difficult to obtain the endorsement of the other firms of a collusive policy that hurt them. If concentration automatically produces collusion only among the leading firms, the incidence of *declines* in concentration would have been substantially greater in this group of industries. As it was, a smaller incidence of declines occurred than would be dictated either by collusion or by the combination of chance and centripetal forces. Other forces must have been at work. Our earlier results on productivity and price changes in concentrated industries suggest that increased efficiency in leading firms and "active" competition played important roles. Perhaps increasing government regulation in this period, which increased fixed and semifixed costs, tipped the balance in favor of larger firms.

The data on the earlier period displayed in Table 4-3 also indicate that when leading firms in concentrated industries were less profitable than their competitors, they were less efficient. They failed to hold their early market shares and declined relative to their industries, as we would expect if competitive behavior prevailed. The leading tire companies were only slightly less profitable than other firms (see Table 4-3), if we can again rely on accounting rates of return to indicate relative profitability within an industry, yet they nevertheless lost 4 percent of the market to other firms.

We see the same forces at work in the unconcentrated industries listed in Table 4-3. The leading firms that were more profitable than other firms increased their market shares in most instances (six out of seven cases). When they were less profitable, their market shares declined.

The Effect of High Industry Profitability on Concentration

The limited number of industries shown in Table 4-3 may not be representative of all industries. High profitability among leading firms will not always lead to an enlargement of their market share. If the profitability of the industry is sufficiently high to attract new entrants, industry output may grow more rapidly than that of the leaders. The appearance of additional firms and additional capacity will erode the market share of the leaders despite competitive behavior on their part—and new firms will appear and small firms will expand if profits are attractive. The costs of rapid expansion by leading firms may be too high to make it worth keeping up with fast industry growth.

A general rule of thumb in managerial lore is that expanding an organization more rapidly than 10 percent a year makes cost go out of control. Corroboration of this rule is provided by Stigler's finding that the fifteen industries with the largest growth rate in number of firms from 1948 to 1956 among the ninety-nine he examined were those in which assets grew 17 percent per year. The number of firms grew 9 percent per year in this group. The fifteen industries with the lowest growth in number of firms had a 4.5 percent annual asset growth rate. The number of firms decreased 4 percent per year in these.[20] This suggests that a 9 percent industry asset growth rate can be accommodated by internal growth of an industry's resident firms without costs and prices rising to a level that attracts new firms. It also suggests that faster growth tends to deconcentrate industries and slower growth to concentrate them.

We saw above that greater profitability of leading firms relative to the rest of an industry is associated with a greater growth of these leading firms. High industry profitability, however, attracts entry and tends to deconcentrate industries. Professor Edwin Mansfield concluded from his study of factors affecting entry that the "entry rate would increase by at least 60 percent if an industry's profitability doubled."[21] Professor Michael Gort ranked *industries* by profitability for the 1947 to 1954 period and examined the fate of leading firms as related to the profitability rank of their industries. He found that in the industries ranked among the top 20 percent by profitability, leading firms suffered marked declines in market share from 1947 to 1954.[22]

However, as K. D. George's data for 1950 to 1960 indicate, profitable leading firms expand more rapidly than less profitable leading firms.[23] To account for the apparent inconsistency, we should note that the leading firms that lost market shares may have been less profitable than other firms in their industries. It is also likely that they may have lost market shares simply because they were unable to expand as rapidly as their industries did from 1947 to 1954 when their industries were among the most profitable and attracted large volumes of investment and new entrants.

Gort's finding that leading firms in the most profitable industries suffered loss of market share may also have been due to the particular circumstances of the period from 1947 to 1954. Data assembled by T. G. Sullivan for the period from 1961 to 1968 showed that the most profitable firms among leading firms *increased* their market shares, again indicating competitive behavior. Using 129 firms listed among *Fortune's* 500 biggest industrial firms, he found that where leading firms were relatively more profitable, they grew more rapidly and achieved increased market shares regardless of the initial level of concentration of their industries.[24]

Again there was no finding of restraint by leading firms in order to maintain the profitability of their industries.

This is not to say that leading firms never yield market share in an attempt to maintain prices. Apparently, this has occurred in a few instances. It seems clear that U.S. Steel allowed its sales to decline by 14 percent, in the 1903–04 recession, in an attempt to maintain prices. But other steel firms maintained and even increased their sales, despite the recession, under the price umbrella held by U.S. Steel. Its market share fell from 65.2 percent in 1902 to 60.7 percent in 1904 despite the acquisition of Troy Steel in 1903 and Clairton in 1904. It never recovered, falling to 50 percent by 1914 and to 42 percent by 1925 (see Table 4-4). The fact that market share must be given up to maintain a supracompetitive price demonstrates the self-defeating character of such activity and the presence of competition. Only if leading firms continually improve processes and products to preserve their relative efficiency, and only if they price competitively, do they succeed in maintaining their positions.

Capital Intensity and Concentration

The lower cost to large firms of raising capital as a result of flotation economies and lower risk, causes an association of capital intensive production with large firms and concentration. Some industries are naturally capital intensive, that is, the most economical technology uses relatively large amounts of capital per employee or per unit of product. Capital costs are a large part of total costs in such industries. As a result, economies in obtaining capital have a more important influence on total cost per unit of product there than in other industries. Large firms in such industries can raise their capital less expensively and therefore offset unfavorable effects of scale caused by other factors. They can frequently offer lower prices than smaller firms in their industries and still be at least as profitable. Their market shares become large, then, because they can attract buyers with better offers. This is a major reason that capital intensity and concentration are associated[25] and that value-added per employee in the thirty-eight most concentrated industries is almost double that in the thirty-seven least concentrated.[26]

Ranking industries by a measure of capital intensity (gross book value of plant and equipment per employee), we find that the 20

Total Ingot Production:
U.S. Steel Corporation and Other Steel Producing Companies

| Year | Production in Thousands of Gross Tons | | | U.S. Steel in Percentage of Total U.S. |
	U.S. Steel	Other Companies	Total U.S.	
1901	8,855	4,618	13,473	65.7
1902	9,750	5,197	14,947	65.2
1903	9,174	5,361	14,535	63.1
1904	8,413	5,447	13,860	60.7
1905	12,006	8,018	20,024	60.0
1906	13,529	9,869	23,398	57.8
1907	13,100	10,263	23,363	56.1
1908	7,839	6,184	14,023	55.9
1909	13,355	10,600	23,955	55.8
1910	14,179	11,916	26,095	54.3
1911	12,753	10,923	23,676	53.9
1912	16,901	14,350	31,251	54.1
1913	16,656	14,645	31,301	53.2
1914	11,826	11,687	23,513	50.3
1915	16,376	15,775	32,151	50.9
1916	20,911	21,863	42,774	48.9
1917	20,285	24,776	45,061	45.0
1918	19,583	24,879	44,462	44.0
1919	17,200	17,471	34,671	49.6
1920	19,278	22,855	42,133	45.8
1921	10,966	8,818	19,784	55.4
1922	16,082	19,521	35,603	45.2
1923	20,330	24,614	44,944	45.2
1924	16,479	21,453	37,932	43.4
1925	18,899	26,495	45,394	41.6
1926	20,307	27,987	48,294	42.0
1927	18,486	26,449	44,935	41.1
1928	20,106	31,438	51,544	39.0
1929	21,869	34,564	56,433	38.8
1930	16,726	23,973	40,699	41.1
1931	10,082	15,863	25,946	38.9
1932	4,929	8,752	13,681	36.0
1933	8,047	15,185	23,232	34.6
1934	8,660	17,375[a]	26,055[a]	33.2
1935	11,131	22,962	34,093	32.6

TABLE 4–4 (Cont)
Total Ingot Production:
U.S. Steel Corporation and Other Steel Producing Companies

| Year | Production in Thousands of Gross Tons | | | U.S. Steel in Percentage of Total U.S. |
	U.S. Steel	Other Companies	Total U.S.	
1936	16,908	30,860	47,768	35.4
1937	18,532	32,036	50,569	36.6
1938	9,397	18,953	28,350	33.1

Source: Corporation records and American Iron and Steel Institute. Data include production of castings.
[a] Figures for 1934 and subsequent years include only that portion of steel for castings used by foundries operated by companies producing steel ingots.
Tennessee Coal, Iron and Railroad Company data included in Corporation figures beginning with January 1, 1908.

percent of industries that were most capital intensive in 1972 were also more concentrated than the rest (see Table 4-5). Four-firm concentration averaged 49 percent in these as compared to 26 percent in the 20 percent of industries that were least capital intensive.

TABLE 4–5
Average Concentration Ratios and Wage Rates in Industry
Quintiles Ranked by Depreciable Assets per Employee, 1972

Number of Industries	Depreciable Assets per Employee	Average Concentration Ratio	Average Hourly Wage
81	$49,285	49	$4.49
82	17,178	42	3.99
82	11,970	36	3.96
82	8,727	33	3.80
82	4,678	26	2.92

Source: U.S., Bureau of the Census, ANNUAL SURVEY OF MANUFACTURERS 1976, INDUSTRY PROFILES, Part 7 (1979).

LCR = 3.90 + .263 LGBV + .319 LINV + .0763 LADV − .422 LTPA − .306 LSH
$\quad$ (15.1) (4.11) $\quad$ (5.36) $\quad$ (3.07) $\quad$ (−6.16) $\quad$ (−3.08)

$\bar{r}^2 = .201$

LCR = log concentration ratio
LGBV = log gross book value of depreciable assets in thousands of dollars
LINV = log inventories in thousands of dollars
LADV = log advertising outlays in thousands of dollars
LTPA = log total payroll in thousands of dollars
LSH = log total shipments in thousands of dollars
Number of industries used in the regression is 307.
The figures in parentheses below the coefficients are t-ratios.

Since several varieties of capital are employed other than depreciable assets (plant and equipment), we examined the effects on concentration of the investment required in inventories and in advertising, allowing for the influence of other factors such as labor intensity and the size of the industry. Holding payroll and shipments constant by means of the multiple regression shown in Table 4-5, we see that if greater investment in inventories and in advertising is necessary for economical production and distribution, this too tends to raise the level of concentration. Every one percent increase in the amount of inventory required per dollar of shipments raises the concentration ratio by 0.3 percent. Every one percent increase in the stock of capital invested in advertising required per dollar of shipments (assuming the stock in each industry is proportional to current outlays on advertising) raises the concentration ratio by .076 percent. That is, an industry which is identical in all respects with another that is 50.00 percent concentrated, except that it must invest 10 percent more in advertising to economically distribute its product, will have a concentration ratio of 50.38 percent instead of 50.00 percent.

Wage Rates and Concentration

The wage level also is higher where the depreciable capital employed per worker is higher (Table 4-5). The wage level itself may be as much a cause as a consequence of the higher concentration and higher capital-per-employee level in high-wage industries. If more highly skilled, higher-cost workers have to be employed to turn out a product, firms will economize on this costly factor by substituting capital for workers, thus increasing the capital-labor ratio. It is also true that a large firm with a lower cost of capital invests more in employee training and pays its trained people more. Higher rates of pay are offered to people in whose training an employer has invested in order to reduce the quit rate and, thereby, to avoid losing the capital invested.[27]

With wage rates rising over time relative to the cost of equipment, more larger-scale equipment using more capital-intensive technology is becoming increasingly economical, and small-scale equipment is becoming increasingly uneconomical. Small tankers are disappearing from the high seas, larger tank trucks delivering larger lots of gasoline to filling stations are replacing small tank trucks, more cows are milked mechanically on larger dairy farms and tomatoes are grown on a much larger scale than previously and sold to larger canneries. Yet this has not decreased the number of enterprises (Table 12-1) nor influenced the *average* level of concentration.

The rise in wage rates is, in part, a consequence of the increasing quantity of capital and the resulting increase in productivity. The average firm uses more capital with the increased quantity available and thus can pay the higher wage. To hold its labor against bids by other firms, which have also raised productivity with the use of additional capital, the average firm has been forced to pay more. But wage rates in some cases have been pushed up artificially, above market clearing levels, by such actions as the passage of minimum wage laws. A consequence has been the demise of many small-scale enterprises in low-wage industries and an increase in concentration. Many of these small labor-intensive enterprises could have adapted and survived if wage rates had risen more slowly at the rate dictated by the market. An irony in this situation is the fact that minimum wage laws have had little effect on the wage level in the long run. While the average wage of those employed increased as a result, it also caused unemployment in the interim until a larger supply of capital and improvements in technology became available. Each increase in the minimum wage was followed by years of slower than normal growth in low wage rates until the old relationship to the average wage level was reestablished.[28]

Professor David Kaun studied the impact of federal minimum wage changes in 1950 and 1956. He concluded that the marked decline in the number of individual proprietorships and in partnership-owned establishments (and in employment) in the tobacco, textile, and leather industries from 1947 to 1958 was a consequence of the rise in the federal minimum wage rate to $.75 an hour in 1950 and to $1.00 in 1956.[29] Individually owned establishments in the tobacco industry, for example, fell by 54 percent from 1947 to 1954 and a further 35 percent by 1958. The decline was not a part of a general trend of corporate establishments displacing individual proprietors. The number of proprietor-operated establishments rose by 30 percent in "all other" manufacturing (see Table 4-6).

The individually owned establishments in tobacco were employing low-wage workers. Their costs were greatly affected by the

111

TABLE 4-6

Changes in Value Added, Employment, and Number of Establishments for Several Low-Wage Industries by Type of Operation: 1947–54, 1954–58

Industry	Percentage Change in Number of Establishments		Percentage Change in Value Added		Percentage Change in Production Workers		Production Workers Annual Income		
	1947–54	1954–58	1947–54	1954–58	1947–54	1954–58	1947	1954	1958
Tobacco									
Individual	−54	−35	−51	−19	−65	−35	$1,181	$1,542	$1,750
Partnership	−61	−35	−7	−17	−42	−38	1,412	1,734	2,077
All other	−20	−6	56	44	−13	−12	1,722	2,551	3,278
Textiles									
Individual	−9	−1	−46	13	−44	−9	1,565	2,127	2,416
Partnership	−27	−16	−6	−13	−21	−27	1,978	2,483	2,817
All other	5	−4	−11	+3	−17	−14	2,150	2,678	2,982
Leather									
Individual	−11	−3	−27	NA	−35	NA	1,861	2,155	NA
Partnership	−33	−25	−23	−9	−33	−27	1,918	2,404	2,824
All other	0	−3	10	17	−5	−2	2,095	2,615	2,950

Apparel									
Individual	3	−9	9	3	5	−18	2,000	2,185	2,527
Partnership	−27	−22	−13	−10	−18	−24	2,193	2,407	2,710
All other	18	1	24	23	19	3	2,046	2,369	2,699
Lumber									
Individual	80	−1	37	−2	−1	−14	1,453	1,786	2,217
Partnership	19	−18	25	−24	−13	−31	1,704	1,927	2,759
All other	56	−20	26	6	0	−8	2,242	3,102	1,617
All other manufacturing									
Individual	30	8	35	22	−2	0	2,145	2,877	3,383
Partnership	−3	−9	39	−7	−3	−23	2,261	3,092	2,677
All other	27	15	71	23	8	−4	2,757	4,028	4,770

Source: David E. Kaun, Minimum Wages, Factor Substitution and the Marginal Producer, 79 Quarterly Journal of Economics (1965) at 484, Table IV, corrected. Copyright by John Wiley & Sons. Reprinted by permission of the publisher.

jump in the legal minimum from 40 cents to 75 cents in 1950 and to $1.00 in 1956. Employment in individually owned establishments declined by 65 percent from 1947 to 1954 and by a further 35 percent by 1958. It should be noted that this did not cause a rise in employment in the higher-wage establishments owned by corporations, although they did greatly increase their output. Employment declined in these as well because they cut their lowest wage positions and substituted other resources for labor.

Lumber production was also a low-wage industry where a large fraction of employees were being paid less than the new minimum established in 1950, but it escaped a decrease in the number of jobs and establishments. Its fate was different because the 1949 amendments to the Fair Labor Standard Act provided an exemption for logging and sawmill establishments employing fewer than twelve workers. The result was a large rise in the number of establishments in the industry with no significant change in the total number of employees.

The Influence of Entry Barriers on Concentration

Some economists argue that centralized industries are concentrated because economic barriers prevent new firms from entering these industries. Economist Douglas Greer, for example, tells us that barriers "help to explain variances in observed concentration, because high barriers tend to be associated with high concentration."[30] He cites Edwin Mansfield's statement that "An oligopolistic industry may not be oligopolistic for long if every Tom, Dick, and Harry can enter." Professor Willard Mueller informs us that

> The height of the "barriers to entry" . . . is even more basic than the degree of market concentration; the ease with which new concerns may enter an industry determines, in the first instance, the degree of market concentration that will ultimately prevail in an industry. Where barriers to entry are few, as in farming, there are generally numerous competitors; where entry barriers are formidable as in autos, there are only a few sellers."[31]

Presumably, few newcomers ever appear in concentrated industries, because barriers shut them out and this keeps those industries concentrated. Many have appeared in the less centralized industries, which made them unconcentrated. The degree of concentration of an industry, from this view, is determined by the height of entry barriers. There have been several attempts to estimate the height of entry barriers in various industries, and to classify industries according to whether their entry barriers are "high, substantial, or moderate."[32] All of the classifiers used subjective standards to categorize industries. The only "barrier" measured by an objective criterion was advertising. In this case, percentage of sales spent on advertising was the measure used. A value less than one percent was termed "moderate," a value between one and perhaps 2 to 5 percent, "substantial," and anything greater a "high barrier."[33]

Oddly, something as vague as "product differentiation" is thought to be the most important entry barrier by many economists of this school of industrial organization theory, although there is no objective standard here either. Since we are interested in finding how likely it is that firms will enter an industry when its profitability makes entry attractive, an objective measure would be an examination of the entry rate in various industries. If entry is barred, the entry rate will be zero. The less effective the barriers to entry, the higher the entry rate. A high entry rate, then, would indicate moderate barriers, a middling entry rate would indicate the existence of substantial barriers, and a low entry rate would indicate the existence of high barriers, assuming the incidence of profitability does not differ across grouped industries.

Suppose we examine the increase in the number of firms from 1947 to 1972 in thirty-five manufacturing industries 60 percent or more concentrated in 1947, all of those for which data are available in both years. The number of firms increased by 51 percent in the average industry in this group, but we cannot tell from this alone whether barriers were high or low. Since most economists of the structuralist school believe that barriers are high in concentrated industries, as illustrated by the statements quoted above, we know that we should expect a higher net entry rate in less centralized industries. Examining the increase in the number of firms in the 126 industries with concentration ratios below 60 percent, we find that the average increase from 1947 to 1972 was 12.3 percent. On the face of it, this suggests that entry barriers were higher in the less concentrated industries. If that is the case, barriers do not account for the high level of concentration that prevails in some industries. They are not the determinant of concentration they are believed to be by the structuralist school.

Perhaps the higher net entry rate in concentrated industries is simply the result of their being more attractive—more profitable

115

—in the 1950s and 1960s. If that is so, then we can expect that high profitability in centralized industries will not persist any more than it will in diffused industries. Apparently that is the case, as shown in Tables 7-2A, 7-2B, and 7-2C. Also, we find that the entry rate in the 80 to 100 percent concentrated industries dropped from the highest rate among all concentration levels for the 1947-72 period to the third highest for 1967-72 (see Table 4-7), indicating that there was a drop in the relative profitability of the most concentrated industries by the latter period. (It seems unlikely that entry barriers became substantial after being so low.) That is the outcome predicted by Telser in his study of concentration and profitability for 1958 and 1963.[34]

TABLE 4–7

Net Entry by Concentration Quintiles, 1947–72 and 1967–72

Four-Firm Concentration Percentage in Initial Year	1947–72		1967–72	
	Entry: Average Percentage Increase in Number of Firms	Number of Industries	Entry: Average Percentage Increase in Number of Firms	Number of Industries
0–19	1.1	34	−3.9	65
20–39	14.7	57	−2.5	138
40–59	19.3	35	6.3	79
60–79	25.5	22	16.9	50
80–100	94.5	13	4.8	20
0–59	12.3	126	−0.4	282
60–100	51.1	35	13.5	70
0–100	20.7	161	2.4	352

Sources: U.S., Bureau of the Census, CENSUS OF MANUFACTURES, 1972, CONCENTRATION RATIOS IN MANUFACTURING, MC76(SR)–2 (Oct. 1975).

Entry (1947–72) = −16.58 + 0.943 CR47

       (−1.34)   (3.51) $\bar{r}^2 = 0.066$

Entry (1967–72) = −9.07 + 0.292 CR67

       (−2.74)   (3.95) $\bar{r}^2 = 0.040$

The Influence of the Postwar Revolution in Distribution on Concentration

Several economists have commented on the fact that trends in concentration in the postwar period have differed markedly between consumer goods and producer goods industries. Professor F. M. Scherer analyzed postwar trends and found that "between 1947 and 1972, concentration fell on average by 1.7 percentage points in 87 producer goods industries . . . It *rose* on average by 6.4 percentage points in 50 consumer goods industries."[35]

The factor accounting for the rise in consumer goods concentration probably lies in the combination of the decreasing cost of advertising with the advent of television in the 1950s and the postwar revolution in distribution—particularly the rise of discount stores. The influences playing a role in the great rise in concentration in the brewing industry were described above. One of these was the shift from distribution by barrel through taverns to distribution by package through supermarkets and liquor stores. In general, consumer goods distribution now relies less on wholesalers and service providing retailers and more on chain and discount stores providing fewer services and less personal selling. Large lots are bought directly from manufacturers instead of small lots from wholesalers. Self-service stores, or discount stores, sell to consumers pre-sold by advertising and by familiarity with goods that are now fairly well standardized with familiar features.

When household laundry equipment was not a familiar good with a few settled designs that had been found to be the most practicable, many producers vied for the trade with differentiated products incorporating unfamiliar features, which had to be displayed, explained, and demonstrated. Advertising could not provide an adequate explanation. Personal selling was required, and the number of retailers was large relative to the volume sold. As some features won the market and others were dropped, designs closed in on common elements packaged in the various combinations tailored to the desires of differing segments of the market. Volume in each of the fewer varieties increased and economies of scale could be achieved, which precluded continuing with as large a number of producers. Also, the buyer now familiar with the no longer innovative elements could be more readily informed of new variants and provided with product assurance by advertising, thus decreasing the amount of personal selling and the number of retailers required. This made scale economies in distribution possible both at the manufacturing and the retailing levels and influenced the structure of manufacturing industries.

No such revolution in the distribution of producer goods occurred. Neither the decreasing costs of advertising, of wholesaling and retailing, or the innovation-concentration cycle had a role to play in influencing concentration in the average producer goods industry. The design and innovation-concentration cycle influenced a few industries, such as printing machinery and paper making machinery. In these, concentration increased. But most suppliers of products continued to make the same basic goods, moderately improved from time to time, distributed in the same ways as in prewar days. New economies of scale did not develop with sufficient rapidity to keep up with the growth of the market. As a consequence, smaller suppliers grew more rapidly than the leading firms who had already reached the far edge of scale economies, and concentration tended to decrease with market growth.

Conclusion

The standard paradigm used by industrial organization theorists argues that the structure of an industry determines its *conduct* and performance.[36] In the standard view, competitive conduct will occur if an industry consists of many firms with little centralization. Competitive conduct produces good performance. On the other hand, a highly concentrated industry structure will cause noncompetitive conduct and poor performance. But this reverses the actual forces at work in the history of most industries.

What we actually find in the history of many concentrated industries is that outstanding performance by a few firms, rapid expansion of their capacity and output, whether by merger or new construction, and competitive conduct produce the concentrated structure. An industry's structure remains concentrated only as long as its largest firms continue to perform outstandingly, do not stagnate technologically, and conduct themselves competitively. The automobile and brewing industries provide prime examples of the reversal of the causation sequence posited in the standard paradigm, according to FTC studies.[37] Where firms of different sizes can be equally efficient, an industry remains diffused. If initially concentrated, it becomes diffused.

The standard paradigm should have its causation flow reversed. Exceptional performance and competitive conduct lead to a concentrated structure. Where no exceptional performance occurs or, even with exceptional performance but no competition in the industry, a diffused structure remains. *Structure is a result, not a cause.* Regulatory constraints often inhibit competition in a way that results in a diffused structure. The stock brokerage industry, for example, until recently operated under rules that restricted competition. With the removal of regulatory constraints, it became more concentrated.

Most of the industries with which we are concerned do not operate under such restraints. In general, we can be sure that where those restraints are absent, industries become and remain concentrated because that is the efficient structure. Industries do not become concentrated where a dispersion of production and marketing facilities among many firms is more efficient, provided governmentally granted franchises or government entry barriers do not prevent the dispersion. The reasons for high concentration, where it occurs, range from economies of scale or superior performance in a few firms to the decreased cost of raising capital for capital intensive technology and the importance of learning.

The similarity of industrial structures in many different countries demonstrates that fundamental technological and economic forces determine concentration levels. The enormous horizontal-merger wave of 1898-1901 and the minor wave of the 1920s have little influence on the current industrial structure in the United States (see Tables 10-1 and 10-3). Only those industries remained concentrated that would have become concentrated by other roads. Where merger for monopoly or oligopoly occurred, the industry soon became deconcentrated (see Tables 3-1 and 3-2). Centralization does not persist where it is inefficient. Neither does low concentration persist where it is inefficient unless competition is prevented by collusion or by government. Rising or persistently high concentration is a demonstration of the presence of competitive behavior. Where major firms do not behave competitively, they soon lose market share.

Appendix: Risk and Concentration

High concentration in an industry may be a consequence of the riskiness of the projects in which it invests.[38] Also, it may be a means of reducing the cost of risk and of reducing the possibility of the failure of the enterprise. American Can reduced its risk of being hurt by crop failures in one or a few regions by acquiring can plants in many regions (discussed in Chapter 3). Similarly, General Motors, by producing multiple models and designing plants to be equally useful in producing different lines, reduced its risk of having to carry the costs of idle plant and of paying workers higher wages as compensation for more layoffs (also discussed in Chapter 3). If Lockheed's business in other lines and other industries had been a larger share of its total business, it might have survived the collapse of its engine supplier for L-1011s without having to call on the federal government for help.

Concentration may be caused by risk as well as be a means of minimizing the cost of risk. The influence of risk in causing concentration (and causing high profitability in successful firms) can be illustrated by a simple example. Suppose a new entrant into petroleum exploration has funds to finance the drilling of only one well. If one out of five wells is the usual success ratio, the new entrant has an 80 percent chance of going broke. If five firms enter the industry with such limited funds, four fail and one succeeds. Assuming that each well costs $1,000, that the probability of success is one-fifth, and that the cost of capital is 10 percent, a successful well must promise a $500 return in perpetuity to attract investment to the exploration industry.[39] That is, since finding a producing well requires a five-well drilling program and a $5,000 investment, a $500 annual return on that one well is necessary to yield a 10 percent return on the $5,000 investment. If it does, the industry can compete for capital. Each company investing $1,000 faces a one-fifth chance of making $500 a year. Each faces an expected return of $100 (one-fifth probability times $500).

With five firms each drilling one well, four fail and one succeeds. The successful company invested $1,000. It earns $500 a year and shows a 50 percent annual return. It is this "high" return on the one successful well that attracts sufficient capital to our hypothetical oil exploration industry to provide a large number of producing wells. Capital will not be invested in drilling, let us say, 500 wells unless the return on investment in successful wells is large enough to provide a probable yield of 10 percent to the investment in each well—dry or wet.

If 100 firms succeed among the 500 who try, the 100 successes will show 50 percent return. The industry will appear to be very profitable indeed. Only the successful firms will be reporting their income each year, the 400 failures having disappeared from the scene.

Does the 50 percent average return in firms producing crude oil mean that consumers are being victimized? Are resources being kept out of the industry by monopolists who are barring entry? Should controls be imposed on the price of oil to reduce returns to

10 percent in these 100 successful firms? If we do impose such controls, the return from a successful well will be reduced to $100 per year. The expected return to a drilling venture will drop to 2 percent (one-fifth probability of a $100 return or a $20 expected return on a $1000 investment). Drilling investment will cease in these circumstances. No further additions to the stock of producing wells will occur.

Of course, not all currently operating petroleum producers produce a uniformly high return. One reason for this is the fact that successful wildcatters usually continue to wildcat. Let us assume that the one hundred successful firms, having succeeded, will all drill a second well. Of these, one out of five succeeds again. Twenty firms will hit a second wet hole, will operate two producing wells, and will continue to earn a 50 percent return. The remaining eighty will each have a $500 return from their successful wells but will now have invested $2000, the second $1,000 having gone into a dry hole. Their return will drop to 25 percent (assuming they do not write off their investment in dry holes). There are now twenty firms, which top the industry in size, earning 50 percent and eighty smaller firms producing half as much and earning a 25 percent return.

A third round of drilling further increases the dispersion and leaves us with even larger firms earning the highest return. Of the twenty largest, on the third round, four succeed in drilling another wet hole. Four firms each operate three successful wells and earn 50 percent on their investment. Sixteen of the former twenty largest each earn $1,000 on their $3,000 investment in two wet holes and one dry hole for a 33 percent return. Of the eighty firms with one producing well, sixteen (one-fifth of the eighty) strike a second producing well and also earn 33 percent. But sixty-four will have drilled two dry holes and will earn 17 percent.[40] We can set out the results in tabular form.

Number of Firms	Number of Wet Holes per Firm	Return (percentage)
4	3	50
32	2	33
64	1	17
400	firms no longer in existence	—

Since current records show only the firms still in business, the industry appears to be very profitable (with an increasing concentration trend) despite the fact that the probable return on investment to any new entrant is still 10 percent and the probable return on any additional wells drilled by currently operating firms is also only 10 percent.[41] If all the firms go into a fourth round of drilling, each investing $1,000 in another well, the distribution shown in the table below will result:

Number of Firms	Number of Wet Holes per Firm	Return (percentage)
1	4	50
9	3	38
39	2	25
51	1	13
400	firms no longer in existence	—

It might be argued—incorrectly—that the one firm earning 50 percent should do no more drilling since it has only a one-fifth chance of maintaining its 50 percent return. But it faces a probable return of 10 percent, the same return that induced it to drill in the first place. Presumably, this return is as attractive as it always was. This is the same chance it faced when it drilled its first, second, third, and fourth wet hole. So let us assume that all firms go into a fifth round of drilling. The distribution shown below is the most likely result.

Number of Firms	Number of Wet Holes per Firm	Return (percentage)
3	4	40
15	3	30
41	2	20
41	1	10
400	firms no longer in existence	—

The surviving 100 firms earn an above-average return as a group. The industry apparently earns an average 18 percent return on the $500,000 invested in sinking 500 wells. The 180 producing wells, however, are the result of sinking 900 wells, 400 by firms that have long since disappeared. If we count the $400,000 investment of the defunct firms, the industry earns only a 10 percent return on its total investment (and has always earned that return).[42] We have 180 producing wells only because each firm hoped to be one of the surviving 100—and, preferably, one of the big three with the four wet holes.

This is the situation we see in the automobile industry, except that the chances of success are slimmer for automobile firms than in the hypothetical oil industry postulated above. The average cost of producing a successful model, taking the cost of failed efforts into account, is even higher there relative to the size of the total market. Perhaps as many as a thousand firms entered the auto industry, but only a handful survived.[43] Some had an initial success, but failed to hit any more. They eventually left the industry. Some had enough successes to survive their Edsels, DeSotos, and La Salles. None has been uniformly successful. All the surviving firms have had failures.

In the early days of the auto industry, successful firms emerged with rich prizes. Henry Ford earned returns in excess of 100 percent.[44] From 1927 through 1929, Nash earned 58 to 76 percent, Hudson 29 to 42 percent, and Packard 36 to 66 percent.[45] Yet, Hudson and Packard did not survive their later failures. The nearly bankrupt General Motors of 1920 has since hit enough wet holes to make it the industry leader. The onetime industry leader, Ford, lost that position and twice nearly foundered. The Federal Trade Commission has pointed out how risky the industry is. "The profits of the motorcar manufacturers have varied greatly according to time and circumstance. The path of the industry's growth is strewn with scores of companies that have failed."[46] The FTC goes on to point out that, "For many years the automobile industry was regarded as highly speculative."[47]

That the risks in the automobile industry are still high is indicated by the fate of the Bricklin, the demise of the Edsel, and the current difficulties of Chrysler. That the cost of attempting to hit a wet hole in the industry is high is indicated by John Z. Delorean's estimate of the cost of bringing his sports car to market. He expected that it would require $90 million, and he has no guarantee of success.[48] If he fails he is unlikely to have a second chance.

Part of the reason for GM, Ford, and Chrysler's survival (although Chrysler's survival in its current circumstances is in doubt) is that none bet all their chips on one model or even one brand. The failure of a model or of a brand has not sunk the company.[49] Each can and has survived one dry hole or even several dry holes. But to practice this risk strategy means each must have a large enough share of the market to support several models in each line and more than one line.

123

Each model must sell in sufficient volume to realize most of the economies of scale. These are significant in the automobile industry.[50] Of the 101 makes selling less than 5,000 vehicles in 1920, only six survived to 1930. Of the 25 makes selling between 5,000 and 25,000 in 1920, eleven survived to 1930. The ten makes that produced more than 25,000 in 1920 all survived to 1930.[51] And some of the economies of scale necessary for survival were achieved by using the same bodies and parts among different lines as well as by exploiting the benefits of volume within each line.

Multiplicity of models and brands has to be balanced against economies of scale. In the pre–World-War-I period when the total volume of automobile sales was low, single-line companies succeeded while multiple-line companies foundered or failed. United States Motors failed (the Maxwell Motor Company was extracted from the wreckage by the creditors and then succeeded as a single-line firm), General Motors foundered and Durant was removed from its stewardship. Pope came to grief with its multiple products. "Companies that had chosen to concentrate on a single car seemed to be doing well—Ford spectacularly so, concerns like Reo, Packard, and Hudson at least respectably."[52] But as total automobile volume grew, all the single-line companies, which had succeeded earlier, came to grief, beginning with the weeding process in the 1920s when the number of producers fell from eighty-eight in 1921 to forty-four in 1926. The culmination of the process came with the withdrawal of Studebaker-Packard in 1963.

Decreasing concentration by mandate in the automobile industry with its high risks[53] would mean that the number of bankruptcies and withdrawals from the industry would increase.[54]

Notes

1. Production economies of scale are not discussed in this book. Most of these are well recognized in the literature of industrial organization. There is no dispute over their existence although they tend to be underestimated. E. A. G. Robinson, THE STRUCTURE OF COMPETITIVE INDUSTRY (1958); John Haldi and David Whitcomb, *Economies of Scale in Industrial Plants*, 75 JOURNAL OF POLITICAL ECONOMY 373 (Aug. 1967); John S. McGee, *Economies of Size in Auto Body Manufacture*, 16 JOURNAL OF LAW & ECONOMICS 239 (Oct. 1973). Finance, marketing, coordination, adaptation, and external relations (primarily with government)

economies are less frequently recognized, yet are of equal importance in bringing product to the market economically. Economies in the provision of information also are important, especially in marketing, yet are sometimes condemned as being counter to the social interest as in the FTC Procter & Gamble-Clorox decision compelling divestiture of Clorox. Also, see F. M. Scherer, A. Beckenstein, E. Kaufer, and R. D. Murphy, THE ECONOMICS OF MULTI-PLANT OPERATION (1975). For a critique of the latter study, see John S. McGee, *Efficiency and Economies of Size* in Goldschmid, Mann, and Weston (eds.), INDUSTRIAL CONCENTRATION: THE NEW LEARNING 55 (1974).

2. "The number of plants affected by combinations was 18 percent of the total number of establishments and 10 percent of the total number of factories and neighborhood industries recorded by the Bureau in 1900." Jesse Markham, *Survey of the Evidence and Findings on Mergers* in National Bureau of Economic Research, BUSINESS CONCENTRATION AND PRICE POLICY 157, n. 32 (1955). In his *Comment,* at 183, Walter Adams says, "These combinations, according to generally accepted estimates, controlled fully 40 percent of the nation's manufacturing capital."

3. Oliver Williamson, *Dominant Firms and the Monopoly Problem: Market Failure Considerations,* 85 HARVARD LAW REVIEW 1512 (Jun. 1972); Book Review, 83 YALE LAW JOURNAL 647 (Jan. 1974). According to a view expressed in judicial opinions (P&G-Clorox, for example), the inertia is in part a consequence of small companies' fear of entering and competing in a market where a giant firm, which has vastly superior financial resources, operates.

4. W. G. Shepherd, THE ECONOMICS OF INDUSTRIAL ORGANIZATION 207 (1979).

5. For a more comprehensive listing of industries in which the four leading firms of 1947 changed ranks or had a different composition by 1958, see Bureau of the Census, CONCENTRATION RATIOS IN MANUFACTURING INDUSTRY, 1958, Part II at 469–72 (1962). For the 204 industries listed, the composition of the four leading firms changed in 81 percent. In only 6 percent was there no change in rank order of the leaders or composition. Jules Backman, *Statement,* ECONOMIC CONCENTRATION, Part 2 at 562 (1964).

6. W. F. Mueller and L. G. Hamm, *Trends in Industrial Concentration, 1947 to 1970,* 56 REVIEW OF ECONOMICS AND STATISTICS 513 (Nov. 1974).

7. For a regression taking account of additional factors (industry growth, industry size, advertising, and whether product was a consumer or producer good) influencing changes in concentration from 1947 to 1972, see F. Scherer, *The Causes and Consequences of Rising Industrial Concentration: A Comment,* 22 JOURNAL OF LAW & ECONOMICS 192 (Apr. 1979). Using Scherer's regression produces the same conclusion.

The regression in Table 4-1 relating four-firm market share changes from 1947 to 1972, to 1947 concentration shows that the average industry 40 points above the 1947 average concentration level experienced a nearly eight-point decline in concentration. The average industry 20 points below the 1947 average experienced a six-point rise by 1972. Despite these changes in averages, however, the declines and rises were fairly random. The coefficient of determination showing the effect of 1947 concentration on 1972 concentration amounted to 17 percent. Eighty-three percent of the typical concentration change appears to have been the result of factors other than the initial concentration level in 1947. Forces other than initial concentration levels were important determinants of 1972 concentration levels.

Apparently, highly centralized industries are more frequently above their equilibrium concentration level than below it. The opposite seems to be true of the dispersed industries. But the more rapid growth in industry sales than in output per plant had a deconcentrating effect in many industries, whatever the initial concentration ratio, while increasing regulation and rising wage rates had a concentrating effect. A near balance between these opposing forces produced stability in average concentration in manufacturing industries despite marked growth in the average output per factory and per firm. (Average output per plant grew by 117 percent from 1947 to 1972. This did not raise concentration since total manufactured output grew even more rapidly, increasing 178 percent.) The average concentration ratio, in the industries with unchanged definitions, rose from 39.6 to 41.2 percent between 1947 and 1972. (The standard deviation decreased slightly from 23.5 to 21.5, a manifestation of the centripetal tendency described above.) The simple average of concentration in all 450 industries in 1972 was 39.1

8. Walter Adams, *Comment*, in BUSINESS CONCENTRATION AND PRICE POL-ICY 190 (1955).

9. Warren Nutter, THE EXTENT OF ENTERPRISE MONOPOLY IN THE UNITED STATES: 1899–1939 (1951).

10. Joe Bain, INDUSTRIAL ORGANIZATION 183 (1968).

11. Leonard Weiss, *An Evaluation of Mergers in Six Industries*, REVIEW OF ECONOMICS AND STATISTICS 172 (1965).

12. D. C. Elliott and J. D. Gribbin, *The Abolition of Cartels and Structural Change in the United Kingdom* in A. P. Jacquemin and H. W. de Jong (eds.), WELFARE ASPECTS OF INDUSTRIAL MARKETS 357 (1977).

13. D. E. Waldman, ANTITRUST ACTION AND MARKET STRUCTURE 47 (1978).

14. Yale Brozen, *Concentration and Structural and Market Disequilibria*, 16 ANTITRUST BULLETIN 248 (Summer 1971). Professor Harold Demsetz adds that, "Under the pressure of competitive rivalry, and in the absence of effective barriers to entry, it would seem that concentration of an industry's output in a few firms could only derive from their superiority in producing and marketing products or in the superiority of a structure of [an] industry in which there are only a few firms." *Industry Structure, Market Rivalry, and Public Policy*, 16 JOURNAL OF LAW & ECONOMICS 1 (April 1973).

15. Harold Demsetz, THE TRUST BEHIND ANTITRUST 4 (March 1978). Emphasis in original.

16. Ann R. Horowitz and Ira Horowitz, *Firms in a Declining Market: The Brewing Case,* 13 JOURNAL OF INDUSTRIAL ECONOMICS 129 (Mar. 1965), reprinted in Y. Brozen (ed.), THE COMPETITIVE ECONOMY: SELECTED READINGS (1975), hereinafter cited as THE COMPETITIVE ECONOMY. For a description of the similar trends in other countries, see Anthony Cackerill, *Economies of Scale, Industrial Structure, and Efficiency: The Brewing Industry in Nine Nations,* in Jacquemin and de Jong, *supra* note 12, at 273.

17. U.S., Federal Trade Commission, Bureau of Economics, THE BREWING INDUSTRY (Dec. 1978), demonstrates how the efficiency of large-scale firms and their competitive conduct lifted concentration to its current 63 percent level in the beer industry.

18. Richard Posner, ANTITRUST LAW: AN ECONOMIC PERSPECTIVE (1976).
19. Darius Gaskins, *Dynamic Limit Pricing*, 3 JOURNAL OF ECONOMIC THE-ORY 306 (Sep. 1971).
20. George G. Stigler, CAPITAL AND RATES OF RETURN IN MANUFACTURING INDUSTRIES 32 (1963).
21. Ed Mansfield, *Entry, Gibrat's Law, Innovation, and the Growth of Firms*, 52 AMERICAN ECONOMIC REVIEW 1043 (Dec. 1962). It should be kept in mind that high profitability in all cases used by Mansfield in arriving at this conclusion was the consequence of unexpectedly rapid increases in demand or decreases in cost. However, sketchy evidence from German cartel experience indicates a similar response to increases in profitability resulting from restraints on output. Also, see Table 1-5 and the discussion there.
22. Michael Gort, *Analysis of Stability and Change in Market Shares*, 71 JOURNAL OF POLITICAL ECONOMY 60 (Feb. 1963).
23. K. D. George, *Concentration, Barriers to Entry, and Rates of Return*, 50 REVIEW OF ECONOMICS AND STATISTICS 273 (May 1968).
24. T. G. Sullivan, *A Note on Market Power and Returns to Stockholders*, 59 REVIEW OF ECONOMICS AND STATISTICS 108 (Feb. 1977).
25. E. W. Eckard, *Concentration and Inflation*, (dissertation, UCLA 1978), reports a 0.24 coefficient of correlation between gross book value of fixed assets per production-worker-hour and concentration in 1972. Higher correlations were found for 1958, 1963, and 1967. Professors J. R. Moroney and J. W. Duggar have found that capital-intensity measured per unit of output or per unit of value-added exhibits a positive relationship with firm size. *Size of Firm and Capital-Output Ratios: A Comparative Study in U.S. Manufacturing*, 15 MSU BUSINESS TOPICS 16 (Summer 1967).
26. Betty Bock, Presentation to the Senate Subcommittee on Antitrust and Monopoly, May 3, 1977.
27. Lester Telser, *Some Determinants of the Returns to Manufacturing Industries*, COMPETITION, COLLUSION, AND GAME THEORY 312 (1972).
28. Y. Brozen, *The Effect of Statutory Minimum Wage Increases*, 12 JOURNAL OF LAW & ECONOMICS 111 (Apr. 1969).
29. David E. Kaun, *Minimum Wages, Factor Substitution, and the Marginal Producer*, 79 QUARTERLY JOURNAL OF ECONOMICS 478 (Aug. 1965).
30. D. F. Greer, INDUSTRIAL ORGANIZATION & PUBLIC POLICY 170 (1980).
31. W. F. Mueller, A PRIMER ON MONOPOLY AND COMPETITION 13–14 (1970).
32. Joe Bain, BARRIERS TO NEW COMPETITION (1956); H. M. Mann, *Seller Concentration, Barriers to Entry, and Rates of Return in Thirty Industries, 1950–1960*, 48 REVIEW OF ECONOMICS AND STATISTICS 296 (Aug. 1966).
33. U.S., Federal Trade Commission, INDUSTRY CLASSIFICATION AND CONCENTRATION (March 1967) says it generally classified industries with advertising expenditures of less than 1 percent as undifferentiated and those with substantial expenditures, "often in excess of 10 percent of sales" as highly differentiated. M. Marcus, *Advertising and Changes in Concentration*, 36 SOUTHERN ECONOMIC JOURNAL 117 (Oct. 1969) relied on the FTC classification, but it placed some less than 1 percent of advertising industries in the highly differentiated group and some in the moderately differentiated group.
34. Lester G. Telser, *Some Determinants of the Returns in Manufacturing Industries*, COMPETITION, COLLUSION, AND GAME THEORY (1972).

35. F. M. Scherer, *The Causes and Consequences of Rising Industrial Concentration*, 22 JOURNAL OF LAW & ECONOMICS 192 (Apr. 1979).
36. For example, Professor R. E. Caves, following the Bain tradition, says, "Market structure is important because the structure determines the behavior of firms in the industry, and that behavior in turn determines the quality of the industry's performance." AMERICAN INDUSTRY: STRUCTURE, CONDUCT, PERFORMANCE 17 (1967). Professors A. C. Johnson, Jr., and Peter Helmberger say "by structure we mean the set of environmental elements that influence market conduct and performance." *Price Elasticity of Demand as an Element of Market Structure*, 57 AMERICAN ECONOMIC REVIEW 1218 (Dec. 1967).
37. U.S., Federal Trade Commission, REPORT ON MOTOR VEHICLE INDUSTRY (1940); THE BREWING INDUSTRY (Dec. 1978).
38. Richard Mancke, *Causes of Interfirm Profitability Differences: A New Interpretation of the Evidence*, 88 QUARTERLY JOURNAL OF ECONOMICS 181 (May 1974).
39. We simplify the arithmetic of the discussion by using perpetual returns. A limited-life well's cash flow can be converted to the equivalent perpetuity and this discussion can be thought of as using perpetuities equivalent to the actual cash flows from a well. In terms of the example used here, a ten-year-life well yielding $500 in perpetuity, given a 10 percent cost of capital (yield on alternative investments), would be one, for instance, that yielded a $5,000 return of capital over the ten years (a uniform return of $500 of capital each year for ten years, for example) plus a uniformly declining income yield, declining from $500 the first year to $50 in the last year. The perpetual income stream of $500 is maintained by the investment of the recaptured capital in the alternative uses yielding 10 percent. This growing income stream from the alternative uses maintains a level total income stream of $500 when combined with the declining net income (income after depreciation) from the well.
40. Lester Telser, after examining the relative size of companies in manufacturing and their profitability in various concentration strata, concluded that "the relatively larger firms are more fortunate than their rivals" and that "success cannot be imitated, at least in the near term, by their competitors. This is not the picture we would expect if the concentration ratio is positively associated with a monopoly return." *Concentration Ratios: What Do They Signify?* 8 (unpublished, 1971).
41. This analysis also shows why studies that use a few large firms from each of several industries and relate industry concentration to the profitability of the firms selected will find a positive correlation between concentration and firm profitability even when there is no causal relationship running from concentration to industry profitability. U.S., Federal Trade Commission, THE INFLUENCE OF MARKET STRUCTURE ON THE PROFIT PERFORMANCE OF FOOD MANUFACTURING COMPANIES, Staff Report (1969), provides an example of this fallacy.

The Report also uses incorrect concentration data. The concentration figure used for beer firms in computing 1950 four-firm concentration ratios was based on "the median of concentration ratios for the individual states." In effect, this assumes that Anheuser-Busch in Missouri sold in a market with characteristics identical with Duquesne in Pennsylvania, Ruppert in New York, et cetera. Further, it assumes that brewers such as Anheuser and Pabst did not sell nation-wide although they did. Regional concentration ratios, which averaged less than 60 percent, would have been preferable to the 87 percent used by the FTC. Using regional beer concentration instead of state beer concentration ratios in the FTC regressions cuts the concentration parameter by one third and significance drops from the 5 percent to the 15 percent level.

42. Given the actual accounting practices of crude-oil exploration and production firms, accounts of successful firms would have to be corrected (and capital invested by defunct firms taken into account) to arrive at the true return in crude oil. S. David Anderson, *Review of F. Allvine and J. M. Patterson, Competition Ltd.*, 82 YALE LAW JOURNAL 1355 (May 1973); Shyam Sunder, *Properties of Accounting Numbers under Full Costing and Successful Efforts Costing in the Petroleum Industry*, 51 THE ACCOUNTING REVIEW 1 (Jan. 1976).

43. The number of firms entering cannot be established. There have been 2,900 makes of cars manufactured in the United States. John B. Rae, AMERICAN AUTOMOBILE MANUFACTURERS: THE FIRST FORTY YEARS 5 (1959).

44. U.S. Federal Trade Commission, REPORT ON MOTOR VEHICLE INDUSTRY 624, 634 (1940).

45. See *id.* at 692, 709, 757.

46. See *id.* at 1061.

47. See *id.* at 1063.

48. *Plans for New U.S. Sports Car Company Disclosed by Former GM Aide Delorean*, WALL STREET JOURNAL 40 (Feb. 1, 1977).

49. Yet, the United States Motor Company went into receivership in 1912 because of "the failure of virtually all of its twenty-eight distinct models of automobiles, produced under seven trade names, to meet with popular approval." L. H. Seltzer, FINANCIAL HISTORY OF THE AMERICAN AUTOMOBILE INDUSTRY 38 (1928).

50. John S. McGee, *Economies of Size in Auto Body Manufacture*, 16 JOURNAL OF LAW & ECONOMICS 239 (Oct. 1973).

51. John W. Scoville, BEHAVIOR OF THE AUTOMOBILE INDUSTRY IN DEPRESSION 24 (1935).

52. See Rae *supra* note 43, at 96.

53. G. R. Conrad and I. H. Plotkin, *Risk/Return: U.S. Industry Pattern*, 46 HARVARD BUSINESS REVIEW 96 (March-April 1968) find the auto industry to be the third-riskiest industry out of fifty-nine, using dispersions of book rates of return among firms in each industry as the measure of risk. This measure tends to understate an industry's relative riskiness in those cases where a large proportion of firms has disappeared. It further understates risk because each of the remaining successful firms has attempted a large number of projects. Consequently, the rates of return among the successful firms tend to converge.

54. There is doubt as to whether the automobile market should even be considered a highly concentrated market. See discussion at note 14 in Chapter 2.

5

Assumptions of the Concentration-Collusion Doctrine

THE Federal Trade Commission began an assault on centralized industry structures in 1972 by filing a complaint against the four major concerns in the ready-to-eat (RTE) cereal industry. Together, the four produced 90 percent of industry output. The FTC staff argued that implicit live-and-let-live (mutually recognized interdependence) pricing of RTE cereals was inevitable, was practiced, and amounted to a "shared monopoly." When asked whether it was accusing the cereal producers of explicitly conspiring to set prices, the FTC staff denied making any such accusation. It argued, however, that prices were higher than they would be if the firms were broken up—by 25 percent according to its press briefing. It recognized that high prices normally attract entry and cause declining concentration instead of the rising trend that had prevailed. According to the FTC staff, the four firms prevented entry by their large advertising expenditures, their brand proliferation, and their control of grocery store shelf space. The FTC relied on the concentration-collusion doctrine—on one version of oligopoly theory—to make its case. Using similar arguments, it issued another complaint against the eight leading oil refiners in 1973, accusing them, too, of engaging in a "shared monopoly."

Two Crucial Assumptions:
Cooperation and Entry Barriers

The concentration-collusion doctrine—the belief that high concentration ends competition among leading firms and leads to the establishment of monopoly prices—rests on an unproved assumption. The assumption is that among firms with large market shares, interdependence in pricing (and in other decisions) is recognized and taken into account differently than where there are many firms with small market shares.[1] This mutually recognized interdependence, it is said, produces a result equivalent to explicit collusion and amounts to tacit collusion. And the cartel prices persist in concentrated industries because entry barriers protect the tacitly colluding firms from the competition of would-be entrants.

We have already shown that objective evidence does not support the view that higher entry barriers prevail in concentrated, than in dispersed, industries. More entry occurred in concentrated industries from 1947 to 1972 than in the less concentrated (Table 4-7). At any given level of concentration, the greater the profitability of an industry, the more firms entered (Table 1-5). Also, as we will show later, many firms do not find it profitable to cooperate with others. The circumstances causing this unwillingness to cooperate are more likely to occur in concentrated industries than in others.[2] An examination of attempts at explicit collusion confirms this unwillingness of some firms to cooperate by the fact that *explicit* agreements to not compete have been impossible to arrange in many cases. Either some competitors refuse to meet with those promoting a collusive arrangement or, when they do meet, refuse to agree to terms acceptable to all. Even when cartel agreements are made, collusion is more notable for its failures than its successes. Members of explicit cartels breach their accords more often than they observe them.

Even where governments bar entry and set price floors, competition breaks out by means of illegal entry and by illegal price shading as well as by the route of legal and illegal competition in other dimensions. Railroads, for example, have been fined repeatedly for charging less than the minimum prices set by the ICC. Also, they have been fined for providing services without charge

131

and for extending credit. The CAB has levied fines on airlines for illegally charging less than the minimum fares it set.[3] The City of Chicago maintains a seven-man police detail that devotes its time to catching illegal taxi operators.

Despite this evidence that unarranged and unspoken collusion is extremely unlikely, belief in the equivalence of oligopoly (in the sense of high concentration) and successful explicit collusion still persists. Its persistence is evidenced by the behavior of the anti-trust agencies as well as by the assertions in recent as well as older textbooks used in economics and antitrust courses.[4] Despite strong evidence supporting alternative hypotheses, studies finding a relationship between concentration and profitability continue to assert that the relationship demonstrates restrictive, cooperative behavior by leading firms.[5] It seems then that it is necessary to dissect oligopoly theory and the evidence offered in its support further.

The Contribution of Oligopoly Theory

What is the theory of collusion that underlies the concentration-collusion doctrine? If the truth be told, there is no generally accepted theory. The two brightest gems in the economist's box of treasures are the classical treatments of a market with many sellers and open entry, and of a market with one seller and barred entry. The behavioral and welfare implications in both cases are clear and not easily disputed (provided one doesn't inquire too deeply into the source of a firm's position as sole seller in the case of monopoly). In contrast, the case in which sellers are few has been the subject of interminable disagreement. As Professor George Stigler notes,

> . . . [t]he theory of price formation with oligopoly is, and for more than a century has been, one of the less successful areas of economic analysis, in spite of the fact that almost every major economist has thought about the problem, and a large number have written on it.[6]

If the problem of finding out what happens in the case of several sellers appears difficult, and one has at hand an accepted analysis of the behavior of the single seller, a logical preliminary step would appear to be to focus on the specific instance of only two sellers.

Yet even here hopes of a solution have been in vain. "In spite of the fact that the literature on duopoly and oligopoly goes back over a hundred years," wrote Professor Gregg Lewis thirty years ago, "there is not now a duopoly theory to which economists generally subscribe."[7] Nor does there exist one today.[8]

What is the source of difficulty? The theory of duopoly has focused on two sellers who have exclusive rights to some resource. This, by assumption, does away with entry, which has murdered so many cartels. How much will the two, in the absence of any explicit communications, decide to sell? The crucial juncture in the analysis occurs when we choose the way a seller responds to his rival's actions. The first attempt to answer this question, that of Augustin Cournot, assumed that each seller views the other's output decision as fixed. He then makes his output decision as though he were the monopolist in the market remaining to him. The focus of the analysis then shifts to the other seller, who now regards *his* rival's output as fixed and makes a similar monopoly decision for the portion of the market remaining. By successive steps an equilibrium implying positive profits for both is arrived at. But it is unlikely that two economic agents could be so short-sighted as not to take into account the other's reaction to his own decision. And it is equally unlikely that sellers can be as sure of their own and their competitor's cost conditions and demand as the analysis assumes. A further objection is that the manner in which the number of firms is determined and competitors are kept out is not specified.

Something instructive may still be gained from this exercise. With Cournot's assumptions it is easy to extend the analysis to cover three or more sellers. Each seller establishes the output of rivals, taking this quantity to be fixed. Each then makes his output decision as though the remaining demand is his and his alone. The solution is again determinate. The surprising result is that as the number of sellers increases, the output approaches the competitive solution rather quickly. Using a simple model with four sellers, each with identical costs of prodution (zero for the sake of simplicity in deriving the effect of changes in the number of sellers), for example, output is four fifths of the competitive output while the monopoly output is one half the competitive output.[9] Thus, the addition of the three sellers increases output by 60 percent and drives price down to very near the competitive level despite 100 percent concentration. Notwithstanding the assertion by some economists that high concentration results in the monopoly price being charged, this model, at least, produces the conclusion that even with 100 percent concentration, the price will be very near the competitive charge. We see, then, that even under the austere and unlikely assumptions of the Cournot analysis, any significant deleterious effect of oligopoly is confined to the case when sellers are very few indeed.

Numerous attempts have been made to use more realistic assumptions about sellers' anticipations of each other's behavior. One line of argument is that both sellers in a duopoly know that maximum profits would be obtained if they somehow managed to reach monopoly pricing and output. Since it is in their interests to do so, they will. Suppose that they have in fact arrived at this point. This provides higher profits for both than Cournot's solution. From the point of view of each, however, some slight shading of price would provide him with the lion's share of the monopoly profit. Put differently, the first obstacle two sellers would face if they decide to run a joint monopoly is how to divide the spoils. They might, for example, decide to do their bargaining once and for all and merge. Then the analysis is back to the case of monopoly and the host of questions raised by it. If instead they remain independent, then caving in to the (considerable) temptation of a slight price reduction would result in: a) one seller getting the whole market if the other doesn't follow suit; or b) in the eventual elimination of any supracompetitive profits for both if he does and similar rounds of price cutting follow. In mathematical language, this is an unstable solution. Any slight disturbance leads to its collapse.[10]

There is an additional objection. If two sellers can arrive at this point, why not three, four, or ten? There seems to be no natural stopping point. Yet this explanation is not advanced for pricing in a market with many sellers. Recall also that we assumed firms reached this point somehow. But starting at the competitive point, each firm has an incentive to let others raise their price first. Who will go first, safe in the knowledge that others will follow? And again, the analysis begs the question of potential entrants.[11] As Stigler points out, ". . . it is clear that the degree of competition . . . varies more closely with the number of potential rivals than with the number of actual rivals."[12]

Other, more complex formulations of a similar vein have been proposed to answer the question of what happens in a market with few sellers. But, as Professor John McGee has noted,

... the attractiveness of these complex classical models is quite superficial. On a logical level, they are really subject to the same criticism that has, historically, been lavishly applied to Cournot: Why would sellers retain and act on even the most complex assumption about rival reactions once it is proved incorrect or less profitable than alternatives?

... [Even] if the theories predicted unambiguously, there are other crucial problems to adapting them to real-world policy making. For example, they assume—but do not explain why—there is no entry; and they do not investigate the relationship between costs and the structure of industry.[13]

The Extension of Oligopoly Models to Actual Markets

These objections to the formal models did not, for the most part, lead others to attempt alternative rigorous formulations with implications supported by empirical tests. Rather they led to a flourishing industry that built yet other, more complex or more "realistic" models subject to the same basic objections. Depending on the behavioral assumptions employed, the outcomes vary here too from the monopoly price result asserted by Professor E. H. Chamberlin to a price below the competitive level. Out of this professionally embarrassing wealth of conjecture has emerged no generally accepted prediction of what we might expect in a market with a few major sellers. Regardless of this lack of an accepted theory of behavior and performance in a market with few firms, the antitrust agencies proceed on the premise that a market without an atomistic structure must be monopolized in character. Monopoly performance must be the consequence.

Any industry's firms—whether few or many—can as a group do better by colluding, *absent new entry*. On that, at least, economists agree. But it is not to the interest of some firms to collude even if the group as a whole will benefit. As a result, it is impossible to persuade firms to even send delegates to a meeting under a grant of antitrust immunity in some cases. Those firms that do meet often cannot reach agreement.[14]

If explicit collusion is difficult to arrange and hard to enforce if arranged, tacit collusion must be next to impossible. Nevertheless, tacit collusion is said to occur in highly concentrated industries. According to Professor E. H. Chamberlin, if a seller

... seeks his maximum profit rationally and intelligently, he will realize that when there are only two or a few sellers his own move has a considerable effect upon his competitors, and that this makes it idle to suppose they will accept without retaliation the losses he forces upon them. Since the result of a cut by any one is inevitably to decrease his own profits, no one will cut, and, although the sellers are entirely independent, the equilibrium result is the same as though there were a monopolistic agreement between them.[15]

Chamberlin explicitly assumed that when competitors are few, they will take *retaliatory* action if any one cuts price or improves his product or provides more information. If the retaliatory action is costly, that is, if it decreases profits, it is as irrational and as unlikely as predatory pricing.[16] If all he means is that competitors adjust to whatever demand situation faces them, then the reaction is rational rather than retaliatory and no different than when competitors are numerous.

The fatal deficiency in the Chamberlinian discussion is the lack of reality either in his assumptions or in the predictions yielded by his models. Not only his guesses about seller behavior but also his implicit assumptions about relative cost, capacity, and demand distribution among firms are unfounded. In addition, he incorporates improbable implicit assumptions about the size and behavior of buyers, the nature of the product and the static character of product design, production techniques, and the market in his analysis. Differences in cost make it impossible to preserve a profit maximizing price for an industry even under circumstances where it is illegal to cheat. This is illustrated by National Steel's behavior in the 1930s described in Chapter 3. Professor David Schwartzman, in his investigation of pricing in the pharmaceutical market shows the effect of two of Chamberlin's assumptions. He argues and demonstrates that

> The wide divergence between the prediction of the [oligopoly] model and the actual behavior of drug manufacturers suggests that the model ignores certain forces which promote price competition in drug markets. These forces are very powerful. A firm which cuts its price will do so for a single product and not for its entire range of products, and the sales of the product will represent a small share of its own total sales. The firm need only obtain a price which is barely above the marginal cost of production in order for the product to contribute to overhead costs. Furthermore, the new product with its reduced price will have a small share of the sales of its generic class, and it must compete against the original product which is familiar to doctors. The firm can expand the sales of this product, which is merely an imitation, only by cutting its price. It is the seller of the

original brand which does not want to cut its price. Thus, we see that the interests of different sellers are not symmetrical, contrary to the assumptions of the model of oligopolistic behavior. It is this asymmetry which leads to price competition. The model of oligopoly is plausible only because it explicitly or implicitly assumes that oligopolists in each market have exactly the same interests. Occasionally, discussions of the model recognized that differences in market shares and in costs lead to disagreements among oligopolists and to price competition. The importance of such disagreements is never evaluated, and the popularity of the oligopoly model which predicts restraint on price competition suggests that such disagreements are viewed as rare. But there is no evidence to support this view. In any case, it is clear that in the drug industry the interests of sellers diverge greatly.[17]

Chamberlin's assumptions of market share symmetry among sellers and no entry are demonstrably absent in the drug industry, as Schwartzman shows, and in other industries. Sultan's analysis of the effects of disparity in size and cost in the triopolistic turbine-generator industry shows that such disparities produce a competitive outcome even with explicit collusion. Collusion was ineffective because of these circumstances despite explicit agreements.[18]

The very notion of behavioral interdependence among sellers when they are few has been questioned. Professor William Baumol, for example, says

. . . in day-to-day decision making, oligopolistic interdependence plays only a small role. Of course, plans for the launching of a really major advertising campaign, or for the introduction of a radically new line of products does usually involve some discussion of the probable competitive response. But often, even in fairly crucial decisions, and almost always in routine policy-making, only the most cursory attention is paid to competitive reactions. This apparently dangerous attitude does not usually lead the businessman into serious difficulty because, I believe, his more ordinary decisions are rarely met by prompt, aggressive countermoves of the sort envisaged in many of our models.[19]

Professor Baumol's casual observations are consistent with a general principle that operates over the short term. Professor Dean Worcester's analysis and empirical investigation of market structures led him to conclude ". . . that profit advantage is obtained by firms which concentrate on maintaining or expanding their output rather than maintaining or increasing industry price."[20]

Chamberlinian and other oligopoly theories do not fit semi-dynamic circumstances where the capacity available is insufficient to provide a supply great enough to bring price into equality with long-run cost. They also overlook the secular dynamics of the market and the effect of buyer size. In the steam locomotive industry, a railroad that was a large buyer could fabricate its own locomotives if prices were high or no suitable design were offered. The Norfolk & Western Railroad chose to design and manufacture its own locomotives to suit its traffic and track condition when it was not offered an acceptable model. Ford Motor Company chose, in 1922, to begin manufacture of its own steel. It also entered glass manufacture and now supplies others as well as itself with steel and glass. The Fisher Body Company was another entrant in the concentrated glass industry, in 1920. (In 1931, General Motors sold its National Plate Glass subsidiary and left the glass industry.) Any of the major automobile firms could supply its own tires and sell in the replacement market and to other motor vehicle producers if the concentrated rubber tire industry failed to sell at a competitive price. A firm in a concentrated industry cannot behave as the oligopoly theories predict, then, if it is faced with a large customer.[21] A buyer has a "make or buy" choice in obtaining supplies. A "make" choice is often followed by a "make and sell" policy.

If the firms in a concentrated industry neglect technological opportunities, they will fall before the new entrant who does not. This is the kind of competition that Professor Joseph Schumpeter called "creative destruction." Firms in the concentrated locomotive industry were wedded to steam, although the steam locomotive was forced to stop frequently for water and coal and had to be changed on long runs to replace boiler tubes and reline fire boxes. They refused to believe that anything could replace steam despite General Electric's success in producing electric locomotives, which could handle the high density traffic along a few miles of the east coast and mountain traffic in especially difficult terrain at low enough cost to be competitive. The producers of steam locomotives dismissed the small, slow diesel switchers, which were produced in the 1920s, since they were unsuitable for road work. Westinghouse attempted to enter the locomotive industry with the Scottish Beardsmore diesel, but it proved inadequate to the task. Finally, after heroic efforts by Charles Kettering and his General Motors research and development group in redesigning and adapting the diesel to railroad conditions, the General Motors Corporation succeeded in breaking into the locomotive market with a passenger and later a freight locomotive. These swept the field while steam locomotive manufacturers continued to proclaim in their advertising that steam would always be king.[22]

The concentrated locomotive industry became even more concentrated by an outsider developing better locomotives that saved railroads billions of dollars and kept them alive in the face of the truck competition that threatened to extinguish them. Firms in the concentrated steam locomotive industry could not charge an "oligopoly" price, although there were only three sellers of steam locomotives. The dynamics of the market produced a competitive outcome in this oligopoly market. "Oligopolists" cannot "oligopolize" unless technology is stagnant. The innovator competed for business, not content to price high and rest on a small market share. GM increased its capacity and priced its product low. Sweeping the market was regarded as the more profitable course to follow. This allowed GM to achieve economies of scale and the gains in proficiency that came with increasing experience in producing more units. Once again, performance and conduct determined structure.

How Many Firms Does It Take to Produce the Competitive Price?

The various oligopoly models purporting to determine the prices and outputs that will result under static conditions, assuming various reactions to each firm's policies by other firms, usually have one common characteristic. *They neglect what will happen to entry when prices are high relative to costs,* making the market attractive to firms not currently supplying the product and for expansion by small firms already resident in the industry.[23] This deficiency was shown by Professor Harold Demsetz to be a crucial flaw in the conventional analysis of natural monopoly, that is, a market that can be supplied at less cost by a single firm than by two or more producers. He concluded that even in markets with only one producer, prices will be driven down to cost (including the cost of capital) if prospective sellers are free to *bid* for the business of the customers of the single seller.

> Rival [prospective] sellers can offer to enter into contracts with buyers. In this bidding competition, the rival who offers buyers the most favorable terms will obtain their patronage; there is no . . . necessary reason for *bidding* rivals to share in the *production* of the goods.[24]

This was demonstrated by Mack Truck's success in winning the bid to produce buses for the City of San Francisco in 1961, although it did not then manufacture buses. Lockheed's success in obtaining contracts to supply wide-body L-1011 tri-jets before it even designed the plane provides another demonstration. Douglas, which was embarking on the production of DC-10s, had to cut its price by $1,000,000 on the contracts it had already signed because of Lockheed's *bidding* competition. Lockheed could not even offer to deliver planes until a year later than Douglas, yet its bidding competition immediately influenced the market.

Professor Robert Bork provides instances in which the presence of a single rival resulted in a competitive price. United Shoe had a patent-protected monopoly in the manufacture of certain shoe machines and only a single small competitor in other machines. On those machines protected by a patent, rental arrangements allowed United to earn as much as 44 percent on its investment in the machines. On machines where it had one competitor, it earned 10 percent (assuming no maintenance cost). When Roche, in England, was compelled to license another firm to produce diazepam, the price fell from £2,000 per kilogram to £1,200, hardly the monopoly price expected by Chamberlin in duopoly or oligopoly markets. Bork points to a number of other instances where a change from a monopoly to a one or two competitor situation contradicted the Chamberlinian analysis.[25] And this is no surprise to Professors Eugene Fama and Arthur Laffer who, after performing a general theoretical analysis, concluded that "a general equilibrium with two or more noncolluding firms per industry is perfectly competitive."[26]

In answer to this analysis, the believers in the concentration-collusion doctrine reply that perhaps tacit collusion will not occur when an industry is concentrated, but then express collusion will. It will because it is cheap to arrange and police collusive agreements among a few firms. The prices that occur in concentrated industries, then, it is asserted, will be the same as those that would prevail if those industries were monopolies.[27] But if express conspiracy occurs, present laws are adequate, and there is no need to outlaw concentration to make this actionable.

140

Evidence of Competitive Behavior and the Interpretation of the Concentration-Collusion Doctrine

The very fact that *overt* collusion occurs in concentrated as well as unconcentrated industries demonstrates the unwarranted nature of the standard oligopoly theory conclusion that mutually recognized interdependence in concentrated industries will produce tacit collusion. If tacit collusion were automatic or possible, this would obviate any need for express conspiracy, and we would never see the instances that occur. The grip of oligopoly theory on some theorists has become so strong that they express puzzlement and grope for ad hoc reasons for such "strange" behavior when confronted with events that contradict their faith in the universality of tacit collusion in concentrated industries. Professor James W. McKie, for example, is nonplused by the fact that

> The highly-concentrated oligopolies include some which are much more dominated by rivalry than . . . less concentrated and less protected against entry industries. . . . Electrical generating equipment is an illustrative case. It is a highly concentrated industry. In turbines, at the time of the electrical equipment conspiracies of the 1950s, there were only three significant producers (since reduced to two) and in heavy-duty switchgear and transformers only four or five. There were high barriers to entry. One would have expected a tight oligopolistic discipline—effective tacit collusion with results approximating maximum joint profits. If the pattern were to take the form of price leadership, General Electric (GE), the largest seller, overall, would be the logical leader. Instead, there have been alternating periods of overt collusion and price warfare; tacit coordination never took hold of the markets.[28]

Other observers, when confronted by evidence of competition in concentrated industries, do not argue that periods of competition are interspaced between periods of collusion. Professor Weiss, an old proponent of the thesis that interdependence in pricing will produce a monopoly result when industries are concentrated, has backed away from the stand that a concentration measure is an index of collusion and instead views it as an index to the ease of collusion. Collusion is the problem, not concentration.[29]

Even easy collusion no longer suffices in Professor Weiss' eyes to produce a noncompetitive result. In addition, there must be barriers to entry. And even these do not automatically result in

CONCENTRATION, MERGERS, AND PUBLIC POLICY

high prices. Instead they raise "the optimal price cost margin," and that rise is "from the point of view of the leading firm or firms." This statement in his latest paper is not only much less assertive about the prices that materialize in concentrated industries than earlier statements; it also speaks of a "point of view" on prices rather than speaking of market prices, and that point of view is that of "leading firms." No assertions are made about the ability to control prices, except at a later point in his paper where he contends that dominant firms "with half or more of the market and *no close* rivals" (emphasis supplied) may have that ability. Also, it is "price cost margin" that is increased, not necessarily prices. Price cost margins may be increased by lowering costs as well as by raising prices. This begins to verge on a retraction of the concentration-collusion doctrine.

As Weiss moves on in his paper from dominant firms to oligopoly theory, his faith in tacit collusion as an economic fact of life seems to falter. In discussing the Cournot analysis of the oligopoly problem (in which a price above the competitive level is derived), Weiss characterizes its "nice neat numerical solution" as its "main appeal." He goes on to observe that

> Its assumptions about the oligopolists' expectations with respect to their rivals' behavior seem just short of inconceivable. Only if by chance all the oligopolists happened to set outputs at the equilibrium level would their expectations be realized. And *while this might be just barely conceivable in a wholly static model, it becomes impossible in a real world where outputs and prices change often.*[30]

Conclusion

Antitrust policy to a large degree has rested on the concentration-collusion doctrine. This doctrine is derived, however, from a body of theoretical literature that has never gained the wholehearted acceptance of economic theorists, nor even a fraction of the empirical confirmation one usually expects for a theory in general. Classical oligopoly theory, which forms the basis of the concentration-collusion doctrine, presents us with nothing more than some interesting speculation. Its speculative character is made quite apparent by the wide range of outcomes it implies, and by the large element of conjecture involved when the theory takes up the issue of how individuals' reactions are formed. Oddly enough, the inadequacies of the theory have not kept several eminent economists from asserting that the suppliers in a market will act *as if* they were a single monopolist, paying little attention to the question of entry and the question of how many sellers it takes before this conclusion is no longer valid. The question of entry in particular is much more subtle than adherents to this school are ready to admit.

Numerous instances can be presented in which competitors spring up to take business from existing firms, that is, *present* industry concentration is no guide to the amount of competition. The concentrated structures we do see are often the result of just such competition, particularly in those cases where a new technology was introduced. The new producers in turn must face the competition of others who could sweep their markets with similar new technologies, as well as by smaller firms similar to the less efficient ones they replaced.

While a number of proponents of the concentration-collusion doctrine have modified their view of the economic significance of concentration, this doctrine has a strong enough hold on segments of the economics profession and the antitrust apparatus to make it imperative that its validity be questioned in all quarters. A complete review of the evidence will, we think, lead to its abandonment altogether.

Notes

1. G. C. Archibald criticizes this assumption and argues that the number of firms is irrelevant. "The argument is simply that, if the individual firm is assumed to believe that the price or output of its rival(s) remains constant, its behavior is independent of whether its rival is supposed to be one firm or many." *"Large" and "Small" Numbers in the Theory of the Firm,* 27 THE MANCHESTER SCHOOL OF ECONOMICS AND SOCIAL STUDIES 104 (Jan. 1959); reprinted in Y. Brozen, THE COMPETITIVE ECONOMY 48.
2. See, for example, Ralph Sultan, PRICING IN THE ELECTRICAL OLIGOPOLY (1974).
3. Dale K. Osborne, *Cartel Problems: Reply,* 68 AMERICAN ECONOMIC REVIEW 947 (Dec. 1978).
4. See, for example, D. F. Greer, INDUSTRIAL ORGANIZATION & PUBLIC POLICY (1980); J. V. Koch, INDUSTRIAL ORGANIZATION AND PRICES (1980); W. G. Shepherd, THE ECONOMICS OF INDUSTRIAL ORGANIZATION (1979). The belief is also evident in a recent OECD report, CONCENTRATION AND COMPETITION POLICY (1979). The report confesses its own inadequacies when it states in its foreword, at 7, that "The report does

not purport to be a complete survey of recent work on concentration by Member countries. It is based primarily upon research undertaken by Government agencies, and there is only limited reference to academic research in this field."

5. John E. Kwoka, Jr., *Market Shares, Concentration, and Competition in Manufacturing Industries,* FTC Working Paper no. 7 (1978).

6. G. J. Stigler, THE THEORY OF PRICE 216 (1966). Joan Robinson and Edward Chamberlin are among those who devoted considerable attention to the question of how markets with few sellers work. Commenting on her book, THE ECONOMICS OF IMPERFECT COMPETITION, Robinson admits "[t]he reason oligopoly is neglected there . . . is not that I thought it unimportant, but that I could not solve it." J. Robinson, *Imperfect Competition Revisited,* 63 ECONOMIC JOURNAL 584 (Sept. 1953). Chamberlin says as much with his comment that "oligopoly has no single solution"; E. H. Chamberlin, *On the Origin of "Oligopoly,"* 57 ECONOMIC JOURNAL ·218 (June 1957). Echoing Stigler, William Baumol writes: "Perhaps the single most remarkable failure of modern value theory is its inability to explain the pricing, output, and other related decisions of the large, 'not quite monopolistic' firms"; W. Baumol, BUSINESS BEHAVIOR, VALUE, AND GROWTH 13 (1967). However, see Lester Telser, COMPETITION, COLLUSION, AND GAME THEORY (1962) for a discussion of conditions under which it pays to compete and those under which it pays to collude.

7. H. G. Lewis, *Some Observations on Duopoly Theory,* 38 AMERICAN ECONOMIC REVIEW 1 (May 1948).

8. Besides Cournot, the list of economists and mathematicians who have attempted to solve the duopoly problem includes Edgeworth, Bertrand, Pareto, von Stackelberg, Chamberlin, von Neumann, Morgenstern, Sweezy, and Nash. For representative discussions of duopoly, see C. E. Ferguson, MICROECONOMIC THEORY (1972); W. J. Baumol, BUSINESS BEHAVIOR, VALUE AND GROWTH (1967); L. W. Weiss, *The Concentration-Profits Relationship and Antitrust,* in H. J. Goldschmid, H. M. Mann, and J. F. Weston, INDUSTRIAL CONCENTRATION: THE NEW LEARNING (1974); J. S. McGee, IN DEFENSE OF INDUSTRIAL CONCENTRATION (1971); W. Fellner, COMPETITION AMONG THE FEW (1949); or F. Machlup, THE ECONOMICS OF SELLERS COMPETITION (1952). Lester Telser has made the most successful attempt to date at a systematic analysis of the parameters influencing the determination of whether duopolists (and oligopolists) will collude or compete, and whether collusion, if attempted, will succeed.

9. See J. S. McGee, IN DEFENSE OF INDUSTRIAL CONCENTRATION 56 (1971). He draws this analysis from E. H. Chamberlin, THE THEORY OF MONOPOLISTIC COMPETITION 32–34 (1948).

10. Stigler provides a more fundamental methodological criticism of this approach:

> A satisfactory theory of oligopoly cannot begin with assumptions concerning the way in which each firm views its interdependence with its rivals. If we adhere to the traditional theory of profit-maximizing enterprises, the behavior is no longer something to be assumed but rather something to be deduced.

G. J. Stigler, *A Theory of Oligopoly,* 72 JOURNAL OF POLITICAL ECONOMY 44 (Feb. 1964), reprinted in Stigler's THE ORGANIZATION OF INDUSTRY

39–40 (1968). As is shown later in this chapter, even in instances of explicit and enforced collusion firms do not reach the monopoly pricing and output point.

11. Attempts have been made to remove some of the indeterminacy and instability of oligopoly theory. One strand of thought, more of interest for the light it throws on analytic methods than for the purposes at hand, is what has come to be called the theory of spatial competition. The dispersion of consumers across space and the existence of transport costs in these models tend to weaken the knife-edge results of duopoly theory. Dispersion over space has also been taken as a metaphor for product differentiation and the effects it might have on oligopoly behavior. See H. Hotelling, *Stability in Competition*, 39 THE ECONOMIC JOURNAL 41 (Mar. 1929); and A. Smithies, *Optimum Location in Spatial Competition*, 49 THE JOURNAL OF POLITICAL ECONOMY 423 (Jun. 1940).

12. G. J. Stigler, *The Measurement of Concentration*, in Stigler, THE ORGANIZATION OF INDUSTRY 29 (1968).

13. See McGee *supra* note 9, at 60–61. For a Cournot analysis enlarged to include entry, see F. M. Fisher, *New Developments on the Oligopoly Front: Cournot and the Bain-Sylos Analysis*, 67 JOURNAL OF POLITICAL ECONOMY 410 (Aug. 1959); and D. E. Farrar and C. F. Phillips, Jr., *New Developments on the Oligopoly Front: A Comment*, 67 JOURNAL OF POLITICAL ECONOMY 414 (Aug. 1959).

14. An example of this was the failure of U.S. airlines to reach agreement on schedules in negotiations held in the early 1970s. See the discussion of this episode in Chapter 6 at note 47.

15. E. H. Chamberlin, THE THEORY OF MONOPOLISTIC COMPETITON 48 (1933).

16. See discussion at note 2, Chapter 13.

17. David Schwartzman, INNOVATION IN THE PHARMACEUTICAL INDUSTRY 252–53 (1977).

18. Ralph G. M. Sultan, PRICING IN THE ELECTRICAL OLIGOPOLY (1974).

19. See Baumol *supra* note 6, at 29.

20. Dean Worcester, MONOPOLY, BIG BUSINESS, AND WELFARE IN THE POSTWAR UNITED STATES 63 (1967).

21. Steven Lustgarten, *The Impact of Buyer Concentration in Manufacturing Industries*, 57 REVIEW OF ECONOMICS AND STATISTICS 125 (May 1975).

22. General Motors Corporation, *The Locomotive Industry and General Motors* in Y. Brozen, THE COMPETITIVE ECONOMY 270. Dale K. Osborne points out that an implicit assumption in one variant of oligopoly analysis —that a limit price will be set above the competitive price—is that, "Technology must not be rapidly changing." *The Role of Entry in Oligopoly Theory*, 72 JOURNAL OF POLITICAL ECONOMY 399 (Aug. 1964).

23. Professors George Stigler and Joe Bain are important exceptions (and of course, Professor Dean Worcester, *supra* note 20, whose investigations focused on the effect of entry, under various types of pricing and output behavior, on industry structure). Stigler pointed out that ". . . when attention is turned to the conditions of entry of new firms and expansion of existing firms in an industry, oligopoly behavior loses much of its arbitrariness and oligopoly price much of its indeterminacy." *Discussion of Papers on "Capitalism and Monopolistic Competition: I. The Theory of Oligopoly,"* 40 AMERICAN ECONOMIC REVIEW 63 (May 1950), reprinted in Y. Brozen, THE COMPETITIVE ECONOMY 21. Bain argued a limit price doctrine where barriers to entry (purportedly cost advantage

of resident firms, scale economies, and product differentiation, usually interpreted as advertising) determined the extent to which the limit prices exceeded competitive prices. He did *not* adopt Chamberlin's conclusion that the monopoly price would prevail when competitors were few. H. F. Lydall, *Conditions of New Entry and the Theory of Price*, N.S. 7 OXFORD ECONOMIC PAPERS 300 (Oct. 1955); and P. Sylos-Labine, OLIGOPOLY AND TECHNICAL PROGRESS (1962) are also credited with considering the effects of potential entry on oligopoly price and contributing to the limit price hypothesis. But as Osborne points out (note 22 *supra*), the limit price notion is more a theory of determinants of concentration than of price. Also, see the discussion at note 19 in Chapter 1.

24. H. Demsetz, *Why Regulate Utilities?* 11 JOURNAL OF LAW & ECONOMICS 56 (Apr. 1968). Reprinted in THE COMPETITIVE ECONOMY 15. For case examples of Demsetz' point, see Gregg Jarrell, *The Demand for State Regulation of the Electric Utility Industry*, 21 JOURNAL OF LAW & ECONOMICS 269 (Oct. 1978).

25. Robert H. Bork, THE ANTITRUST PARADOX 182 (1978). Neither of these examples should compel us to conclude that patent or licensure protection to the original single producer was inequitable or inefficient, only that two firms do not behave as one. From the standpoint of social welfare, a patent monopoly may be quite desirable for its effect on innovation.

26. Eugene F. Fama and Arthur B. Laffer, *The Number of Firms and Competition*, 62 AMERICAN ECONOMIC REVIEW 679 (Sept. 1972), reprinted in COMPETITIVE ECONOMY 43. Also, see John P. Gould, *Inventories and Stochastic Demand: Equilibrium Models of the Firm and Industry*, 51 JOURNAL OF BUSINESS 1 (Jan. 1978), which develops a formal model in which competitive price and output occurs when there is one firm in an industry.

27. "When a small number of firms control most or all of the output of an industry they can individually and collectively profit more by cooperation than by competition. . . . These few companies, therefore, will usually cooperate." George Stigler, *The Case Against Big Business* 45, FORTUNE 123 (May 1952). Stigler later retracted this statement. See discussion following note 21, Chapter 15.

28. J. W. McKie, *Market Structure and Function: Performance versus Behavior* in J. W. Markham and G. F. Papanek (eds.), INDUSTRIAL ORGANIZATION AND ECONOMIC DEVELOPMENT 12 (1970).

29. Wesley J. Liebeler, *Market Power and Competitive Superiority in Concentrated Industries*, 25 UCLA LAW REVIEW, n. 9 at 1235 (Aug. 1978). U.S., Federal Trade Commission, Office of Policy Planning and Evaluation, *1976 Budget Overview*, ATRR, no. 692 at E-4 (Dec. 10, 1974).

30. L. Weiss, *The Structure-Conduct-Performance Paradigm and Antitrust* 3 (unpublished, University of Pennsylvania antitrust conference, 1978). Emphasis supplied.

6

The Likelihood of Tacit Commercial Conspiracy

CONCERN about concentration's effect on pricing and rates of return (allocative efficiency) is, in the end, a concern about the degree to which sellers effectively collude. The charge that a concentrated market structure inflicts damage on society loses much of its sting unless a plausible theory of commercial conspiracy can be advanced and supported by fact. This is especially true since the collusion alleged to take place among firms is said often to be a result of unspoken agreements (mutually recognized and acted-upon interdependence), or communication conducted in such a fashion as to leave little hope of its ever being detected.

In situations where no evidence of agreement exists, the question of whether collusion is occurring must be answered by resorting to an economic analysis. This analysis must go beyond establishing correlations between variables. As has been pointed out repeatedly—but, it seems, to little avail in the eyes of some antitrust fans—a correlation between profits and concentration supports the view that leading firms in concentrated industries are more efficient or innovative, as well as the view that they collude. In other words, the analysis must present a coherent economic theory of unspoken commercial conspiracy and provide some empirical test or set of tests that jointly support the theory. The concentration-profits correlation no more supports a collusion

147

hypothesis than it does efficiency, high risk, or disequilibrium hypotheses.

One way to begin an investigation of tacit collusion is to look at instances of express collusion. Cartels, price-fixing rings, and other arrangements designed to restrict output and raise prices have been examined in detail for a variety of circumstances. Express agreements to collude usually leave traces in the form of memoranda, minutes of meetings, and price lists. Particularly in instances where such agreements are not illegal, as in some European countries and in certain protected industries in the United States, sufficient evidence exists to establish how such agreements are carried out.

There is considerable evidence establishing the fragility and the usually short-lived character of collusive agreements. Cheating and entry are the two biggest problems facing any cartel.[1] Restriction of output creates an economic inefficiency. The fact that we observe cheating and new entrants lends additional support to an already powerful economic insight: inefficiencies tend to be removed when it is to someone's benefit to do so. While the agreement to collude can frequently be established, the effectiveness of collusion is usually in doubt. Professors G. W. Stocking and M. W. Watkins, after studying the records of a large number of cartels, many of which were established and supported by governments that used their powers to prevent competition or disobedience to cartel orders, concluded that:

> Cartels differ greatly in form, effectiveness, and duration. Many control experiments have been short-lived. Others, though lasting longer, have exerted little influence on prices. Some have represented more the expression of hope than the achievement of a goal. Beside structural weaknesses three factors tend continually to limit the influence of cartels: (1) internal defection, (2) outside competition, and (3) technological displacement.[2]

Does tacit collusion exist? Again and again, proponents of the market-concentration doctrine assert that it does and that it is prevalent. In making the argument that competitors reach an unvoiced agreement to restrain their behavior, they note the obvious, namely, that all the firms in a market can be made better off by charging a higher-than-competitive price and splitting the gains. This is true enough, but it does not occur automatically. In view of (1) the difficulty of even getting the members of an industry to a meeting to negotiate an agreement, (2) the difficulty of arranging explicit agreements, and (3) the further difficulty of enforcing them, how plausible is it to assert that competitors will hold back when the appropriate restrictive behavior expected of each firm is left for it to decide? The problem of cheating must pose an even greater obstacle than in express collusion.

Successful tacit collusion should leave roughly some of the same traces we see from time to time in instances of explicit collusion, and yet no such evidence has been presented. If tacit collusion exists, one would expect to find strong evidence of it in (1) divergences of prices from what an analysis of the underlying market conditions implies, or (2) absolutely stable market shares, or (3) universal refusals to deal with customers of other firms or outside of specific geographic areas, each unique to a specific firm, or (4) greater declines of output from leading firms than from minor firms in times of falling demand, or (5) persistent price discrimination with stable patterns of price differences unaccounted for by cost differences.

The accusation that prices in concentrated industries have diverged from those indicated by underlying market conditions has been made frequently, but substantiation has been rare (see, however, the American Tobacco case discussed below). Stable market shares not explained by economic factors have been found only in cases of patent licensing. Yet, even here, shares frequently have not been stable despite explicit requirements in licenses. Refusals to deal with competitors' customers have been required in some explicit collusion agreements, but these agreements have been more often breached than honored. It is highly unlikely that tacit collusion would work in such instances when explicit agreements fail so frequently. Assignment of geographic areas is a common feature in explicit international conspiracies. In the absence of patent or governmental protection, however, buyers have sought out low-cost sources and prevented the agreements from being effective. Major firms in concentrated industries maintain output nearer to their capacity than minor firms in times of falling demand (see, for example, the discussion below of the rayon industry) because of their greater capital intensity and lower marginal cost, a conclusion substantiated by the greater variability of price-cost margins in concentrated than in less centralized industries. And price discrimination outside the industries regulated by governments has been sporadic—which is what we would expect in competitive markets—not persistent.

There are three levels of argument in support of the theory of

tacit collusion in concentrated industries. First, even what we regard as tacit collusion is really explicit collusion. It's just carried
out in such a clever and subtle way, with interlocking directorates
and chit-chat at gentlemen's clubs, that it cannot be detected nor
prevented under existing antitrust laws. With mutually recognized interdependence in pricing, the executives of large firms
signal each other what prices to charge by speaking before public
gatherings about the need to increase prices and by circulating
price lists. Second, big business is fat and lazy, and it would do
everybody a world of good if it were transformed into scrambling
atomistic competitors. And third, there is something disquieting
and ominous about x firms "controlling" y percent of the market
for widgets. It leaves some people feeling helpless, and it is not
democratic. It is not atomistic competition and, therefore, it must
be (shared) monopoly. The paucity of this reasoning and the evidence in support of tacit collusion has not, however, noticeably
dampened the frequency with which deconcentration measures
are proposed.

The plan of this chapter is first to examine the economic factors
that effect the likelihood of commercial conspiracies, then to provide examples of explicit collusion in the hope of gaining some
notion of its effectiveness, then to turn to what evidence there is
of tacit collusion, and finally to examine the view that economic
conspiracies can be unspoken along with the part this view plays
in contemporary thinking on policy.

The Economics of Explicit Collusion

Two issues need to be taken up in an analysis of explicit collusion among sellers. The first is: under what circumstances are
such agreements made? The evidence is that they occur sporadically and in markets with as many as twenty sellers. They are
likely to occur when demand for the product in question is slack
and firms are earning unusually low returns. Also, it appears to be
necessary for certain technical factors to be present, such as product uniformity and a simple price, credit, and distribution structure, which reduce the likelihood of cheating (that is, make it more
easily detected). Also, the demand for the product of the colluding
group must be fairly inelastic and costs must be fairly uniform. (If
there is a firm with significantly lower costs, it has reason to refuse

to agree to the higher price that will serve the interests of other firms, as in the case of National Steel described in Chapter 3.)

Second, how well are collusive agreements observed? The evidence is that firms entering into collusive agreements are as ready to defraud each other as they are to defraud their customers. In fact, the suspicion that this will be the case often keeps firms from entering into agreements in the first place. The history of cartels and similar arrangements is a history of double-crossing. If internal friction and rivalries don't lead to a cartel's dissolution, then it is typically brought about by the downward pressure on price that new entrants exert with their additions to capacity and supply of the product.

It will simplify matters if we focus our attention on the most common type of collusive agreement, price fixing.[3] Through one means or another, firms agree to sell their output at some price higher than the competitive level. With several hundred years of recorded commercial history and the insights of economic analysis to draw on, the conditions that influence both the chance that an agreement will be reached and the chance that agreements will be kept can be summarized as follows.

Number of Firms

A small number of firms in an industry is the most frequently mentioned condition facilitating collusion, but, as will be shown, it is only one of several conditions, and never enough by itself. If only a few firms are in a market, it is easier to come to an agreement about the manner in which they are to collude and how any eventual group profits are to be split. In addition, it is easier to detect cheaters. If all but one of the firms that are party to an agreement to raise prices notice that their share of the market is eroding while one firm's share is increasing, they are likely to suspect price cutting. Random changes in patronage would be unlikely to go only in one direction. With fewer firms, the decrease in market shares of faithful members will be greater, assuming all the firms are approximately the same size.[4]

Despite the prominence given to this factor, no systematic relationship between the number of firms and the occurrence of collusion has been found. In their investigation of antitrust cases in which guilty or *nolo contendere* pleas were submitted, Professors

Asch and Seneca find "no significant association . . . between the number of firms in the industry and collusion."[5]

Elasticity of Demand

The greater the increase in price that a small reduction in output causes, the greater the gains to colluders. In other words, if there are no close substitutes for the good whose price is being raised, the gains to the group are likely to be larger. Conversely, elastic demand for a good (that is, a large response in sales follows a change in price) means that there are likely to be only small gains from raising its price above the competitive level.

The elasticity or responsiveness of demand also affects the likelihood with which price-cutting will be detected. If the demand for a product is inelastic, a price-cutter's new business will come largely from other firms. If elastic, the new business may in large part be that which is attracted to the industry by the lower prices offered. In the latter case, existing firms need not notice any decrease in their sales if the price-cutting firm has found a way of locating those who would buy only at a slightly lower price.

In addition, the cost of capacity adjustments is lower if demand is inelastic. Since quantity varies relatively little as prices are raised, only a small fraction of capacity will be left idle. If capacity is retired, the costs are again small if demand is inelastic. Note, however, that the process is symmetric. It is also easier for firms to expand to the competitive output should the agreement break down. And to the degree that inelastic demand favors the formation of a cartel, it also contributes to its dissolution since the resulting higher gains attract other firms into the field.

Level of Industry Profits

The less existing firms are earning, the less the danger of firms entering as prices rise above their competitive level. Not surprisingly, attempts at cartelization are most common during business recessions and during periods of falling prices. In American history, cartels were common in the recession of the 1890s and in earlier recessions. Cartelization was more prevalent around the world during the Great Depression of the 1930s.

An attempt at cartelization, apparently motivated by a recession, was described by Professor Arthur Dewing in the following way:

During the period in which the yarn business was growing in New Bedford and the surrounding towns, no effort was made to establish a trade agreement or other form of price-regulating association. But following the general trade depression of 1894, when the yarn mills were suffering from over-production, drastic price-cutting became so prevalent that a number of the mills were selling yarn for less than the gross cost. To prevent the sale of yarn at unremunerative prices, an Association was formed which comprised a large proportion of the yarn mills of the country. This Association did not have great success it achieving the purpose the managers had in view, although its members tried to enforce a "gentlemen's agreement" regarding prices.[6]

A second possible reason for the appearance of cartels during business downturns is that slack demand is often expected to be temporary. The alternative to a cartel agreement is pricing at short-run marginal cost and the possibility that one or another firm will go under. The cost in ordinary circumstances of cheating and being discovered is that the industry returns to its competitive situation, with firms more or less in the precollusion positions. In depressed circumstances, the strong likelihood emerges that one firm, perhaps the cheater's, will not survive a breakdown of the agreement. As an empirical matter, however, cheating is frequent during the darkest days of a business slump, as exemplified in this description of the history of the Cotton Duck Manufacturers Association.

As early as 1884, a "gentlemen's agreement" had existed among the duck manufacturers to restrict their output. At first this agreement was very loose, and accomplished little in the way of a control of the market. Gradually the "understanding" among the mill owners became more precise, and by the early nineties, it had reached the form of a definite pooling agreement. At first, there was a Cotton Manufacturers Association, and later a Cotton Duck Manufacturers Association. These pooling agreements were very informal in character. Each mill was assigned its output, and expected to keep within the limit. Those manufacturers who exceeded their assigned production paid into "the pool" a certain number of cents per pound of over-production; those that fell below were paid by "the pool" proportionately. As in the majority of such agreements, there was always friction caused by alleged dishonest methods of conduct. Frequently, the extreme anxiety of salesmen to make sales led to practices which broke the spirit, if not the letter, of the pooling agreements. At one time, it was proposed to introduce a system of fines for bad faith, but the plan was never adopted. Competition in the middle nineties was so severe that the agreements were of little value in maintaining the stability of the market.[7]

Asch and Seneca found a "consistently negative and significant relationship between firm profitability and the presence of collusion."[8] They dismiss the notion that collusion leads to lower profits and focus instead on an alternative explanation. Poor profits motivate collusion, and, one might add, even collusion that might some day be detected. Interpreted this way, their results also provide confirmation of the view that new entrants provide a strong check on collusive behavior. The relatively less frequent collusion among firms in industries making average or above average profits is a straightforward implication of a model of competitive behavior that relies in part on new entry to maintain competitive prices and competitive returns to owners of inputs.

Product Homogeneity

If a good is easily defined and consumers are indifferent between a unit from producer X or one from producer Y, then firms will find it difficult to cheat by offering better quality for the same price. The goods most suited for collusive agreements are items such as refined minerals, standard chemical compounds, and agricultural goods. It is difficult to define and enforce collusion at the manufacturing level in the case of products such as automobiles, household appliances, and clothing. Even if a manufacturer of one of these items kept to an agreed-upon price, he would have an incentive to offer more product in the form of extra features or greater durability in order to lure buyers from other firms. Since extra refinements are costly, the returns for all firms will be driven to the competitive level as all parties to an agreement adopt this tactic.

In fact, one sees the same tendency at work even in markets where the good is quite homogeneous. Reciprocal purchases and extra services, for example, can be used to lower the actual price below the cartel price for a good that is indistinguishable across firms.[9] In the case of railroad transportation services, the Interstate Commerce Commission (ICC) had to lay down rules on credit terms to prevent railroads from shading rates by allowing longer payment periods. Numerous other restrictions on the provision of services, such as loading and unloading, use of boxcars to store goods, and care for perishable items during transport have been imposed by the ICC to prevent the use of these indirect means for shading rates. The Civil Aeronautics Board from time to time imposed restrictions on airlines on spacing and width of seats, meal service, and lounge space to prevent indirect price shading.

Fixed Costs

The greater the amount of industry-specific capital required, the less likely other firms are to enter the industry if the collusive behavior is not expected to last indefinitely or if collapse is expected as a consequence of new entry. Note, however, that an early collapse is a necessary part of the sequence of events that keeps potential entrants out. In a modern economy at least, it is an easy matter to raise large sums for investment in a project, if investors familiar with the field expect the project to be profitable. The power of the interest rate is considerable. The prospect of large returns for as short a period as three to five years can attract considerable capital into an area.

Yet another consideration serves to dampen the influence of fixed costs in deterring entry. While some industries do perform most efficiently with a large stock of fixed capital, at the cartel price production can be remunerative for temporary entrants on a more makeshift basis.

The ease with which capital can be moved into or out of industry-specific uses plays another role in cartel formation and dissolution. The same factor that makes it easy to restrict output—alternative uses of capacity—typically makes it easy for others to enter. Conversely, the existence of large fixed costs will make firms reluctant to cut back operations. Moreover, if they don't retire capacity, they will be eager to put it back to work on slight provocation. The existence of fixed costs also usually implies that any given firm has an optimum output, and significant restrictions of output will raise the average cost to the firm.[10] Fritz Voight found, in his examination of the behavior of German cartels, that the larger the proportion of fixed costs, the more quickly a cartel broke down.[11]

Transportation Costs

The less it costs to transport an item, the less likely is an effective conspiracy. If transport costs are small enough, an effective conspiracy to raise prices would have to be worldwide. Even with substantial transportation costs, the limit on the price of any effective local conspiracy is the nearest noncollusive price plus the cost of transporting the items. Note also that, while a producer who is protected from competition elsewhere by transportation costs and who is successful in barring new entrants locally can raise prices to consumers nearby, he can do so only at the expense of losing those farther out who were previously indifferent between his product and that of someone else. More importantly, in most industries where collusive practices have been thought to be widespread, such as steel and lumber, certain sites are favored over others by their natural advantages. With clustering of producers at a few sites, the problem of collusion is more difficult than if producers are more widely dispersed and each has only a few regional competitors.

Pace of Technological Change

Collusive agreements are costly to make and costly to enforce. These costs are greater in the industries whose technology and product design undergo large or frequent changes. With lowered production costs, the appropriate collusive price is changed (usually lowered), but if firms differ in the rates with which they adopt such technology, disagreement will arise about the right price. Firms differ in their rate of innovation because of such factors as firm size and local conditions. One is unlikely, consequently, to find collusive arrangements for such items as calculators or stereo components.

It should be emphasized that large firms are usually those most likely to benefit from new technologies and to introduce them sooner. The benefit to them is directly related to their scale of operation. If, as is often supposed, these large firms are the leaders in a collusive arrangement, they would be raising their own costs in order to perpetuate an agreement that would benefit all firms in the industry.

Support for this line of analysis comes from Professor Edwin Mansfield's study of the relationship of technological innovation and firm size. He finds that "other things equal, the length of time a firm waits before using a new technique tends to be inversely related to its size."[12] He attributes this to three factors: 1) larger firms can handle risk more easily; 2) a given technique has wider applicability in a large firm; and 3) a larger firm has more equipment being replaced in any given time period. On the basis of his empirical findings, Mansfield predicts that

> ... if one firm is four times as large as another (the profitability of the investment in the innovation being the same for both), the chance that it will introduce an innovation more rapidly than its smaller competition seems to be about .80.[13]

A large firm, in order to take advantage of the benefits that large size confers, such as superior risk-taking ability and greater machine turnover, and to balance off the losses it incurs as a result of span-of-control problems, must innovate. By holding back, in a field where technological innovation is taking place, large firms would be damaging themselves more than would the typical firm in that industry.

Variations in Production Costs

If output has to be reduced considerably, variations among firms in the cost of production will give rise to relative profitabilities different from those they experienced in the competitive situation. This increases the scope for conflict among firms in negotiating and in carrying out the agreement.

Availability of Price Information

The easier it is for firms to collect information about how much buyers pay, the less the gain to the firm that breaks ranks (since the cartel dissolves when its members learn they are being underbid). Hence there is less likelihood of such behavior. The best possible situation occurs when sealed bids are taken and publicly announced, because the price-cutter is exposed immediately and unambiguously.

Number and Size of Buyers

If there are buyers of the product who purchase large quantities, any attempt to maintain prices above the long-run competitive level will cause these buyers to examine the alternative of making the product. Large buyers generally are well informed about the costs of producing the product and are potential entrants. Once they are induced to enter by collusively set prices, they may become sellers as well as supplying themselves.

Potential Competition and Entry Barriers

In our enumeration of the conditions governing the formation of price-fixing conspiracies, the only deterrent to entry cited was fixed costs (and they tended to deter entry only if the cartel's collapse was likely to occur soon). Yet entry barriers are a crucial ingredient in the formation and successful conduct of a cartel. What constitutes a barrier to entry? Strictly speaking, it would be anything that makes cost greater for new entrants than for existing firms.[14] (Barriers to entry should not be confused with low returns, which make entry unattractive.) Most barriers to entry, in fact, are not economic but institutional. License requirements, government regulations, and similar devices are often used to keep out other firms. Barriers created by government are not, however, what is usually meant by the term. Rather, the barriers are "natural" or spontaneously generated features of economic life.

From a tactical standpoint it is clear why barriers to entry have been proposed. Acceptance of the argument that fixed capital costs alone prevent entry makes it difficult to sustain the conclusion that economic conspiracies are widespread and effective. First, one would be relying on the proposition that capital markets do not function well, that some pervasive and chronic malfunction of the financial markets keeps capital from going to areas where high returns can be expected. Second, one would be relying on the view that production is an inflexible, capital-intensive activity. In fact, the possibilities for alternative, less capital-intensive production at a slightly higher price are often considerable. Third, and probably most important, the argument that fixed capital costs are a barrier is useless if, in addition, one would like to make the point that collusive behavior occurs over a wide range of industries, not all of which use much industry-specific capital.

As Professor Harold Demsetz has shown, the analysis of the question of barriers to entry turns out to provide an answer to the original question of how many competitors it takes to make a market competitive.[15] If *potential* sellers are free to negotiate sales with buyers, then a market with only one seller will do. Let the existing single seller charge a higher than competitive price. If buyers can freely offer their business to someone else, then he will lose their trade. Demsetz' analysis is principally directed to the argument that an industry with declining costs must necessarily consist of one seller and that the seller will charge the monopoly price. As we see here, declining costs can imply one efficient seller charging the competitive price. The importance of this for our purposes is exactly that a single-seller market does not imply monopoly pricing, and that *the conditions that allow a firm to charge a higher than competitive price must be sought in something other than market structure.* Barriers to entry are an essential ingredient of any argument supporting the view that monopoly and collusion are widespread.

What can protect a seller or group of sellers from potential competitors? Under the general rubric of "barriers to entry," the following hypotheses have been offered.

Advertising

The essence of the argument that advertising constitutes a barrier to entry is that a new firm finds it difficult to gain customers because advertising ties them to existing firms. A new entrant, it is argued, faces the "prohibitively" expensive task of advertising to offset the prior advertising of existing firms. This view is naive and, in some of its renditions, moralistic. Presumably, firms advertise because it is in their interest to do so. But advertising is expensive to existing firms as well as to potential entrants. It must be productive in some way to be justified. It is not a net social loss; if it were, other firms could provide the same service without advertising and charge less. If a new firm finds it necessary to advertise, it is because whatever advertising does, customers want done. It is certainly cheaper to pick up a newspaper to look for bargains than to visit a half-dozen stores. If the ads prove unreliable, they won't be believed and will be a waste of the firm's funds.[16] The error that creeps into much thinking about advertising—and that lies at the root of the conception of advertising as a barrier to entry —is to think of advertising as warfare: both sides bloody each other's noses just to stay even and thereby incur a private cost and cause a social loss.

The advertising-as-barrier-to-entry argument, if one wants to analyze it seriously, rests on the same foundation as explanations of collusive pricing. Working on the assumption that advertising is unnecessary, firms must agree to throw these barriers up, incurring costs in so doing. But once brand name recognition is established, the gains to any one firm, which succeeds in reducing its advertising expenditures, are matched almost dollar for dollar by the amount of the reduction. In effect, each firm is motivated to cheat on the tacit agreement to advertise heavily to shut out new entrants. *The fact that explicit cartel agreements do not specify that each firm must spend at least some given amount on advertising casts suspicion on the view that advertising is a method of barring entry,* despite the FTC's assertions in its cereal industry complaint that advertising was tacitly used in this way.

The most fruitful way of looking at advertising is as a capital stock. Producers spend money to build a stock of product recognition and product information. It is productive because consumers' time and effort are scarce resources. As Professor Wesley Liebeler has noted,

> . . . [I]n economic terms . . . it is hard to distinguish the capital asset of a favorably recognized name from the plant in which the product is produced or from any other capital asset held by an existing firm. Obviously it will take time for a new entrant to build up a reputation, just as it will take time and money to build a plant. But the real question is whether it will take longer or cost more than it took or cost the existing firm to reach the position it now enjoys.[17]

Product Differentiation

A variant of the idea that advertising presents an obstacle to new firms is the notion that product differentiation and brand proliferation are undertaken among the existing firms to cover all possible forms of the product and so foreclose any lucrative position to new firms.[18] The similarity is that both rest on the contention that it is possible to affect consumer behavior (and welfare) through the introduction of spurious product qualities. A particularly "insidious" subspecies of product differentiation is the yearly automobile model change. Again, this presumably is something that consumers don't really want, but which is foisted on them by tacit collusion in order to keep potential producers of the sensible cars consumers really need out of the market.[19] Evidence from the American auto industry, however, runs contrary to this hypothesis. A model is not replaced until its sales begin to fade. Styling changes occur annually in order to keep a model attractive and to introduce mechanical improvements, but these changes are no more frequent than those in some of our least concentrated industries, such as the apparel industry, which cannot be accused of oligopolistic tacit collusion.

There is now a well-established branch of economic thinking that presents a contrary view.[20] Product differentiation, when it occurs, is the response of firms to what consumers with varying incomes and with varying capacities to benefit from products of a given quality demand. Someone with a large lawn will tend to buy a sturdier and more expensive model lawn mower and the man eager to impress his friends will buy the latest style car each year (and pay for his weakness). The notion that product differentiation and advertising represent an impediment to new firms rests on the belief that people don't know what's good for them, that they can't be convinced to find out, and that it costs more for a new firm to fool them. This notion also neglects the fact that the new firm can design a product variant of its own as a means of entry— as a way of attracting customers whose preferences are not satisfied by existing products.

A further point is that product differentiation works at cross-purposes to the aims of a commercial conspiracy. Suppose each of five manufacturers of refrigerators conspires to fix the price of his 15-cubic-foot model. Suppose, in addition, that these refrigerators vary with regard to the amount of effort devoted to aesthetic features, convenience items such as defrosting mechanisms, and energy efficiency. Since these features are costly to produce, the makers of the more costly models will argue, justifiably, that the price they fix should reflect the higher costs they incur. Suppose some agreement is reached on the relative prices reflecting these costs. Even so, each maker will have an incentive to add yet other features, which amounts to price-cutting. Similar effects can be achieved by offering better service and longer warranties.

The role of model changes is minimized by even as perennial an advocate of the entry-barriers school of thought as John Blair. He did contend that "obviously the greater the cost of model changes, the stronger is the position of the leader and the greater the competitive disadvantage of the lesser oligopolists."[21] Without attempting a reconciliation, he also contends that "model changes have ᵤcen a formidable barrier to entry."[22] (General Motors is so crafty that it has apparently hit upon a technique of keeping new entrants out and getting its rivals to agree to a system imposing costs on them, all without doing much harm to itself.) The analogy to warfare, with the industry giant incurring large retooling and research and development expenses in order to keep lesser competitors at bay and new entrants out, is again evident. But industry is not warfare and Pyrrhic victories win no laurels. Blair asks us to sympathize with the vice-president of Ford who testified before the Hearings on Administered Prices about the lengths to which GM's yearly policy changes were pushing him: "in our experience we find when the model is not changed substantially, the customers do not buy it."[23]

But that model changes "have had anything like a comparable effect in other industries is far less sure," admits Blair.[24] He goes on to note that "efforts by refrigerator manufacturers to shorten the time span between style changes had run up against an impenetrable wall of consumer resistance."[25] But what, apart from consumer whimsy, makes model changes work in one case and not the other?

Economies of Scale

Suppose demand for a particular good is not large enough to sustain more than one or two producers operating at minimum average cost. In such a case, it is said, economies of scale prevent more entrants and give firms resident in the industry market power, both short-run and long-run. As pointed out earlier, the first flaw in this argument is that while economies of scale may determine how many firms there are in an industry—perhaps only one or two—these economies do not imply anything about *which firms* will do the producing if *potential* suppliers compete.[26]

The economies-of-scale argument is overworked. True enough, in some markets, two or three efficient producers alone can supply world demand. The diesel locomotive and the jet engine industries appear to be such cases.[27] But can economies of scale reasonably be invoked in the case of automobile manufacture, for example, as leading to monopoly? First, producers of varying sizes exist side-by-side in the United States as well as in the (more relevant) world market. Second, one has seen entry in the American market, both in the form of new firms selling from foreign plants and new producers in the United States (Volkswagen). Equally important, there have been expansions of capacity of existing producers.

162

The fact that we do see firms of varying sizes in the same industry indicates that scale economies are really something different from what we normally conceive them to be. Small firms are selling their products in the same market as large firms. Why, if economies of scale are so prevalent and such a technologically straightforward matter, don't we see the merger of the small firms or competition among them until the survivors are as large as the "efficient" firms? The fact that this doesn't happen and that we do often see large and small firms in any particular industry indicates that other factors in addition to particular technologies and products govern firm size. The distributions of firm size may be governed by something of a more general nature, such as the distribution of managerial ability (as well as a demand for a variety of products).[28] The best managers manage the largest firms. Their salaries reflect the rent for their talent, that is, the difference between the cost of the item they produce and the price that the firm managed by the least talented manager may charge and still break even. Where scale economies arise from these considerations, it is clear that those economies do not represent a barrier to entry.[29]

The suspicion with which arguments relying on the assumption of barriers should be viewed is reinforced by the evidence from a related issue in industrial organization. Another instance of alleged anticompetitive and economically inefficient behavior is predatory pricing. Predatory pricing rests on this same barriers-to-entry argument—what would be the use of driving out competitors if others appear to take their place? Yet, as Professors Areeda and Turner, two advocates of strong antitrust policies, admit, "proven cases of predatory pricing have been extremely rare."[30] If only the weakest form of the entry barrier argument is assumed, namely, imperfections in the capital market, then we should observe occasional (and *not* "extremely rare") instances of predatory behavior. If capital markets function well, victim firms would find it easy to find investors who would help them finance their fixed costs while the would-be predators incurred losses selling large quantities below cost. If, however, a breakdown of the capital market occurs that allows some efficient, but poorly financed, firms to go out of business, a similar malfunctioning in the market financing new entrants would be necessary for the whole scheme to work. As it happens, this is the same breakdown that the barriers-to-entry argument requires when predatory pricing is not an issue. Yet, as mentioned, such price warfare is rare.

In commenting on "the absence of a well worked out theory supporting the link between industry structure and monopoly power,"[31] Harold Demsetz has provided the following criticism of the role and origin of barriers to entry:

> It was decided—largely by intuition, not analysis—that the use of advertising and capital, as well as the existence of economies of scale, created what Bain called barriers to the entry of resources from outside the industry. No clear rationale was given as to why the use of particular kinds of inputs should create such barriers when these same inputs are available to firms inside and outside the industry.[32]

One piece of evidence on the empirical importance of barriers to entry comes from Professor Kenneth Elzinga's study of the gunpowder trust (discussed in Chapter 4), which existed at the beginning of this century. In fact, firms entered during the period the trust was active and left during the period following its dissolution.[33] This evidence is, of course, consistent with the view that firms can and do respond in a fairly flexible fashion to differentials in the rates of return among various activities.[34]

A full discussion of barriers to entry brings us back again to the question of whether we expect price-fixing to be successful even if new entrants are kept out. The most persuasive evidence on this issue comes from the various regulated industries, where clearly defined and legally enforced barriers to entry exist. Not only are these barriers to entry prescribed by the government, but what would ordinarily be called price conspiracy is enforced by the same regulatory agencies that keep new entrants out. Do we expect these firms to earn unusually high rates of return? The evidence is that they do not where there is more than one firm in the market. One of the more pampered industries until recently, domestic commercial aviation, chronically suffered low rates of return. The railroad industry rate of return has not exceeded 4 percent in any year since World War II despite price *floors* set and enforced by the ICC, together with price floors set by the ICC for the major competitor of railroads, common-carrier motor trucking. Banking, similarly protected from "cutthroat competition" by interest rate ceilings and regulated entry, has not shown itself to be a particularly lucrative investment. These restrictions do generate inefficiencies. But they show that even a combination of restricted entry and enforced minimum prices, the essential ingredients in collusion, do not yield the extortion typically claimed.[35]

American Price-Fixing Conspiracies

A classic price-fixing conspiracy may be found in the Trenton Potteries case, in which the respondents, twenty individuals and twenty-three corporations, were convicted of violating the Sherman Anti-Trust Act.[36] Together, the defendants supplied over 80 percent of the U.S. market for vitreous plumbing fixtures in 1922. The firms had joined in the Sanitary Potters' Association, which assembled, at the instruction of its "price list committee," what were intended to be the list of prices that members should charge for particular fixtures. That there was such an agreement is not in doubt, nor was it substantially denied by the defendants. The Supreme Court, giving very strong reinforcement in this decision to the per se illegality doctrine, found the defendants guilty for the *attempt* to fix prices.

While the defendants did agree to fix prices in this way, the agreement, it turns out, was "more honor'd in the breach."[37] Extensive evidence was presented that buyers did not pay attention to the price bulletins and that transaction prices tended to be considerably below list prices.

> [A]n analysis of the actual sales invoices of 21 of 23 defendants between June 1, 1918, and July 31, 1922, showed that 26 percent of the tanks sold by the defendants sold at bulletin prices, while 64 percent sold below bulletin and 10 percent above bulletin. Of the bathroom bowls invoiced, only 28 percent sold at bulletin prices, while 68 percent sold below bulletin and 4 percent above bulletin.[38]

The testimony of fifteen buyers of the association's output corroborated the evidence from the invoices. One sample:

> Question: "Did you find differences in prices for the same goods?"
> Answer: "Yes, naturally. When the agent came around I got the price from him. The salesman would come to me and I would get the price of him. . . . I have about five or six before I gave an order. . . . I did not make use of the bulletins except to put them in the waste basket because I went around shopping and bought just as I found the market ripe to buy."[39]

Such evidence was immaterial from the Court's point of view. The economic point, however, is that the low bidder got the order and that the prices offered by low bidders were not those fixed by

165

the cartel. Not to cheat on the bulletin price was simply to invite someone else to do so.

Another example of a price-fixing agreement with no substantial effect on prices is given by the attempt of rayon producers to support prices during the early 1930s. Rayon would seem to be an ideal product for such a conspiracy since market concentration was high and the nature of the product is such that differentiation is confined to standard denier and filament-count specifications. In 1930, the four largest firms had 73 percent of capacity, and in 1935 this figure was still 71 percent.[40] Moreover, *list* prices conformed to the price leadership caricature in which a large firm initiates a change and others follow. As the account of Professor Jesse Markham shows, however, the list price was almost never the one that was actually charged.[41]

Prices were falling in the industry during the period 1930–39, causing firms to get together in a rayon association with the aim of placing lower bounds on prices. Although the ten members of the association undertook the expense of hiring an accounting firm to make monthly checks of their stocks, sales, and prices charged, price-cutting was so severe that even the largest firms were selling rayon at 30 percent below list prices.[42] In addition to outright discounts from list price, firms resorted to misbranding, in particular, to selling current production as discounted, "obsolete" material. The failure of large firms to maintain prices is indicated by the fact that with their 71 percent of capacity in 1935, they produced 74 percent of the rayon sold in that year. Two of the smallest firms shut down by 1933 and five by 1935, an occurrence opposite to what would occur if a cartel or a dominant price leader were successfully maintaining prices.

One of the most well-known price-fixing rings of recent years involved several makers of electrical equipment. The charges were that various producers of standard electrical equipment held regular meetings during the period 1956–59 to fix the prices of these items. Again, so much is acknowledged in the testimony of company officials themselves.[43] Yet the evidence fails to support the contention that the agreements were lived up to. This seems largely due to the absence of any enforcement mechanism (not that the firms would willingly have submitted themselves to one even if they thought it would have raised the chances of success). On the subject of medium voltage switchgear, for example, the industry witness at the Senate hearings investigating the electrical equipment conspiracy reported that the agreements weren't observed. "Basically, the thing wasn't working. In other words, everybody would come to the meeting, the figures would be settled, and they were only as good as the distance to the closest telephone before they were broken."[44]

Similar testimony was offered by General Electric's manager of the transformer division:

> My experience in meeting with competitors, as I have said before, indicated to me that it was a rather fruitless endeavor. It might be one day, it might be two days, after a meeting, before jobs would be bid all over the place, and there seemed to be no real continuity that came out of those meetings in the way of stabilizing prices at my level.[45]

The electrical equipment agreements also demonstrate the effectiveness of marginal producers in undermining agreements. In this case potential entrants were the so-called tin-knockers, producers of inferior goods, and foreign competitors, neither of which groups would abide by agreements, even if, as in the case of the tin-knockers, they participated in making them.

These twentieth-century attempts at price fixing suffered difficulties and failures that were simply a replay of the experience of various nineteenth-century attempts. Typical of the earlier experience is the following description of the numerous attempts of cordage manufacturers to mitigate competition among themselves.

> The first trade agreement among cordage manufacturers was consumated February 23, 1861. The object was "to establish certain customs in the trade," correct abuses and misbranding, and to come to an understanding regarding prices. Weekly meetings were held in all eastern cities where the cordage manufacturers had secured a foothold. In July, 1874, the old agreements were entirely rewritten, and the "manufacturers pledged themselves, as men of honor and integrity, to the true and faithful observance of the rules." This proved ineffectual to prevent underselling, and the agreement was strengthened in 1875. Since this, too, proved of little avail as competition became stronger the manufacturers concluded to adopt a pooling system. The first pool was established January 1, 1878. A committee in conference with the manufacturers agreed that certain percentages of the total production of the country should be assigned to each manufacturer. "The percentages ranged from eleven and one-fourth percent to one percent." When the business of a concern for a given month exceeded the assigned percentage, that concern paid into the

pool 2 cents a pound on the excess. The manufacturers whose production fell below their assigned percentages drew out from the pool
2 cents per pound on the difference. "In 1880, the amount of the pool
was reduced from 2 cents to 1 cent per pound, and in June of that
year to ½ cent; but in January, 1881, the pool was abolished." Associations, conducted along the same lines, were formed in 1882 and in
1885. The last was to exist until February, 1888, but was broken up
about a year previous . . . on account of price cutting and false returns. Indeed, the reason for the failure of all these pools seems to
have been that always some men would undersell their competitors,
or make false returns to the organization. There seems no doubt that
competition was particularly severe during this period and the manufacturers regarded the agreements as means of mitigating its severity.
Yet the ease with which they were broken up shows clearly that their
influence was nominal.[46]

The difficulty of obtaining agreement among firms was illustrated recently in the airline industry. That industry was heavily
regulated, with interstate fares considerably higher than would
prevail in the absence of regulation. This has been demonstrated,
for example, by comparing charges for unregulated flights between points in the same state with flights of equal distance between points located in different states. The consequence of
mandated minimum fares was that when two or more airlines
served the same route, competition was conducted by offering
more frequent service. As a result, planes flew half empty. Within
the framework of a regulated industry it was possible, however, to
undertake coordinated cutbacks that would ordinarily result in
antitrust action. In 1971, the Civil Aeronautics Board granted permission to carriers to discuss service reductions in twenty-one
markets. Professor George Eads' vivid description of that case illustrates the problems faced by a price-fixing ring.

It is clear that if the [airline] carriers in a market can agree, either
tacitly or overtly, to exercise restraint in scheduling, load factors can
be raised and profits improved. . . . Experience with cartels leads us
to believe that it would be extremely difficult to negotiate and even
more difficult to enforce such voluntary agreements. Recent experience bears this out. . . . [I]n late 1970 TWA suggested that carriers be
allowed to meet and negotiate schedule cutbacks on certain city-pairs.
Formal requests for permission were filed early in the Spring of 1971.
The Board issued the necessary approval . . . and . . . twenty-one
"over-served" markets were identified. However, in eight of the
twenty-one markets, at least one carrier objected to even a discussion

of limitations. Therefore, the Board approved discussions for only thirteen markets. . . . Agreements could be reached on a formula for capacity reduction on only four of these routes.[47]

The failure to collude occurred despite the fact that restriction on only one dimension of competition—schedule frequency—was sought and competitors in each market were few. If such explicit collusion among a small number of competitors protected by CAB entry barriers cannot be arranged in the majority of these twenty-one instances, it must be exceedingly rare with multidimensional competition—the kind of competition that prevails in the vast majority of industries. The four markets for which it was possible to reach an agreement were transcontinental routes served by only the big three (American, TWA, and United). In the cases where no discussions were held or in which discussions broke down, the primary reason for failure seems to have been the fear on the part of at least one of the airlines that it would not be able to expand its share of the market.

Experience from Abroad

It is of interest to examine what happens to price-fixing arrangements among sovereign states or among producers located in countries that do not have blanket prohibitions of price-fixing. Typically, agreements among states are not subject to any law. International law, if it has any effectiveness, does not concern itself with price-fixing. Agreements among producers located in different countries are also not policed as closely as agreements among domestic producers. In fact, producers often receive the encouragement of their governments, who view such arrangements as a way of transferring resources from abroad or helping with balances of payments problems.

International Agreements

During the 1930s, the leading wheat exporting countries attempted, under the auspices of the League of Nations, to raise the world price of wheat by regulating their exports. The failure of this endeavor has been chronicled by Professor Alfred Plummer.[48]

Under the Wheat Agreement of 1933, the leading export coun-

169

tries, Argentina, Canada, Australia, and the United States, obtained the cooperation of wheat-importing countries. The latter promised to lower their tariffs once prices reached certain levels. The exporting countries promised each other to restrict exports by 15 percent for the 1934–35 season. One large exporter, Russia, was reluctant to be saddled with export limitations and excluded itself from any specific promise. The wisdom of such a policy is, of course, that it is better to be the one nonmember in a collusive industry. But the arrangement proved to be troublesome for other, more basic, reasons.

> One of the leading export countries, Argentina, having harvested an unusually large crop, broke the Agreement by exceeding her export quota, and the International Wheat Advisory Committee, meeting in London in May, 1935, found themselves still faced with a large, though reduced, world wheat surplus, and with the task of squeezing from the quota of Canada, Australia, and the United States sufficient to satisfy the insistent demands of Argentina for a larger export quota. At the same time the United States Secretary for Agriculture dangled a sword of Damocles by stating that in the event of a complete breakdown of the Wheat Agreement the vast stocks of wheat held by the United States would be thrown upon the world market. . . . It is not surprising that the Committee were forced to admit that "the operative clauses of the Agreement had in practice ceased to be fully applied," and could only suggest the continuance of the Committee until 31st July, 1936, and the preservation of the framework of the old agreement so that representatives of the twenty-one States might still be able to explore the possibilities of designing effective methods of international collaboration "to solve the wheat crisis" in the near future.[49]

What was accomplished at further meetings? It was agreed that more meetings should be undertaken so that: 1) "periodical reviews of the world wheat situation" could be prepared; 2) investigations of "further possibilities of encouraging the use of wheat" might be made; and 3) "a survey covering the fundamental economic and social factors affecting wheat production, consumption, and exports" could be undertaken.[50] These are hardly the essential ingredients of a successful price-fixing ring.

Plummer chronicles a similar failure to prop up the international price of sugar. Attempts to do so were initiated by Cuba, the world's leading exporter, in 1926. Cuba restricted its exports, and

> . . . a small rise in the world price of sugar took place in 1927, possibly as a result of Cuba's action, but it soon became evident that without

corresponding restriction of output on the part of other exporting countries, the effort would fail, as increased production in other countries would fill the gap left by Cuban restriction.[51]

Representatives of Cuba, Czechoslovakia, Germany, and Poland met and agreed on a method for restricting production. All countries agreed to limit their production by specific amounts for the 1928–29 season.

The effects of this agreement, however, to a large extent, negatived by the fact that Java persistently refused to cooperate . . . Cuba renounced her restricted measures for the 1928–29 crop, while the three European countries considerably extended their sowings.[52]

A large 1929 crop and the resulting low prices alarmed even Java and in 1930 all the major producers met in Brussels. This meeting resulted in the International Sugar Agreement of May 1931.

This was an agreement between the producers' association in each country and not between their Governments, but the latter were in full sympathy and undertook to pass any legislation necessary to make the agreement effective.[53]

The fatal flaw in this agreement was that several major producers, notably producers in the British Empire, the United States, Russia, France, Italy, and Japan, were not included. At most, 40 percent of world output was controlled by the cartel. Not surprisingly, when the conspiring countries managed to reduce their production by about 5 million tons per year, nonmember countries as a group increased their production by almost the same amount. "It is now quite clear," wrote Plummer in 1938, "that the Plan completely failed to raise prices and that it only partially succeeded in reducing stocks."[54]

International cartels have been formed in dozens of instances for agricultural products and natural resources. Agreements have been attempted for natural rubber, quebracho, platinum, tin, rubber, coffee, tea, and phosphate rock, among other items. Professor Paul MacAvoy has surveyed the research on these cartels, finding fifty-three cartel agreements in eighteen industries.

Of the 53 significant cartel organizations only 19 achieved price controls which raised the level of charges to consumers significantly above what they would have been in the absence of the agreements.

171

The efficient cartels did not seem to last very long. Although formal organizational agreements (to set up cartel management, for example) lasted longer in the efficient cartels, the average length of effective controls on price was not more than two to three years. . . . The more important products, such as rubber in the 1930s or aluminum, copper or sulfur before World War II, experienced cartel longevity from one to four years.[55]

Nearly forty years earlier, at the peak of international cartel activity, Charles T. Hallinan presented a similar, although more rhetorically embellished summary.

The international cartel, though nominally guided by a mere handful of men, often is actually as racked with discussion as though, like the early English "unions," it had some sixty men on its Board. Alarmist views to the contrary notwithstanding, the international cartel has proved thus far to be a rather fragile affair. If trade reports are to be trusted, some of the most conspicuous of them are frequently on the point of angry dissolution. Individual and national jealousies over quotas provoke disputes requiring patient negotiations to smooth out. Glue manufacturers composing "Epidoes," the international glue combine, took more than a year to settle their differences and to reach a detailed agreement (secret), which is known to fill many pages of foolscap. The European heavy rail cartel has broken up repeatedly and has re-formed, and is reported on the point of breaking again. The quinine "trust," with headquarters in Amsterdam, has had a checkered career quite as much afoot as horseback.[56]

European Cartels

Price-fixing conspiracies have been more common in European countries in large part because such arrangements enjoy a more favorable legal climate. One country that allowed cartels in the 1950s, as long as their prices were judged reasonable, was Denmark. Bjarke Fog undertook a study of cartel agreements there. He found that larger firms favored lower prices than smaller firms during negotiations.[57] Although he attributes this to the "more circumspect long-run policy of the larger firms," our analysis suggests that small firms stood to gain more from a high price enforced by the large firms. Their costs were higher and their cheating was less likely to be discovered, which would provoke a breakup of the cartel. In fact, Fog notes that "[a]s a general rule, the large and well-known firms hesitated to circumvent an agreement—or at least maintained that this was so—while the smaller

172

firms did not have so many scruples about this, chiefly because they have a better chance of doing it secretly."[58]

Another source of difficulty among firms noted by Fog was how the spoils were to be divided.

> The cartel negotiations I have been informed about have been characterized by reciprocal suspicion and distrust, not only as to what would be the optimum level for the others, but also regarding their motives and sincerity. Each participant seemed to concentrate on gaining advantages at the cost of the others, and to be unwilling to give any concession without due reward, and only paying slight attention to anything like maximizing joint profits. . . . In the two cases, where the negotiations were unsuccessful, it was fairly clear to a neutral observer that a cartel would have been to the benefit of all within the industry.[59]

Fog concludes from his study that for most cartels, the cartel price is merely the "full cost price," and that it is difficult to raise cartel prices substantially above the competitive level.

In a similar examination of German cartels, Fritz Voight found that most of them did not last long. Besides cheating, the cartels were faced with new entrants. "The duration of cartels, with few exceptions, was strikingly short," he writes. A major reason for this, aside from failure to abide by agreements, was that

> . . . [i]f a cartel succeeded in raising prices for its members . . . new firms entered the industry. . . . the greater the pressure of fixed costs, the more rapidly the cartel collapsed. . . .[60]

The Economics of Tacit Collusion

The focus of attention in the early writings of economists on collusion and in the original antitrust laws themselves was explicit agreements among competitors to restrict trade. That competitors might treat each other with caution in the absence of some explicit arrangement must have seemed unlikely to turn-of-the-century observers, given the charges, during a period of falling prices, of cutthroat competition and predatory pricing. During the 1930s, the notion of tacit collusion began to gain ground, however. In its subsequent elaborations, it came to be accepted by a substantial portion of the economics profession, as well as many makers and critics of policy.

The appearance of Professor Edward H. Chamberlin's *The Theory of Monopolistic Competition* marks the beginning of the period during which the idea of tacit collusion was taken seriously and considered to be a pervasive aspect of contemporary economic life. A closer look at his ideas and their subsequent elaboration and acceptance is in order.

Chamberlin believed he had turned a good deal of economic theory on its head.

> The book deals, not with a special and narrow problem but with the whole of value theory. Its thesis is that both monopolistic and competitive forces combine in the determination of most prices, and therefore that a hybrid theory affords a more illuminating approach to the study of the price system than does a theory of perfect competition, supplemented by a theory of monopoly.[61]

In particular, Chamberlin stressed the role of product differentiation. It was a concatenation of this and small numbers that caused prices to be higher than a world of pure competition would permit.

> The general conclusion must be that the considerations relevant to competition between small numbers are much more generally applicable than might at first be supposed. Certainly, over a wide range of economic activity, the price not only must, on account of a differentiated product be higher than the purely competitive level by at least, an amount corresponding to what has been called "a sort of ideal"; it *may* rest at any higher point up to a figure which would maximize the joint profits of those whose markets are related.[62]

This idea was further developed by Professor Fritz Machlup in *The Economics of Sellers' Competition* and Professor William Fellner in *Competition Among the Few*. Fellner's basic contention is that in a market with few firms "there is a tendency toward the maximization of the joint profits of the group."[63] His model was based on classical oligopoly theories. By ignoring the difficulties these theories pose and by relying on made-to-order jargon such as "spontaneous coordination" and "conjectural interdependence" (the latter pressed into service from the classical oligopoly literature), Fellner elaborated his point, similar to Chamberlin's, that the prices we actually encounter will be higher than those in a purely competitive model. Not surprisingly, Fellner predicts the possibility of any price, depending on which of several "limitations" on joint maximization are in effect. New entry is mentioned only in passing.

Of particular interest for our purposes here is the claim made by Fellner that there is little analytical distinction between tacit and express collusion.

> [T]here is no fundamental difference between these instances of conjectural interdependence which lead to explicit bargaining and those which do not. In the one case, explicit negotiations are carried on, and, in the course of these, the parties concerned attempt to find out by direct observation what the most favorable agreement is which they can reach with the others. In the other case, each party tries to find out what the ultimate consequences of its own pattern of behavior are; and each party tries to discover which of the alternative patterns of behavior results in mutual reactions that are in the nature of a tacit agreement (or convention), and are more favorable from his point of view than any other tacit agreement acceptable to the others.[64]

This is a remarkable assertion. Recall our examples of collusion, which were characterized by formal agreements on price and means of policing and enforcement that required the cooperation of participating members. Recall also the frequency with which such agreements were in the main arrived at by producers of relatively homogeneous goods. Now Fellner's assertion rests on the unstated belief that explicit collusive agreements are more successful and more stable than the ones we have record of, and second, the belief that tacit agreements are just as successful and stable as he thinks explicit ones to be and are arrived at without any of the costly, time-consuming meetings, negotiations, and conspicuous apparatus of formal price-fixing.

Putative empirical support of such a view was not long in coming. Beginning in the 1930s, various researchers claimed to have found evidence supporting the notion that firms in concentrated industries "administer" prices. Concentration, which led to tacit understandings, was claimed to cause higher profits and inflation.

Support for the hypothesis of tacit collusion would have to come to us indirectly, that is, through economic evidence such as the behavior of prices, market shares, and profits. But, as we will see in Chapter 7, the evidence advanced was based on faulty statistics, list instead of transactions prices, accounting profits (which did not correspond to economic profits), and restricted samples (which contained serious biases).

Furthermore, certain statistical regularities, which were advanced as support for the tacit collusion hypothesis, are consistent with either collusion (tacit or express) or competition. That two steel firms charge the same price is by no means evidence of collusive behavior as long as buyers decide in favor of the item with the lower price. Nor is it conclusive evidence that the two change their prices at the same time. It is the nature of economic life that prices must be changed, and if the price of iron ore, let's say, increases, a competitive market will raise the price of steel. Suppose two firms are in the industry and one raises its prices. If the other doesn't follow, all business goes to the firm pricing lower. But with higher iron ore prices, the firm pricing lower will incur a loss. If both firms see it in their interest not to operate at a loss and not to incur costs in changing the size of production runs that resulting equilibrium prices cannot sustain, "parallel" price behavior is fully consistent with competitive behavior. Prices are the same because both firms match their competitors' prices, and prices change and reflect resource conditions because the firms are in competition with each other.

The large nonsense quotient contained in the argument that parallel pricing must imply collusion is quite apparent when we look at what has actually happened in steel. As shown in Chapter 13, U.S. steel makers have lost a large part of their share of the world steel market to Japan. Japanese firms are considered to be the stiffest competitors of American producers. Yet at the same time, pricing policies of domestic producers are naively interpreted as evidence that collusion prevails. In view of the competition those firms face, how plausible is it to contend that they practice oligopoly pricing?[65] They simply price at the level their competition permits (although that competition is limited by restraints on imports).

The fundamental impasse that a theory of tacit collusion encounters bears emphasis. What evidence there is of explicit arrangements suggests that they are most likely to be undertaken when the output of colluding producers is easily defined, when nonprice competition can be prevented, and when entry is expected to be slow. These appear to be the minimum requirements for a remunerative collusive arrangement, yet, as shown, by no means a guarantee of success. But if tacit collusion works well, why would firms ever resort to the time-consuming and costly technique of explicit agreement? Recall that the international cartels we looked at attempted to control the price of products for which it was an easy matter to define a unit of output. In Adelman's study of international cartelization attempts, the products were all of this nature. Why doesn't one see attempts to fix the prices of clothing, automobiles, and meals at restaurants? As Professor Stigler has noted, "Collusion is less feasible, the less clear the basis on which it should proceed."[66]

Alleged Instances of Tacit Collusion

The issue of tacit collusion has rarely come before the Supreme Court. In fact, the Court professed indifference to the question of whether tacit collusion occurred when the leading cigarette manufacturers were found guilty of keeping prices up during the Depression.[67]

American Tobacco Co. v. United States

In June of 1931, the R. J. Reynolds tobacco company raised its wholesale price of Camel cigarettes from $6.40 to 6.85 per thousand. American Tobacco and Liggett raised the price of Lucky Strikes and Chesterfields to the same level the same day. As we saw earlier, parallel price behavior does not constitute evidence of conspiracy by itself, nor has legal opinion construed it this way.[68] Yet in this case the Court gave considerable, even crucial weight to such parallel behavior. The other evidence that appears to have been relied on was the attempt by the defendants, all manufacturers of higher-priced cigarettes and originally possessing 90 percent of the market, to stipulate to dealers what sorts of prices they were to maintain in relation to the 10-cent brands.

The Court held even a "meeting of minds" to be possible and illegal, but it left open the question of whether the alleged agreement was tacit. A number of plausible explanations that do not rely on tacit or express collusion may be advanced, however, for what was observed.

One explanation is that the decision was simply a mistake. Table 6-1 shows the net sales of the leading manufacturers. The defendants produced the cigarettes in the first three columns. The ten-cent brands introduced at the beginning of the Depression are in the fourth. Note the drastic drop in 1932 of the amounts sold by the leading firms, and the simultaneous increase of the ten-cent brands. Professor Richard Tennant, in his study of the tobacco industry, notes that in November of 1932 the ten-cent brands had 22.8 percent of the total market. Only by reducing their prices to first $5.29 and later $4.85 per thousand did the leading firms manage to get back their old positions.[69] If the decision was a mistake (leaving aside the issue of whether it was a collusive mistake or merely stumbled into), the evidence indicates that it may have been a costly one. Although 1931 profits were high, the action cost them a substantial fraction of the market. Costly or not, the evidence also indicates that here, as in the cases of express collusion that we examined earlier, new entry occurred.

TABLE 6–1
Sales of Leading Cigarette Brands, 1930–39
(Billions of Cigarettes)

Year	Lucky Strike	Camel	Chesterfield	Ten-Cent Brands
1930	43.2	35.3	26.4	0.1
1931	44.5	33.3	22.8	0.4
1932	36.7	23.9	20.9	10.7
1933	36.7	25.6	29.3	10.1
1934	32.1	33.3	31.9	13.8
1935	30.7	39.4	31.8	15.8
1936	33.1	46.4	34.4	16.7
1937	34.5	47.7	34.7	19.6
1938	36.4	43.7	33.7	23.4
1939	38.3	42.8	33.0	25.6

Source: R. Tennant, THE AMERICAN CIGARETTE INDUSTRY (1950), Table 18 at 88. Copyright by Yale University. Reprinted by permission of the publisher.

A second factor was nonprice competition, in particular competition conducted through advertising. In his study of the cigarette industry, which covered this period, Professor Lester Telser concludes as follows:

> The picture that emerges is one of competition by means of advertising, and I see no reason to doubt its effectiveness for some products, cigarettes being a case in point. The behavior of consumers in the market is consistent with the view that they demand the advertising.[70]

The Court unwittingly touched on the same point in its opinion when it cited the claim of Liggett officials who believed the price increase to be a mistake. The officials thought, however, the Court goes on to note, that "unless they also raised their list price for Chesterfields, the other companies would have greater resources to spend in advertising and thus would put Chesterfield cigarettes at a competitive disadvantage."[71]

Simply put, this was very likely a case in which nonprice competition was important (but the weight given to it by leading firms was a mistake). Although the manufacturers took pains to ensure that their prices were the same and that they stood in a certain relation to what were generally regarded as inferior brands, such behavior should establish no presumption of collusion. What manufacturers did offer buyers for their money was advertising, an image of what it meant to be a Lucky Strike smoker. The Court, in addition to having failed to establish whether the conspiracy was tacit or explicit (and the issue is important because it affects the interpretation to be assigned to certain kinds of evidence), also failed to take into account the possibility of nonprice competition, and so whether a conspiracy of any kind existed.

The Rayon Industry

Let's take another instance in which tacit collusion is alleged to have taken place. In his study of the rayon industry, Professor Jesse Markham contends that it was one in which price leadership existed. This variant of the tacit collusion hypothesis holds that the leading firm sets prices and others follow because they know it is in their interest to do so. In part, he bases this conclusion on the behavior of list prices, despite the considerable evidence he himself amasses that list prices were not adhered to. In part also, he bases this conclusion on the following suspect piece of reasoning:

> By the usual definition, rayon prices are administered—they do not move to equate short-run demand and supply. The seasonal demand pattern for rayon yarn contains fairly high peaks and low troughs but there is no corresponding response observable in the rayon price series.[72]

But one would not expect marked seasonal pricing patterns to emerge for a good that can be produced and stored all year-round, regardless of the nature of demand conditions, unless storage or capacity costs are high relative to price. Producers faced with seasonal peaks and troughs in demand may: a) curtail and expand production if the marginal cost of extra units over the relevant range is constant, or b) produce at a constant level all year and place output in inventory during the slack period.

The Brewing Industry

An industry in which one would expect to find tacit collusion if it exists anywhere is the brewing industry. The demand for beer is fairly price inelastic (although not for particular classes or qualities), the number of firms has declined sharply over the last thirty years, and transportation costs play an important role. For a significant portion of the last thirty years, the beer industry was also a declining industry. As we saw earlier, collusion is facilitated when new entrants would do poorly. Professor John Blair, for example, contends that "the superior performance of the industry's largest and third-largest firms (Anheuser-Busch and Pabst Brewing) was probably the result of both superior efficiency and monopoly power."[73] Yet Ann and Ira Horowitz, in their study of the brewing industry, conclude that increased concentration has increased what might be termed the competitive spirit of the industry. The existence of fewer firms

> . . . is not at all a sign of a decrease in the need of any one firm to temper its market behavior to both realized and potential actions of other firms in the industry. Rather, it signifies a stronger competitive position for a greater number of firms in which, through technological necessity, only the larger firms can survive.[74]

A particular feature of the industry, which might lead some observers to infer tacit collusion, is its pricing structure. The demand for any particular beer is very sensitive to price, especially its price compared to other beer in its class. The result has been that a special effort has been made by brewers to price their beers close to their rivals. Yet, as the Horowitzs found, the importance of pricing policies implies that much competition takes place though attempts to offer more quality or, as we saw in the case of cigarettes, through advertising.

180

Conclusion

While tacit collusion, mutual forbearance, and spontaneous co-ordination are frequently alleged, attempts either to provide a model of how such behavior could occur or to substantiate the claim with economic evidence have failed. The fundamental problems of any attempted collusion, namely, the definition and the enforcement of the participants' behavior, must be resolved in some way. Professor Stigler points out that

> Tacit collusion based upon "oligopolistic rationality" is as inferior in efficiency and flexibility to overt collusion as mental telepathy is to a telephone. A large industry must make an intricate pattern of decisions at any time for the many product and geographical areas in which it operates, and these decisions must be revised fairly often. It has not yet been shown that effective cooperation would be possible without leaving a dozen large evidences in the institutions and practices of the industry.[75]

That these matters could be agreed on without explicit communication is not an idea that should be dismissed out of hand. It is, however, extremely unlikely. And, as Keynes observed, "the fact that all things are *possible* is no excuse for talking foolishly."[76]

Notes

1. Dale K. Osborne, *Cartel Problems,* 66 AMERICAN ECONOMIC REVIEW 835 (Dec. 1976); D. E. Mills and K. Elzinga, *Cartel Problems: Comment,* 68 AMERICAN ECONOMIC REVIEW 938 (Dec. 1978).
2. G. W. Stocking and M. W. Watkins, CARTELS OR COMPETITION 94 (1948). Cited in N. H. Jacoby, *Perspectives on Monopoly,* 59 JOURNAL OF POLITICAL ECONOMY 517 (Dec. 1951).
3. The emphasis on price-fixing is motivated here by considerations apart from its pedagogical advantages. While other forms of output restriction exist, such as assigning geographical areas and establishing common sales agencies, price fixing is most closely related to what is believed to occur in alleged instances of tacit collusion. The competing products are sold side by side, but competitors practice price restraint because they know it is in their common interests to do so.
   It should also be noted that the distinction between tacit and explicit collusion is being made to facilitate an analysis of the economic, and not the legal, aspects of the problem. Particularly now that the economics of

information costs is coming of age, as seen, for example, in innovations in the theory of the firm, much would be lost by failing to take into account why it is that explicit agreements are found to be necessary at all.

4. See G. J. Stigler, *A Theory of Oligopoly,* 72 JOURNAL OF POLITICAL ECONOMY 11 (Feb. 1964), reprinted in Stigler, THE ORGANIZATION OF INDUSTRY 39 (1968), for a model of price cutting. For traditional expositions of factors leading to cartel formation, see, for example: D. Dewey, MONOPOLY IN ECONOMICS AND LAW 18–24 (1957); G. A. Hay and D. Kelley, *An Empirical Survey of Price Fixing Conspiracies,* 17 JOURNAL OF LAW AND ECONOMICS 13 (Apr. 1974); J. Kuhlman, *Nature and Significance of Price Fixing Rings,* 2 ANTITRUST LAW AND ECONOMICS REVIEW 69 (Spring 1969); R. A. Posner, ANTITRUST LAW: AN ECONOMIC PERSPECTIVE 55–61 (1976); and G. J. Stigler, THE THEORY OF PRICE 219–27, 230–36 (1966).

5. P. Asch and J. J. Seneca, *Is Collusion Profitable?,* 58 REVIEW OF ECONOMICS AND STATISTICS 1 (Feb. 1976).

6. Arthur S. Dewing, CORPORATE PROMOTIONS AND REORGANIZATIONS 306–7 (1914).

7. See *id.* at 336.

8. Asch and Seneca *supra* note 5, at 7.

9. That is why, for example, as long as interest ceilings were in effect in commercial banking on savings deposits, banks tried to attract customers with "gifts." Despite a mandate from the government, which, by the way, stems from Depression-era concerns about ruinous price-cutting, and which allows them to charge depositors a "higher price" (lower interest payments in this case), banks do not earn supracompetitive returns.

10. One way of keeping plants operating at their optimal capacity while restricting industry output is to close some plants. This, it seems, has rarely been tried. "Authentic cases where a cartel, lacking government support, has so restricted an industry's output that closing of some plants was necessary to achieve its ends are difficult to discover. Cartels apparently are seldom this ambitious or foolhardy." D. Dewey, MONOPOLY IN LAW AND ECONOMICS 14 (1959).

11. Fritz Voight, *German Experience with Cartels and Their Control During Pre-War and Post-War Periods,* in J. P. Miller (ed.), COMPETITION, CARTELS, AND THEIR REGULATION 171 (1962).

12. E. Mansfield, *The Speed of Response of Firms to New Techniques,* 77 THE QUARTERLY JOURNAL OF ECONOMICS 291 (May 1963).

13. See *id.* at 309

14. See U.S., Federal Trade Commission, Office of Policy Planning and Evaluation, 1976 BUDGET OVERVIEW E-8 (published by The Bureau of National Affairs, Inc., 1974).

15. H. Demsetz, *Why Regulate Utilities?,* 11 JOURNAL OF LAW AND ECONOMICS 55 (Apr. 1968), excerpted in Y. Brozen, THE COMPETITIVE ECONOMY 15 (1975). A curious aspect of at least one antitrust case was that the sole supplier was found in violation of the Sherman Act *because* he priced output at the competitive level. See the discussion of the Alcoa case in Chapter 2.

16. "The crucial questions are whether advertising creates value and whether it creates monopoly. If it pays to advertise, this must mean that the increase in total revenues brought about by advertising is greater

than the increased cost it entails. Consumers are clearly willing to pay as much or more for the advertising than it cost." J. S. McGee, IN DEFENSE OF INDUSTRIAL CONCENTRATION (1971).

17. W. J. Liebeler, *Market Power and Competitive Superiority in Concentrated Industries,* 25 UCLA LAW REVIEW 1243 (Aug. 1978). Also, see Harold Demsetz, *Accounting for Advertising as a Barrier to Entry,* 52 JOURNAL OF BUSINESS 345 (Jul. 1979).

18. For an application of this line of reasoning, see R. Schmalensee, *Entry Deterrence in the Ready-to-Eat Breakfast Cereal Industry,* 9 THE BELL JOURNAL OF ECONOMICS 305 (Autumn 1978).

19. See J. Blair, ECONOMIC CONCENTRATION: STRUCTURE, BEHAVIOR, AND PUBLIC POLICY 334–38 (1972).

20. S. Rosen, *Hedonic Prices and Implicit Markets: Product Differentiation in Pure Competition,* 82 JOURNAL OF POLITICAL ECONOMY 34 (Jan. 1974). K. Lancaster, *A New Approach to Consumer Theory,* 74 JOURNAL OF POLITICAL ECONOMY 132 (Mar. 1966).

21. See Blair *supra* note 19, at 337.

22. See *id.* at 338.

23. See *id.* at 337.

24. See *id.* at 338.

25. See *id.*

26. "Concentration and barriers to entry are in a sense different sides of the same coin: the reason that economies of scale explain the existence of a concentrated industry is that they make entry by other firms unprofitable." U.S., Federal Trade Commission, Office of Policy Planning and Evaluation, *supra* note 14, at E-8.

27. See General Motors Corporation, *The Locomotive Industry and General Motors,* in Brozen *supra* note 15, at 270.

28. See M. Friedman, *Comment,* BUSINESS CONCENTRATION AND PUBLIC POLICY 213 (1955); R. E. Lucas, Jr., *On the Size Distribution of Firms,* 9 THE BELL JOURNAL OF ECONOMICS 508 (AUTUMN 1978); JOHN S. MCGEE, IN DEFENSE OF INDUSTRIAL CONCENTRATION (1971).

29. Such an interpretation does not imply, however, that there are no costs to breaking up the larger firms. It might be argued that there are no social costs to a policy that reduces all firms to the size of the marginal entrant, since the market price would be the same. Such an argument does not take into account, however, that rents to managerial talents and organizational factors are rewards for resources saved (producers' surplus). Social cost before restructuring would be represented by the area under a rising industry supply curve; social cost after by the (larger) area under the horizontal line passing through the demand curve at the same point.

30. P. Areeda and D. F. Turner, *Predatory Pricing and Related Practices under Section 2 of the Sherman Act,* 88 HARVARD LAW REVIEW 699 (Feb. 1975).

31. H. Demsetz, *Two Systems of Belief About Monopoly* in Goldschmid, Mann, And Weston, INDUSTRIAL CONCENTRATION 167 (1974).

32. See *id.* at 168.

33. K. Elzinga, *Predatory Pricing: The Case of the Gunpowder Trust,* 13 JOURNAL OF LAW & ECONOMICS 223 (Apr. 1970).

34. See discussion at note 19, Chapter 1.

35. There are, of course, numerous indisputable instances of collusion sanctioned by specific exemptions from the Sherman Act, as in the case of

the Reed Bulwinkle Act, which shelters the railroad industry. The fact that collusion in these cases is not accompanied by higher profit rates shoud lead us to question the use of profit rates as proxy for collusion in the first place. See U.S., Federal Trade Commission, Office of Policy Planning and Evaluation, *supra* note 14, at E-6. As this article points out, the economic crime is misallocation of resources and not high profits. One might pause to wonder whether the certain and sustained social losses in regulated areas do not overshadow the losses that occur from occasional false trades and sporadic price-fixing agreements.

36. *United States v. Trenton Potteries Company et al.*, 273 U.S. 397 (1927).
37. See D. T. Armentano, *Price Fixing in Theory and Practice,* in Y. Brozen, *supra* note 15, at 310 to 314; A. Winston, JUDICIAL ECONOMICS 1–20 (1957); and A. Phillips, MARKET STRUCTURE, ORGANIZATION, AND PERFORMANCE 161–76 (1962).
38. See Armentano *supra* note 37, at 313.
39. See Winston *supra* note 37, at 6.
40. J. Markham, COMPETITION IN THE RAYON INDUSTRY 47 (1952).
41. See the evidence Markham has assembled at 72 to 81. Surprisingly, Markham insists on characterizing the rayon industry as one in which price leadership (and hence, noncompetitive pricing) occurs. As is shown in the next section, simultaneous changes in price are consistent with competiton.
42. See Markham *supra* note 40, at 77.
43. See Armentano *supra* note 37, at 314.
44. See *id*. at 318.
45. See *id*. at 319.
46. Arthur S. Dewing, CORPORATE PROMOTIONS AND REORGANIZATIONS 114–15 (1914).
47. GEORGE EADS, *Competition in the Domestic Trunk Airline Industry: Excessive or Insufficient?* in Almarin Phillips, Competition and Regulation of Industry (1974), excerpted in Brozen *supra* note 15, at 325.
48. A. Plummer, INTERNATIONAL COMBINES IN MODERN INDUSTRY 120–24 (1938).
49. See *id*. at 123
50. See *id*. at 123–24.
51. See *id*. Ministry of Agriculture, *Report of the Sugar Beet Industry at Home and Abroad* (1931) in Plummer, *supra* note 48, at 23–24.
52. See *id*. at 24
53. See *id*. at 24.
54. See *id*. at 39.
55. P. MacAvoy, A REVIEW OF RESEARCH FINDINGS ON THE LONGEVITY OF INTERNATIONAL CARTEL AGREEMENTS 2 (Memorandum prepared for U.S. Federal Energy Office, no date).
56. C. T. Hallinan, Introduction to R. Liefman, INTERNATIONAL CARTELS, COMBINES, AND TRUSTS 15 (1927).
57. B. Fog, *How Are Cartel Prices Determined?* 5 JOURNAL OF INDUSTRIAL ECONOMICS 20 (Nov. 1956).
58. See *id*.
59. See *id*.
60. See Voight, *supra* note 11, at 17.
61. H. Chamberlin, THE THEORY OF MONOPOLISTIC COMPETITION ix (1933).
62. See *id*. at 104, footnote omitted.
63. W. Fellner, COMPETITION AMONG THE FEW 33 (1949).

64. See *id.* at 15–16.
65. For a statement of the theory of parallel pricing behavior, see Blair *supra* note 19, at 462–63.
66. Stigler *supra* note 4 at 55.
67. *American Tobacco Co. v. United States,* 328 U.S. 781 (1946).
68. "This Court has never held that proof of parallel business behavior conclusively establishes agreement or, phrased differently, that such behavior itself constitutes a Sherman Act offense. Circumstantial evidence of consciously parallel behavior may have made heavy inroads into the traditional judicial attitude toward conspiracy, but conscious parallelism has not yet read conspiracy out of the Sherman Act entirely." *Theatre Enterprises, Inc. v. Paramount Film Distributing Corp.,* 346 U.S. 537 (1954).
69. R. Tennant, THE AMERICAN CIGARETTE INDUSTRY 89 (1950).
70. L. Telser, *Advertising and Cigarettes,* 70 JOURNAL OF POLITICAL ECONOMY 498–99 (Oct. 1962).
71. See note 67 *supra.*
72. See Markham *supra* note 40.
73. See Blair *supra* note 19, at 179. If the leading firms did share a monopoly position, why didn't the second largest firm also have "superior performance"?
74. A. R. Horowitz and I. Horowitz, *Firms in a Declining Market: The Brewing Case,* excerpted in Brozen, *supra* note 15, at 299.
75. George J. Stigler, *Discussion of Report of the Attorney General's Committee on Antitrust Policy,* 46 AMERICAN ECONOMIC REVIEW 506 (May 1956).
76. J. M. Keynes, ESSAYS IN PERSUASION 14 (1931).

7

Do Leading Firms in Concentrated Industries Possess Market Power?

Before the 1930s, few economists viewed even a single firm selling the bulk of any product as possessing market power. J. B. Clark expressed the widely shared opinion that potential competition produces a competitive result at least as satisfactory as that occurring when a large number of existing firms compete for the market.

> Let any combination of producers raise the prices beyond a certain limit, and it will encounter this difficulty. The new mills that will spring into existence will break down prices; and the fear of these new mills, without their actual coming, is often enough to keep prices from rising to an extortionate height. The mill that has never been built is already a power in the market: for it will surely be built under certain conditions, the effect of this certainty is to keep prices down.[1]

Even when more than 70 percent of an industry's capacity was combined to form a single firm, most economists dismissed the notion that a monopoly or near-monopoly result would ensue. J. B. Clark and J. M. Clark expressed this view.

> The key to the situation is the position of the consumers, rather than that of the producers. Has every consumer a choice of efficient and independent producers to buy from? If so, there is no monopoly, even if one combination should control three quarters of the output.[2]

Some even felt that competition would be more rugged with only a few firms in an industry than with many. Eliot Jones voiced this opinion in writing about the petroleum refining industry.

> In 1904 there were some seventy-five independent refiners all told. ... Had the total independent output been concentrated in a few large refineries, competition with the Standard Oil Company would have been much more vigorous and successful.[3]

To these views expressed by economists can be added the opinion of a scholar turned President, the signer of the Clayton and Federal Trade Commission Acts, Woodrow Wlson. In his book, *The New Freedom* (1913), he wrote

> ... any large corporation built up by the legitimate processes of business, by economy, by efficiency, is natural; and I am not afraid of it, no matter how big it grows. It can stay big only by doing its work more efficiently than anybody else.[4]

Professor George Stigler, a student of the history of economic doctrine, observed that, "When the Sherman Act . . . was passed in 1890, most economists and most non-economists believed that an industry with a modest number of firms could be tolerably competitive."[5] Firsthand knowledge of the nearly industry-wide combinations around the turn of the century had a profound effect on the opinions of pre-1930 economists. This, and the common conclusion derived from experience, that efficiency and price reductions earned greater profits than industry-wide mergers and price increases, account for their lack of concern when confronted with increasing concentration and the emergence of dominant firms.

Memory of the fate of early twentieth-century dominant firms that had tried to set monopoly prices faded, however, and reports produced in the 1930s through the 1960s changed the common view among economists. They began to believe that concentration and collusion were synonymous. While the previous generation had noted that the "mill not yet built" could police prices, the new generation grew confident in its belief that dominant firms would have monopoly power and use it. First, reports on "administered-prices" associated price rigidity with concentration.[6] Later, several studies reported correlations, albeit weak, between accounting rates of return and concentration.[7] One analysis found that output per worker hour rose more rapidly in industries where concentration decreased and in those in which it was low. This too had some influence.[8] Then the "administered price" hypothesis was revised to include upward price flexibility to explain inflation, as well as downward price rigidity, which had been used to explain falling production and employment in recessions. An addendum incorporating "unliquidated monopoly power" was later added to explain "stagflation."

The Administered Price Hypothesis

The "administered price" hypothesis launched by Gardiner Means posits greater price stability in highly concentrated industries than in others. It blames declining employment in recessions on the failure of prices in concentrated industries to decline when demand declines. Also, it blames the great depth of the depression in the 1930s on greater price rigidity than in earlier periods. And it blames the downward rigidity of prices in times of falling sales on a lack of competition in industries with few firms.

A series of analyses demonstrating the inaccuracy of the data used in the studies that had concluded that prices are rigid in centralized industries toppled that hypothesis. David Qualls' 1977 study of the flexibility of price-cost margins and an analysis by Steven Lustgarten and Alan Mendelowitz showing that employment is more stable in concentrated than in other industries administered the coup de grace.[9] Prior to Qualls and Lustgarten-Mendelowitz, a number of other studies dissected Gardiner Means' administered price tract. Among these, a study of a larger sample of prices than that used by Means showed no relationship between concentration and the rigidity of realized prices.[10] Another study showed the work by Means to be deficient because it relied on Bureau of Labor Statistics (BLS) price data. These data, it was demonstrated, did not accurately reflect actual prices paid.

The BLS data suffered from two crucial flaws. First, the smaller the number of firms used in gathering reports on the price of any specific commodity, the less frequently changes appeared to occur. This had caused prices of some goods to show a spurious rigidity. Also, the association between the spuriously rigid prices and concentration was considerably weaker than reported by Means because he had made a careless and subjective classification of price changes by concentration class.[11] Second, the prices gathered were list prices provided by sellers. Since actual transaction prices frequently departed, sometimes widely, from list prices, the BLS prices were not the actual prices charged. They did not represent what was actually going on in the nation's markets. (See Table 7-1 for a startling contrast between BLS reported prices for tranquilizers and the actual prices charged. The actual prices charged are listed under "NBER.") A study by Professors George Stigler and James Kindahl found the prices actually charged in concentrated industries to be more flexible than was indicated by BLS reports.

> The main thrust of the doctrine of administered prices is that contractions in business lead to no systematic reduction of industrial prices, and, much more equivocally, expansion in business may only tardily lead to price increases.Whether because of a simple desire for stability, or more subtly because perhaps profits are better protected by stable prices, it has been argued that prices have at best only one-way flexibility, and that upward. The finding of Gardiner Means in his original study that numerous prices changed not at all, twice or a few times in a decade including the Great Depression was the sensational part of his study.
>
> A great majority of economists have accepted this finding even though no explanation for this behavior of oligopolists commands general assent. Prices of concentrated industries . . . do not respond to reductions in demand, or so it is believed. We raise grave doubts of the validity of this belief. . . .
>
> Even the BLS price indexes are not especially cordial to this view of cyclical rigidity, and our price indexes are emphatic in their contradiction of it.[12]

Although no explanation or rationale for price rigidity in concentrated industries "commands general assent," one was offered, which still appears in textbooks. The "kinked" demand curve explanation is still put forward to account for the supposed character of prices in concentrated markets, although the hypothesis has been shown by Stigler to be an unworkable theoretical concept with no empirical foundation.[13] A number of studies of price behavior in highly concentrated industries have appeared since, testing the kinked-demand theory. All have substantiated Stigler's findings.

Capping this series of studies, Qualls' 1977 analysis of price-cost margins in ninety-four industries produced results that "conflicted

TABLE 7-1
Bureau of Labor Statistics Price Indexes for Tranquilizers and National Bureau of Economic Research Price Indexes Based on Transaction Prices, 1957–66
(price indexes, 1964 = 100)

	1957	1958	1959	1960	1961	1962	1963	1964	1965	1966
			Bureau of Labor Statistics							
January	100.00	100.00	100.00	100.00	100.00	100.00	100.00	100.00	100.00	100.00
February	100.00	100.00	100.00	100.00	100.00	100.00	100.00	100.00	100.00	100.00
March	100.00	100.00	100.00	100.00	100.00	100.00	100.00	100.00	100.00	100.00
April	100.00	100.00	100.00	100.00	100.00	100.00	100.00	100.00	100.00	101.40
May	100.00	100.00	100.00	100.00	100.00	100.00	100.00	100.00	100.00	101.40
June	100.00	100.00	100.00	100.00	100.00	100.00	100.00	100.00	100.00	101.40
July	100.00	100.00	100.00	100.00	100.00	100.00	100.00	100.00	100.00	101.40
August	100.00	100.00	100.00	100.00	100.00	100.00	100.00	100.00	100.00	101.40
September	100.00	100.00	100.00	100.00	100.00	100.00	100.00	100.00	100.00	101.40
October	100.00	100.00	100.00	100.00	100.00	100.00	100.00	100.00	100.00	101.40
November	100.00	100.00	100.00	100.00	100.00	100.00	100.00	100.00	100.00	101.40
December	100.00	100.00	100.00	100.00	100.00	100.00	100.00	100.00	100.00	101.40

National Bureau of Economic Research

January	113.94	113.94	113.34	110.87	110.10	109.06	105.89	101.86	97.42	95.71
February	113.94	113.94	113.15	111.05	110.30	109.02	105.87	100.57	97.41	95.80
March	113.69	113.94	112.92	110.87	110.49	109.04	105.84	101.49	96.83	95.80
April	113.69	113.94	112.73	111.06	110.69	109.10	105.81	101.36	96.81	95.85
May	113.69	113.94	112.55	111.27	110.89	109.12	105.78	100.26	96.81	95.62
June	113.69	113.94	112.37	111.45	111.06	109.16	105.75	100.13	96.85	95.59
July	113.69	113.94	112.57	111.39	110.38	109.29	104.58	99.91	96.35	94.88
August	113.69	113.94	112.77	111.32	109.76	109.26	104.52	99.78	96.35	94.93
September	113.94	113.59	112.84	111.26	109.68	109.00	104.46	99.18	95.93	93.77
October	113.94	113.59	113.05	111.21	109.55	108.97	104.33	98.55	95.84	93.77
November	113.94	113.59	113.25	111.16	109.50	108.95	103.81	98.46	95.84	93.77
December	113.94	113.59	113.45	111.12	109.45	108.91	103.31	98.44	95.84	93.77

Source: George J. Stigler and James K. Kindahl, The Behavior of Industrial Prices (1970) at 162. Copyright by the National Bureau of Economic Research. Reprinted by permission of the publisher.

Note: The NBER index is a weighted group index employing rough estimates of weights for the following commodities: meprobamate (Miltown, Equanil, etc.), Librium, Thorazine, Compazine and Stedazine.

radically with conventional administered pricing lore." Qualls found "a statistically significant, positive relationship between *cyclical* variability of price-cost margins and concentration."[14] The finding could be viewed as consistent with the hypothesis that concentrated industries are *more* competitive than the more nearly atomistic industries, that collusion is less common in concentrated industries, and that concentrated industry prices are more responsive to variations in demand. This is what we would expect in more competitive industries, but it is probably simply a result of the greater capital intensity and larger fixed costs in concentrated industries. In any case, these results should spell the end of any belief in the concentration-collusion doctrine, even among its most doctrinaire adherents.

Concentration and Profits

Belief in the concentration-collusion doctrine was supported by another line of studies that found a weak correlation between concentration and profitability. Professor Richard Miller summarized the argument that higher profits indicate noncompetitive performance by an industry: "Firms in the search for profit restrict output, raise price, and earn supernormal profit if the market structure in which they find themselves permits."[15] But there is plausible contrary reasoning, which goes as follows: firms in the search for profits increase efficiency and reduce costs. Above average profits, when they occur, are the result of innovations in technology or organization. A concentrated market structure and profits are a consequence of superior competitive performance by a few firms in that market.

By this line of reasoning, if a few firms are relatively more successful, the industries that they occupy will thereby become concentrated. There will be an initial association between profits and concentration, and the association will continue until a long-run equilibrium is reached. But the association will be maintained and the equilibrium will not be reached as long as the leading firms in concentrated industries continue to maintain their innovative activities at a rate giving them a continuing decline in real costs or product improvement equal to or exceeding that in other firms.

We face, then, two questions: first, is there an association between profits and concentration? And second, which explanation of any association of profits and concentration is correct, if indeed there are only two possible explanations?

Is There a Concentration-Profit Correlation?

Professor Joe Bain produced the first of many studies that concluded that there is an association between industrial concentration and profitability.[16] In an examination of forty-two industries (out of 281 manufacturing industries whose data he might have used), he found that those that had eight-firm concentration ratios greater than 70 percent earned higher accounting rates of return, on the average, than those that were less concentrated. This, he argued, was consistent with the hypothesis that successful collusion, tacit or explicit, occurred more often in highly concentrated industries (at least in those that are sheltered from entry by various sorts of "barriers").[17]

Evidence contradicting Bain was presented in Stigler's investigation of manufacturing rates of return. He reported no significant difference in rates of return between concentrated and unconcentrated industries.[18] Stigler used a larger sample of industries than Bain, arousing the suspicion that Bain's study used an unrepresentative sample. Also, Stigler's data included all corporations reporting to the IRS. Bain had used as few as three companies in many industries. The small number of corporations used by Bain and his use only of companies registered with the Securities and Exchange Commission (SEC) were also possible sources of bias.

Further, for the sixteen of Bain's forty-two industries that correspond closely to Stigler's industries, both Bain's and Stigler's data for the pre-1940 period showed the same relationship between concentration and profitability. The relationship in the sixteen industries disappeared, however, in 1947–54.[19] That Bain's finding held for the similar *portion* of Stigler's group of industries in 1938–40, but not for the total group, again suggested small-sample bias in Bain's study. The fact that the relationship for the small group of sixteen industries disappeared in 1947–54 suggested that Bain had mistaken a temporary disequilibrium phenomenon in a small number of industries for a permanent relationship in all industries.

When, in 1968, the White House Antitrust Task Force recommended new legislation to deconcentrate industries with four-firm concentration ratios of more than 70 percent, it justified its proposal on the basis of a purported relationship between concentration and *persistent* profitability.[20] We reexamined the reports on which the Task Force had relied. First, we analyzed them to see if the weak correlations that they found between concentration and profitability might be the result of temporary disequilibria, as had been implied by Stigler's study. If they were, high profit industries would attract entry.[21] With the growth of capacity and supply in those industries, rates of return would, over time, converge to the average. This would occur whether the high-profit industries were in the concentrated or the unconcentrated groups. (Some of the high-profit industries were in the unconcentrated part of the samples employed). We computed accounting rates of return in later periods for the industries that the studies used. Rates of return did indeed converge![22]

The higher profit rates of concentrated industries, and of some unconcentrated ones, were the result of disequilibrium. They were not the result of concentration with concomitant collusion sheltered by entry barriers as assumed in the studies relied upon by the Task Force. (See Tables 7-2A, 7-2B, and 7-2C for these results.)

There remained the question of why concentrated industries in Bain's and in other authors' data so often enjoyed higher than equilibrium rates of return. Why were less concentrated industries so often below equilibrium? Bain had reported that in thirty-four industries, excluded from his sample because he had data for fewer than three firms in each, the relationship between concentration and profitability was negative. This observation and Stigler's data made it seem probable that Bain's findings, and those of other authors relied on by the Task Force, were a consequence of bias resulting from small samples.[23]

The Federal Trade Commission's profit data on seventy-eight industries in 1939 and seventy-five industries in 1940, for which concentration data were available, provided a *ready-made* enlarged sample. In this enlarged sample, we found no significant difference in profitability between more and less concentrated industries.[24] Bain's observation that, in the prewar period, concentrated industries tended to earn higher rates of return again was shown to be a result of small sample bias. It was not true for the universe from which the sample was selected.

Since the FTC data covered only 1939 and 1940 while the Bain data covered the period 1936 through 1940, a further analysis was

194

TABLE 7-2A
Profitability Trends in Selected High-Concentration Industries, 1953–57 to 1962–66

Industry	Concentration Ratio 1954	Percentage Rate of Return on Net Worth (Number of Companies)		
		Stigler	Brozen	
		1953–57	1953–57	1962–66
High-return group				
Sulfur mining	98	23.85 (4)	25.5 (4)	11.3 (3)
Automobiles	98	20.26 (3)	19.2 (3)	19.6 (3)
Gypsum	90	20.26 (2)	15.6 (2)	9.4 (2)
Domestic laundry equipment	68	17.76 (2)	18.1 (2)	19.7 (2)
Chewing gum	86	17.06 (2)	17.7 (2)	13.9 (1)
Flat glass	90	16.17 (3)	16.5 (3)	10.7 (3)
Rubber tires	79	14.02 (9)	12.6 (13)	9.9 (11)
Aluminum	98	13.46 (4)	16.9 (3)	8.5 (3)
Average rate of return			17.8	12.9
Low-return group				
Corn milling	75	11.55 (3)	11.8 (4)	14.2 (4)
Industrial gases	84	11.53 (3)	11.7 (3)	11.0 (3)
Cigarettes	83	11.18 (5)	11.5 (5)	13.7 (5)
Metal cans	80	13.90 (4)	10.2 (5)	9.9 (3)
Carbon black	73	9.97 (2)	10.5 (2)	6.5 (1)
Floor covering, hard surface	87	7.59 (3)	8.3 (3)	12.9 (3)
Distilled liquors	64	7.55 (6)	6.4 (12)	7.2 (12)
Rayon fiber	76	6.62 (4)	8.0 (4)	11.8 (2)
Typewriters	83	5.39 (3)	5.1 (3)	7.6 (2)
Average rate of return			9.3	10.5

Sources: George J. Stigler, A Theory of Oligopoly, 72 JOURNAL OF POLITICAL ECONOMY (1966) at 58; Report of the Federal Trade Commission, RATES OF RETURN FOR IDENTICAL COMPANIES IN SELECTED MANUFACTURING INDUSTRIES (1940, 1947–1960); Standard and Poor's Compustat Tapes, 1966, 1968; Moody's INDUSTRIAL MANUAL 1952–1958. Figure in parentheses is number of companies used in computing rate of return.

Note: Brozen return figures are a simple average of the weighted return for each year (return computed on average equity). Stigler figures are a weighted average return on end of year equity.

195

TABLE 7–2B

Movement of Averages of Industry Profit Rates Within
Concentration Deciles for 42 Selected Industries,
1936–40 to 1953–57

Concentration Range, 1935 (Percentage of Product Supplied by Eight Firms)	Number of Industries	Average of Industry Percentage Profit Rates[a]	
		1936–40	1953–57
90–100	8	12.7	11.3
80–89.9	10	9.8	11.3
70–79.9	3	16.3	13.8
60–69.9	5	5.8	8.9
50–59.9	4	5.8	12.0
40–49.9	3	8.6	12.5
30–39.9	5	6.3	9.3
20–29.9	2	10.4	10.9
10–19.9	1	17.0	11.7
0– 9.9	1	9.1	11.7
0–100	42	9.6	11.1
70–100	21	11.8	11.7
0–70	21	7.5	10.6
Difference		4.4	1.1

Source: Y. Brozen, *The Antitrust Task Force Deconcentration Recommendation,* 13 THE JOURNAL OF LAW AND ECONOMICS 283 (Oct. 1970). Copyright by the University of Chicago. Reprinted by permission of the University of Chicago Press.
[a] Average of net profits after taxes as percentage of net worth.

TABLE 7–2C

Movement of Average Accounting Rate of Return on
Net Worth for 19 Selected Concentrated Industries
Classified by Barriers to Entry,[a] 1950–60 to 1961–66

Barriers to Entry	Percentage Rate of Return	
	1950–60	1961–66
High barriers class mean (eight industries)	16.1	13.1
Substantial barriers class mean (seven industries)	11.3	8.9
Moderate-to-low barriers class mean (four industries)	12.7	10.0
All manufacturing corporations	11.3	11.2

Source: Y. Brozen, *Barriers Facilitate Entry,* 14 ANTITRUST BULLETIN 852 (1969).
[a] These industries were selected and classified by H. M. Mann, *A Note on Barriers to Entry and Long-Run Profitability,* 14 ANTITRUST BULLETIN 845 (1969).

undertaken. Profitability data from 1936 through 1940 for ninety-eight industries were assembled, including the forty-two industries used by Bain.[25] In this enlarged sample, industry rates of return were not found to vary with concentration (see Table 7-3).[26] This reinforced the view that Bain's results were the consequence of small sample bias.

The Bain and FTC data related to the prewar period. Two of the studies on which the Task Force relied (and which also used small samples) were for the postwar period.[27] Professor James Ellert, using a larger sample of 141 industries, undertook the task of measuring the concentration-profitability relationship for the 1947–68 period and for various subperiods. He found no significant difference for the entire period between returns in the industries with high concentration and those with low concentration. In one subperiod (1947–51), there was a significant difference, but the sign was *opposite* to that predicted by the Bain hypothesis. Ellert's eighty-eight unconcentrated industries earned a higher average rate of return than his fifty-three concentrated industries in that subperiod (see Table 7-4).[28]

Regressions that measure the returns from investments in depreciable assets (GBV), inventories (INV), advertising (ADV), and in recruiting and training personnel (TPA) and allow for the influence of concentration on industry profitability show that *concentration and profitability are not correlated* when the influence of the amount of investment on total return to providers of capital is taken into account (see Table 7-5). These regressions, which use a sample of industries more than double the number used in Table 7-4, show that overhead and profits are entirely accounted for by the capital required in each industry.[29] These results for 1972 and 1963 confirm Ellert's findings.

Does Concentration-Profit Correlation Prove Collusion?

Whether or not concentration and profitability are correlated, there remains the question of what a positive correlation would mean if one were found. Many economists have *assumed* that a positive correlation is evidence of collusion among the few firms that "dominate" any concentrated industry. But as Professor Peltzman points out

[I]f concentration and profitability are indeed related, what market process produces the relationship? The traditional answer has been

TABLE 7-3

Average of Industry Profit Rates Within Concentration Deciles, 1936–40
(42 and 98 Industries)

Concentration Range, 1935 (Percentage of Product Supplied by Eight Firms)	Bain 42 Industry Sample		98 Industries	
	Average of Industry Profit Rates (Percentage[a])	Number of Industries	Profit Rates (Percentage[a])	Number of Industries
90–100	12.7	8	10.0	14
80–89.9	9.8	10	9.7	14
70–79.9	16.3	3	11.9	10
60–69.9	5.8	5	8.2	11
50–59.9	5.8	4	14.8	6
40–49.9	8.6	3	9.5	10
30–39.9	6.3	5	10.4	16
20–29.9	10.4	2	12.0	9
10–19.9	17.0	1	13.4	5
0– 9.9	9.1	1	7.6	3
0–100	9.6	42	10.5	98
70–100	11.8	21	10.4	38
0–70	7.5	21	10.6	60
Difference	4.4	—	-0.2	—

Source: Y. Brozen, Concentration and Profits: Does Concentration Matter? in F. Weston (ed.), THE IMPACT OF LARGE FIRMS ON THE U.S. ECONOMY (1973) at 69. Copyright by D. C. Heath and Company. Reprinted by permission of the publisher.

[a] Average of net profits after taxes as percentage of net worth.

TABLE 7–4

Rates of Return, Standard Deviations of Rates of Return, and Concentration-Return Correlations for 141 Manufacturing Industries, 1947–68

Line	Variable	1947–68	1947–57	1958–68	1947–51	1952–56	1957–60	1961–64	1965–68
1.	ROE^c	12.32	13.50	11.90	14.92	11.75	10.77	11.32	13.10
2.	ROE^u	12.87	13.90	11.39	16.78	11.88	11.21	10.61	12.65
3.	(1–2)	−0.52	−0.40	+0.51	−1.86	−0.13	−0.44	+0.71	+0.45
4.	S.D.^{c}	3.93	4.54	4.90	5.32	4.10	4.49	5.68	4.70
5.	S.D.^{u}	4.67	5.21	4.33	8.15	4.82	5.80	5.38	4.00
6.	(4–5)	−0.74	−0.67	+0.57	−2.83	−0.72	−1.31	+0.30	+0.70
7.	r^c	−.09	−.20	−.25	−.26	−.15	−.10	−.23	−.21
8.	r^u	−.02	+.07	−.13	+.09	+.10	−.02	−.14	−.05
9.	CR	1958	1954	1963	1947	1954	1958	1963	1966
10.	Cos^c	199	200	181	159	200	199	183	180
11.	Cos^u	366	365	384	406	365	366	382	385
12.	Ind^c	50	53	53	50	53	50	53	54
13.	Ind^u	91	88	88	91	88	91	88	87

Source: James C. Ellert, *Concentration, Disequilibria, and the Convergence Pattern in Industry Rates of Return.* (Presented before the University of Chicago Industrial Organization Workshop, October 1971).

Notes: The superscript "C" indicates that the sample is composed of industries where the eight-firm concentration ratio is in excess of 70 percent; "U" denotes a sample of unconcentrated industries (the eight-firm concentration ratio is less than 70 percent).

ROE: Group mean industry return on book equity for subperiod. Industry mean return is a simple average of annual industry weighted averages.

S.D.: Standard deviation of industry returns.

r: Simple correlation coefficient between industry returns and concentration levels.

CR: Eight-firm concentration ratio—year specified.

Cos: Number of Companies in group sample.

Ind.: Number of Industries in group sample.

Table 7–5

Regressions Measuring the Influence of
Several Variables on Profitability[a]

Constant		CR	Log GBV	Log INV	Log TPA	Log ADV	$\bar{r}^2$
			1972 N = 307				
(1)	.467 (4.1)	.0004 (0.4)	.360 (11.7)	.171 (5.8)	.348 (9.3)	.120 (9.7)	.925
(2)	.488 (4.8)		.363 (12.1)	.173 (5.9)	.342 (10.0)	.121 (9.9)	.925
			1963 N = 318				
(3)	.317 (1.1)	.0001 (0.1)	.364 (8.8)	.125 (3.2)	.400 (7.8)	.105 (5.5)	.870
(4)	.326 (1.2)		.362 (9.2)	.125 (3.2)	.398 (8.6)	.105 (5.6)	.871

Sources: U.S., Department of Commerce, Bureau of Economic Analysis, The Detailed Input-Output Structure of the U.S. Economy: 1963 (1969); U.S., Bureau of the Census, Annual Survey of Manufacturers 1976, Industry Profiles, Part 7 (1979); Concentration Ratios in Manufacturing (1975); Census of Manufacturers, 1972 (1975).
CR = four-firm concentration ratio; GBV = gross book value of depreciable assets; INV = book value of inventories; TPA = total payroll (excluding central offices and auxiliaries in 1972); ADV = advertising expenditures; VA = value added. Figures in parentheses below coefficients are t-ratios. N = number of four-digit industries for which data are available.
[a] The dependent variable, profitability, is measured as the log of (VA − TPA − ADV). More precisely, this is the contribution to overhead and profits earned in each industry.

that high concentration facilitates collusion and hence super marginal-cost pricing, for which some profitability measure is a proxy. Unfortunately, this answer does not logically follow from the usual evidence, so its acceptance by economists and practitioners of antitrust policy is little more than an act of faith.[30]

The correlation, rather than signifying collusion and *pricing* above competitive levels, may signify socially desirable performance in reducing *costs*. In industries with significant scale economies, the largest firms can grow by reducing prices, enlarging sales, and increasing capacity and output, thereby reducing costs. The leading firms in these industries innovate by pressing the frontiers of large-scale operation. The continuing application of scale innovations in production and organization can keep them profitable as they grow, despite falling prices. Also, superior managements may apply innovations more quickly. As a consequence, their firms grow more rapidly and their industries become concentrated. This socially desirable performance results in higher levels of concentration. Above-average profits occur in these concentrated industries until scale and other innovations dry up and the old innovations become widely known and imitated, as in the case of the meat packing industry described in Chapter 1.[31]

It is notable that the early combinations that held onto a large market share were those that installed research programs producing a continuing stream of product innovations and cost-reducing improvements. Eastman installed an experimental depa, :ment in 1896.

> By that date companies in less technologically sophisticated industries including American Cotton Oil and National Lead had research departments with their own laboratories separated from those used to test pi ducts and control production processes. By the first decade of the new century Western Electric, Westinghouse, General Electric, Electric Storage Battery, McCormick Harvester (and then International Harvester), Corn Products, Du Pont, General Chemical, Goodrich Rubber, Corning Glass, National Carbon, Parke Davis, and E. R. Squibb all had extensive departments where salaried scientifically trained managers and technicians spent their careers impre ving products and processes. Other companies soon followed suit. The research organizations of modern industrial enterprises remained a more powerful force than patent laws in assuring the continued dominance of pioneering mass production firms in concentrated industries.[32]

If greater profitability in concentrated industries is the consequence of collusion or of the dominance of a firm behaving as a partial monopolist, then concentration should be correlated with profitability in small- and middle-size firms as well as with industry profitability. We could even expect that the correlations would be stronger for smaller firms than for larger firms if collusion (or partial monopoly behavior by a dominant firm) is the primary factor enhancing profitability in concentrated industries. Small firms operating under the price umbrellas held by the largest firms would not have to bear the costs of excess capacity that might accrue to the large firms.[33] In declining industries or in downturns, for example, the colluding or dominant firms would have to cut production disproportionately below capacity to maintain prices at supracompetitive levels, incurring a cost not borne by the sheltered, smaller firms. (In the steel industry, for example, U.S. Steel cut output in the 1903–4 recession by 14 percent from its 1902 level while other firms with 35 percent of 1902 output raised production by 5 percent.)[34] For these reasons, we would expect small firms in concentrated industries to be more profitable than those in other industries if dominant-firm partial-monopoly behavior or collusion among leading firms is common in concentrated industries.

Professor Harold Demsetz, seeking to determine whether profits in concentrated industries are the consequence of collusion or of superior performance, examined data on profitability of firms at various size levels. He came to the conclusion that "[t]hese data . . . fail to provide evidence that collusion in the absence of superior performance is easier or more successful in concentrated industries than in unconcentrated industries."[35] In those instances in which there is a correlation between concentration and profitability in leading firms, as there has been in some years in studies using three-digit industries,[36] the profitability of the leading firms in concentrated industries was demonstrated to be a result of superior performance. This was shown by the negative correlation between concentration and profitability in smaller firms and by the correlation of profitability differences between first- and second-tier firms with concentration (Table 3-11). We cannot attribute the industry correlations to collusion alone, if at all.

Demsetz found that, "Most of the correlation between concentration and [industry] profit rates is attributable . . . to variation in firm size."[37] Earlier work done by Professors Peter Asch and M. Marcus not only demonstrated this to be the case; it also showed all the correlation to be "attributable to variation in firm size." They separated firms into size classes. To their surprise, they found a "nonsignificant statistical performance of the concentration ratio" in determining the profits of firms of a given size class. Yet they also found that, "When all sizes are consolidated, . . . the concentration ratio becomes statistically significant for profit rate variations among industries." They concluded that:

> This finding strongly suggests that the explanatory power of the concentration ratio may be due to its correlation with the average firm size within industries; and not, as has been thought, with the degree of monopoly control. More specifically, it might be hypothesized that: (a) rates of return are related to absolute firm size; and (b) the concentration ratio is a proxy for average firm size in an industry.[38]

202

Professor Baruch Lev's work supports Demsetz's conclusion that the correlation between concentration and profits, when it occurs, is not the result of collusion. If "dominant" firms maintain supracompetitive prices, their profit performance should be more erratic than that of the smaller firms sheltered under the large firms' price umbrella (for the reasons given above). Examining the leading firm in each of twenty-one industries in which the leading firm had more than 50 percent of industry sales in 1960, Lev reported

> . . . the serial correlation coefficients of profits in these twenty-one firms to be statistically indistinguishable from the rest of the sample. In addition, the 410 sampled firms (82 four-digit industries) were classified by five groups; largest firms in their industry, second largest firms, etc. Again, no significant differences could be detected among the group's average correlation coefficients and the number of significant correlations. We conclude therefore that the rank of the firm within its industry appears to be unrelated to the time-series behavior of earnings.[39]

Professor John Carter has provided a further test of the Demsetz hypothesis that a positive relationship between concentration and profitability occurs because large firms are more efficient than smaller firms and are a larger factor in concentrated industries and not because of collusion in concentrated industries. Carter compared the relationship of price-cost margins to concentration in the leading four firms with that in the next four firms in 356 industries (1963), 350 industries (1967), and 306 industries (1972). Some of the deficiencies in the usual price-cost margin studies were avoided by comparing margin relationships among leading firms with those among secondary firms. In this way, he avoided drawing the unsustainable inferences drawn when non-stratified margins across industries are compared. Using four-digit industries and partially allowing for the influence of tangible capital (plant and equipment) intensity and for intangible capital (advertising) intensity, Carter found a positive relationship between margins and concentration for the leading firms but no relationship (in 1963 and 1967) or a negative one (in 1972) for secondary firms.[40] The leading firms in concentrated industries were not collusively holding a price umbrella high enough to benefit secondary firms. If anything, they were competitve enough to force prices down to levels that depressed margins in secondary firms in concentrated industries (also see Table 3-10).

Since Carter lacked advertising data for 1972, he used 1967 advertising data in his 1972 regression. Also, he used depreciable assets from 1971 for forty industries in his 1972 regression for lack of the 1972 data. Replacing his 1967 and 1971 data with that for 1972, concentration shows a negative (but insignificant) influence on margins in the leading four firms and a negative and significant influence on margins in the second four firms in each industry. Competition among leading firms in concentrated industries was sufficient to make their margins the same as those in less concentrated industries, allowing for differences in capital intensity. The negative relationship between concentration and margins in secondary firms confirms the fact that the relative efficiency of leading firms is greater in concentrated industries; and that is why they are concentrated.

In a 1978 study using data on production shares of individual firms, John Kwoka concluded that "only the largest two or three firms are generally important explanators of performance. Furthermore while [increasing shares of] the two leading firms both raise industry margins, the third depresses them in the few cases where it is very large."[41] The usual caveats should be raised concerning Kwoka's use of "price-cost margins" (which should be called "contribution to overhead" margins, a practice followed by Professor Lester Telser) as a proxy for profitability. He partially took the caveats into consideration by using a gross-fixed-depreciable-assets to output ratio as a separate variable. However, this only partially allows for differences in capital intensity since he omits capital in the form of land, inventories, receivables, and intangible capital (investment in worker training, research and development, provision of information, development of a distribution network and business connections, et cetera). Neither does the price-cost margin (value added minus payroll in establishments classified in an industry by their primary product) allow for the payroll in central offices, field sales offices, and warehouses (which are a larger part of cost in concentrated industries), royalties, or for variations in taxes and the ratio of depreciation to gross depreciable assets.

Kwoka found that industry margins rise (weakly) with an increase in the output share of the largest firm and especially with the output share of the second largest firm, but decline with a rise in the share of the third largest. He interprets this as confirming the hypothesis that "The ability of an industry to secure above-competitive returns depends on . . . successful collusion [which is more likely] the greater the output control by the leading firm or firms. . . . Output control confers price-setting and enforcing powers generally related to large market shares."[42] Kwoka believed that larger margins result from price-raising power. He never considered whether they can be explained by cost reductions or by greater investment in capital other than fixed assets. He found, for example, that large market shares in the hands of each of three leading firms is associated with lower industry price-cost margins than where only the two largest firms have large market shares. This suggests a number of possibilities in addition to collusion. It might be the case that the learning curve effect or economies of scale may be substantial. If there are three leading firms in an industry, the firms taken as a whole are likely to be less diverse. Consequently, special circumstances such as rapid innovation by some firms will have had less influence on industry structure. Investment by the two leading firms in research and development (R&D) or other intangible capital may occur that does not occur in those industries where three firms are equally large.[43] That two firms grow large relative to the market while a third does not suggests a cost advantage in being large relative to the size of the market (in the industries where this occurs) that comes from accumulated experience or size. The cost advantage decreases average cost and, the two firms being a large share of the industry, causes large industry margins. Evidently competition between two leading firms (or by one with all others) depressed price enough that it does not pay the third firm (or all firms) to increase output sufficiently to take share away from the first and second firms.

Kwoka found that if the production share of an industry's leading firm (S1) exceeds 26 percent (.26), "industry price-cost margins are higher by about 4 percentage points. . . . [I]f both S1 ≥ .26 and S2 ≥ .15, margins are higher yet . . . produc[ing] price-cost margins nearly 9 percentage points higher." From this he concluded that,

> . . . interfirm bonds are tighter, coordination efforts more successful, and/or the power to enforce industry discipline more effective than with lesser output control. For any or all of these reasons, it is these industries that achieve price-cost margins most in excess of competitive levels.[44]

As we have shown, productivity has risen and prices have fallen in the industries with large increases in concentration and in high concentration industries relative to other industries. Consequently, Kwoka's conclusion does not follow from his data. The conclusion that does fit his data (and the other data from the Census of Manufactures, which he neglects) is that a rise in productivity as the leading firm grew to a more than 26 percent share reduced wage cost per dollar of value added and increased margins. The increase in margins was *not* caused by a rise in price. Price fell as productivity went up with the growth in size and experience of the leading firm (see Table 3-5).

This suggests another interpretation of Kwoka's findings. Since the leading firm's influence on industry margins is proportional to its weight in the industry, industry margins rise by only 4 percentage points. If the second firm also grows and accumulates experience, or takes advantage of scale economies, its margins also will grow large through increased productivity. As a result, the combined weight of the two leading firms in the computation of industry margins raises the industry margin by 9 percent in this instance.

Kwoka, as Peltzman pointed out, simply *assumed* that any rise in industry margins accompanying an increase in the shares of the two leading firms must be the consequence of the exercise of market power to raise prices. Alternative hypotheses are never considered and, consequently, not tested. Since an alternative hypothesis fits Kwoka's and other data better, his hypothesis should be discarded.

Professor Leonard Weiss has concluded that a correlation between concentration and profits probably indicates that forces other than those assumed by Kwoka must be at work. If profits in concentrated industries are higher than in the unconcentrated, it is unlikely that tacit collusion (mutually recognized interdependence) holding prices above the competitive level is the cause. As Weiss points out, "Oligopoly theory really predicts high prices and not necessarily high profits. If the high prices attract too many resources into the industry, the result will be excess capacity and only normal profits."[45] Since above-cost prices attract entry, and the data analyses of Telser and of Mansfield indicate that this is the case, then higher than average profits in concentrated industries must imply that innovation or positive disequilibria from other sources cause the relationship between price-cost margins and the market shares of the leading firms. As we argued in the last chapter, entry barriers cannot account for the relationship.

Telser's findings on the association between the number of firms, profitability, and concentration substantiate this conclusion (also see Table 1-5).

The Negative Collusion-Profit Correlation

In the 1930s it was usually argued that low-profit and low-margin industries are more likely to be characterized by collusion than high-profit industries. That argument has been repeated since.[46] This can be expected to be the case since increasing profits by collusion or "dominance" in low-profit industries does not invite cartel-destroying or dominance-destroying entry as it does in industries where profits are already attractive.

A study by Professors Asch and Seneca confirms the view that there is a negative relationship between profitability and explicit collusion. They conclude that "a poor profit performance by the firm . . . increases the probability of collusion."[47] They also find that industry concentration is statistically insignificant in affecting the probability of collusion in consumer goods industries and strongly significant, but *negatively,* in affecting the probability of collusion in producer goods industries. It seems that concentrated industries are less likely to collude than the unconcentrated. The antitrust agencies, in focusing their recent investigatory efforts and complaints on concentrated industries, are pursuing the wrong quarry in a search for tacit collusion.

Professor Alex Hunter, analyzing concentration in the United Kingdom, reached a similar conclusion concerning the relationship, or lack of relationship, between concentration and collusion.

> Whether high concentration assists the formation of collusive practices, thus extending the incidence of monopoly power, is an open question. *A priori,* a high concentration ratio for the largest three-four firms of an industry suggests that collusive practices will probably occur either in the form of tacit understandings on prices, outputs, market shares, etc.; or in restrictive agreements operated through a trade association. It seems equally reasonable to suppose that, the larger the number of enterprises in an industry and the lower the degree of concentration, the more difficult it becomes to secure stable lasting agreements of any kind. In practice, however, there are examples of concentrated industries which obviously are very competitive. . . . (Motor vehicles, soap and detergents, office machinery,

biscuits and margarine.) And, on the other hand, there are many low-concentration industries with a fairly wide membership which, as Monopolies Commission reports and Restrictive Practices Court cases show, operate price agreements which are remarkably well-organized and well-observed (bread, book publishing, copper semi-manufactures, sand and gravel, timber imports, etc.). It is *difficult to perceive any systematic connection between concentration and collusion.*[48]

Concentration and Productivity

A third line of studies, which contradicted the Schumpeter view that productivity would grow most rapidly in concentrated industries, supported the belief that concentration might be an index to monopoly power or to the frequency of collusion. These studies related the rate of change of productivity and the degree of concentration. Using data for twenty-nine industries, Professor Stigler found that output per worker hour rose more slowly from 1899 to 1937 in high concentration industries than in those with low concentration. It rose most rapidly in declining concentration industries during this period.[49]

However, this and other studies reaching similar conclusions suffered from two faults. The sample of industries was small. In addition, no attention was paid to the influence of growth on both concentration and productivity. In Stigler's declining concentration industries, total output grew much more rapidly than in other industries. The rate of growth in this group was *five times greater* than the rate of growth in either the high or low concentration group. Both the concentration decline and the rapid growth in productivity were probably caused by rapid sales growth.

Recent studies, by Professor J. Fred Weston, Professor Steven Lustgarten, and Professor Sam Peltzman, using large samples of industries and incorporating data for the postwar period, found results opposite those of the study described above. Industries with increasing concentration and highly concentrated industries show more rapid growth in productivity than the declining or low concentration industries (Table 3-5).[50] Also, industries with decreasing numbers of firms, after allowing for the influence of growth, show more rapid rises in productivity than those with an increasing number of firms.[51]

208

The Profitability of Monopolizing by Dominant Firms

The merger movement in the 1890s and the subsequent experience of the resulting consolidations have several lessons to offer to proponents of the market-concentration and dominant-firm doctrines—lessons that were learned by pre-1930s economists but forgotten since. Most of the large mergers of that era consolidated more than 50 percent of the capacity in their respective industries into a single firm.

> . . . [T]he mean share of the market controlled by the mergers studied by the Industrial Commission was 71 percent (one in the 25 to 50 percent range, 11 in the 50 to 75 percent range, and 10 in the 75 to 100 percent range). In the ninety-two large mergers studied by Moody, the distribution by share of market was similar: seventy-eight controlled 50 percent or more of the output of the industry; fifty-seven controlled 60 percent or more; and twenty-six controlled 80 percent or more.[52]

According to either the concentration-collusion or the dominant-firm doctrine, these consolidations should have been very profitable, given their large market shares and the high levels of concentration in their industries (see the predicted rate of return column in Table 7-6 computed by Professor W. G. Shepherd). Most of the mergers produced "dominant" firms. The share of industry capacity in a single firm's hands exceeded the level that would today be called "high" concentration when spread among four firms. Presumably, it was not even necessary to engage in collusion to obtain supracompetitive prices. Yet 40.4 percent of the consolidations with very large market shares failed (Table 3-2) and an additional 6.4 percent were forced into "voluntary" reorganization by inadequate earnings.[53]

Even in the combinations successful enough to avoid bankruptcy or reorganization for at least ten years, *profits were not enhanced* by their dominant positions or by the high concentration in their industries. Contrary to the predictions of the market-concentration doctrine, the profits of thirty-five combinations created between 1893 and 1902 joining five or more firms were lower in the first year after combination, in the tenth year after, and, on the

TABLE 7–6

Predicted (1910) and Actual Rates of Return of
Leading "Dominant" Firms

Firm	Predicted Rate of Return[a] 1910	Actual Rate of Return[b] 1909–16	Actual Rate of Return[b] 1901–8
		Percentage	
U.S. Steel	22.0	8.8	5.2
American Tobacco	27.0[c]	13.8	14.2
International Harvester	25.5	8.7	5.7
Central Leather	21.0	6.3[d]	—
Pullman	29.3	9.4	10.7
American Sugar	21.0	5.9	7.0
General Electric	23.0	11.1	11.3
Corn Products	21.0	3.0	3.2
American Can	22.0	5.1	2.9
Westinghouse Electric	20.5	9.5[d]	—
E. I. du Pont	29.5	8.2[e]	—
International Paper	18.5	3.0	4.7
National Biscuit	18.5	6.8	6.3
Western Electric	33.0	6.0[d]	—
United Fruit	27.0	12.0	13.9
United Shoe Machinery	31.7	18.1	—
Eastman Kodak	29.5	31.2	16.4
Average	24.7	9.8	—

[a] "Profit rate that this firm would . . . realize if its market share and entry barriers exert their normal influence." W. G. Shepherd, THE ECONOMICS OF INDUSTRIAL ORGANIZATION (1979) at 219, Table 10A-3.

[b] Shaw Livermore, *The Success of Industrial Mergers*, 50 QUARTERLY JOURNAL OF ECONOMICS (1935) at 94–95.

[c] This "predicted" rate of return should be compared with the 1901–08 figure since American Tobacco no longer had its 1910 market share following its dissolution compelled by an antitrust decree in 1911.

[d] Computed from data in MOODY'S.

[e] Computed for 1909–11. Company was dissolved in 1912 by antitrust decree.

average, during the ten years after, than the profits of the constituent firms before consolidation.[54] The total profits of the constituent firms before consolidation were 18.2 percent higher than the first-year profits and 1.3 percent higher than the tenth-year profits of the combinations they entered. Despite the additional investment made in new facilities by the combinations, their profits failed to rise above those earned by their constituent companies before they were combined. The profits of the constituent companies before consolidation averaged 16.2 percent more than the annual average profit of the ten years following the mergers.

The largest single firm created in this period, U.S. Steel, was typical of the thirty-five combinations. Its constituent firms before merger earned 9.6 percent more than U.S. Steel in its first year, 0.1 percent more than U.S. Steel in its tenth year, and 16.2 percent more than U.S. Steel averaged in its first ten years despite its investment in additional facilities. Republic Iron and Steel and Crucible Steel, which were among the thirty-five combinations examined by Professor Arthur Dewing, were made up of firms where earnings before consolidation exceeded Republic's ten-year average by 28.1 percent and Crucible's by 113 percent. High market share and high concentration did not raise earnings in the steel industry despite a short episode of explicit collusion (the Gary dinners). This resort to explicit collusion indicates that tacit collusion—the presumptive basis for antagonism to industrial concentration—was not practiced or effective and supports the general conclusion that a large market share does not confer market power.

Although a large proportion of the consolidations of the period were promoted, publicly at least, as a means of reducing cost by eliminating the "wastes of competition" and achieving the efficiencies of large scale, it appears that a major motive in many of the mergers was monopolization. The fact that most of the combinations of the period were produced by the *simultaneous* merger of several firms selling to the same market points in this direction.

To achieve scale economies or to place assets in the hands of superior managers, successive mergers will do as well as simultaneous mergers (except, perhaps, to the extent that new securities had to be floated to obtain additional capital for the purpose of achieving economies). Successive mergers might even be preferable, if the mergers are for cost-saving purposes, since the economies achieved in early mergers and the resulting increased output could improve the terms on which later mergers could be made.[55] But if mergers are for the purpose of monopolizing, the opposite would be necessary. As Professor Stigler has pointed out, if a combination is being formed to monopolize

> . . . it is more profitable to be outside a merger than to be a participant. The outsider sells at the same price [as the combination] but at the much larger output at which marginal cost equals price. Hence the promoter of a merger is likely to receive much encouragement from each firm—almost every encouragement, in fact, except participa-

211

tion. In order to overcome this difficulty, it will often be necessary to make the participation of each firm contingent on that of other firms and execute the merger in a single act.[56]

Despite the obviously monopolizing intent of a large number of the turn-of-the-century mergers, they did not succeed judging by the profit data reported by Professor Dewing and Professor Shaw Livermore, and by the large number of financial failures among the consolidations reported by these two students of the merger movement. Livermore, who investigated the experience of 409 companies listed by previous investigators as important consolidations, found 157 "could rightfully claim to be mergers with power enough to influence markedly conditions in their industry."[57] Of these, 40 percent failed, costing their stockholders their investment (Table 3-2). Six percent had to be "rejuvenated" by financial reorganization and 11 percent "limped" along following their formation. Only 6 percent were "outstanding successes." The successes succeeded by competing, some after suffering losses by trying to monopolize.

Professor Shepherd, a long-time student of industrial organization and a proponent of the concentration-collusion doctrine, estimated that the firms formed by merger at the turn of the century should have earned 24.7 percent "if market share and entry barriers exerted their normal influence" (see Table 7-6). If we disregard the negative returns of the consolidations that failed, those that had to be rejuvenated, and the "limping" mergers, the actual returns were 9.8 percent for the firms that were successes and were listed by Shepherd in his table showing the "average degree of market power" possessed by these firms in 1910 (see Table 7-6). The prediction of this believer in the market power of large firms missed the actual returns earned by 150 percent, disregarding all the failures and the limping firms. His predictions of returns in dominant firms for 1935 missed the actual returns earned by an equally wide margin (see Table 7-7).

It could be argued, in view of the accusations of "watering" of common stock book values, that actual returns are understated by using book value of equity. However, the removal of "water" still leaves a wide gap between the predictions of the concentration-collusion doctrine and the returns actually realized by dominant firms. The U.S. Steel return for 1901–8, for example, rises from 5.2 percent to 7.8 percent with the "water" removed from book

TABLE 7–7

Predicted (1935) and Actual Rates of
Return of "Dominant" Firms

Firm	Predicted Rate of Return[a]	Actual Rate of Return	
	1935	1935	1936–40[b]
	Percentage		
U.S. Steel	17.0	0.1	4.0
Standard Oil (N.J.)	15.3	5.7	9.0
American Tobacco	13.3	10.6	11.5
International Harvester	15.0	6.5	7.5
Central Leather[c]	6.0	2.1	−8.1
Pullman	27.0	−0.1	3.0
American Sugar	14.7	3.5	3.0
Singer	19.7	11.5	7.2
General Electric	21.8	8.1	14.8
Corn Products	17.3	7.6	9.2
American Can	19.7	9.6	10.5
Westinghouse Electric	19.3	6.7	8.4
du Pont	13.5	11.8	13.8
International Paper	11.0	−1.9	5.4
National Biscuit	11.0	9.1	10.7
Western Electric	33.0	1.7	11.7
United Fruit	27.0	6.7	9.0
United Shoe Machinery	30.5	9.7	10.2
Eastman Kodak	29.5	11.3	13.2
Alcoa	29.5	5.5	16.6
Average	19.5	6.3	8.5

[a] "Profit rate that this firm would . . . realize if its market share and entry barriers exert their normal influence," W. G. Shepherd, THE ECONOMICS OF INDUSTRIAL ORGANIZATION (1979) at 219, Table 10A-3.

[b] Securities and Exchange Commission, SURVEY OF AMERICAN LISTED CORPORATIONS: DATA ON PROFITS AND OPERATIONS, 1936–1942 (1944). Rates of return calculated on beginning-of-year equity.

[c] Central Leather was merged into United States Leather, June 23, 1927. The actual earnings reported here are for the United States Leather Company.

values. This is still far short of Shepherd's predicted return of 22.0 percent. It is worth remembering that U.S. Steel annual profits were less in the ten years following its formation than those its constituent firms earned in the year preceding the merger ($108 million) despite its additional investments in plant and equipment. Shepherd's prediction of total earnings for U.S. Steel amounting to $397 million in 1910, using market share, entry barriers, and assumed "dominance" as his basis for the prediction,[58] can be contrasted with actual earnings amounting to only $108 million in

1910 and average annual earnings from 1901 through 1910 of $93 million. The promoters of U.S. Steel, incidentally, estimated annual earnings would be $100 million, certainly a conservative prediction. There appeared to be no expectation of monopoly gains from the merger since the constituent companies were earning $108 million prior to consolidation.[59]

The Perishability of Market Shares of Dominant Firms

Many of the combinations operated in the same way as the cartels they replaced. Typically they allocated specific markets to the units making up the combination or set production quotas and industry-wide price schedules.[60] They failed to improve efficiency and quickly lost ground to other firms when they attempted to maintain or raise prices. Even Standard Oil, noted for the economies it achieved by erecting large-scale refineries,[61] introducing assembly-line methods of packaging, and constructing pipe lines, slipped from 88 percent of petroleum product production in 1899 to 67 percent in 1909 as its methods were imitated by others.

The combinations that relied on initially large market shares to set and maintain supracompetitive prices had almost as little luck as the cartels they succeeded. They were not able to hold their market shares and their influence on prices faded quickly. The American Sugar Refinery Trust, formed in December 1887, from companies with 80 percent of the industry's capacity, cut output and forced a two-thirds increase in sugar refining margins. Its share of the country's output fell abruptly to 72.7 percent in 1888. In an attempt to maintain margins in 1889, American cut its output further from 23,000 barrels per day in 1888 to 19,915 barrels in 1889. Its share of production fell to 66 percent. The Trust's situation continued to worsen. By 1890, so much additional capacity had come into the industry that sugar margins fell 6 percent *below* those prevailing before the trust was formed, although American still produced more than 60 percent of total U.S. output.[62]

The same story was repeated following mergers late in 1891 and in mid-1892 that gave the American Sugar Refining Company, no longer a trust, 98 percent of the capacity east of the Rockies. By cutting production it raised refining margins 25 percent in 1892 (which raised the price of sugar by 5 percent). Its 1888–89 experience, when it raised margins by two thirds, had taught it to be less greedy. But by 1894, expansion of output by other firms forced margins back nearly to 1891 levels, despite output reductions by American. American's market share fell one quarter by 1894. It was still a dominant firm by today's FTC definition with its 75 percent share of market. It had lost most of its influence over price and output, however, regardless of its remaining 85 percent share of capacity. Although it improved efficiency by using large refineries and consolidating purchases, its share of market continued to fade. American's share fell to 49.3 percent in 1907 and 28 percent in 1917—although it continued to acquire other firms up to 1907.[63] And even with the high level of concentration in the industry, neither tacit collusion nor price leadership could maintain sugar margins. An explicit cartel agreement had to be arranged in 1896 to regulate production and restore margins. Nevertheless, margins dropped in 1898 and by 1899 deteriorated to the lowest level in the industry's history.

The history of American Can provides another episode illustrating the inability of a dominant firm to maintain supracompetitive prices and hold its market share. American Can was created in 1901 by merging 90 percent of all capacity in the can business. It raised prices by one quarter. In short order, American Can lost one third of its market, although it bought up more competitors and their output.[64] The independents' share of business rose from 10 percent preceding the merger to 40 percent within two years, even as their ranks were depleted by American's continuing acquisitions. Prices fell back to the pre-merger level, in spite of the 60 percent of the market remaining as an outlet for American Can's production.

Similar episodes are recorded for other industries. American Tobacco, formed in 1890 with 91 percent of the cigarette market, declined to 83.6 percent by 1893. Additional acquisitions in 1894 and 1895 brought it back to 85.6 percent of the market, but it dropped to 80.9 percent in 1896. More acquisitions brought it back to 93 percent in 1899. This position faded to 75.9 percent by 1903.[65]

Professor Whitney examined the fate of combinations formed in six different branches of the paper industry. He found that they all fared ingloriously.

> . . . Union Bag Machine Company of Pennsylvania acquired various patents which enabled it to make the first successful paper bags. In 1875 it took the name Union Bag and Paper Company. Its original 90

percent share of the market dropped sharply when the company, by restricting output in order to raise prices, began to attract competitors. . . .

The American Strawboard Company, organized in 1889, soon acquired or leased mills with 85 or 90 percent of the total output of paperboard. . . . New companies sprang up for the purpose of selling out to the combine. In 1897, 1901 and 1903 the combine and the remaining independents formed a common selling agency, but each time the emergence of new competition put an end to the agency. Meanwhile, wood pulp [paperboard] largely replaced straw [paperboard], and American Strawboard Company's share of the shrinking straw division fell to one-third by 1919. . . .

After the wallpaper manufacturers had tried a profit-pooling experiment which collapsed in 1888, firms controlling 60 percent of the industry combined in 1892 into the National Wallpaper Company. After this in turn failed, 98 percent of the industry established the Continental Wall Paper Company . . . in 1898. The new combine was liquidated in 1900. . . .

The United Paper Company, organized in 1892, was called the "Tissue Paper Trust." It raised prices, whereupon other mills turned to making tissue, and the merger was dissolved in 1899.

In 1898 . . . sixteen paper mills and a number of pulp mills . . . united as the International Paper Company. International had capacity to produce two-thirds of the newsprint made in North America and an unstated percentage of the coarse paper. By 1911 the newsprint proportion was down to about 30 percent. Commentators attribute this decline to the . . . umbrella of high costs and prices that invited new mills to compete . . .

In 1899 the American Writing Paper Company consolidated twenty-six separate producers; but its policy of reducing output opened the way to new firms, some of them founded by its own defecting officers. Between 1899 and 1952, during which time it underwent two reorganizations, the company's share of the market dropped from about 75 percent to less than 5 percent.[66]

A large market share or high concentration can be maintained only if the leading firms continually improve their efficiency and produce enough to keep prices at levels unattractive to efficient would-be entrants—whether those would-be entrants are new firms, old firms from other industries intent on finding profitable uses for talent and capital, customers who integrate backward to escape high prices, suppliers who integrate forward to obtain outlets for their production, or smaller firms in the same industry eager to obtain larger market shares.

The 1968 Task Force on Antitrust Policy recommended that leading firms in more than 70-percent-concentrated industries be dissolved if high concentration has been *persistent*. The Task Force selected with unerring precision the most inappropriate targets for antitrust action, namely those in which prices had been brought down to a level at which incentives to entry or expansion by small firms did not exist. Although the Task Force proposed that loss of economies be allowed as a defense against dissolution, it is easier and less costly to society to rely on the fact that the sheer persistence of concentration demonstrates that this is the most economical structure for an industry.

> The comparative private costs of firms of various sizes can be measured in only one way: by ascertaining whether firms of the various sizes are able to survive in the industry. Survival is the only test of a firm's ability to cope with all the problems: buying inputs, soothing laborers, finding customers, introducing new products and techniques, coping with fluctuation, . . . , etc. A cross-sectional study of the costs of inputs per unit of output in a given period measures only one facet of the firm's efficiency and yields no conclusion on efficiency in the large. Conversely, if a firm of a given size survives, we may infer that its costs are equal to those of other sizes of firms, being neither less (or firms of this size would grow in number relative to the industry) nor more (or firms of this size would decline in number relative to the industry).[67]

Turn-of-the-century combinations were often created in order to monopolize and, less often, to economize and improve service to customers. Where managements tried to use dominant positions to extract supracompetitive prices, however, the consolidations did not long remain dominant or viable (see Tables 3-1 and 3-2). Only where they quickly gave up monopolizing and price-raising activities and turned their attention to improving efficiency, product quality, product design, and marketing, and succeeded in matching or exceeding actual and would-be competitors, did they endure.

American business learned a lesson from this experience, which, perhaps, has not yet been learned by the proponents of market-concentration and dominant-firm doctrines. The royal road to profits is *not* to attempt to control markets but to compete. Professor Chandler's citation of the following excerpt from the 1901 annual report of National Biscuit, formed in 1898 by a merger of three regional consolidations (New York Biscuit, American Biscuit, and United States Baking Company), exemplifies the shift from the attempt at horizontal control to the competitive strategy that was necessary for successful survival.

> This Company is four years old, and it may be of interest to shortly review its history . . . When the company started, it was an aggregation of plants. It is now an organized business. When we look back through the four years, we find that a radical change has been wrought into our business. In the past, the managers of large industrial corporations have thought it necessary, for success, to control or limit competition, and that to do this we must either fight competition or buy it. The first meant a ruinous war of prices and great loss of profits; the second, constantly increasing capitalization. Experience soon proved to us that, instead of bringing success, either of these courses, if persevered in, must bring disaster. This led us to reflect whether it was necessary to control competition . . . We soon satisfied ourselves that within the company itself we must look for success.
>
> We turned our attention and bent our energies to improving the internal management of our own business, to getting the full benefit from purchasing our raw materials in large quantities, to economizing the expense of manufacture, to systematizing and rendering more effective our selling department, and above all things and before all things, to improving the quality of our goods and the condition in which they should reach the consumer . . .
>
> It became the settled policy of this company to buy out no competition.[68]

Conclusion

In Chapter 1, a rise in concentration was shown to be consistent with an increase in number of rival sellers in local markets even though the number of sellers in the nation decreases. Just as a series of chain mergers in which a dairy company, let us say, acquires a series of local dairy firms—one in each of the localities in which it makes acquisitions—may increase national concentration while leaving local concentration unchanged, so an expansion by a seller into a series of local markets may actually decrease local concentration while increasing national concentration. A leading firm in a concentrated industry may be faced with more competitors than a minor firm in a diffused industry.

Charles Keithahn, in his study of the brewing industry while on the FTC Bureau of Economics staff, concluded that

> . . . one must be careful in the inferences and conclusions drawn from an increase in national concentration. Most consumers face markets which are and always have been more concentrated than is indicated

by the level of national concentration. The rise in national concentration [from 11 percent to 63 percent] reflects a displacement of local and regional brewers by the [more efficient] national brewers rather than a dramatic decrease in the number of sellers faced by consumers. In short, few if any beer consumers were ever served by 400 brewers.[69]

But even an increase in local concentration does not imply a decrease in competition. Competition is not a function of the number of firms selling in a given market. The presence of a large number of firms may mean that competition has been suppressed. Attempts to maintain a large number frequently call for noncompetitive behavior and blunted competition. Superior performance and competitive behavior may decrease the number of sellers as the market grows more competitive. The resulting rise in concentration cannot bring noncompetitive pricing in its wake, however. Prices cannot be raised above the levels that would prevail with a larger number of firms since to do so would invite the larger number into the market and knock prices down. The data bear out the fact that either a decrease in number of sellers or a rise in concentration, when it occurs, brings a decline in cost and a fall in prices.

Professor Walter Adams warns us that

> . . . concentration must not be confused with monopoly. The mere fact that an industry is highly concentrated is not positive proof that the industry is monopolized or that its firms are in active collusion. . . . [I]t is even conceivable that as few as two companies are enough to provide effective competition in an industry.[70]

Some leading firms with large market shares have believed that they could behave monopolistically. The market informed them of their error and, frequently too late for the health of their enterprises, taught them and other businessmen that the attempt to monopolize is more often the road to losses than to profits, absent the government as an ally.

Notes

1. J. B. Clark, THE CONTROL OF TRUSTS 13 (1901).
2. J. B. Clark and J. M. Clark, THE CONTROL OF TRUSTS 184–85 (1912).
3. Eliot Jones, THE TRUST PROBLEM IN THE UNITED STATES 59 (1929).
4. Woodrow Wilson, THE NEW FREEDOM (1913).
5. George J. Stigler, PROCEEDINGS OF THE MONT PELERIN SOCIETY (1968).

6. "A major factor in the cycle phenomenon is the quite unequal flexibility of different sets of prices and, more explicitly, the stickiness of prices. . . . This stickiness of prices reflects, first; competition-restraining organization and, second, a wide-spread disposition to sacrifice volume to price—which is the characteristic exercise of monopoly power." Henry C. Simons, A POSITIVE PROGRAM FOR LAISSEZ FAIRE 20 (1934). Gardiner C. Means proceeded to equate concentration with restraint of competition and sticky prices with concentration. INDUSTRIAL PRICES AND THEIR RELATIVE INFLEXIBILITY (1935).

7. The studies are summarized by L. W. Weiss, *The Concentration-Profits Relationship and Antitrust* in Goldschmid, Mann, and Weston (eds.), INDUSTRIAL CONCENTRATION: THE NEW LEARNING 184 (1974).

8. George J. Stigler, *Industrial Organization and Economic Progress* in L. D. White (ed.), THE STATE OF THE SOCIAL SCIENCES 269 (1956). Donald F. Turner cites evidence from this study in his reply to FORTUNE's proposal that antimerger policy be made less restrictive. *The Antitrust Chief Replies*, 73 FORTUNE (April 1966).

9. P. David Qualls, *Market Structure and Price-Cost Margin Flexibility in American Manufacturing, 1958-1970*, FTC Working Paper no. 1 (Mar. 1977); Steven Lustgarten and Alan I. Mendelowitz, *The Covariability of Industrial Concentration and Employment Fluctuations*, 52 JOURNAL OF BUSINESS 291 (Apr. 1979).

10. W. F. Crowder and W. L. Thorp, *Concentration and Product Characteristics As Factors in Price-Quantity Behavior*, 30 AMERICAN ECONOMIC REVIEW 390 (Feb. 1941). Not only was there no relationship between price rigidity and concentration, but there had been no increase in rigidity, as claimed by Means, between earlier periods and the 1930s. Professor Dennis Carlton remarks, in his *Contracts, Price Rigidity, and Market Equilibrium*, 87 JOURNAL OF POLITICAL ECONOMY 1036 (Oct. 1979), on this curious claim by Means as follows:

> It is unclear why the earlier work of Mills (1927) is not cited as the research which discovered administered prices. Perhaps it was because Means attracted widespread political attention by arguing that changes in the U.S. economy had altered the laws of supply and demand, made prices rigid, and were responsible in part for the severity of the depression. In contrast, Mills mainly presented data, drew few dramatic conclusions about market behavior, and found that prices had become more flexible in the 1920s. By 1940, several researchers (Humphrey 1937; Pedersen and Petersen 1938; Tucker 1938) had shown that, as Mills had suggested, inflexible prices had characterized many sectors of the U.S. and other economies as far back as 1800. Means's claim that the rise of large firms had been making prices more and more rigid over time is therefore false. Still, Means's arguments continue to attract attention and support.

11. H. J. DePodwin and R. T. Selden, *Business Pricing Policies and Inflation*, 71 JOURNAL OF POLITICAL ECONOMY 116 (Apr. 1963).

12. G. Stigler and J. Kindahl, THE BEHAVIOR OF INDUSTRIAL PRICES 7 (1970).

13. G. Stigler, *The Kinky Oligopoly Demand Curve and Rigid Prices*, 55

JOURNAL OF POLITICAL ECONOMY 439 (Oct. 1947), reprinted in Stigler, ORGANIZATION OF INDUSTRY 208 (1968).

14. See note 9 *supra.*
15. Richard A. Miller, *Market Structure and Industrial Performance,* 17 JOURNAL OF INDUSTRIAL ECONOMICS 104 (Apr. 1969).
16. J. S. Bain, *Relation of Profit Rate to Industry Concentration: American Manufacturing, 1936–1940,* 65 QUARTERLY JOURNAL OF ECONOMICS 293 (Aug. 1951).
17. J. S. Bain, BARRIERS TO NEW COMPETITION (1956); H. M. Mann, *Seller Concentration, Barriers to Entry, and Rates of Return in Thirty Industries, 1950–1960,* 48 REVIEW OF ECONOMICS & STATISTICS 296 (Aug. 1966).
18. George J. Stigler, CAPITAL AND RATES OF RETURN IN MANUFACTURING INDUSTRIES (1961).
19. See Stigler *supra* at 68 n. 22.
20. U.S., *White House Task Force Report on Antitrust Policy,* reprinted in TRADE REGULATION REPORTS (CCH) Supp. to N. 415 (May 26, 1969).
21. Entry should be understood as the entry of additional capacity. Whether the additional capacity is created by firms already resident in an industry or by newly entering firms is irrelevant. Lester Telser corroborates the fact that entry occurs in the form of additional firms as well as by expansion of capacity of resident firms. See discussion at note 21 in Chapter 1. Also, see Daryl N. Winn and Dick Leabo, *Rates of Return, Concentration, and Growth—Question of Disequilibrium,* 17 JOURNAL OF LAW & ECONOMICS 97 (Apr. 1974).
22. Y. Brozen, *The Antitrust Task Force Deconcentration Recommendation,* 13 JOURNAL OF LAW & ECONOMICS 279 (Oct. 1970), reprinted in Y. Brozen, THE COMPETITIVE ECONOMY 113 (1975). The convergence phenomenon, which is a result of capacity being attracted to high-return industries and capital leaving low-return industries, should not be confused with the regression phenomenon. The latter is a consequence of chance variations.
23. The study by Mann had used thirty industries, that by Stigler seventeen —even fewer than Bain had used for his sample. *Infra* note 27.
24. Y. Brozen, *Bain's Concentration and Rates of Return Revisited,* 14 JOURNAL OF LAW & ECONOMICS 351 (Oct. 1971).
25. Actually, forty-three industries were used by Bain, but he combined the cosmetics industry and the soap industry (and used the soap concentration ratio for the combination). The two were separated in the 98-industry list.
26. Y. Brozen, *Concentration and Profits: Does Concentration Matter?* 19 ANTITRUST BULLETIN 381 (Summer 1974), reprinted in Brozen *supra* note 22, at 135. For additional examples of the bias resulting from the use of small samples of industries to measure the concentration-profitability relationship, see Brozen, *The Persistence of "High Rates of Return" in High Stable Concentration Industries,* 14 JOURNAL OF LAW & ECONOMICS 501 (Oct. 1971).
27. Bain's 1956 study for the postwar period 1947–51 found larger differences between rates of return in concentrated and unconcentrated industries than in the 1936–40 period. The finding was, however, based on only twenty industries, a small sample with a greater likelihood of small sample bias than that used for the 1936–40 period. See Brozen *supra* note 24. The two studies for the postwar period mentioned in the

Antitrust Task Force Staff Director's letter were those by Mann *supra* note 17.

28. Using two-digit industries, G. Gambles, *Structural Determinants of Profit Performance in United States Manufacturing Industries, 1947–1967* (dissertation, University of North Carolina, 1969) also finds an occasional negative relationship between profitability and concentration. This also appears to be the case for three-digit industries in 1969. H. Demsetz, THE MARKET CONCENTRATION DOCTRINE 19 (1973).

29. The sum of the coefficients of the logs of GBV, INV, TPA, and ADV add up to 0.999 in 1972 and in 1963. We would expect the sum of the coefficients to be 1.0 if these independent variables accurately represent all the capital used in each industry. That they do add up to very near 1.0 is a surprise since the investment in receivables, land, and in research and development is omitted from the equation for lack of industry data. Also, TPA and ADV are imperfect proxies for the investment in human capital and information. If investments in land, receivables, and R&D are correlated with GBV, INV, and ADV, and it seems reasonable to believe that they are, this accounts for the sum of coefficients behaving as it does.

30. Sam Peltzman, *The Gains and Losses from Industrial Concentration,* 20 JOURNAL OF LAW & ECONOMICS 229 (Oct. 1977). An example of the process, which produces lower cost and increased concentration, is discussed in Morris Adelman, *The A&P Case,* 63 QUARTERLY JOURNAL OF ECONOMICS 238 (May 1949).

31. Y. Brozen, *Significance of Profit Data for Antitrust Policy,* 14 ANTITRUST BULLETIN 119 (Spring 1969), reprinted in S. Peltzman and J. F. Weston, PUBLIC POLICY TOWARD MERGERS 110 (1968).

32. A. D. Chandler, THE VISIBLE HAND 375 (1977).

33. George Stigler, THEORY OF PRICE (1952); *Monopoly and Oligopoly by Merger,* 40 AMERICAN ECONOMIC REVIEW 23 (May 1950); Dean A. Worcester, Jr., *Why Dominant Firms Decline,* 65 JOURNAL OF POLITICAL ECONOMY 338 (Aug. 1957).

34. The accounting rate of return earned by U.S. Steel from 1901 through 1908 amounted to only 5.2 percent. Even if we use the capitalization of the constituent firms from which U.S. Steel was formed, its return was less than 8 percent and its average annual profits were less than those that had been earned by its constituent firms despite the additional plant and equipment added by U.S. Steel.

35. H. Demsetz, THE MARKET CONCENTRATION DOCTRINE 21 (1973). Similar evidence for 1959–61 may be found in Asch & Marcus, *Returns to Scale on Advertising,* 15 ANTITRUST BULLETIN 37, Table 1 (Spring 1970). Also, Richard Osborn, *Concentration and the Profitability of Small Manufacturing Corporations,* 10 QUARTERLY REVIEW OF ECONOMICS AND BUSINESS 15 (Summer 1970) demonstrates "that the apparently greater profitability of . . . concentrated industries is really a function of size distribution rather than of concentration." Using 1963 data, he finds that the larger firms in all industries, grouped by concentration quartile, are more profitable than the smaller firms, but that the largest firms in concentrated industries are no more profitable than in the low-concentration industries. Concentrated industries appear more profitable, then, because they have many fewer small firms.

36. H. Demsetz, *Two Systems of Belief About Monopoly,* in Goldschmid, Mann, and Weston, *supra* note 7 at 180, Table 9. The partial correlations

found in Table 9 are more accurate than those in Table 8 since the introduction of an advertising variable allows for the relatively greater understatement of assets and overstatement of profitability of advertising-intensive firms and industries. The use of an R&D variable, in addition, would have provided an even more accurate measurement of the relationship.

37. H. Demsetz, *More on Collusion and Advertising: A Reply,* 19 JOURNAL OF LAW & ECONOMICS 205–6 (Apr. 1976).
38. Asch and Marcus *supra* note 35, at 36.
39. B. Lev, *Economic Determinants of Some Time-Series Properties of Earnings* (Working paper, presented at the University of Chicago accounting workshop, unpublished, Jan. 1977).
40. John R. Carter, *Collusion, Efficiency, and Antitrust,* 21 JOURNAL OF LAW & ECONOMICS 435, (1978).
41. John E. Kwoka, Jr., MARKET SHARES, CONCENTRATION, AND COMPETITION IN MANUFACTURING INDUSTRIES (1978).
42. See *id.* at 24.
43. Bradley T. Gale and Ben Branch, SCALE ECONOMIES: THE EVIDENCE FROM BUSINESS-UNIT DATA 14 (Sept. 1979).
44. See Kwoka *supra* note 41, at 33.
45. See L. Weiss *supra* note 7, at 199.
46. B. Erickson, *Economics of Price Fixing,* 2 ANTITRUST LAW & ECONOMICS REVIEW 83 (Spring 1969). The point is implied in George Stigler's statement that, "the restriction of output by quotas, the introduction of common sales agencies, and the other paraphernalia of cartels . . . often arise as defensive measures against progressive industries." Stigler, *supra* note 8, at 272.
47. P. Asch and J. J. Seneca, *Is Collusion Profitable?* 58 REVIEW OF ECONOMICS & STATISTICS 1 (Feb. 1976). It has also been shown that collusion, or rather the difficulties of reaching agreement, which causes agreements once made to be left unchanged in the face of change in circumstances depressing profits, itself causes low profits in some instances. B. Fog, *How Are Cartel Prices Determined?* JOURNAL OF INDUSTRIAL ECONOMICS 16 (Nov. 1956).
48. A. Hunter, COMPETITION AND THE LAW (1966). Emphasis supplied.
49. See Stigler *supra* note 8.
50. Franklin Fisher, *The Demand for Aluminum Ingot in the United States,* A PRIORI INFORMATION AND TIME SERIES ANALYSIS (1961); G. W. Stocking and W. F. Mueller, *The Cellophane Case and the New Competition,* 45 AMERICAN ECONOMIC REVIEW 54 (Mar. 1955); Kaiser Aluminum & Chemical Corporation, AT ISSUE: THE CONTROVERSY OVER CONCENTRATED INDUSTRIES 12 (1978).
51. Steven Lustgarten, INDUSTRIAL CONCENTRATION, PRODUCTIVITY GROWTH, AND CONSUMER WELFARE (forthcoming). More rapid productivity growth in industries with a declining number of firms might be expected because of a decline in the number of plants of suboptimal capacity, as pointed out by Professor Leonard Weiss.
52. See Stigler, *Monopoly and Oligopoly by Merger, supra* note 33, reprinted in Stigler, THE ORGANIZATION OF INDUSTRY 102 (1968).
53. Shaw Livermore, *The Success of Industrial Mergers,* 50 QUARTERLY JOURNAL OF ECONOMICS 68 (Nov. 1935).
54. Arthur Dewing, *A Statistical Test of the Success of Consolidations,* 31 QUARTERLY JOURNAL OF ECONOMICS 84 (1921–22), reprinted in Y.

Brozen *supra* note 22, at 124. See W. G. Shepherd, THE ECONOMICS OF INDUSTRIAL ORGANIZATION at 196, Figure 10-2, and at 219, Table 10A-3 (1979), for estimates of rates of return expected under the market-concentration approach from various market shares and levels of concentration.

55. An exception could be the case if a single large-scale plant would replace most or all the small plants in the industry and the customer relations and brand-name capital of all firms are needed to utilize the plant.

56. See Stigler *supra* note 52, at 98. J. M. Clark suggested that "The outstanding motives to combination include monopoly profits, defense against cut-throat competition and economic stability, promoters' profits from the reorganization of combinations, as distinct from their operation, the economies of combination, and the lust of economic empire." J. M. Clark, SOCIAL CONTROL OF BUSINESS 378 (1939). The most remarkable of these to modern readers is perhaps the prevention of cutthroat competition, which Clark deduced as "the result of an over supply of fixed and specialized investment and may be defined as a condition in which prices are forced below 'cost'," *id.*, at 379. Modern theoretical economists are familiar with the difficulties that fixed costs pose for competitive equilibria, and in this light Clark does point to a fundamental economic issue in industries with specialized equipment and fixed costs. Whether it is true that the consolidations, and the trusts and cartels that preceded them, were in part a response to the problems caused by such circumstances is an interesting and unresolved problem.

57. See Livermore *supra* note 53.

58. See Shepherd *supra* note 54.

59. See Dewing *supra* note 54.

60. A. D. Chandler, THE VISIBLE HAND: THE MANAGERIAL REVOLUTION IN AMERICAN BUSINESS 320 (1977).

61. Chandler reports that the Standard Trust, formed in 1882, consolidated refinery capacity, decreasing the number of refineries from 53 to 22 between 1882 and 1885, with over two fifths of the trust's output concentrated in three huge new refineries at Bayonne, Philadelphia, and Cleveland, and cut the average cost of producing a gallon of refined oil by two thirds (from 1.5¢ to 0.5¢). See *id.* at 324.

62. Richard Zerbe, *The American Sugar Refinery Company, 1887–1914: The Story of a Monopoly*, 12 JOURNAL OF LAW & ECONOMICS 353 (Oct. 1969).

63. See Chandler *supra* note 60, at 328–29.

64. S. Whitney, ANTITRUST POLICIES 197, 199 (1958); and speech by William C. Stock, *Revolution in Containers*, before Newcomen Society (New York, 1960), cited by Harold Fleming, 10,000 COMMANDMENTS (1951).

65. U.S., Bureau of Corporations, REPORT OF THE COMMISSIONER ON THE TOBACCO INDUSTRIES 329 (1909).

66. See Whitney *supra* note 64, at 356–57.

67. See Stigler *supra* note 52, at 98–99.

68. Cited in Chandler *supra* note 60, at 335.

69. Charles F. Keithahn, THE BREWING INDUSTRY 19 (Dec. 1978).

70. Walter Adams, THE STRUCTURE OF THE AMERICAN ECONOMY 546 (1961).

8

Are U.S. Manufacturing Markets Monopolized?

Dɪscᴜssɪᴏɴs of monopoly in the United States dwell almost exclusively on manufacturing industries. Typically, a collection of learned inquiries on monopoly, such as *Monopoly Power and Economic Performance*[1], has not one paper dealing with the licensing of occupations or with limitations on entry into plumbing contracting, liquor and drug retailing, taxi operation, banking, sale of electricity, or truck transportation. Nor do such collections include studies discussing Interstate Commerce Commission (ICC) rate floors, sponsorship of cartels by the Department of Agriculture and the Federal Maritime Commission, minimum wage law effects on the size structure of firms and concentration, limitations on entry and on the introduction of new products imposed by the Food and Drug Administration, or even that mother of monopoly, tariffs. Also, this anthology omits any analysis of the performance of government monopolies such as the Postal Service, the Tennessee Valley Authority, the uranium enrichment service of the Department of Energy, or the numerous local government monopolies of water, electricity, and mass transit. Nor is the monopolization of jobs by the Airline Pilots Association, the Teamsters, or the railroad brotherhoods mentioned.

If one were to believe what is said in the majority of studies analyzing the monopoly problem, any increase in the size of a firm or in concentration must be anticompetitive. The price of general merchandising services in rural areas, according to those studies, must have increased as a consequence of the growth of large mail order organizations, such as Sears, Roebuck and Montgomery Ward. The concentration of a large share of this business in their hands must have produced higher prices. Henry Ford was lionized for what he did to reduce the price of automobiles and raise wages, but the 60 percent share of the market attained by his company in 1921 would be frowned on today as obvious evidence of oligopoly or dominance. The extraordinary returns earned by the Ford Motor Company, frequently exceeding 100 percent, would confirm its antisocial character. That the nearly bankrupt General Motors Company of 1921 would ever surpass Ford or that the then unborn Chrysler Company would beat Ford by the late 1930s would be inconceivable.[2]

Professor John Kenneth Galbraith's *The New Industrial State* tells us that a success story like Henry Ford's could never happen in modern America. Today's industrial giants are not as profit-minded as Ford and his ilk, and they do not serve the market as he did. From Galbraith's view, a sort of corrupted socialism prevails in the United States. The economy is planned, and that is good. But it is planned by private organizations—the 500 largest industrial corporations—and that is bad. To improve the situation, ". . . the educational and scientific estate . . . [must] become a decisive instrument of political power [under a strongly creative political hand]."[3] The author is not concerned with his "fact" that markets are controlled, but only with who does the controlling. Consumer sovereignty does not shine in his firmament of values.

Galbraith equates severely constrained private planning with dictatorial state planning. He "slips from the proposition that the firm plans to the proposition that the economy is planned without realizing that such statements possess only a verbal similarity."[4] He recognizes no difference between the ability of a steel firm, for example, to force the market to conform to its plan and the ability of the state, with its powers, to force conformance. Galbraith insists that private organizations, if they are "big in an industry" can influence "prices and costs and command capital [because they have] access to advertising, and selling resources, and possess . . . the other requisites of market power."[5]

Galbraith tells us that half of all economic activity in the United States is controlled by the 500 largest industrial corporations.[6] His data are not quite accurate. Half of all *manufacturing* employment occurs in the 500 largest. Manufacturing provides only one fourth of all employment in the United States. This means that the 500 largest industrial corporations provide one eighth of all employment rather than one half—a 300 percent error in his assertion.

The problem before us, however, is not to determine how inaccurate he is but how to measure monopoly—the ability of a business to control the market. This we must first settle. Then we can move on to a determination of whether the market controls U.S. business or these businesses control the market.

The Structural Test for Monopoly

Galbraith follows a forty-year-old tradition still prevalent among economists. He uses a simple structural test as a measure of market power. His approach is simpler than that of almost all economists in that he uses aggregate concentration, rather than percentage of a market, as his measure of market power. American Motors is among the biggest 500 industrial companies in the United States, ranking in the top quarter of the 500, but its 2 percent share of domestically produced new automobiles and its 0.6 percent of the domestic market for all automobiles (new and used) sold in any given year would hardly be regarded as giving it much influence over the price, quantity, or quality of automobiles. A Woodward Governor or a Sanborn Map Company, each "dominant" in its market (engine governors and fire insurance maps) but neither qualifying for the list of 500 largest companies, would be said by many economists to have more market power selling 80 to 100 percent of the product offered in their markets. This is a larger market share by far than that of American Motors, one of the 150 largest concerns in the United States.

The typical approach among members of the "bust-'em-up" school to the determination of which markets are monopolized is exemplified by the 1968 report of the antitrust task force headed by Professor Phil Neal. It tells us that an oligopolistic industry is one in which four or fewer firms produce 70 percent or more of its product. It advises amending the antitrust laws to make it possible to break up any oligopolistic firm; that is, any firm that turns out more than 15 percent of its industry's domestic output where the biggest four firms do 70 percent or more of the industry's business and the value of the industry's sales exceeds $500 million (1.3 billion at today's prices).[7]

Economists frequently use the simple structural test used by the

227

Neal Commission as their method of categorizing markets.[8] However, most no longer argue that an oligopolistic market, defined in the manner of the Neal Commission, is necessarily or automatically a cartelized or monopolized market.[9] They readily concede that "seller concentration is a necessary, but not sufficient, condition."[10] They do argue that the cost of arranging and policing explicit collusion is less and cartelization (shared monopoly) more likely in concentrated markets.

Analyses of the extent of competition and monopoly in the United States use this same simple structural test in classifying markets.[11] They sometimes include industries in the monopoly category that are not concentrated but in which cartelization is compelled or supported by a government agency. The fluid milk, trucking, and the 1960s air transport markets, for example, fall in this category. Automobiles, photographic equipment, locomotives, chewing gum, corn syrup, biscuits, cigarettes, newsprint, newspapers, primary aluminum, and copper mining are all classed as monopolized in 1939 in a study by Professor Stigler on the basis of their high concentration ratios.[12]

We may believe the cost of collusion to be low in a concentrated industry, suspect that undetected collusion occurs in some of these industries, and we may even find actual instances of collusion (as in the electrical products conspiracy), but it does not follow that all concentrated industries should be classed as monopolistic or oligopolistic.[13] It can be argued that an industry is not necessarily monopolized even with the actual presence of a scheme for regulating prices and output. Lower output and higher prices may not occur even with a formal agreement among competing firms to privately regulate a market.[14]

The members of a highly concentrated industry may explicitly agree to adhere to assigned quotas and to avoid cutting prices and yet have no influence over their market. If there are no arbitrary barriers to entry and the number of entrepreneurs is abundant[15] or if customers are large,[16] a cartel will not succeed in controlling the market despite a small number of firms in the industry. The Organization of Petroleum Exporting Countries (OPEC) enjoys an unusual success. Its success came to it in part because of the hindrance of expansion of producing capacity outside the OPEC by price and allocation controls in the United States.[17] Also, the increasingly onerous tax treatment of oil firms in the United States, the United Kingdom, Norway, Indonesia, and, especially,

Alaska restrains the growth of non-OPEC capacity. For instance, the Alaskan state government enacted thirteen tax increases in ten years. These reduced private returns on investment in North Slope production to 9 percent—less than could be earned by the purchase of U.S. Treasury issues. As a consequence, operators on the North Slope in 1979 abandoned efforts that would have added a million barrels a day to the U.S. supply.[18] Similarly, exploration in the British sector of the North Sea was cut back because of governmental greed. As a result, annual output planned for the 1980s has fallen by 800,000 barrels per day. These factors plus the 90 percent reduction in Iranian shipments in 1979 and 1980 as a consequence of civil disorder and the reduction in Iraqi output following the outbreak of the Iraqi-Iranian War have supported and increased the OPEC's prices.

A Dynamic Test for Monopolization

We need better means for determining the presence or absence of monopoly than simple structural measures. Stigler proposed a test that is somewhat more useful and indicative than the usual structural approach: if an industry is monopolized, it will tend to earn at least the average rate of return and, frequently, above average returns on its capital. If monopoly is present, above average rates of return will frequently tend to stay above the average.[19] This test is not a sufficient condition for showing the presence of monopoly.[20] The long-run equilibrium position in a competitive market may also move as the industry moves toward its long-run equilibrium position. Recurring unforeseen positive movements in demand or declines in cost could keep a competitive industry more profitable than the average.[21] But sustained above-average profitability is a condition, which, if it occurs, is consistent with the presence of monopoly although it is not a proof of the absence of competiton.[22]

The test is difficult to apply because the readily available data are not as informative as we need. The accounting rates of return on equity in various industries compiled by the Internal Revenue Service, the Securities and Exchange Commission, the Federal Trade Commission, and the First National City Bank are not economic rates of return. They are biased upward, more for some industries than for others, because of the necessarily conservative approach of accountants. They do not capitalize several types of investment (spending on research, advertising, development of dealer networks, training of the work force, breaking in plant); they do not revalue assets to correct for changes in the price level; and they write off investment in the projects that fail.[23] Accounting rates of return are biased downward in rapidly growing industries, in which a large proportion of assets are new, relative to rates of return in slowly growing or declining industries, in which a large proportion of assets are more fully depreciated.[24]

Professor Fritz Machlup warns us:

> Although many monopolistic firms may make profits, there are several fundamental pitfalls in the idea that the accounting rate of profit can show the degree to which monopoly power is exercised.
>
> That the accounting rates of profit, the only ones that may be available to the statistician, are such unreliable indices of economic excess profits and monopoly situations is unfortunate, since the relationship between supernormal profits and monopolistic barriers against potential entrants into the industry is highly significant. Firms sheltered against newcomers' competition are likely to earn higher returns on their investments than firms in industries wide open to anybody willing to start a new business.
>
> Before results of investigations of "adjusted profit rates" become available we cannot say whether and how it will be possible to separate monopoly elements. But we know for certain that such a separation is not possible on the basis of the unadjusted accounting rates of profit and that these rates cannot be accepted as a measurement of the degree of monopoly.[25]

We may still learn something by examinining *trends* in the accounting returns on net worth in leading manufacturing corporations grouped by industry, however. If returns remain high in high-return industries and low in low-return industries without being demonstrably the result of arbitrary accounting conventions, then we can at least say that we have failed to show that manufacturing is not monopolistic. The implication would follow that Galbraith *may* be correct in saying that each of the 500 biggest industrial companies controls its market and that U.S. markets are monopolized, at least in the case of manufactured products. If, however, high rates of return erode and low returns improve with returns converging on the average rate, then we may be entitled to suspect that the market is competitive. We may assert that the market does manage to reallocate resources to the goods most preferred by consumers and away from the production of less preferred goods. The assertion will rest on better evidence than the absolute or relative sizes of firms.

What the Data Show

Let us examine the most profitable industries of 1948, a cycle peak year. Then let us look at their earnings ranks eight years later, the next year in which a cyclical peak occurred without the distortions introduced by the price controls that prevailed during the Korean War. Doing this, we find that the average rank of the top twenty in 1948 out of forty industries fell. They ended in 1956 with a random distribution among the forty ranks, ranging from fourth to bottom rank instead of top to middle rank (see Table 8-1). The average earnings rank among the 1948 top twenty dropped to very near the average for all forty industries (from an average rank of 10.5 to 19.6). Similarly, the average industry in the bottom half did not remain in the middle of the bottom half. Its rate of return rank rose from the average for the bottom half to very near the average for all the industries ranked (from 30.5 to 21.4). This is exactly what is supposed not to occur in monopolized markets. What happened is what we would expect in a group of competitive industries.

That this result is not peculiar to the period is demonstrated by the behavior of the ranks of forty industries from 1966 to 1979. The average industry in the 1966 top twenty dropped from a 10.5 rank in 1966 to 18.2 in 1979. The average industry in the 1966 bottom twenty rose from a 30.5 rank in 1966 to 22.8 in 1979 (see Table 8-2).

The years 1948, 1956, 1966, and 1979 were all business cycle peaks. It is surprising to find such marked convergence of industry profitability ranks from one peak year to another. Cyclically sensitive industries, such as automobiles and machinery, tend to have high returns in prosperous years (and low returns in depressed years). They would be top-ranked industries in these peak years. As a result, we would not expect the average ranks of the top and bottom groups of industries to converge as completely as they did from one prosperous year to another. That they did despite the use only of prosperous years (and use of accounting rates of return) for the comparison is strong evidence of an absence of pervasive monopoly. As the White House Antitrust Task Force pointed out, "the persistence of high profits over extended time periods and over whole industries . . . suggest artificial restraints on output and the absence of fully effective competition."[26] But persistence of high profits did *not* occur.

While shifts in the rate-of-return ranks among manufacturing industries provides evidence that production ebbs and flows are dictated by competitive markets, the question might still be raised whether the pattern differs between concentrated and diffused industries. Stigler hypothesizes that

> Competitive industries will have a volatile pattern of rates of return, for the movements into high-profit industries and out of low-profit industries will—together with the flow of new disturbances of equilibrium—lead to a constantly changing hierarchy of rates of return. In the monopolistic industries, on the other hand, the usually profitable industries will be able to preserve their preferential position for considerable periods of time.[27]

TABLE 8–1

Return on Net Worth in Leading Manufacturing Corporations and Rank by Industry Group, 1948 and 1956
(Return Measured on Beginning of Year Net Worth)

Industry	Number of Firms		Percentage Return on Book Net Worth		Rank by Book Return	
	1948	1956	1948	1956	1948	1956
Lumber	29	26	29.3	12.6	1	20
Appliances	45	36	26.6	12.1	2	25
Textiles	126	80	26.2	6.6	3	39.5
Automobiles and trucks	28	14	26.0	14.6	4	12.5
Distilling	12	12	24.8	6.8	5	38
Office equipment	27	27	24.3	17.5	6	7.5
Automobile parts	68	57	23.5	13.3	7	19
Brewing	31	24	22.8	8.1	8	35
Petroleum products	44	116	22.1	14.6	9	12.5
Baking	24	18	21.4	12.2	10	22.5
Drugs, soap, cosmetics	32	46	21.3	19.9	11	4
Building and plumbing equipment	77	81	21.0	11.2	12	30
Soft drinks	17	15	20.4	13.9	13.5	14.5
Pulp and paper	85	73	20.4	13.8	13.5	16.5
Electrical equipment, radio, and television	80	97	20.3	11.8	15	27.5
Machinery	166	168	18.6	14.9	16	11
Furniture	18	19	18.3	11.8	17	27.5
Other stone, clay	45	55	18.2	15.8	18	9
Total Manufacturing	1,710	1,843	18.2	13.9	—	—

232

TABLE 8–1 (Cont.)

Return on Net Worth in Leading Manufacturing Corporations
and Rank by Industry Group, 1948 and 1956
(Return Measured on Beginning of Year Net Worth)

Industry	Number of Firms		Percentage Return on Book Net Worth		Rank by Book Return	
	1948	1956	1948	1956	1948	1956
Chemicals	65	69	17.7	15.5	19.5	10
Other metal products	94	112	17.7	12.1	19.5	25
Cement	31	30	17.0	20.6	21	2
Other food	82	88	16.9	11.7	22	29
Hardware and tools	47	51	16.3	12.2	23	22.5
Glass	13	18	15.5	17.7	24	6
Nonferrous metals	34	46	14.9	17.8	25	5
Shoes	25	25	14.7	10.3	26	32
Printing and publishing	34	42	14.3	13.8	27.5	16.5
Tobacco products	23	20	14.3	12.1	27.5	25
Tires, rubber products	25	29	14.0	13.6	29	18
Iron and steel	54	56	13.9	13..	30	14.5
Apparel	33	49	13.8	7.8	31	36
Agricultural implements	12	10	13.6	8.3	32.5	34
Leather	9		13.6	10.8	32.5	31
Paint	19	22	13.1	17.5	34	7.5
Dairy products	18	12	13.0	12.4	35	21
Sugar	23	23	12.2	6.6	36	39.5
Shipbuilding	6	8	11.7	20.0	37	3
Railway equipment	27	21	9.2	9.9	38	33
Meat packing	21	15	7.2	7.7	39	37
Aircraft	27	41	2.9	21.4	40	1

Source: First National City Bank MONTHLY ECONOMIC LETTER, April issues, 1949, 1950, 1957, 1958.

Note: The average rank of the industries may be summarized as follows:

	Average Rank	
	1948	1956
Industries 1–20 (1948)	10.5	19.6
Industries 21–40 (1948)	30.5	21.4
All industries	20.5	20.5

If entry into concentrated industries is difficult and firms in these industries restrain output to elevate profitability to supracompetitive levels—that is, if monopoly and concentration are correlated —we can expect profitable concentrated industries to maintain their returns. There will be little scrambling of profit ranks among concentrated industries in successive years. If atomism and competition are correlated, then attractive profits induce new entry and expansion by resident firms in unconcentrated industries.

The resulting expansion of capacity and output erode high profits and drop the ranks of the relatively higher profit industries, thus causing a greater scrambling of industry profitability ranks with time because of the reallocation of resources in response to profits and the effects of random disturbances.

For the 1919–28 period, the correlation of profit ranks for successive years in concentrated industries (four-firm concentration ratio 60 percent or greater) is significantly *poorer* than in the unconcentrated industries (less than 50 percent concentrated) or those that are 50 to 60 percent concentrated (see Table 8-3). Monopoly was not a correlate of concentration in that period.

TABLE 8–2

Return on Net Worth in Leading Manufacturing Corporations
and Rank by Industry Group, 1966 and 1979
(Return Measured on Beginning of Year Net Worth)

Industry	Number of Firms		Percentage Return on Book Net Worth		Rank by Book Return	
	1966	1979	1966	1979	1966	1979
Soft drinks	17	13	22.0	22.4	1	4
Instruments and photographic goods	114	79	21.2	19.6	2	10
Drugs and medicines	39	25	21.0	22.5	3	3
Hardware and tools	44	18	19.2	18.3	4	16
Office equipment, computers	51	42	18.1	20.7	5.5	8
Printing and publishing	89	41	18.1	19.2	5.5	13
Soaps, cosmetics	34	24	17.9	19.5	7	11
Automobiles and trucks	15	6	17.8	18.2	8	17.5
Electrical equipment, radio and television	339	132	16.7	16.8	9	24
Machinery	210	101	16.0	18.2	10	17.5
Clothing and apparel	85	52	15.9	16.5	11	27
Aircraft and space	55	25	15.7	21.8	12.5	6.5
Nonferrous metals	66	23	15.7	16.5	12.5	27
Chemical	79	52	15.1	17.3	14	21
Appliances	21	13	15.0	16.5	15	27
Agricultural implements, construction equipment	44	39	14.7	17.0	16	23
Automobile parts	41	23	14.5	21.8	17	6.5
Furniture	37	23	14.2	9.7	18	39
Other metal products	63	62	14.0	16.6	19	25
Paint and varnish	22	8	13.9	11.4	20.5	37
Total Manufacturing	—	1,280	14.2	18.4	—	—

TABLE 8–2 (Cont.)
Return on Net Worth in Leading Manufacturing Corporations
and Rank by Industry Group, 1966 and 1979
(Return Measured on Beginning of Year Net Worth)

Industry	Number of Firms		Percentage Return on Book Net Worth		Rank by Book Return	
	1966	1979	1966	1979	1966	1979
Baking	15	7	13.9	17.9	20.5	19
Tobacco products	12	7	13.8	22.1	22	5
Other food	84	24	13.3	17.4	23	20
Shoes and leather	25	16	13.1	14.4	24	34.5
Tires and rubber products	58	35	13.0	7.1	25	40
Brewing	17	10	12.8	15.3	26	31.5
Glass	15	12	12.7	14.4	27	34.5
Petroleum products, refining	106	86	12.6	22.9	28	1
Dairy products	13	6	12.4	15.7	29	29.5
Miscellaneous manufacturing	99	32	12.1	19.4	30	12
Textile products	70	36	11.9	10.0	31.5	38
Building and plumbing equipment	60	12	11.9	22.6	31.5	2
Paper	75	49	11.8	17.1	33	22
Lumber and wood products	27	33	11.0	20.1	34	9
Distilling	13	3	10.6	14.9	35	33
Iron and steel	82	46	9.3	11.5	36	36
Other stone, clay	44	19	9.2	15.7	37	29.5
Sugar	15	12	9.1	15.3	38	31.5
Cement	17	11	7.0	19.0	39	14
Meat packing	27	10	5.5	18.9	40	15

Source: First National City Bank, MONTHLY ECONOMIC LETTER, April issues, 1967, 1968, 1980.

	Average Rank	
	1966	1979
Industries 1–20 (1966)	10.5	18.2
Industries 21–40 (1966)	30.5	22.8

In the 1947–57 period, the correlations in the concentrated and unconcentrated sets are not significantly different until we reach those between rates of return separated by seven years. Then they become significantly poorer in the concentrated industries (Table 8-3). This is also inconsistent with the concentration-monopoly hypothesis. In the 1958–68 period, the correlations are signifi-

TABLE 8–3

Intertemporal Correlation of Rates of Return for Concentrated, Unconcentrated, and Ambiguous Industries, 1919–28, 1947–57, and 1958–68

Four-Firm Concentration	Average Correlations		
	1919–28 [a]	1947–57 [b]	1958–68 [b]
Rates of Return in Year T and (T+1)			
Greater than 60	0.51	0.74	0.88
Less than 50	.64	.63	.83
50 to 60	.85	.82	.86
Rates of Return in Year T and (T+2)			
Greater than 60	.42	.59	.80
Less than 50	.57	.49	.66
50 to 60	.77	.70	.71
Rates of Return in Year T and (T+3)			
Greater than 60	.29	.54	.74
Less than 50	.54	.49	.41
50 to 60	.63	.67	.69
Rates of Return in Year T and (T+4)			
Greater than 60	.17	.50	.70
Less than 50	.45	.50	.49
50 to 60	.50	.68	.66
Rates of Return in Year T and (T+5)			
Greater than 60	.15	.47	.65
Less than 50	.31	.39	.34
50 to 60	.46	.60	.54
Rates of Return in Year T and (T+6)			
Greater than 60	.13	.29	.55
Less than 50	.26	.27	.22
50 to 60	41	.52	.61
Rates of Return in Year T and (T+7)			
Greater than 60	−.02	.16	.46
Less than 50	.13	.47	.13
50 to 60	.47	.43	.54
Rates of Return in Year T and (T+8)			
Greater than 60	−.02	.18	.39
Less than 50	.29	.38	.33
50 to 60	.50	.42	.50
Rates of Return in Year T and (T+9)			
Greater than 60	−.25	.17	.46
Less than 50	.08	.22	.34
50 to 60	.31	.34	.52

cantly better in the concentrated than the unconcentrated until
eight years after any given year.

Can we take this to mean that concentrated industries were
more competitive than the diffused industries until 1958 and then
became less competitive? There is no direct evidence suggesting
greater competitiveness in concentrated industries in the two earlier periods. There was greater cyclical instability in those periods.
Qualls found greater cyclical instability of price-cost margins in
concentrated than in diffused industries.[28] This is, perhaps, the
explanation for the difference in the latter period from the two
earlier. Also, firms in concentrated industries have become more
diversified in recent years. This, too, may have stabilized their
returns.

Another explanation can be offered that has some slight supporting evidence. Unrecorded intangible capital is, on average,
relatively greater in recent times in concentrated than in unconcentrated industries. Telser found that concentrated industries invest more in human capital than the unconcentrated.[29] Since
training programs within industry have been growing relative to
other magnitudes in the economy in the postwar period, it would
appear that this unrecorded asset may be increasingly biasing accounting rates of return upward in some concentrated industries,
thus creating a spurious recent stability in the pattern of relative
profitability in concentrated industries. In other words, some industry rates of return are pushed upward more than others by the
accounting bias. Hence, the range in which an industry profit rate
moves is separated from the range of movement in other industries. A spurious stability in the relative rank of the industry's
return results.

A hypothetical example may help clarify the issue. Suppose an
industry, half of whose assets consists of unrecorded intangibles,
reports a 20 percent return. Suppose another with no intangibles

[a] Calculated by Aldy Keene from data on earnings on equity for 2,046 identical lead-
ing corporations classified in seventy-two industries reported in Ralph C. Epstein,
INDUSTRIAL PROFITS IN THE UNITED STATES (1934). Concentration classification
according to data in National Resources Committee, THE STRUCTURE OF THE AMERI-
CAN ECONOMY (June 1939). Classification scheme that used by G. J. Stigler, CAPI-
TAL AND RATES OF RETURN IN MANUFACTURING INDUSTRIES (1963).
[b] James C. Ellert, CONCENTRATION, DISEQUILIBRIA, AND THE CONVERGENCE PATTERN
IN INDUSTRY RATES OF RETURN (multilith, 1971). Compustat data for 565 corpora-
tions classified in 141 industries used.

reports an 8 percent return. If current outlays on intangible investments (which are expensed) equal depreciation of unrecorded intangibles, then the true return in the first industry is 10 percent (assuming no other accounting biases). Now suppose that events occur that reduce returns in the high-accounting-return industry by half and in the low-return industry by one quarter. The reported returns will show the first industry earning 10 and the second 6 percent. The first industry will continue in its number one rank and the second in number two and the correlation of ranks will be persistent. If rates of return were not differentially biased by the accounting treatment of intangible outlays, however, the first industry would sink from a 10 to 5 percent rate of return while the second sinks from 8 to 6 percent. The ranks of the two would reverse and the pattern of relative profitability would not show the spurious stability that is caused by differential accounting biases.

The pharmaceutical industry provides an example of the spurious stability in rank and the apparent persistence of a high accounting rate of return caused by the omission of a major portion of an industry's capital from its accounting statements. It is the most research-intensive industry in the American economy and one of the most promotion-intensive. Since research and other information-providing activities are expensed as incurred, despite the returns appearing in later accounting periods, its book capital understates its actual capital by a larger proportion than in any other industry. As a result, its accounting return is high and the industry ranks among the top three most of the time in the 40-industry list used in Table 8-2. In the last three decades (1950–79), it was number one on the list six times, number two nine times, and number three seven times. It did not drop below number ten at any time.

A recomputation of the drug industry rate of return by Professor Kenneth Clarkson, capitalizing research and the advertising portion of promotion expenditures, dropped the industry's average return for 1959–73 from 18.3 to 12.9 percent, the largest drop among the eleven industries for which Clarkson recomputed rates of return. The average decline in the other industries was 1.2 percentage points as compared to the 5.4 point drop in pharmaceuticals.[30] The industry consistently ranks high, then, simply because accounting conventions cause a much larger departure of the accounting from the economic rate of return than in any other industry.

Other evidence also supports the view that the high rank of the drug industry and its persistence was spurious. The number of pharmaceutical firms dropped from 1,123 in 1947 to 680 in 1972. This occurred in the face of a rapid growth in sales from $0.9 billion in 1947 to $7.1 billion in 1972. If the industry was in fact as profitable as indicated by the accounting rate of return for leading corporations (the data used for computing the industry rate of return come from twenty-eight to forty-two corporations in various years), firms would not have departed as rapidly as they did. Only an unusually wide dispersion in rates of return among firms, indicating an unusually risky industry with many firms failing while others did unusually well, could have caused an above average economic return with a simultaneous decline in number of firms. If that was the situation, then the high returns could encompass a risk premium with the risk-adjusted rate of return being below average.[31]

Has American Manufacturing Grown Less Competitive?

The great merger wave at the end of the nineteenth century involved a proportion of manufacturing assets that has never been remotely approached in any merger wave since. According to some authors, the consolidations of that time and of the 1920s set an oligopolistic stamp on American manufacturing that makes it non-competitive by comparison with the atomistic structure of the pre-1890 era.[32]

In contrast to this view. Professor Ambrose Winston observed that

> . . . competition has in our day become intense and swift and sure beyond all previous human experience.
>
> What do we mean by competition? We ought to mean the ready movement of the factors of production—labor or productive instruments—toward those employments in which prices are exceptionally high and profits large. That is, competition is substantially "mobility." . . .
>
> New capital—the current accumulation of surplus income—is unspecialized industrial protoplasm quickly turning in any direction, attracted by the hope of profit, creating new competing products with a promptness and certainty unknown in the age of handicraft.
>
> The owners of investment capital and their advisers are looking incessantly for the most profitable opportunities for its employment. The earnings from oil, from steel, from the packing industry, from automobiles, from sugar, from commerce and shipping, flow into steel or automobiles or oil, or whatever gives greatest promise of high earnings.[33]

We used the test of competition proposed by Professon Winston to examine the rate at which industries ranked high or low by profitability converged on the middle rank. We saw the average rank of the top-ranked industries of 1948 move 91 percent of the distance toward the average rank by 1956 (Table 8-1). The top-ranked industries of 1966 moved 77 percent of the distance toward an average rank by 1979 (Table 8-2) in spite of the tendency of cyclical industries to be in a top rank in all such years as 1948, 1956, 1966, and 1979. By performing a similar test on pre-1890 manufacturing industries, perhaps we can judge whether the alleged oligopolization of manufacturing has occurred, ending an idyllic, competitive era.

Professors Atack, Bateman, and Weiss have extracted profitability data from the 1850, 1860, and 1870 Manuscript Censuses. Using the twenty-one industries for which they computed returns, we find that the top-ranked industries of 1850 moved only 36 percent of the distance toward an average rank by 1860 (see Table 8-4), half the rate of movement which occurred in recent years. And this was no quirk of monopolistic rigidity. The top-ranked group of 1860 went only 52 percent of the distance toward an average rank between 1860 and 1970 (see Table 8-5), despite the enormous economic changes in the Civil War and Reconstruction era.

TABLE 8–4

Profit Rate in Major Manufacturing Industries, 1850–60

Industry	Profit Rate (Percentage)		Profit Rank	
	1850	1860	1850	1860
Blacksmithing	39.5	30.2	1	6
Tin, copper, and sheet iron	35.4	22.8	2	12
Saddlery	33.5	39.7	3	2
Printing	33.1	31.3	4	4
Books and shoes	31.8	34.1	5	3
Meat packing	29.0	42.7	6	1
All Industries	26.1	25.9	—	—
Furniture	25.1	21.1	7	14.5
Agricultural implements	23.0	21.3	8	13
Leather	22.7	23.4	9	9
Lumber milling	22.4	23.3	10	10.5
Flour milling	22.1	23.3	11	10.5
Pig iron	22.0	9.2	12	21

Cast iron	21.8	24.2	13	7
Wagons and carriages	21.6	23.8	14	8
Machinery	16.8	31.0	15	5
Cooperage	14.2	19.1	16	18
Clothing	12.9	21.1	17	14.5
Woolen textiles	10.0	20.6	18	17
Brick making	0.8	13.5	19.5	20
Bar iron	0.8	21.0	19.5	16
Cotton textiles	0.2	13.6	21	19

Source: Jeremy Atack, Fred Bateman, and Thomas Weiss, *Risk, the Rate of Return and the Pattern of Investment in Nineteenth Century American Industrialization.* Paper presented May 25, 1979, at the University of Chicago.

Note: The movement of the average rank of industries in the top and bottom half of the 1850 list is shown below.

	1850	*1860*	*1870*
Industries 1–11 (1850)	6.0	7.8	8.0
Industries 11–21 (1850)	16.0	14.2	14.0
All industries	11.0	11.0	11.0

TABLE 8–5

Profit Rate in Major Manufacturing Industries, 1860–70

Industry	Profit Rate (Percentage)		Profit Rank	
	1860	*1870*	*1860*	*1870*
Meat packing	42.7	63.1	1	1
Saddlery	39.7	38.5	2	4
Books and shoes	34.1	62.0	3	2
Printing	31.3	32.2	4	5
Machinery	31.0	18.5	5	14.5
Blacksmithing	30.2	55.2	6	3
All Industries	25.9	29.3	—	—
Cast iron	24.2	18.0	7	16
Wagons and carriages	23.8	25.7	8	9
Leather	23.4	21.3	9	11
Lumber milling	23.3	17.3	10.5	17
Flour milling	23.3	19.3	10.5	13
Tin, copper, and sheet iron	22.8	28.4	12	7
Agricultural implements	21.3	12.4	13	19
Furniture	21.1	31.0	14.5	6
Clothing	21.1	27.0	14.5	8
Bar iron	21.0	5.1	16	20
Woolen textiles	20.6	14.0	17	18
Cooperage	19.1	21.8	18	10
Cotton textiles	13.6	18.5	19	14.5
Brick making	13.5	20.6	20	12
Pig iron	9.2	−1.6	21	21

Source: Jeremy Atack, Fred Bateman, and Thomas Weiss, *Risk, the Rate of Return and the Pattern of Investment in Nineteenth Century American Industrialization.* Paper presented May 25, 1979, at the University of Chicago.
Note: The movement of the average rank of the industries in the top and bottom halves of the 1860 list is shown below.

	Average Rank	
	1860	1870
Industries 1–11 (1860)	6.0	8.6
Industries 11–21 (1860)	16.0	13.7
All Industries	11.0	11.0

It seems that there was less fluidity of "industrial protoplasm" in the days before the rise of large corporations and "dominant" firms than there has been since. Judging by these data, the American manufacturing economy is more competitive today than ever before.

Conclusion

Two dynamic tests for the existence of monopoly, one applied to forty manufacturing industries and the other applied to concentrated and to unconcentrated manufacturing industries separately, both produce results inconsistent with the presence of monopoly. Manufacturing industries do not show the stability of relative profitability that would be expected if many industries were monopolized. When concentrated industries were separated from the unconcentrated industries, and profit ranks in successive years were correlated within the concentrated group and within the unconcentrated group, the differences in the rates of decay of the two correlations were not those expected if monopoly or collusion were characteristic of the concentrated group. The share of domestic production turned out by the leading four firms in an industry is a poor index to the degree of monopoly, yet that is the proxy for monopoly used in unnumerable studies.

The attention devoted by academics and government officials to hunting monopoly in manufacturing is out of proportion to the importance of the problem. Monopoly in manufacturing receives inordinate attention largely because of a misplaced faith in concentration ratios as a monopoly index and because big companies, which are always suspect, abound in this sector. Every attempt to measure monopoly misallocation in manufacturing has indicated that the degree is slight even when using the most unfavorable assumptions.[34]

Those concerned with the monopoly problem in the United States tend to neglect the important monopolies, which cause a substantial misallocation of resources. The Air Line Pilots' Association, by creating a monopoly of pilots in the service of scheduled airlines, has won returns on private investment in pilot training far exceeding those earned by manufacturing industries. Despite its obvious monopoly power, it is seldom studied.[35] The legislative and regulatory support given to cartels in agriculture, transportation, and trades such as barbering and drug retailing receive little or no space in the collections of readings on the monopoly problem. The monopoly problem is far from trivial in the non-manufacturing areas of the economy and in the industries composed of small firms such as taxi operations,[36] yet it receives little attention in comparison to the effort devoted to manufacturing.

Notes

1. E. Mansfield (ed.), MONOPOLY POWER AND ECONOMIC PERFORMANCE (1968).
2. W. G. Shepherd, THE ECONOMICS OF INDUSTRIAL ORGANIZATION 207 (1979).
3. J. K. Galbraith, THE NEW INDUSTRIAL STATE 294 (1967).
4. S. Gordon, *The Close of the Galbraithian System*, 76 JOURNAL OF POLITICAL ECONOMY 640 (Aug. 1968).
5. See Galbraith *supra* note 3, at 206.
6. See Galbraith *supra* note 3, at 1–2.
7. U.S., *White House Task Force Report on Antitrust Policy*, TRADE REGULATION REPORTS. Supplement to No. 415 at II-13, A-9, A-18 to A-21 (May 26, 1969).
8. For example, R. Evely and I. M. O. Little, CONCENTRATION IN BRITISH INDUSTRY 8–25 (1960); also Stigler *infra* note 12.
9. R. M. Cyert and K. D. George, *Competition, Growth, and Efficiency*, 79 ECONOMIC JOURNAL 25 (Mar. 1969); George J. Stigler, *Discussion of Report of the Attorney General's Committee on Antitrust Policy*, 46 AMERICAN ECONOMIC REVIEW 506 (May 1956).
10. H. M. Mann, *Seller Concentration, Barriers to Entry, and Rates of Return in Thirty Industries, 1950–1960*, 48 THE REVIEW OF ECONOMICS AND STATISTICS 269 (Aug. 1966).
11. G. J. Stigler, *Competition in the United States*, FIVE LECTURES ON ECONOMIC PROBLEMS 46 (1950). (Stigler follows the classification of C. Wilcox, COMPETITION AND MONOPOLY IN AMERICAN INDUSTRY (1941), which is largely based on concentration ratios).

12. Stigler adds an industry such as rubber boots and shoes to the Wilcox list of monopoly markets because, "The concentration ratio is relatively high." See *id.* at 58.
13. "And the systematic disregard of inter-product competition renders almost all of the work with concentration ratios worthless." Stigler *supra* note 11 at 48, n. 2. "The availability of substitutes, the size of the market (local, national, and international), the extent of collusion, and other factors will influence the correspondence between concentration and monopoly." See *id.*, at 53. Also see Claire Wilcox, *The Alleged Ubiquity of Oligopoly*, 40 AMERICAN ECONOMIC REVIEW 67 (May 1950).
14. Ambrose P. Winston, JUDICIAL ECONOMICS (1957); James C. Ellert, ANTITRUST ENFORCEMENT AND THE BEHAVIOR OF STOCK PRICES (1975).
15. H. Demsetz, Why Regulate Utilities? 11 JOURNAL OF LAW & ECONOMICS 55 (April 1968).
16. G. J. Stigler, *A Theory of Oligopoly*, 72 JOURNAL OF POLITICAL ECONOMY 44 (Feb. 1964), reprinted in G. J. Stigler, THE ORGANIZATION OF INDUSTRY 39 (1968); Steven H. Lustgarten, *The Impact of Buyer Concentration in Manufacturing Industries*, 57 REVIEW OF ECONOMICS AND STATISTICS 125 (May 1975).
17. D. K. Osborne, *Can OPEC Crack?* THE WHARTON MAGAZINE 40 (Summer 1977). When U.S. price ceilings on crude oil were allowed to start rising in 1980, the drop in crude oil output in the lower forty-eight states, which had been going on for more than a decade, stopped. A. J. Parisi, *Oil Output in U.S. Picking Up*, NEW YORK TIMES D1 (Aug. 15, 1980).
18. *The Great Alaskan Oil Freeze*, BUSINESS WEEK 74 (Feb. 26, 1979).
19. G. J. Stigler, CAPITAL AND RATES OF RETURN IN MANUFACTURING 3–6 (1963).
20. This is the only alleged evidence offered by the Neal Commission for its contention that high concentration is an index to oligopoly. ". . . studies have found a close association between high levels of concentration and persistently high rates of return on capital . . ." See U.S., *White House Task Force Report on Antitrust Policy supra* note 7, at II-8.
21. See Stigler *supra* note 19.
22. For some exceptions, see William Jordan, *Producer Protection, Prior Market Structure, and the Effect of Government Regulations*, 15 JOURNAL OF LAW & ECONOMICS 151 (Apr. 1972).
23. G. J. Stigler, *A Note on Profitability, Competition, and Concentration*, in Stigler, THE ORGANIZATION OF INDUSTRY, *supra* note 16, at 142.
24. Y. Brozen, *Significance of Profit Data for Antitrust Policy*, 14 ANTITRUST BULLETIN 119 (Spring 1969); reprinted in J. F. Weston and S. Peltzman (eds.), PUBLIC POLICY TOWARD MERGERS (1969).
25. F. Machlup, THE POLITICAL ECONOMY OF MONOPOLY 493 (1952).
26. See U.S., *White House Task Force Report on Antitrust Policy supra* note 7, at 70.
27. See Stigler *supra* note 19.
28. P. David Qualls, *Market Structure and Price-Cost Margin Flexibility in American Manufacturing*, 1958–70, FTC Special Paper (March 1977).
29. Lester Telser, *Some Determinants of Returns to Manufacturing Industries*, COMPETITION, COLLUSION, AND GAME THEORY 312 (1972).
30. Kenneth Clarkson, INTANGIBLE CAPITAL AND RATES OF RETURN, Table 16 at 64 (1977).
31. Y. Brozen, *Foreword* to *id.* at 11–16.
32. See Shepherd *supra* note 2.

33. Ambrose P. Winston, *The Chimera of Monopoly,* THE ATLANTIC MONTHLY (Nov. 1924); reprinted in THE FREEMAN 39 (Sept. 1960).

34. A. Harberger, *Monopoly and Resource Allocation,* S44 AMERICAN ECO- NOMIC REVIEW 77 (May 1954); D. Schwartzman, *The Effect of Monop- oly on Price,* 67 JOURNAL OF POLITICAL ECONOMY 361 (Aug. 1959).

35. The only study of the Air Line Pilot's Association monopoly return is that by S. Sobotka, ECONOMIC IMPLICATIONS OF JET OPERATIONS (1958). He found that the monopolized sector of airline piloting provided a lifetime income whose present value, at that time, exceeded the present value of pilots' lifetime earnings in less monopolized sectors by 32%, with duty hours required in the monopolized sector amounting to only 50% of the duty hours required in the less monopolized sector.

36. The capitalized value of the monopoly return in the New York City taxicab industry alone exceeds $600 million. Fleet medallions sold for $45,000 and independent medallions for $68,000 in 1979. There are nearly 12,000 New York City taxi medallions. The capitalized value of the monopoly returns in ICC-regulated household goods transportation has been estimated at $60.8 million. Denis A. Breen, *The Monopoly Value of Household-Goods Carrier Operating Certificates,* 20 JOURNAL OF LAW & ECONOMICS 153 (Apr. 1977).

9

Does Advertising Create Business Power?

When the Federal Trade Commission (FTC) ordered Procter & Gamble to divest itself of the Clorox Company, which Procter & Gamble had acquired a few years before, it did so on the ground that economies in the purchase of advertising serve no social purpose. The economies arising out of Procter & Gamble's merger with Clorox were, therefore, not an allowable defense. The FTC argued that advertising benefits only the seller by entrenching his market position. Advertising, it said, is of no use to the consumer (at least in the liquid bleach market).

Although the FTC did not go so far as to argue that advertising produces detrimental effects for consumers, there are critics who do. The complaint is that advertising induces people to spend their money differently than they otherwise would. Not only that, they spend their money for purposes that the complainers question. For example, the cars people buy, it is said, flourish "unnecessary" features and styling, and heavily advertised soft drinks don't taste nearly as good as people are led to think they do. On this view consumers left to themselves would not demand the particular mix of goods they do and would be happier for it. In a more nearly perfect world, which is perhaps within reach if only we passed the right laws, we could avoid the social "waste" generated by advertising.

This view of advertising, it is fair to say, receives most of its support from self-appointed censors who are pained by advertising's appeal to human weaknesses. If human nature is not fundamentally corrupt, the corrupt habits of the typical person—at least his commercial habits—must be the result of misdirection or indoctrination. Advertising's play on the susceptibility to cajolery, entertainment, and the most implausible claims, the desire to escape from the mundane and the inescapable, and the apparent willingness to be beguiled by the unscrupulous and the greedy seem to some to be its worst aspect. And whether weak or not, it is "irrational" to want things that the censors do not want, or, at least, to want things that people "should" not want. And it is advertising that creates these irrational desires.

Professional economists of a generation ago translated the uneasiness of intellectuals about advertising into the most serious charge that economists can make. They contended that advertising creates and sustains monopoly power. This is accomplished through the generation of irrational brand loyalties. Analytically, advertising does two things if this view is correct. First, it makes each firm's demand curve less elastic (that is, makes each firm's rate of sales less responsive to price changes) by making consumers less price conscious in the case of heavily advertised goods. Second, it increases the cost of entry. New producers not only have to cover the usual expenses of doing business, but also they must spend extra amounts to break down irrational brand loyalties and woo consumers away from established firms. These costs make operating expenses for entrants higher than the costs for heavy advertising firms already in the industry. They also raise the investment required to enter an industry and, therefore, constitute a barrier to entry.[1]

The New Economics of Advertising

There are a number of difficulties with this view, not the least of which is that it is not developed in a consistent and formal framework supported by, and consistent with, the relevant data. In fact, a systematic economic approach to advertising, which was developed only recently, is largely at odds with this line of thinking. Although the issues have by no means been resolved to the satisfaction of all involved, a number of important strands of thought can be identified.[2]

247

1. *The provision of information is an unavoidable aspect of economic life.* Information is valuable to economic actors but costly to produce and assimilate. This should come as no surprise to anyone who has ever spent an afternoon shopping for a new coat, a pair of shoes, or a stereo. Consumers in a modern economy want to be informed about what goods are available, how much they cost, and their relative merits. This is particularly true in the case of products that they use only occasionally or use first when they reach a certain age. Advertisements for toys and acne medicines, for example, are important means of informing groups of potential buyers whose memberships are constantly changing.

2. *Information about products cannot be provided without cost, and an important question is who pays for it.* Some information is produced by sellers, who make known the existence of their products and make claims about the virtues of those products. Other information is produced by buyers who talk to acquaintances, read articles (as well as advertisements) in newspapers and magazines, and do comparison shopping. Some information is also provided indirectly. For example, the existence of highly regarded brand names or respected department stores assures shoppers of quality and conserves time and effort that would otherwise be spent searching for it. More generally, a variety of commercial institutions provide information about product quality. Brand names, trademarks, guarantees, and extensive "non-informational" advertising—advertising that makes the brand well known as an advertised brand—all serve as guides to quality for consumers.[3]

3. *The possibility of fraud, misrepresentation, and distortion exists whenever information is transmitted.* Consumers may indeed be misled in advertising provided by those who sell products. But it would be quite mistaken to say that the information offered in the market for commodities is particularly fraudulent. The gains from deception are often great in politics, in intellectual matters, even in art and love. Indeed, deliberate misrepresentation may occur whenever people write or speak. In business, however, the apparent incentives for the seller to create falsehoods are matched by the incentives buyers have not to be misled. Note also that the law provides recourse in some cases. In many cases, considerable social waste would arise if buyers entering a transaction had to verify information provided by the seller or could uncover it only after purchase. In such cases a failure to perform as promised or to reveal crucial information is illegal.

248

For a wide variety of transactions, the efficient solution has the seller providing some information voluntarily, making his product terms as appealing as possible, subject, however, to certain limitations. The limits on distortion arise because what is claimed must be reasonable at first glance, and must, in those cases where repeat purchases are important, also stand up when the product is purchased. In addition, it should be realized that hyperbole and showmanship are not necessarily attempts to defraud. "The Best Pizza in Town" is not a literal claim, but rather an invitation to do some testing. It may not be true that a particular brand of razor can shave sandpaper, nor should anyone care, because the purpose of an advertisement that "claims" such a fact is to get people to try the product. Furthermore, what often appears to a naive observer to be advertising deception is instead part of the image that is being sold. In bygone ages only the aristocracy could purchase flattery and illusion. Now, the unsuccessful, the homely, and the bored of modest means can infuse their lives with suggested action, beauty, and excitement. None of these can be purchased in a disembodied state, but they can be bought in small doses along with ordinary purchases. Few of us don't every now and then find ourselves wishing we were free-spirited cowboys, beauty queens, or jet setters.

4. *Information provided to a mass audience must be repetitive, entertaining, limited in scope, and memorable.* This arises from the finite capacity of people to absorb, analyze, and retain information that might be useful. This is a fundamental fact recognized by anyone who presents information to large groups of people, particularly people absorbed by a host of other concerns. An advertisement for an automobile that contains densely packed technical information is unlikely to interest the typical car buyer. People who do want such information can turn to the many publications that cater to those who are willing to spend the time and effort required.

5. *Property rights in information are difficult to establish and enforce.* In some cases copyright and patent protection bestow property rights to those who invest resources in providing valuable information. However, the information that consumers might find useful is not always of the sort that allows people generating the information to recover their cost fully. Who has the incentive to tell consumers about the hazards associated with certain products? A large part of such information is provided by consumers themselves, their physicians, insurance companies, and the news-

papers and magazines they buy. Similarly, no single producer has an incentive to tell consumers what the benefits of a broad class of products may be since he is unlikely to reap any gain. Such information often comes from sources outside the industry or from producers' associations, which are formed with this end in mind.

6. *A firm's advertising expenditures are best viewed as invest-ment.* Current advertising is an investment, and the stock of de-preciated past investments should be viewed as a capital asset. Past advertising depreciates at some rate that depends on factors such as buyer turnover and the rate of product innovation in a market. The greater the depreciation rate of past advertising and consumer information, the higher the required level of current advertising needed to keep buyers informed.

This introduction to the issues raised by an economic analysis of advertising is a necessary prelude to the task at hand: assessing the charge that advertising contributes to, or is associated with, economic concentration and monopoly power. It is alleged that there is social waste above and beyond that presumed to occur in paying the costs of "unneeded" advertising. Competition is im-paired because firms in concentrated industries construct barriers to entry with advertising. These barriers keep the concentrated industries concentrated, lead to higher prices, and cause resource misallocation.

Origin of the Entry Barrier View of Advertising

In most workaday applications economic science proceeds on an "as if" basis. The theory of competition taught to generations of students asks us to assume that economic agents possess knowl-edge of the products that are available and the prices being charged by each seller. It is true enough that if we have informa-tion about supply and demand, and if markets clear by means of costless recontracting or a hypothetical auctioneer, then we can define the resulting "competitive" equilibrium as a notional opti-mum. This useful abstraction nicely demonstrates some central propositions in economics.

The case of "perfect competition" is of course not a faithful representation of what we find in economic life. What we see in fact is differentiation among products and widespread ignorance about markets and prices. In the absence of knowledge about alternatives, every seller has a monopoly. One of the ways such ignorance is overcome is by advertising. Early analyses of advertising dismissed this function. Rather, it was argued that if competition with advertising wasn't "perfect" as defined by one type of competitive model (the one in which consumers are all-knowing), then it must be imperfect as we find it in the case of the monopoly model, and advertising helped make it so. The fact that advertising was used when ignorance was widespread was interpreted as if the correlation was a demonstration of causation. In retrospect it seems clear that a better understanding of advertising was possible only after economists came explicitly to incorporate information in their models, and after an attempt was made to analyze the economics of product differentiation.

What happened, in fact, was that the view of each firm as a monopoly gained ground.[4] On this view, the world of perfect competition in which each buyer and each seller has complete information and transactions are costless defines the perfect allocation of resources. Advertising, for which there is no function if buyers have complete information, serves merely to tie consumers to specific brands of products. The analytical premise (perfectly competitive markets do not have advertising) makes the conclusion (the existence of advertising in a market implies that it is not competitive) inescapable.

This view of advertising as either a generator or symptom of anticompetitive impulses gained followers in professional circles with the publication in 1933 of *The Economics of Imperfect Competition* by Joan Robinson, and *The Theory of Monopolistic Competition* by Edward Chamberlin. Robinson's book was not directly concerned with advertising, but with the apparatus used by economists to look at monopoly and competition, and the relative weight that should be attached to the two types of analysis. Her thesis was that monopoly is more prevalent than economists of the classical school supposed. She went astray when she argued that monopoly was deliberately made prevalent by techniques such as product differentiation and advertising, phenomena that, on her view, the classical school could not explain. "The traditional assumption of perfect competition is an exceedingly convenient one for simplifying the analysis of price, but there is no reason to expect it to be fulfilled in the real world," she asserted. The demand curve facing each firm is less than perfectly elastic. Among the forces making this true is advertising. "The customer will be influenced by advertisement, which plays upon his mind with studied skill, and makes him prefer the goods of one producer to those of another because they are brought to his notice in a more pleasing or forceful manner."[5]

Chamberlin treated this theme at greater length. He distinguished between selling costs and production costs. Selling costs on his definition encompass "advertising of all varieties, salesman's salaries and the expenses of sales departments, margins granted to dealers . . . window displays, etc."[6] Their purpose is to change a product's demand curve. By their very existence they indicate that particular markets are characterized by monopoly elements. Chamberlin asserted that "selling costs cannot be defined without a theory which recognizes the monopoly elements responsible for them."[7] A little reflection and a small dose of common sense makes this view one that implies that advertising makes markets competitive. By eroding ignorance (the monopoly element), advertising erodes the power of a firm to the extent that a firm's power rests on its customers' ignorance of alternatives. In the language of economists, advertising by any one firm makes the demand facing all other firms more elastic as well as the demand facing the firm doing the advertising.

This is Chamberlin's conclusion when he says:

> Buyers often do not know or are but dimly aware of the existence of sellers other than those with whom they habitually trade or of goods other than those they habitually consume; they are ill-informed of comparative prices for the same thing sold by different merchants; they are ignorant of the quality of goods, in themselves, compared with other goods, and compared with prices asked. . . . By spreading this knowledge, advertising makes the demand for a seller's product *more* elastic.[8]

Unfortunately, a selective and distorted reading of Chamberlin's look at the role of advertising and competition came rapidly to be included in the corpus of economic wisdom. The Robinsonian view was accepted, although it was only an aside in her book and lacked support. In addition, the charge was expanded. Not only did advertising lead to changes in the demand facing a firm making it *less* elastic; it also kept potential entrants out of the industry. As we have seen in previous chapters, a large segment of learned opinion linked economic concentration and monopoly throughout

252

the 1940s and 1950s. But how can concentrated industries charge monopoly prices in the many industries to which entry is open? Entry barriers had to be found to make the concentration-collusion supposition plausible. In one of the standard post–World-War-II books on welfare economics, Professor Tibor Scitovsky contends that in markets in which consumers are "uninformed," advertising is an obstacle to entry. Also, the "reserve" of consumers toward the products of new producers creates this barrier. "There are indications," according to Scitovsky, "that these two factors are formidable obstacles in the way of newcomers to many markets in our economy."[9] But he never tells us how advertising makes consumers "uninformed" or keeps them uninformed.

It was a natural step to link advertising and concentration. Professor Joe Bain did just that, becoming the most prominent spokesman for the view that advertising is one of several largely wasteful methods of nonprice competition contributing to concentration.[10] As with other hypotheses purporting to link concentration with monopoly, allegedly supporting empirical evidence was soon at hand. A number of studies found relationships between advertising and measured profits, and between advertising and concentration. These relationships, it was claimed, supported the view of advertising as an anticompetitive device, both directly in its influence on buyer habits and indirectly in its effect on industry structure.

This line of reasoning gained ground, in part because of what was regarded as strong empirical confirmation, and came to be incorporated in economics textbooks. What one author calls "non-informational advertising" provides "little positive information" and costs many billions of dollars each year.[11] Why do firms do this? Advertising, it is claimed, shifts demand at the expense of other products. Firms may get so carried away with this that "it seems quite possible for competitive advertising to be carried to irrational lengths," a tendency that cannot be checked because it is a "serious heresy" to question the usefulness of advertising. Moreover, heavy advertising may not be all that irrational because it raises the cost of entry to others. "*Market penetration* costs more per unit of sales than does *protection* of an established market position. . . . There are important *economies of scale* in advertising. . . . The newcomer must raise funds for advertising investment as well as plant and equipment investment."[12]

Is advertising really a barrier or is it a means of entry? There are compelling arguments for the view that advertising is a means of matching buyers and sellers, of providing information, and, therefore, of entry. To provide a basis for this conclusion we will survey the empirical literature on this question. On the basis of the data, it does not appear that advertising is systematically associated with high profits, barred entry, or other evidence or measures of monopoly power. There may be a weak statistical relationship between the level of advertising—which, it should be emphasized, is one of several promotional techniques—and concentration. There are reasons to believe, however, that the relationship is not an indication of cause and effect, but rather a statistical artifact. In any case, concentration cannot be a consequence of entry barriers since, as we have seen, the entry rate is higher in the more concentrated industries (Table 4-7).

Advertising and Profits

One way of determining the effect of advertising on competition is to look at the profitability of industries with different amounts of advertising. If advertising establishes an entry barrier, then higher rates of return with greater durability should appear in industries with heavier advertising. As a naive empirical approach this has appeal, but it begs the question, as do all correlations of advertising and monopoly indicator X (such as durable high profits), of why some industries use this method of monopoly creation and others do not. It also rests on the assumption that the producers in an industry will practice restraint toward one another. Existing firms are a source of "entry" in an industry (since "entry" simply and operationally means expansion of capacity). Even if the view of advertising as a barrier to entry had a valid and unambiguous economic interpretation, it does not stand to reason that we should expect firms in an industry protected by such barriers to keep their capacities in check and to practice both restraint and cooperation. If, in order to bar entry, advertising is pushed beyond the rate that best serves each firm in attracting customers, then what is to prevent some firms from cheating by reducing their advertising to increase profitability? Cooperation in creating an entry barrier is as unlikely to succeed as cooperation in restricting output, if it is profitable to cheat, as we pointed out in Chapter 6.

If advertising serves other purposes, such as making the customers of other firms disloyal and attracting them to sample the product of the firm doing the advertising, then advertising is an anti-cooperative (pro-competitive) activity. It is evidence that restraint designed to raise the industry's profit level is not being practiced. We may be free to imagine that each firm's advertising makes its demand curve less elastic (although the evidence indicates the opposite),[13] but we also have to admit that advertising by other firms would cause a given firm's demand curve to shift inward. Advertising aside, there are many other ways in which firms can and do compete with each other. These make high returns, even with barred entry, unlikely.[14] To repeat, in the absence of collusion on all matters, one would not expect the industry of firms that engage in artificial product differentiation through advertising to earn more on average than the economy-wide or competitive rate of return.

Yet another criticism of this approach is that accounting rates of return are a biased measure of true profits. The extent of this bias correlates with the amount of advertising a firm does. A common measure of profits is net income divided by net worth (assets minus liabilities). Conventional accounting practices exclude the stock of advertising from the measure of assets. Consequently the net worth of the firm that has invested in advertising is understated.[15]

The first in a series of studies that attempted to establish a relationship between profitability and advertising was that of Comanor and Wilson in 1967.[16] They found a positive relationship between industry accounting rates of return and advertising-to-sales ratios (and no relationship between concentration and profitability). Similar results were reported by a number of other researchers, among them Vernon and Nourse, whose data relating measured profits and advertising-to-sales ratios of firms are presented in Table 9-1. Profits are measured as the firm's net income divided by stockholders' equity, averaged over the years 1963–68. The firms included in the study are chiefly producers of consumers' nondurable goods. Although a loose association between advertising intensity and the measured profit rate is evident, a careful look at the data indicates that a few firms with advertising-to-sales ratios in excess of 10 percent form the basis for a large part of the relationship.[17] An examination of Table 9-1 shows that the few firms with advertising ratios above 10 percent also tended to have high rates of return. Note, however, that these firms had

TABLE 9–1

Profit Rates and Advertising Intensity

Company	Net Income Divided by Shareholders' Equity, Average for 1963–68	Weighted Average Industry Advertising-to-Sales Ratio 1969[a]	Advertising-to-Sales Ratio of Firm; 1969	Weighted Average of Percentage Changes in Industry Sales in Firm's Product Markets (1968 Sales/1963 Sales)
Alberto Culver Company	.30	16.5	28.0	1.67
American Bakeries Company	.09	0.9	0.4	1.16
American Sugar Company	.11	0.2	0.5	1.13
Anheuser-Busch Inc.	.13	3.3	2.6	1.37
Armour & Company	.09	0.2	0.4	1.34
Avon Products Inc.	.37	17.0	1.5	1.69
Campbell Soup Company	.13	2.6	4.1	1.31
Helme Products Inc.	.13	3.2	1.0	1.15
Beatrice Foods Company	.16	1.7	0.8	1.18
Borden Inc.	.12	1.3	1.1	1.22
Bristol Meyers Co.	.30	12.9	16.4	1.59
Brown Forman Distillers Corp.	.17	10.6	7.9	1.36
Del Monte Corporation	.11	2.2	1.7	1.35
Associated Brewing Company	.03	3.3	4.2	1.37
Faberge Inc.	.28	17.0	8.3	1.69
Fairmont Foods Co.	.10	0.4	0.1	1.12
Falstaff Brewing Corp.	.08	3.3	4.0	1.37
General Mills Inc.	.14	7.8	8.8	1.31
General Foods Corp.	.17	4.1	6.4	1.22
Gerber Products Company	.17	2.9	2.0	1.29
Green Giant Company	.10	2.0	4.1	1.40
G. Heileman Brewing Company	.15	3.3	14.1	1.37
Helene Curtis Industries Inc.	-.02	17.0	4.6	1.69
Heublein Inc.	.19	7.1	10.4	1.31
George A. Hormel & Company	.10	0.2	0.7	1.34
Hygrade Food Products	-.05	0.2	0.2	1.40

Hershey Foods Corporation	.19	5.9	0.2	1.17
Keebler Company	.04	1.2	2.9	1.24
Kellogg Company	.22	14.2	10.1	1.40
Kraftco Corporation	.12	1.5	2.1	1.30
Libby, McNeill & Libby	.04	2.0	2.9	1.38
Oscar Mayer & Company, Inc.	.11	0.2	3.2	1.39
National Biscuit Company	.18	2.2	2.0	1.26
Pabst Brewing Company	.13	3.3	2.2	1.37
Pet Inc.	.10	1.9	1.2	1.31
Peter Paul Inc.	.16	6.0	8.1	1.16
Philip Morris Inc.	.15	11.4	10.6	1.18
Procter & Gamble Company	.16	9.5	10.4	1.33
Quaker Oats Company	.12	6.9	6.2	1.32
Rath Packing Company	.17	0.2	3.1	1.45
Revlon Inc.	.22	17.0	5.0	1.69
Riviana Foods Inc.	.12	1.4	1.2	1.31
Royal Crown Cola Company	.27	9.3	15.4	1.56
Helena Rubinstein Inc.	.09	17.0	5.6	1.69
Jos. Schlitz Brewing Company	.10	3.3	4.4	1.37
Shulton Inc.	.16	17.0	6.5	1.69
Standard Brands Inc.	.16	4.8	3.0	1.31
Stokely-Van Camp Inc.	.10	2.3	2.4	1.38
Swift & Company	.05	0.2	0.3	1.34
Tasty Baking Company	.16	0.9	2.2	1.16
Tobin Packing Company, Inc.	.08	0.2	8.4	1.33
United States Tobacco Company	.16	3.6	3.8	1.13
Ward Foods Inc.	.06	1.3	1.1	1.22
Wm. Wrigley Jr. Company	.14	11.7	13.4	1.42
American Brands Inc.	.13	10.2	7.8	1.20
Liggett & Meyers Inc.	.10	9.9	8.8	1.22
Reynolds, Inc.	.19	10.1	10.9	1.20

Source: John M. Vernon and Robert E. Nourse, Profit Rates and Market Structure of Advertising Intensive Firms, 22 JOURNAL OF INDUSTRIAL ECONOMICS (1973) at 17–18. Copyright by Basil Blackwell Publisher, Ltd. Reprinted by permission of the publisher.
a This represents the weighted average of industry advertising-to-sales ratio of a firm's product markets. The weights are the firm's share of its sales in each market.

on the whole high rates of growth. The nine firms with growth rates in excess of 50 percent had an average profit rate of 25 percent, substantially above the typical value. If monopoly power accounted for the high profit rates, we would expect output restriction and low growth rates for these firms. Also, Vernon and Nourse find that the weighted average *industry* advertising-to-sales ratios of a firm's product markets and the weighted average growth rates of a firm's product markets have a correlation of .68. To the extent that growth is associated with the promotion of new products and with high profits, the relationship between advertising and profits is spurious.

More important than this, however, is the fact that the rates of profit used are book net income divided by book equity. As we noted, this produces an overstatement because measured assets don't include investments in advertising. We can be sure that at least part of the observed association between advertising and profits, as loose as it is, is an artifact of accounting techniques. To see why, look at the case of Avon, which is noted for its door-to-door cosmetics sales. Avon's recorded profit rate is high, but its advertising to sales ratio is low. Why? Because in Avon's case a good deal of promotional capital is in the form of its "door-to-door advertising," which is not recorded in the measure of advertising intensity.

Various researchers have attempted to correct for the accounting bias, beginning with Weiss.[18] He found that when advertising expenditures were capitalized over six years, a significant positive relationship between advertising and recalculated profits remained. He assumed, however, that the rate of depreciation of advertising is constant across industries. In fact, others have found that advertising depreciates at different rates for different industries. The assumption of a too large constant rate across industries results in a computed capital stock of advertising that is too small for the high advertising firms. The resulting profit rate is still spuriously high. To correct for this bias, Robert Ayanian estimated actual rates of depreciation for six industries. He found rates were typically less than that used by Weiss. Using these rates to calculate a true profit rate for firms, Ayanian found no relationship between advertising and profits.[19]

Similar findings have been presented by Harry Bloch, who used data at the firm level from an earlier Federal Trade Commission study in which advertising and profitability were found to be related. Bloch gathered data on advertising expenditures for the same firms the FTC study used. The FTC study used figures for each firm based on industry advertising in a firm's markets instead of the firm's own advertising. Bloch constructed profit rates that took into account the investment in, and depreciation of, advertising in each firm. These adjusted profit rates were found to be unrelated to the advertising-to-sales ratios.[20]

Professor Harold Demsetz provided confirmation of the results presented by Ayanian and Bloch. Using industry data, Demsetz found that the strength of the relationship between measured profits and advertising as a percentage of equity depends on the degree of accounting bias.[21] He also considered another possibility. If advertising poses a barrier to entry, then its value as such is also not capitalized in the usual accounting measures of assets. Corrections for accounting bias may indicate that firms that advertise heavily earn only a competitive rate of return, but it could still be true that advertising serves to prevent new entry.

Demsetz brought two pieces of evidence to bear on this question. He first compared the relationship between advertising and measured profits in producer and consumer industries. His results confirmed findings in earlier studies showing that the relationship was as strong in producer goods industries as in consumer goods industries. This finding undermines the notion that the profitability of advertising depends on the creation of *consumer* loyalties that serve as a barrier to entry. No one argues that advertising cements the loyalties of professional purchasing agents buying producer goods.

A more important source of evidence on this question is the correlation of industry profits in a given year with profits several years ahead. This test determines whether advertising insulates firms from competition and protects an industry's profit position over time. Using data for forty-eight low advertising bias industries, Demsetz found that relative profitability in industries with high advertising intensity undergoes as much scrambling as it does in low advertising industries. These results indicate that the accounting bias does not reflect returns to "barrier-to-entry capital." Profit rates that are more or less correctly measured do not tend to be more stable or secure when advertising intensity is high.

Table 9-2 presents the intertemporal correlations calculated by Demsetz. Note that if a relatively broad category is chosen, that is,

TABLE 9–2
Average Intertemporal Correlations of Profit Rates
for Restricted Values of the Bias Indicator (BI)

Time Interval in Years	−.04 < BI < .04 Advertising Intensity			−.02 < BI < .02 Advertising Intensity			−.01 < BI < .01 Advertising Intensity		
	Low (20)	Medium (11)	High (17)	Low (13)	Medium (5)	High (9)	Low (7)	Medium (2)	High (7)
T + 1	.72	.78	.77	.78	.84	.62	.83	1.00	.60
T + 2	.60	.63	.74	.69	.79	.73	.78	1.00	.68
T + 3	.46	.60	.62	.61	.78	.47	.74	1.00	.40
T + 4	.42	.61	.55	.65	.85	.53	.81	1.00	.44
T + 5	.42	.58	.43	.59	.76	.17	.88	1.00	.03
T + 6	.43	.51	.39	.57	.75	.27	.84	1.00	.10
T + 7	.32	.33	.33	.38	.58	.09	.71	1.00	−.15
T + 8	.28	.30	.38	.30	.43	.17	.60	1.00	−.11

Source: Harold Demsetz, *Accounting for Advertising as a Barrier to Entry*, 52 JOURNAL OF BUSINESS (July 1979) at 356. Copyright by the University of Chicago. Reprinted by permission of the publisher.

Note: Number of industries in parentheses.

one covering a rather large range of accounting bias, it appears that profits are slightly more stable for the more advertising-intensive firms for periods of two to four years. This appears to provide support for the view that advertising stabilizes market shares and prevents competition. The correlation coefficient between present profits and profits three years hence is .62 for high advertising firms, only .46 for low advertising firms. On reflection, however, this should not be surprising if we consider the influence of accounting bias. For any given industry the bias in measured profit rates is likely to remain unchanged from one year to the next, that is, profits in a given industry will be consistently biased. This alone would lend a bogus stability to measured profits. Industries with a high ratio of advertising to equity (one important source of this bias) would in particular appear to have stable relative profit rates.[22]

One's suspicions on this matter are confirmed by looking at the results for industries with the bias measure more clearly restricted to a narrow interval about zero. Already for the case where the bias indicator is between −.02 and +.02, we see that high advertising industries have profits that are less serially correlated. For the industries with the narrowest range of bias, profit rates for high advertising firms are actually negatively correlated after seven years.

Advertising and Entry

A more direct test of the competitive effects of advertising can be made by looking at what happens to entry when advertising is more intensive. An entry barrier worthy of the name should, of course, have a chilling effect on potential new entrants.[23]

Although much has been written on advertising as an impediment to entry, there is an alternative view. It is possible, and a good deal of evidence supports the contrary hypothesis, that advertising promotes entry. To provide confirmation for this view we would have to find greater advertising in markets where there is considerable growth, product innovation, and a high turnover or growth in number of firms.

What sort of evidence is there for the view that advertising blocks entry? If advertising barricades markets, heavily advertised products would have more stable market shares—the result of the blockage of competition presumed to be the consequence of advertising. Using data on recalled brand shares (shares from consumer surveys), Professor Lester Telser found that more heavily advertised products have less stable market shares.[24] These are particularly strong results. Data from recall surveys tend to overstate the true market shares of heavily advertised brands, and more importantly, overstate the stability of market shares. Using three categories of products—food, soaps, and cosmetics and toiletries—Telser found the least stability of market share among the most heavily advertised group, cosmetics and toiletries, and the most stability in the least advertised group, food products.

> Since the recalled shares are more stable than the actual market shares, these results show that the market shares of the more advertised products—cosmetics and toiletries—are probably much less stable than the market shares of food products—a much less advertised activity. These results refute the view that advertising stabilizes market shares . . . Despite heavier advertising, brands of cosmetics and toiletries are unable to maintain consumer acceptance for as long a time as branded food products.[25]

The liquor industry is another in which high advertising expenditures are believed to contribute to monopoly power. In fact, one of the leading exponents of the view that advertising is a barrier to entry, Professor Joe Bain, placed liquor in a group of industries with very high barriers simply on the basis of its advertising.[26] Professor James Ferguson examined entry in this industry. He found that twenty-two of the seventy-six distilled spirit plants in operation in 1965 had entered in 1944 or later. Of the thirty-five firms that owned registered distilleries producing whiskey in 1965, twelve were new entrants.[27]

Pharmaceutical markets are also among those in which many believe oligopolistic "market structure" and advertising inhibit competition. Telser et al. studied entry in the supply of ethical pharmaceutical products. They found that higher promotional intensity is associated with higher rates of entry into pharmaceutical markets.[28] Moreover, categories of therapeutic drugs that have a high four-firm concentration ratio also have significantly lower promotional intensity. Evidence from this industry, or rather group of industries, confirms the view that advertising often aids entry, and that it is used by firms who might be noticed less without it.

This view of advertising as an aid to entry was confirmed in a study by William Lynk. He found that with the coming of television, which decreased the cost of communicating with the buyers of some products, markets in which television was a lower cost alternative to other means of advertising showed a decrease in disparity of market shares. Market shares became more equal with a rise in the shares of smaller firms relative to the leaders in the typical product group.[29] Lynk compared changes in market structure of a variety of consumer products, as measured by summary statistics based on brand shares in a survey of household spending, for the period from 1952 to 1970. It was during these years that television grew from a seldom used advertising medium to one that absorbed 70 to 80 percent of a firm's advertising outlays for a typical household product.

Lynk used several measures of market structure in addition to the four-firm concentration ratio on which we focus in this book. The chief advantage of these other measures is that they are sensitive to changes in the size distribution of market shares, which is not always true of concentration ratios. The two most common of these measures are the Herfindahl index, which is the sum of the squares of individual market shares, and entropy, which is a geometric mean of the market shares with weights equal to the market shares used. (If s_i is the market share of firm i then the measure of entropy is $s_1^{s_1} \cdot s_2^{s_2} \cdot \ldots \cdot s_n^{s_n}$ for an industry with n firms.) Lynk also used the standard deviation of market shares as a measure of structures. The chief advantage of these three measures Lynk used is that they take into account disparity in the sizes of firms. In all three cases, the measure is greater the greater the disparity in firm sizes.

A fourth measure used by Lynk was also intended to measure size disparity. If we calculate the ratio of sales of the second to the first largest brand we have an index of their relative size. We can calculate this for all successive comparisons (third to second, fourth to third, and so on) and then take the average of the ratios. The smaller the final number, the greater the disparity in a market. If all firms are of equal size, this measure will equal one.

Lynk hypothesized that the role of an innovation such as television was to reduce the cost of providing advertising messages to consumers. If advertising does provide information about products, it will, among other things, acquaint consumers with less widely known brands. As a result, we expect that with an increase in advertising volume, smaller firms will tend to gain customers relative to larger ones. Consequently, we expect market structure to be influenced to a greater degree in those markets that have been better able to take advantage of television advertising's low cost per message.

In addition to an influence derived from television advertising, there is also likely to be some effect on market structure arising from a change in the number of brands and from a change in the fraction of consumers who use the product. Both of these are also expected to decrease diversity in firm size.

Lynk's results, presented in Table 9-3, are consistent with the hypothesis that increased advertising promotes expansion by smaller firms to a size comparable to that of leading firms. Although an increase in the percentage of consumers who used a particular product had no effect on structure, television advertising and an increase in the number of brands tended to reduce the disparity in firm size, judging by all measures except the four-brand concentration ratio, for which advertising did not have a significant effect. Practically the whole change in concentration was explained by the change in the number of brands. This suggests that the *direct* effect of advertising was confined to bringing about a greater uniformity of market share for all the firms in a market without affecting the aggregate share of the four leading

TABLE 9-3

Regressions Explaining Changes in Market Structure, 1952–70
(Dependent Variable: Change in Measure of Market Structure)

Measure of Market Structure	*Constant*	Independent Variables			R^2
		Change in Number of Brands	*Change in Percentage of Consumers Using Product*	*Percentage of Advertising Expenditures Going to TV*	
Herfindahl	.4083 (2.22)	−.7701 (−8.965)	−.0593 (−.752)	−.5501 (−2.610)	.679
Entropy	.2532 (2.198)	−.9445 (−17.539)	−.0296 (−.598)	−.3182 (−2.408)	.869
Standard deviation of market shares	.4624 (2.054)	−.7866 (−7.474)	−.0710 (−.734)	−.6340 (−2.455)	.609
Four-brand concentration ratio	.0789 (.978)	−.4468 (−11.836)	.0076 (.220)	−.0832 (−.896)	.732
Average of sales ratios of successively ranked brands[a]	−.1950 (−.451)	.3178 (8.542)	−.0111 (−.324)	.2440 (2.673)	.635

Source: William J. Lynk, *Information, Advertising, and the Structure of the Market* (dissertation, University of Chicago, 1978), Table 1 at 91. Also, see Mark Horschey, *The Effect of Advertising on Industrial Mobility*, 54 JOURNAL OF BUSINESS 329 (1981).
[a] See text for explanation.
Note: t-ratios are shown in parentheses.

firms. Note, however, that the number of brands tended to increase in markets where television could be used and that the introduction of new brands is not by any means independent of advertising technology. The coefficients of advertising measure only the direct effect of advertising in bringing about a change in market structure (predominantly greater uniformity of firm size); they do not measure the indirect effect stemming from the introduction of new brands, captured largely in the variable measuring the change in new brands itself. In any event, these results provide ample support for his conclusion that "an increase in the real volume of advertising messages causes an increase in the sales of smaller sellers relative to the sales of larger sellers."[30]

Thus Lynk's study provides additional support to the interpretation of advertising as a competitive practice and aid to entry. It illustrates in particular that the introduction of a new, low-cost advertising technology serves to enlarge the markets of smaller firms and to increase the number of brands of a product by lowering the cost per message smaller firms must incur in order to acquaint consumers with their products.

Advertising and Prices

Another strand of thinking has sought to link advertising with higher prices in an attempt to buttress the argument that advertising causes monopoly. Note again that the mere finding of a statistical relationship between advertising and the price of products would not establish that advertising is a monopoly-creating device, nor would it establish that advertising is wasteful. If advertising economizes on consumers' search costs and their costs of assuring quality, for example, then one might expect the observed price of advertised items in the same market with unadvertised items to be higher. But the total cost to consumers, taking these search costs into account, may very well be lower. Several studies have shown that some heavily advertised products are priced higher than non-advertised counterparts in the same market.[31] Are they in fact the same product? Adjusting for quality and saved search costs is a difficult task and such data must be viewed carefully. Also, without the advertising done by some firms, the prices of unadvertised items might be higher.[32]

As an empirical matter, one need not go this far. In a number of instances the prices of identical goods are in fact lower with advertising than without. This becomes apparent where institutional differences allow us to compare otherwise identical markets with varying levels of advertising. Such instances provide us with a better measure of the effect of advertising. In a study of the effect of advertising on the price of eyeglasses, Professor Lee Benham compared the price paid for eyeglasses in states with differing restrictions on advertising.[33] Comparing states in which advertising was completely banned with states in which there were no restrictions, Benham found prices nearly $20 higher for the year 1963 in the states that banned advertising. Benham attributed the difference to the ability of high-volume retailers to attract sufficient customers under a regime of advertising. Benham also found that eyeglass prices were only slightly higher in states that prohibited only price advertising than in states that had no advertising restrictions. This is strong evidence for the view that advertising can be useful and pro-competitive even if it confines itself to providing information not related to pricing.

Similar findings were presented by Robert Steiner in the case of toy sales.[34] With the adoption of television advertising for toys in some markets in the mid-1950s, toys with a $5 retail list price typically sold for $3.49 while the same toys in areas without television advertising sold for $4.98. In addition, an FTC order resulting in the removal of price information from toy advertisements did not push retail prices up. Again, price information was not as important in promoting consumers' welfare as general information about location and availability.

Advertising and Concentration

Advertising has been linked to industrial concentration in a number of hypotheses. The original argument, advanced by Professor Nicholas Kaldor, was that advertising enjoys significant economies of scale. He argued that its use in an industry would increase the average size of firms and decrease the number of firms.[35] On this view the purported technological influence of advertising makes industrial structure more concentrated and, presumably, less competitive.

The attempt to establish a causal link running from advertising to concentration has proceeded beyond the hypothesis offered by

Kaldor. Professor Joe Bain added brand loyalty induced by advertising as a mechanism whereby markets are made less competitive, specifically less open to entry, in addition to making them more concentrated. By focusing on a theory in which consumer preferences were shaped, largely through the creation of advertising-induced product differentiation, Bain placed himself squarely in the tradition founded by Robinson and Chamberlin. Others have tried to advance more detailed explanations of why higher levels of advertising should link with greater concentration, but the connection between decreased competition and increased concentration is not more compelling there than in those explanations that attempt to link these in other ways.

What is the evidence on the relationship between advertising and concentration? In summarizing the results, it is fair to say that a weak positive relationship between measured advertising-to-sales ratios and the level of concentration in an industry has been found. A number of problems with data have plagued researchers in this area, however. The results are sensitive, for example, to the level of aggregation chosen, whether three-digit or four-digit SICs. Also, the association between advertising and concentration occurs in producer goods industries, where it is unexpected.

An example of the relationship between advertising and concentration is presented in Table 9-4. This is from one of the more extensive sets of data in which a positive relationship has been found and includes 329 industries. Oddly enough, although a weak relationship between the advertising-to-sales ratio and the level of industry concentration can be detected (the coefficient of determination is only .02), the relationship for nondurable producer goods is similar to that for consumer goods. Since Bain's hypothesis applies only to consumer industries, the finding of a similar relationship in producer industries suggests that some other hypothesis may be more appropriate.

Apart from the issue of how the evidence from producer nondurables should be interpreted, is this evidence sufficient to support the inference of a causal relationship between advertising and concentration? The cautious investigator would have to say no. There are numerous reasons why one might expect industries with high concentration to also have high advertising-to-sales ratios. These other explanations impute no unfavorable influence to either concentration or advertising.

TABLE 9–4

Regressions of Industry Advertising-to-Sales Ratios on
Concentration Ratios, 1963

Sample	Intercept	Four-Firm Concentration Ratio	R^2
Total (N = 329)	.9177	.0191[b] (2.45)	.02
Consumer (N = 90)	1.7509	.0509[a] (2.08)	.04
Producer, Nondurable (N = 189)	.6535	.0057[a] (1.89)	.01
Producer, Durable (N = 50)	.9054	−.0022 (0.30)	.02

Source: Stanley I. Ornstein, INDUSTRIAL CONCENTRATION AND ADVERTISING INTENSITY (1977), Table 2 at 49. Also, see R. M. Bradburd, *Advertising and Market Concentration: A Re-examination of Ornstein's Spurious Correlation Hypothesis,* 47 SOUTHERN ECONOMIC JOURNAL 581 (1980).
[a] Significant at .05 level
[b] Significant at .01 level
N = number of industries
Figure in parenthesis is the t-ratio.

Concentration and advertising may be related because of the effect of firm size on promotional activity. Suppose that large firms in some lines of business rely to a greater extent on advertising and small firms on promotion by sales personnel. Holding other factors constant, one would then expect a positive correlation within such an industry between size and the advertising-to-sales ratio. Across industries, this would imply a weak positive relationship between concentration and advertising-to-sales ratios (if such industries are distributed independently across various concentration levels) because more concentrated industries have a greater portion of their output produced by larger firms.

We might do well to consider the reasons for a positive relationship in some industries between size (especially size defined in relation to the market) and advertising. First, it is more likely that a large firm serves a larger geographic market. It can, then, make better use of advertising messages. Fewer messages are lost, that is, directed at buyers who would find it impractical to purchase the product. Substantial geographic mobility makes an advertiser's size an important issue also, but in the opposite direction. To the extent that an advertiser distributes over a large area, the advertising messages received by consumers in one area are not lost when they move to another. To that extent, an advertiser selling over a large area suffers less depreciation and will not need to advertise as intensively.

Second, a large producer in a market may stand to gain more by skewing his promotional efforts toward advertising on purely statistical grounds. Someone sampling goods of a given type at random will be more likely to buy one of a large producer than a small producer. If the large producer has advertised in advance, then the claims he makes for his wares in advertising will be examined with greater care. As a related implication, it would also be the case that the large, more advertising-intensive firms would also tend to have the better products. They are, by this statistical sampling theory, in better position to make claims and to have them verified by purchasers.

Third, it may well be the case that large firms in some industries introduce innovative products more frequently. Evidence presented in Chapter 3 indicates that this indeed is the case. Large firms may be better able to handle the associated risk, or to assess whether consumers will buy a new product. They may also be more research intensive, or have the necessary expertise to introduce new products. Since new products require promotional efforts, including advertising, a relationship between concentration and advertising may spring in part from the nature of product innovation. Greater advertising intensity in some industries may simply reflect the greater innovation there.

We would need such systematic forces asserting themselves in only a few industries. Statistically speaking, changes in the level of concentration account for only about 1 to 4 percent of the changes in advertising. For many industries, we find that size and advertising intensity are not related. Professor Ferguson found this lack of relationship for the twenty leading brands of whiskey.[36] Advertising per case corresponds roughly to the measure we have focused on, the advertising-to-sales ratio. Ferguson found that the leading brand ranked twelfth in advertising per case among the twenty leading brands. The leading advertiser was only the sixteenth largest seller. The absence of a strong relationship between advertising intensity and size suggests that the protection of market position is not a determinant of advertising expenditures. Professor Douglas Greer has presented evidence on advertising per barrel of beer that reveals a similar scrambling of sales rank and relative advertising intensity across firms.[37]

The most likely explanation of the correlations, albeit weak, between advertising and concentration—an explanation which, unlike the brand loyalty rationalizations, fits the case of both producer and consumer good industries—is the same as that that explains the correlations between depreciable capital per dollar of sales and concentration and the correlation between inventories per dollar of sales and concentration. Where it decreases costs most markedly to supply the market by use of a capital intensive technology or inventory intensive methods of production and distribution, industries tend to be more concentrated since larger firms can raise capital at lower cost than smaller companies. Firms do not deliberately choose a capital intensive technology to raise a barrier to entry. If they did, they could be undersold by others using a less capital intensive technology. Capital intensive technologies are chosen when they are the low-cost method of production.

Similarly, advertising per dollar of sales is high in some industries because of such exogeneous forces as newness of product, buyer turnover, and methods of distribution (direct sales versus sales through retailers, for example). Where a large investment in advertising is required—and the spending on advertising is an investment—industries tend to be more concentrated for the same reason as when capital intensive technology is required for economical production. Large firms can raise capital at lower cost and offer lower prices to buyers.

The relationship between industry concentration and advertising is shown in Tables 9-5 and 9-6. The 1972 regression in Table 9-6 shows that, other things being equal, a one percent increase in advertising outlays in an industry (in outlays per dollar of sales, since shipments are held constant) was associated with a .076 percent increase in concentration. An industry with a 50 percent concentration ratio would, if changes in methods of distribution required, let us say, a doubling of advertising outlays per dollar of sales, rise to 54 percent concentration in the new equilibrium, assuming no decrease in capital requirements for inventories or depreciable assets and no rise in the industry's total volume of sales or in labor requirements. (It is likely, however, that in these circumstances, retail prices would fall, manufacturing shipments would increase, and a smaller rise in concentration would occur than that described above for no change in other things.)

In view of results such as these, the interpretation to be placed

TABLE 9-5
Investment and Payroll per Dollar of Shipments in Industries Ranked by Concentration Ratios

Four-Firm Concentration Percentage	Number of Four-Digit Industries	Gross Book Value of Depreciable Assets ÷ Shipments	Book Value of Inventories ÷ Shipments	Current Outlays for Advertising[a] ÷ Shipments	Total Payroll[b] ÷ Shipments
				1963	
80–100	17	$.486	$.172	$.027	$.206
60–79	36	.418	.183	.023	.219
40–59	74	.355	.190	.016	.249
20–39	129	.342	.171	.018	.249
0–19	62	.282	.119	.009	.258
0–100	318	.349	.167	.017	.251
				1972	
80–100	18	$.396	$.192	$.029	$.189
60–79	39	.495	.174	.020	.208
40–50	88	.403	.202	.018	.259
20–39	103	.355	.155	.014	.232
0–19	59	.331	.132	.010	.274
0–100	307	.385	.169	.016	.242

Sources: U.S., Department of Commerce, Bureau of Economic Analysis, The Detailed Input-Output Structure of the U.S. Economy: 1972 (1979); Input-Output Structure of the U.S. Economy: 1963 (1969); U.S. Bureau of the Census. Annual Survey of Manufacturers 1976, Industry Profiles, Part 7 (1979); Concentration Ratios in Manufacturing (1975); Census of Manufacturers, 1972 (1975).

[a] Proxy for investment in advertising.
[b] In establishments in 1972; in establishments and central offices and auxiliaries in 1963.

TABLE 9–6
Regressions with the Log of the Four-Firm
Concentration Ratio the Dependent Variable

Constant	Log Gross Book Value of Depreciable Assets	Log Book Value of Inventories	Log Current Outlays for Advertising[a]	Log Total Payroll[b]	Log Shipments	$\bar{r}^2$
			1972 N = 307			
3.90 (15.1)	.263 (4.11)	.319 (5.36)	.076 (3.07)	−.422 (−6.16)	−.306 (−3.08)	.201
			1963 N = 318			
5.63 (14.6)	.326 (5.87)	.331 (5.87)	.071 (2.77)	−.458 (−6.79)	−.381 (−4.14)	.272

Sources: U.S., Department of Commerce, Bureau of Economic Analysis, THE DE-
TAILED INPUT-OUTPUT STRUCTURE OF THE U.S. ECONOMY: 1972 (1979); INPUT-
OUTPUT STRUCTURE OF THE U.S. ECONOMY: 1963 (1969); U.S., Bureau of the
Census, ANNUAL SURVEY OF MANUFACTURERS 1976, INDUSTRY PROFILES, Part 7
(1979); CONCENTRATION RATIOS IN MANUFACTURING (1975); CENSUS OF MANUFAC-
TURERS, 1972 (1975).
N = number of industries. Figure in parentheses is the t-ratio.
[a] proxy for investment in advertising.
[b] in establishments in 1972; in establishments and central offices and auxiliaries in
1963.

on any connection that might exist between advertising intensity
and concentration in an industry is not the view that advertising
is an exclusionary device used to monopolize. The argument
against reading monopoly into an association between the two was
concisely stated by William Comanor and Thomas Wilson, who
are the authors of *Advertising and Market Power* and who rank
prominently among those who say that advertising has anti-competitive effects.

Unfortunately, concentration is a poor measure of monopoly, which
surely depends on the height of entry barriers as well as other factors.
Even where heavy advertising leads to increased barriers to entry,
concentration is not necessarily altered. The rate of entry of new
firms, which should influence concentration, depends as well on the
pricing practices of established firms, and in particular, whether
prices are set low enough to limit entry. As a result, correlations
between advertising and concentration represent a poor test of the
effect of advertising on competition.[38]

Whether advertising and market structure are related is an interesting area of inquiry; research on this topic may provide insights into the size distribution of firms and how information costs are incurred. But it will not, as Comanor and Wilson affirm, tell us very much about the relationship between advertising and competition.

Conclusion

Our theme in earlier chapters, amply supported by empirical evidence, has been that concentration is a poor measure of monopoly power or the state of competition. We see this theme repeated when we look at the issue of advertising. Economic analyses of advertising show it to be an aid to competition, one of the devices for overcoming consumers' ignorance and inertia.

The amount of advertising done by a firm is largely determined by consumer needs for information and the relative cost of providing information by advertising and by other means. New products and new models of old products are advertised more extensively than old products and old models since buyers are less well informed about new items. Firms do not waste their resources providing information that buyers already possess. In the case of goods whose qualities cannot be determined before purchase by examination, the fact that they are advertised provides assurance that the product will perform as desired. For a few products, advertising attempts to build associations that consumers desire and provides these buyers with inexpensive ways of achieving satisfactions otherwise beyond their reach.

Advertising, as we see it used, is a least-cost means to an end. It is a substitute for more expensive means of informing consumers and distributing products. Broadly speaking, we know that if it were not so, other market arrangements would spring up to replace it. As economic circumstances change, certain forms of promotion and distribution replace others. We see, for example, that door-to-door salesmen are no longer common as they once were. More working women, the increasing technical sophistication of household items, and the increased value of the time of sales personnel led to the general abandonment of door-to-door selling. In addition, the advent of self-service merchandising reduced the provision of information by retail sales personnel. At the same time, the spread of literacy and the introduction of television lowered the cost of carrying messages to the home. Lower-cost methods of distribution and lower-cost means of advertising each contributed to the use of the other, and consumers gained through the resultant decrease in prices. In short, advertising is a response to consumers' desire for information, and the form in which we see it reflects the costs of providing it.

How strong is the evidence that links advertising with monopoly? It turns out that the purported relationship between advertising and the rate of return is based on an accounting artifact. When profit is measured correctly, profit instability is as large in high advertising industries as in those with little advertising. This suggests that advertising is used in industries in which competition is fairly keen, and in which the fortunes of individual firms are somewhat more volatile than on average. Evidence of market shares in different types of business confirm this view. High advertising intensity is associated with unstable market shares. What is more, promotional intensity is associated with higher rates of new entry and greater industry growth. An additional important piece of evidence linking advertising with competition is that in cases where the level of advertising has been affected by institutional or technical changes, increased advertising results in lower prices.

In view of such findings, the continued attempt to link advertising and concentration and to interpret an ambiguous statistical relationship between the two as evidence of monopoly is surprising. A rich array of hypotheses, none of them relying on monopoly or anticompetitive impulses, explains the observed correlations. The correlations are consistent with a number of interpretations. But the competition hypothesis explains a broader array of phenomena than the monopoly hypothesis. What makes the particular hypothesis connecting advertising and restraints on competition implausible is the wealth of evidence that refutes the monopoly interpretation.

Notes

1. O. Williamson, *Selling Expense as a Barrier to Entry*, 77 QUARTERLY JOURNAL OF ECONOMICS 112 (Feb. 1963).
2. For an introduction to these issues see David G. Tuerck (ed.), ISSUES IN ADVERTISING (1978); Y. Brozen, *Is Advertising a Barrier to Entry?* Y. Brozen, ed., ADVERTISING AND SOCIETY 79 (1974); and John S.

McGee, In Defense of Industrial Concentration 47–52 (1971). The modern debate on advertising may be traced by reading Nicholas Kaldor, *The Economic Aspects of Advertising,* 18 Review of Economic Studies 1 (Jan. 1950); Joe S. Bain, Barriers to New Competition: Their Character and Consequences in Manufacturing Industries (1956); Lester G. Telser, *Advertising and Competition,* 72 Journal of Political Economy 537 (Dec. 1964); and Phillip Nelson, *Advertising as Information,* 82 Journal of Political Economy 729 (Aug. 1974).

3. Marshall Goldman, *Product Differentiation and Advertising: Some Lessons From Soviet Experience,* 68 Journal of Political Economy 346 (Aug. 1960), provides an interesting study of how trademarks and other marks identifying the plant of manufacture promote the production of quality in the Soviet Union.
4. The basis of this view is to be found in Joan Robinson, The Economics of Imperfect Competition (1933), especially at 5 and the chapter entitled *A World of Monopolies.*
5. See *id.* at 88 and 90.
6. Edward Chamberlin, The Theory of Monopolistic Competition 117 (1933).
7. See *id.* at 174.
8. See *id.* at 118 (emphasis supplied). Telser adds that advertising attracts customers with weaker preferences for the brand who are sensitive to price, thus further increasing the elasticity of demand. *Advertising: Economic Aspects* 1 International Encyclopedia of the Social Sciences 106 (1968).
9. Tibor Scitovsky, Welfare and Competition 377 (1951).
10. See Bain *supra* note 2.
11. Lloyd G. Reynolds, Microeconomics: Analysis and Policy 173 (1979).
12. See *id.* at 174. James Ferguson finds that there are no important economies of scale in advertising and that a survey of the data shows diminishing returns. Advertising and Competition (1975).
13. Dick Wittinck, *Advertising Increases Sensitivity to Price,* 17 Journal of Advertising Research 39 (1977); G. J. Eskin and H. P. Baron, *Effects of Price and Advertising in Test-Market Experiments,* 14 Journal of Marketing Research 499 (Nov. 1977).
14. Lester Telser demonstrated that just such advertising competition was at work in the case of the cigarette industry. See his *Advertising and Cigarettes,* 70 Journal of Political Economy 471 (Oct. 1962).
15. Lester G. Telser, discussion, 59 American Economic Review 121 (May 1969).
16. William S. Comanor and Thomas A. Wilson, *Advertising, Market Structure, and Performance,* 49 Review of Economics and Statistics 423 (Nov. 1967).
17. Professor Thomas Nagle also finds this to be the case with Comanor and Wilson's sample of 41 three-digit consumer goods industries. *Consumer Information, Advertising, and Industry Profitability* (dissertation, University of California, Los Angeles, 1978).
18. Leonard W. Weiss, *Advertising, Profits, and Corporate Taxes,* 51 Review of Economics and Statistics 421 (Nov. 1969).
19. Robert Ayanian, *Advertising and Rate of Return,* 18 Journal of Law & Economics 479 (Oct. 1975).

20. Harry Bloch, *Advertising and Profitability: A Reappraisal*, 82 JOURNAL OF POLITICAL ECONOMY 267 (Apr. 1974).
21. Harold Demsetz, *Accounting for Advertising as a Barrier to Entry*, 52 JOURNAL OF BUSINESS 345 (Jul. 1979). Demsetz uses a measure of accounting bias equal to

$$\frac{\pi}{\epsilon} - \frac{r}{1 + r}$$

where π/ϵ is the measured after-tax rate of return, and r is the rate of growth of advertising expenditures. Accounting bias is positive, zero, or negative as this expression is positive, zero, or negative. This measure of bias was deduced by Weiss *supra* note 18, and applies to the case where advertising expenditures are growing at a constant rate. Demsetz used the advertising to equity ratio because the theoretical claim is that advertising is a capital asset.
22. See discussion preceding note 30 in Chapter 8.
23. Note that a conceptually thorough notion of entry would include the entry coming about by the expansion of existing firms. A related issue is that in many areas the market shares of firms seem stable, although when we look closely at categories of goods that are more narrowly defined than the standard industrial classification, considerably more fluctuation in firm shares occurs. Entry in a particular market often appears in the form of entry by existing producers in a related field. When broad categories are examined this type of competition and entry is often obscured.
24. See Telser *supra* note 2.
25. See *id.* at 550.
26. See Bain *supra* note 2, at 169–70, 293.
27. James M. Ferguson, *Advertising and Liquor*, 40 JOURNAL OF BUSINESS 414 (Oct. 1967).
28. Lester G. Telser et al., *The Theory of Supply with Applications to the Ethical Pharmaceutical Industry*, 18 THE JOURNAL OF LAW & ECONOMICS 449 (Oct. 1975).
29. William J. Lynk, *Information, Advertising, and the Structure of the Market* (dissertation, University of Chicago, 1978).
30. See *id.* at 114.
31. See Telser *supra* note 2, at 542, n. 3, for a discussion of sources on this question.
32. See Y. Brozen *supra* note 2, at 96–99.
33. Lee Benham, *The Effects of Advertising on the Prices of Eyeglasses*, 15 THE JOURNAL OF LAW & ECONOMICS 337 (Oct. 1972).
34. Robert Steiner, *Does Advertising Lower Consumer Prices*, 37 JOURNAL OF MARKETING 24 (Jan. 1973).
35. See Kaldor *supra* note 2.
36. See Ferguson *supra* note 27, at 426.
37. Douglas F. Greer, *Product Differentiation and Concentration in the Brewing Industry*, 10 JOURNAL OF INDUSTRIAL ECONOMICS 214 (Jul. 1971).
38. W. S. Comanor and T. A. Wilson, *The Effect of Advertising on Competition: A Survey*, 17 JOURNAL OF ECONOMIC LITERATURE 458 (Jun. 1979).

10

An Empirical Test of Oligopoly Theories

In its complaints against the four major ready-to-eat (RTE) cereal companies and the eight largest petroleum refiners, the Federal Trade Commission (FTC) adopted the notion that a large share of the market in the hands of a small number of firms results in shared monopoly behavior (i.e., tacit collusion).[1] The FTC and the Antitrust Division have devoted resources to investigating concentrated industries apparently on no other grounds than the *presumption* that high concentration and shared monopoly are cause and effect. A strong belief prevailed within the antitrust agencies that structure determines behavior and performance.[2]

In addition to suspecting that evil consequences flow from concentrated structures, the antitrust agencies also viewed certain practices as monopolizing in character when used by major firms in concentrated industries despite the acceptance of these practices as innocent, normal competitive behavior when used by smaller firms in the same industries or by those in less concentrated industries. Judge Hand, in the Alcoa decision, provided one of the judicial precedents for the double standard.[3] Recall there that the Court held Alcoa guilty of monopolizing by building capacity to serve aluminum ingot customers as their demand grew. Any competitive firm is expected to build additional capacity if it anticipates an increase in the demand for its product and expects the costs of additional capacity will be covered by the price of the product.

The conduct of the Marblehead Lime Company provides a specific example of such behavior. In 1960, it risked investing $15 million in additional capacity in anticipation of the then uncertain increase in demand it expected from the expansion of basic oxygen furnace capacity for making steel. It was not evoking the increased demand, as Alcoa did by its research and its development of additional uses for aluminum, but it was responding to an anticipated increase in demand as Alcoa did. Marblehead's foresight vaulted it from number sixty among ninety-four lime companies to number one. It is today undertaking a gamble, investing $55 million in additional capacity, building in anticipation of a further increase in demand. It is expanding from its number one position among 68 firms. In doing so, it may be risking an antitrust attack. That this is no idle fear can be seen from the recent FTC action against du Pont. The FTC brought a case against du Pont for expanding its titanium dioxide capacity by building an additional plant at De Lisle, Mississippi. Although the administrative law judge has found in favor of du Pont, the FTC staff is appealing to the Commission to reverse the finding.

The wrong committed by a monopolist, and the essence of monopoly behavior, is its failure to add more production when the cost of the added output is less than the expected price. Adding to capacity and output when the *addition* will be profitable is the essence of competitive behavior. Yet, as Professor Donald Turner, a former chief of the Antitrust Division, points out, Hand's characterization of Alcoa's normal response to expected demand growth as preemptive—as a creation of a barrier to the entry of other firms—made competitive behavior in the concentrated primary aluminum industry illegal.

> One would think . . . expansion of capacity to meet existing or anticipated demand . . . is obviously one of the most important responses that we expect a competitive market to generate. Yet this is precisely the kind of conduct which Judge Hand cited as the principal element in Alcoa's offense.[4]

It could not have been Judge Hand's intention to force oligopolists and dominant firms to behave as some economists conjectured they would conduct themselves, yet that is the effect of his

1945 decision. When the Department of Justice, following the Alcoa decision, brought its case against du Pont in 1947 for "monopolizing" cellophane, du Pont canceled plans to build additional capacity and expand its output.[5]

On Hand's analysis, Alcoa would have been held innocent if it had refrained from adding capacity and output. It should have restrained output and let prices rise to the level that would invite entry.[6] His decision invites ridicule when it says "the successful competitor having been urged to compete, must not be turned upon when he wins." He recognized that Alcoa behaved competitively, yet he ruled that it had monopolized by conducting itself competitively. Aaron Director and Edward Levi pithily summarize the net effect of the opinion in Alcoa: "Perhaps now the successful competitor can be turned upon when he wins because he has been told not to compete."[7]

The Federal Trade Commission staff, in a perhaps unconscious attempt to force noncompetitive behavior on leading firms in concentrated industries, adopted the Hand doctrine in interpreting the major cereal companies' response to anticipated market demands for new varieties of ready-to-eat cereals. It argued that they preempted the market by their "brand proliferation."

If twenty firms had each successfully brought out four brands of cereals, proliferating the number of brands and thus "preempting" the market and "barring" entry, this, presumably, would be viewed as a normal response to market demands and opportunities.[8] But the same response to the market by four firms with 78 percent of the industry's 1954 sales, who increased their share of this growing market to 82 percent by 1967 (see Table 10-1), is viewed as somehow different and iniquitous.[9] The FTC viewed "brand proliferation" as a part of the "shared monopoly's" tacit conspiracy to bar the market to potential entrants.

If there were tacit conspiracy, it would rationally take the form, "my refraining from putting out a new brand should be understood to mean that you will not bring out a new brand either." In this way, the costs and risks of developing and launching new varieties could be avoided. The profits of the "shared monopoly" would be increased. The fact that cartel agreements provide for standardizing products and terms suggests that proliferating products is evidence of an absence of tacit collusion.

A study by R. D. Buzzell and R. E. Nourse demonstrated that the costs and risks of launching new cereal brands are on a par

TABLE 10-1

Industry, Product Group, and Value-Added Four-Firm Concentration Ratios, 1935–72, in Industries 76 Percent Concentrated or More at Some Point

Four-Firm Share of Industry and Product Group Shipments and of Value Added

1972 SIC Number[b]	Industry[c]	1935 a1(a2)a3	1947 a1(a2)a3	1954 a1(a2)a3	1958 a1(a2)a3	1963 a1(a2)a3	1967 a1(a2)a3	1972 a1(a2)a3
2043	Cereal breakfast foods[d]	68(—)72	79(—)77	88(78)—	83(80)—	86(82)87	88(82)90	90(84)91
2046 (2094)	Wet corn milling (A)	79(—)82	77(—)—	75(71)—	73(68)—	71(65)73	68(64)71	63(63)69
2052	Biscuits and crackers	—(—)—	72(—)—	71(—)—	65(61)—	59(58)—	59(56)66	59(58)64
2066 (2072)	Chocolate and cocoa (C)	67(—)65	68(—)—	70(65)—	71(69)—	75(71)80	77(74)83	74(72)83
2067 (2073)	Chewing gum (C)	97(—)94	70(—)72	86(84)85	89(83)—	90(86)92	86(81)89	87(84)89
2085 (133)	Distilled liquor (B)	51(—)55	75(—)78	64(63)62	60(60)—	58(56)62	54(52)58	47(50)50
20994(2091)	Leavening compounds (C)	57(—)59	83(—)—	80(77)—	86(78)—	—(86)—	—(81)—	—(89)—
2111 (1652)	Cigarettes (C)	89(—)93	90(—)88	82(82)80	79(80)—	80(D)79	81(D)80	84(84)84
2141	Tobacco stemming (C)	—(—)—	88(—)—	79(81)—	73(75)—	70(72)49	63(67)57	67(66)51
2271	Woven carpets and rugs (C)	—(—)—	—(—)—	—(—)—	—(50)—	65(61)67	71(60)76	76(62)78
2282	Wool felt hats (C)	—(—)—	76(—)—	73(67)—	70(—)—	—(—)—	—(—)—	—(—)—
2296	Tire cord and fabric	—(—)—	—(—)—	—(—)—	—(64)—	79(71)77	83(74)81	84(81)85
2646 (2964)	Pressed and molded pulp	—(—)—	86(—)—	72(76)—	69(67)—	72(70)73	71(71)73	75(75)75
28193/2811	Sulfuric acid	—(—)—	—(—)—	82(D)—	79(58)—	—(60)—	—(54)—	—(55)—
2813 (2896)	Industrial gases (B)	79(—)79	83(—)—	84(77)—	79(78)—	72(71)71	67(65)70	65(67)67
28655/2821	Cyclic crudes (C)	—(—)—	91(—)—	94(89)—	93(89)—	D(95)D	—(95)—	—(92)—
2823 (2825)	Cellulose manmade fibers (C)	74(—)75	78(—)77	80(79)81	78(71)—	82(79)84	86(79)86	96(84)D
2824 (2825)	Organic fibers, noncellulose	—(—)—	—(—)—	—(D)—	—(D)—	(94(D)95)	84(82)87	74(73)78
2833	Medicinals and botanicals	—(—)—	—(—)—	72(51)—	64(53)—	68(51)71	74(52)75	59(49)67
2841	Soap and glycerine (A)	76(—)75	79(—)—	83(63)—	90(—)—	—(—)—	—(—)—	—(—)—
2861	Hardwood distillation (C)	—(—)—	73(—)—	76(74)—	75(—)—	—(—)—	—(—)—	—(—)—
28611/2862	Softwood distillation (C)	—(—)—	86(—)—	88(83)—	89(80)—	—(D)—	—(85)—	—(90)—
2892 (2826)	Explosives (C)	82(—)83	80(—)—	79(79)—	77(73)—	72(70)75	67(69)66	67(69)69
20931(2882)	Linseed oil mills (C)	87(—)88	75(—)—	85(84)—	81(77)—	—(84)—	—(86)—	—(98)—
2895 (2895)	Carbon black (C)	81(—)84	78(—)—	70(69)—	73(75)—	72(72)73	72(72)72	74(74)74
28991(2898)	Salt (C)	60(—)63	81(—)79	86(83)84	81(81)—	—(77)—	—(75)—	—(70)—

Code	Product							
3011 (3011)	Tires and inner tubes (B)	80(—)82	77(—)75	79(78)78	74(71)—	70(72)71	70(71)71	73(73)74
3021 (801)	Rubber footwear	81(—)82	81(—)80	72(74)72	65(66)—	62(62)65	59(59)61	59(56)62
3031	Reclaimed rubber	—(—)—	84(—)—	73(66)—	87(66)—	93(73)93	87(73)84	78(74)77
3211	Flat glass	88.1(—)—	—(—)—	90(D)89	92(90)—	94(87)93	94(85)94	92(83)92
3275 (3272)	Gypsum products (C)	76.1(—)78	85(—)86	90(89)85	88(86)—	84(82)85	80(78)81	80(79)81
3296 (3275)	Mineral wool (C)	—(—)—	57(—)52	66(63)63	65(63)—	67(68)63	71(70)69	75(72)77
(3294)	Graphite	—(—)—	77.4(—)—	—(79)—	—(—)—	—(—)—	—(—)—	—(—)—
3313	Electrometallurgical products (C)	—(—)—	88(—)—	77(D)—	73(67)—	79(70)83	74(71)75	74(72)79
3331	Primary copper	—(—)—	80.0(—)93	—(—)86	—(NA)87	85(NA)78	71(NA)77	74(60)72
3332	Primary lead	—(—)—	D(—)—	D(—)D	D(—)D	D(D)D	D(D)D	88(D)93
3334	Primary aluminum	—(—)—	100(—)—	100(99)—	D(82)—	D(93)D	D(91)91	79(80)83
(3352)	Aluminum rolling and drawing (C)	—(—)—	94(—)93	88(82)89	78(75)—	68(67)67	65(64)61	—(—)—
3463 (3392)	Nonferrous forgings	80(—)78	78(—)75	—(63)—	—(70)—	84(56)82	77(54)73	71(51)68
3411	Metal cans (C)	85(—)86	—(—)75	80(80)80	80(80)—	74(73)75	73(70)72	66(66)64
(3424)	Files	84(—)86	92(—)—	94(92)—	D(—)—	D(D)D	D(D)D	—(89)—
34991(3492)	Safes and vaults (C)	—(—)—	85(—)—	90(86)—	91(87)—	—(—)—	—(—)—	90(D)91
(3497)	Metal foil	—(—)—	73.2(—)—	75(67)77	62(39)—	93(83)92	88(78)88	—(—)—
3511 (3511)	Turbines and generators (C)	—(—)—	88(—)89	87(85)91	87(86)—	67(63)63	—(—)—	73(63)74
(3568)	Mechanical stokers	—(—)—	55(—)69	78(D)—	67(—)—	—(—)—	83(74)83	—(—)—
3571	Computing related machines (B)	D(—)—	69(—)69	74(74)70	77(77)—	76(79)75	81(81)80	59(58)60
3574	Calculating machines	—(—)—	79(—)81	83(78)—	79(79)—	68(65)73	65(64)68	80(79)77
35797(3572)	Typewriters (C)	—(—)—	73(—)74	78(75)81	71(71)—	83(82)82	86(84)84	—(—)—
3612 (3615)	Transformers (A)	—(—)—	87(—)86	86(82)82	87(84)—	74(73)79	73(69)79	—(—)—
3624 (3612)	Carbon and graphite products (C)	—(—)—	—(—)—	—(—)—	—(—)—	78(71)85	78(74)84	—(—)—
3632	Household refrigerators and freezers	56(—)58	40(—)—	68(58)—	—(65)—	81(64)86	76(62)80	85(75)89
3633 (3581)	Household laundry equipment (C)	—(—)—	—(—)—	—(—)—	71(67)—	D(82)D	81(80)83	83(76)86
3635	Household vacuum cleaners	78(—)73	77(—)78	81(76)—	—(64)—	92(89)92	91(88)91	75(66)78
3636 (3583)	Sewing machines	—(—)—	92(—)91	93(93)94	D(D)—	69(68)72	58(58)62	84(80)89
3641 (3651)	Electric lamps (A)	—(—)—	79(—)91	70(69)—	92(90)—	92(D)92	93(D)92	90(87)91
3652 (3663)	Phonograph records	—(—)—	96(—)95	89(89)90	76(74)—	86(83)88	94(89)93	48(47)50
3661 (3664)	Telephone apparatus	—(—)—	—(—)—	—(79)—	—(—)92	91(81)91	84(84)90	D(D)D
3671	Receiving tubes	—(—)—	—(58)—	—(58)—	—(76)—	89(83)89	85(85)86	95(90)94
3672	Cathode ray picture tubes	—(—)—	76(—)77	75(80)—	—(64)—	—(—)—	92(93)92	83(82)82
3692	Primary batteries (A)	—(—)—	—(—)—	—(—)—	84(84)—	—(—)—	—(—)—	92(91)91
3711	Motor vehicles	—(—)—	—(—)—	—(—)—	—(—)—	—(—)—	—(—)—	93(93)92

281

TABLE 10-1 (Cont)

Industry, Product Group, and Value-Added Four-Firm Concentration Ratios, 1935–72, in Industries 76 Percent Concentrated or More at Some Point

1972 SIC Number[b]	Industry[c]	Four-Firm Share of Industry and Product Group Shipments and of Value Added						
		1935 a1(a2)a3	1947 a1(a2)a3	1954 a1(a2)a3	1958 a1(a2)a3	1963 a1(a2)a3	1967 a1(a2)a3	1972 a1(a2)a3
(3717)	Motor vehicles and parts (C)	—(—)—	66.8(—)56	82.7(—)75	—(—)75	84(—)79	—(—)—	—(—)—
3721	Aircraft (C)	—(—)—	—(—)—	—(55)—	59(62)—	60(58)59	69(76)70	66(69)66
3724 (3722)	Aircraft engines and parts (C)	—(—)—	—(—)—	—(—)—	—(—)—	—(—)—	—(—)—	77(74)74
37285(3723)	Aircraft propellers (C)	—(—)—	—(—)98	—(90)91	—(NA)97	D(87)D	—(77)—	—(81)—
(3741)	Locomotives and parts	—(—)—	91(—)—	91(89)—	95(92)—	97(92)96	97(D)97	—(—)—
3795	Tanks and components	—(—)—	—(—)—	—(—)—	—(—)—	—(—)—	—(—)—	95(83)94
39312(3932)	Organs (C)	57.0(—)59	78(—)—	81(78)—	71(61)—	—(5)—	—(57)—	—(56)—
39313(3933)	Piano and organ parts (C)	41.4(—)40	71(—)—	76(71)—	73(74)—	—(48)—	—(50)—	—(64)—
24994(3982)	Cork products	76 (—)76	82(—)—	84(D)—	77(67)—	—(58)—	—(46)—	—(73)—
3993 (3983)	Matches	70 (—)65	80(—)—	74(72)—	64(63)—	71(70)75	—(72)—	—(73)—
3982	Hard surface floor covering (C)	81.6(—)84	80(—)—	87(84)—	83(79)—	87(85)90	89(86)90	91(90)93
(3996)	Tobacco pipes (C)	62 (—)65	52(—)—	63(63)—	81(—)—	—(—)—	—(—)—	—(—)—

Sources: Bureau of the Census, CONCENTRATION RATIOS IN MANUFACTURING INDUSTRY, 1958 (1962), Part II at 469–72; CONCENTRATION RATIOS IN MANUFACTURING (1975); CONCENTRATION RATIOS IN MANUFACTURING, Part 3 (1971); CONCENTRATION RATIOS IN MANUFACTURING, Part I (1966); Ralph Nelson, CONCENTRATION IN THE MANUFACTURING INDUSTRIES OF THE UNITED STATES (1963).

a1 First figure under each year is industry shipments concentration.

a2 Second figure is product concentration (shown in parentheses).

a3 Third figure is value added concentration.

b Number is italicized (and corresponding concentration ratios) where the industry definition changed in 1958. Where an industry's SIC number in earlier years differed from its 1972 number, the earlier number is shown in parentheses.

c Letter designation in parentheses following industry name indicates four largest companies were the same in 1947 and 1958 and their sales ranked in the same order (A), were the same but ranked in an order in 1958 that was different from that in 1947 (B), or the four largest companies in 1947 were not all among the four largest in 1958 (C). Industry 2045 omitted from the list despite its 76 percent value-added concentration in 1972 because it produced the same product, although made from purchased ingredients, as industry 2041, which produced the product from ingredients made in the same establishment.

d Figures given in the table are from the Bureau of the Census. A recomputation from Census records by Ralph Nelson found the 1947 industry four-firm shipments ratio to be 85.6. Id. at 111.

D = Datum withheld by the Bureau of Census to avoid disclosing operations of individual companies.

with those of "wildcatting" in the oil industry. They found that the median cumulative contribution of ten new RTE cereals to fixed costs and profit by the end of the third year after introduction was *minus* 13 percent of cumulative sales. Of the ten, only four made a positive contribution by the end of the fourth year after introduction. The contribution was measured without any allowance for loss of contribution from other brands as a consequence of the introduction of the new brands. Nor was any interest cost on the capital invested considered as part of the cost.[10]

If the RTE cereal companies were sharing a monopoly and tacitly colluding, each would, by refraining from product innovation, avoid stealing business from its old brands and the brands of other firms. Because they do not have a monopoly of the RTE cereal business and because they compete with each other for the market, they each introduce new brands to compete for RTE business. "Brand proliferation" is evidence against tacit or express collusion in the cereal industry, but the FTC staff said this behavior indicated collusion. In effect, the FTC staff was arguing that a failure to invade each other's markets—which would be equivalent to an agreement to divide markets—would be evidence of competitive behavior. In other antitrust cases, such agreements to divide markets have been ruled per se violations of the antitrust laws.

Even the practices of buyers from concentrated industries are viewed differently than those same practices when engaged in by buyers from less concentrated industries. In its complaint against General Motors' alleged monopolization of the production and sale of common-carrier monocoque buses, the Antitrust Division accused General Motors and bus buyers of conspiring with each other to shut out GM bus competitors. Buyers shut out GM's competitors, said the Division, by specifying such features as three-eighths-inch bumpers and ribbed brake drums.[11] Equipping buses with these items is more costly than equipping them with thinner bumpers and non-ribbed brake drums, but the Antitrust Division never attempted to show that this was *necessarily* more costly for GM's competitors than for GM. Neither did it attempt to demonstrate that it was in the interest of buyers of buses to conspire with GM to prevent other firms from competing for their business.

In 1977, Attorney General Bell, following in the path trod earlier by Senators Hart and Harris, the White House Antitrust Task Force, Professors Kaysen and Turner, and Professor Simons, suggested that Congress should pass legislation outlawing high concentration. His ground for this recommendation was the difficulty of proving to a court that a major firm in a highly concentrated industry has violated the antitrust laws. Therefore, it should be subject to divestiture without bothering with the formality of a trial.[12] Bell evidently believed that collusion, tacit when not explicit, automatically occurs in concentrated industries. Therefore, the joint possession by a few firms of a large market share should join formal price conspiracies as a per se violation of the antitrust laws, regardless of its effect.

Market Share Trends Postulated by Oligopoly Theory

Many analysts doubt the automatic equivalence of high concentration and collusion.[13] Posner speaks of

> The impermissible analytical leap (which proponents of the interdependence theory of oligopoly often make) . . . from the proposition that concentration is probably a necessary condition of clandestine collusion to the proposition that it is a sufficient condition. There is nothing in the theory of cartels to suggest that if there are just a few major sellers in a market competition will automatically disappear. Each seller must still decide whether to limit output, and this implies at least tacit agreement with his major competitors. The problems of arriving at a mutually agreeable price and then maintaining it in the face of temptations to cheat exist whether few or many sellers are trying to collude.[14]

Posner goes on to list eleven other conditions, in addition to high concentration, for indicating a potentiality for successful collusion.[15] Concentration alone is not a sufficient ground for suspecting collusion, implicit or explicit. Legislation that presumes the equivalence of concentration and collusion would be ill founded. Even with the eleven criteria plus concentration present as predisposing conditions, Posner does not suggest that the search for collusion end there or that legislation be enacted. These are the beginning of the search for industries to be brought to heel. These are to "help the enforcement agencies to identify those markets in which collusion was likely and therefore in which the agencies should concentrate their search for evidence of price fixing."[16]

Posner then argues that "even though no overt acts of collusion are detected . . . it may be possible to demonstrate the existence of collusive pricing. Here he lists and discusses twelve varieties of "evidence of collusive behavior relevant to such a demonstration."[17] Among these are (1) fixed relative market shares of major firms (whether by fixing geographical zones or sales quotas or by assignment of customers), and (2) declining market shares of leaders.

The latter criterion was examined for concentrated industries in the periods 1947–58 and 1947–63 first by Shepherd and then by Kamerschen. They also examined concentration trends in industries thought to be collusive ("consensus" oligopolies) by various investigators.[18] Their conclusions concerning concentration trends in "oligopolies" differ. Kamerschen says that

> Although Shepherd's first survey using the narrow CR definition [industries with four-firm concentration ratios of 75 percent or higher in 1947] of "oligopoly" was somewhat ambiguous, he concludes primarily on the basis of the broad BSS definition [thirty-five four-digit industries isolated by Bain, Shepherd, and Stigler as "oligopolies"] that the concentration level of the thirty-five "oligopolies" shows a greater tendency to increase or remain constant than to decline appreciably. In contrast, this study does not confirm his finding. Indeed, it appears that Stigler's hypothesis of falling market shares or the static version of Bain's theory that predicts constant shares has as much, if not more, support than the rising share theories over the 1947–63 period.[19]

Inasmuch as "a long-term decline in the market shares of the leading firms in a market . . . is a symptom of price-fixing, though an ambiguous one since it may be attributable to other factors,"[20] it would be useful to settle the question of whether a "long-term decline in the market share of leading firms" is characteristic of concentrated industries. If it is, then we have evidence that provides some support to the notion that firms in concentrated industries frequently collude. If it is not, we may be entitled to be skeptical about proposals to deconcentrate industries by legislative fiat because of a need to end implicit or explicit collusion. We may also be entitled to view the idea that a trend toward concentration should be nipped in its "incipiency" with even greater skepticism. If concentration once attained does not then lead to supracompetitive pricing, it may cause a loss of efficiency gains if we prevent a trend toward concentration.

It is possible now to extend the tests of Kamerschen and Shepherd with data that have become available from the 1972 Census of Manufacturers. Perhaps this can help settle the question debated by Kamerschen and Shepherd, although it does not necessarily end the debate concerning the equivalence of high concentration and collusion.[21] Even if we find that a concentrated industry is more likely to remain concentrated than it is to become less concentrated over time, it may still be argued that collusion among major firms occurs and yet concentration persists despite supracompetitive prices. Scale innovations could lower costs and collusion could prevent these lower costs from being passed on to buyers.[22]

Collusion in concentrated industries, it may be argued, occurs and results in supracompetitive pricing, but the umbrella is not held high enough to encourage entry by small firms who would be producing with substantial diseconomies. Peltzman, in his study of *The Gains and Losses from Industrial Concentration*,[23] concludes that deconcentrating the more-than-50-percent-concentrated industries would raise costs by 20 percent and prices by 10 to 15 percent. This is consistent both with collusion among the largest firms and with Demsetz' finding that rates of return in small firms are sometimes negatively correlated with concentration.[24] If the collusion hypothesis holds, then prices are 5 to 10 percent higher in concentrated industries than they would be if the firms in these industries were competing with one another. This, however, is cold comfort to antitrusters and to deconcentrators. Prices in concentrated industries are 10 to 15 percent lower than if deconcentration were forced on these industries by legislation. Deconcentration would worsen the allocation of resources.[25] It would leave buyers worse off even if it ends collusive arrangements.

If the scale economies are the result of innovations (where the innovations may simply be successful operation at larger scale than had previously been attempted), then the higher than long-run competitive equilibrium prices simply manifest *temporary* innovation profits for the largest firms.[26] Increasing concentration (more than 5 percentage points increase), which was found by Kamerschen in five of his twenty-two highly concentrated industries, is consistent with the introduction of scale innovations or superior management in one or a few firms and competitive behavior (or of structural disequilibrium from whatever source and competitive behavior).[27] Also, Peltzman's finding that most of the cost savings from concentration above the 50 percent level are passed on to buyers suggests that these industries must be fairly competitive. The residual not yet passed on in 1967 may have occurred either because firms had not yet attained a long-run competitive equilibrium or because they continued to innovate moving the long-run equilibrium position sufficiently rapidly (or unexpectedly) to prevent the concentrated industries from reaching a position of full, long-run adjustment.

Whether concentrated industries are on the whole oligopolies or are simply normally competitive can be tested, then, by examining trends in four-firm concentration ratios. If an abnormally large proportion of the centralized industries display long-term declining concentration—a proportion greater than would be expected by chance and the operation of the regression phenomenon—we may be justified in looking more closely at those industries for oligopoly behavior.

Replication of the Shepherd-Kamerschen Tests

The Kamerschen and Shepherd lists of CR oligopolies (that is, industries 75 percent concentrated or more in 1947) is enlarged here for the 1947–58 and 1947–1963 periods to include industries that they omitted.[28] With the enlarged list (see Table 10-1), we can reexamine the trends in concentration ratios reported by Shepherd and by Kamerschen. Kamerschen and Shepherd were trying to determine whether concentrated industries behaved and performed as Stigler hypothesized they would under circumstances that permit them to collude. The test was also intended to determine whether firms in concentrated industries collude instead to practice limit pricing.

Shepherd reported fourteen industries with increasing or approximately constant concentration and twelve with decreasing concentration. Kamerschen examined twenty-two industries for the longer period from 1947 to 1963 and found an increase in the proportion of declining concentration industries. Where Shepherd found that 46 percent fit this category in 1947–58, Kamerschen found that 64 percent did in 1947–63 (see Table 10-2). This led him, in contrast to Shepherd, to lean toward the view that the Stigler hypothesis fit the behavior of major firms in concentrated industries.

Among those industries with falling concentration in Kamer-

TABLE 10–2
Summary of Concentration Changes in
High-Concentration Industries
(Concentration 75 Percent or Higher in 1947)

Change in Concentration	Shepherd 1947–58 (1)	Kamerschen 1947–63 (2)	Enlarged Samples	
			1947–58 (3)	1947–63 (4)
	Number of Industries			
Increasing or constant	14	8	22	9
Increasing	—	6	12	7
Constant (±2)	—	2	10	2
Decreasing	12	14	17	16
Erratic	5	2	5	7
Steady	7	12	12	9
By 7 percent or more	3	6	8	6
Total	26	22	39	25
	Percentage			
Increasing or constant	54	36	56	36
Decreasing	46	64	44	64
Total	100	100	100	100

Sources: Column (1) from W. G. Shepherd, *Trends of Concentration in American Manufacturing Industries,* 1947–1958, 46 REVIEW OF ECONOMICS AND STATISTICS (May 1964), Table 8 at 210. Column (2) corrected from D. R. Kamerschen, *An Empirical Test of Oligopoly Theories,* 76 JOURNAL OF POLITICAL ECONOMY (1968), Table 2 at 621. Columns (3) and (4) computed from data in Table 10-1.

schen's 1947–63 sample, six decreased steadily from census year to census year (or leveled for only a pair of census years) for a total decrease of 7 percentage points or more. This was twice the number found by Shepherd in his larger, twenty-six industry group for 1947–58, lending more support to Stigler's hypothesis than the Shepherd data.

Enlarging the Shepherd sample of twenty-six concentrated industries for 1947–58 to thirty-nine does not increase the proportion of industries showing decreases (compare columns 1 and 3 in Table 10-2). Neither does the slight enlargement of Kamerschen's sample for 1947–63 change his proportions (columns 2 and 4). The disagreement between Kamerschen and Shepherd concerning the proportions of declining industries remains unresolved by enlarging the groups of industries for the periods they analyze. For the moment, we must be content to attribute the difference in their conclusions to the underlying differences in the data they use.

288

It should be remarked, however, that Shepherd points out that the seven industries in his sample exhibiting a steady decline "are mostly characterized by standard products and relatively little change over the period (pulp goods, corn wet milling, explosives, rubber footwear, electrometallurgical products, tires and inner tubes, and wool-felt hats and hat bodies)."[29] To Shepherd's mind, these appeared to be the wrong industries to corroborate Stigler's hypothesis. Shepherd tells us that: "They do not include any of the oligopolies which would generally be thought to be of major importance."[30] But these are precisely the industries Stigler expected might possibly exhibit such behavior, although he did not express certainty that they would.

> . . . young industries which are still experiencing rapid changes in technology and markets are less likely to follow collusive policies with respect to technology and marketing and hence fundamentally with respect to price. Moreover the number of firms will usually grow for a time with the size of the industry. In older industries with low rates of growth of output and slower changes in technology, the margin of uncertainty as to the most profitable monopolistic policy narrows, and the likelihood of collusion increases.[31]

Posner agrees with Stigler that standardized, unchanging products are precisely the kind to which this hypothesis might apply and that it was less likely to apply to other industries.

> The less standardized (more customized) a product is . . . the more difficult it will be for the sellers of the product to collude effectively . . .
> Where the product is a fungible commodity, cutting prices may be the only way of getting business away from a competitor; if so, eliminating price competition is sure to yield higher profits.[32]

Although the declining fraction of output produced by the top four firms might indicate collusion in these industries, this interpretation is hard to sustain because the firms involved also tended generally to change their relative positions. Movement in the relative positions of the four leading firms from 1947 to 1958 in the standard product industries points to a lack of collusion (or recognized interdependence producing the equivalent). As Posner indicates, we expect "fixed relative market shares" among colluding firms.

We have information on changes in rank and composition of the four leading firms in five of the seven steadily declining concentration industries named by Shepherd (Table 10-1). In one (tires and inner tubes), the ranks of the four leading firms changed between 1947 and 1958. In three (wool-felt hats, explosives, and electrometallurgical products), the identities of the top four firms in 1958 differed from that in 1947. Only in corn wet milling did rank or composition of the four leaders fail to change.[33] The evidence against Stigler's collusive-price-umbrella hypothesis provided by Shepherd's sample of industries is stronger than Shepherd realized. He does not need his misinterpretation of Stigler to support his conclusion.

The larger sample of industries that we have introduced shows that in twelve out of thirty-nine (31 percent), the four leading firms steadily lost market shares instead of only seven out of twenty-six (27 percent). Also, the large sample shows eight of the thirty-nine losing 7 or more percentage points (21 percent) instead of only three out of twenty-six (12 percent). There are more concentrated industries whose market share performance fits Stigler's hypothesis than Shepherd reported.[34] However, in the five industries added to the category of steady losers of market share (cigarettes, tobacco stemming, industrial gases, aluminum rolling, and matches) the first four firms change rank in two cases and composition in three cases. *Stiglerian oligopoly behavior is not a pervasive phenomenon in the 1947–58 period for concentrated industries.* The minority position of the concentrated industries, which had steady declines in the market share of their leaders, and the changes in the composition of leading firms in the declining concentration industries suggest that aggressive competition is present in concentrated industries. This conclusion receives additional support from the fact that the composition of the top four firms changed in 73 percent of the thirty more-than-74-percent-concentrated industries for which data for 1947 and 1958 were available (see Table 10-1). The leading four firms in only 13 percent suffered no change in composition or rank.

Regression Accounts for the Average Change in Concentration

The shifting ranks and composition of the major firms in those industries with declining concentration in the 1947–58 period leads to skepticism concerning that decline as evidence of collusion. Even the preponderance of declines in concentration in the 1947–63 period (64 percent) should be viewed skeptically as evidence of collusive maintenance of supracompetitive prices by the major firms in concentrated industries. The preponderance may simply be a regression phenomenon.[35]

If we examine the relationship of changes in concentration to initial concentration, there is a significant movement in industries at both high and low levels of concentration toward the average. There appears to be a centripetal tendency in operation. Examining Table 10-3, we see a greater proportion of the industries with low concentration in 1948 (zero to 24 percent four-firm concentration) than of those with high concentration (75 to 100 percent) rising in concentration. The proportion rising among low concentration industries of 1947 increases relative to the proportion rising among high concentration industries the longer the time allowed for change. The opposite behavior is exhibited for decreases in concentration. The proportion of low concentration industries exhibiting decreases in concentration is always less than one third and declines as the time span lengthens. The proportion exhibiting decreases in the highest concentration group is always at least one half and rises with the length of time span. In the two groups of industries in the middle of the concentration range, a smaller proportion of the industries in the higher concentration category exhibit increasing concentration and a higher proportion exhibit decreasing concentration than in the lower concentration category, also confirming the regression phenomenon.[36]

Table 10-4 presents statistical relationships that indicate the link between the change in concentration ratios since 1947 and the degree to which an industry's concentration was high or low that year. These results show us that the highly concentrated industries became less concentrated while those at low levels became more centralized on average. Roughly speaking, industries that had concentration 30 percentage points above the 1947 average declined from roughly 70 percent concentration to about 67 percent by 1958 on average. By 1972 those industries moved, on average, to 65 percent concentration.

The centripetal tendencies displayed might be thought to be a consequence of the net entry of firms occurring in highly concentrated industries and the net exit occurring in the more atomistic industries (see Table 4-7). By adding a term measuring net change in numbers of firms to each of the simple regressions in

TABLE 10-3

Percentage of 163 Selected Four-Digit Industries Showing Rising, Stable, or Declining Concentration by Concentration Quartiles, 1947–72

1947 Concentration	More than 2 Percent Increase in Concentration				Stable Concentration				More than 2 Percent Decrease in Concentration			
	1947–1958	1947–1963	1947–1967	1947–1972	1947–1958	1947–1963	1947–1967	1947–1972	1947–1958	1947–1963	1947–1967	1947–1972
	Percentage of Industries											
0–24 (58)	33	54	62	71	39	25	23	14	28	21	15	15
25–49 (52)	43	39	41	42	22	20	22	25	35	41	37	34
50–74 (33)	27	27	33	24	10	24	12	15	55	48	55	61
75–100 (20)	30	25	20	15	20	10	15	10	50	65	65	75

Source: U.S., Bureau of the Census, Special Report Series: CONCENTRATION RATIOS IN MANUFACTURING, MC72(SR)–2 (1975).

Number in parentheses is the number of industries.

The industries selected are those for which concentration data are available in every census year.

$$C72_i - C47_i = 1.62 - .228 (C47_i - 39.6) \qquad \bar{r}^2 - 0.173$$
$$ (1.79) \ (-5.90)$$

$C72_i$ = four-firm concentration in 1972 in industry i (i = 1 to 163).

$C47_i$ = four-firm concentration in 1947 in industry i.

t-value in parentheses below coefficient.

An Empirical Test of Oligopoly Theories

TABLE 10–4

Regression of Changes in Industry Concentration on 1947
Deviation of Concentration from the All-Industry Average[a]

Period During Which Concentration Changed (Dependent Variable)	Estimated Coefficients for			$\bar{r}^2$
	Constant	Deviation of Concentration in 1947 from 1947 Mean	Percentage Change in Number of Firms	
1947–58	−0.454	−.0792		.047
	(−0.73)	(−2.96)		
	0.195	−.0776	−.062	.126
	(0.32)	(−3.03)	(−3.89)	
1947–63	0.748	−.121		.078
	(1.01)	(−3.78)		
	1.27	−.118	−.054	.142
	(1.75)	(−3.81)	(−3.55)	
1947–72	1.69	−.226		.170
	(1.84)	(−5.70)		
	2.49	−.194	−.040	.225
	(2.73)	(−4.92)	(−3.56)	

Source: U.S., Bureau of the Census, CENSUS OF MANUFACTURERS, 1972, SPECIAL REPORT SERIES: CONCENTRATION RATIOS IN MANUFACTURING, MC 72 (SR)-2 (1975).
Note: Number in parentheses is t-ratio.
[a] The all-industry average and the regressions use 158 4-digit industries whose definitions did not change from 1947 to 1972 and for which both concentration ratios and numbers of firms are available in each census year.

Table 10-4, we can see the net effect of deviations of concentration from the average while holding the rate of entry constant. The centripetal tendency is still present and little diminished by allowing for the influence of entry separately. The 70 percent concentrated industries of 1947 with no entry of additional firms drop to a slightly under 67 percent concentration ratio, on the average, by 1972.

Although the regression results summarize the change in concentration for the typical industry (whose definition remained unchanged from 1947 to 1972), they do not hold for the highly concentrated industries whose definition did not change from 1947 to 1958. The average 1947 concentration ratio of the thirty-nine industries, which were 75 percent or more concentrated in 1947, used to examine trends in the 1947–58 period is 83.1 percent. We expect concentration to decline by 3.9 percentage points to 79.2 percent according to the relationship shown in Table 10-4. The actual decline was only 2.6 percentage points to an average 80.5 percent in 1958. On the test proposed by Stigler, we expect collusive industries to have larger declines in four-firm concentration ratios than industries do as a whole, yet the decline was less than the expected normal regression toward the mean. Should we take this to mean that leading firms in concentrated industries are *more* "competitive" than leading firms in less concentrated industries or that collusion among leading firms is less frequent in concentrated industries than in those less concentrated? Concentration increased more than 2 percentage points in a third of the group, presumably indicating that leading firms were too competitive even to keep prices as high as the limit level, much less the monopoly level.

The average concentration of the twenty-five industries used for the 1947–63 period was 83.3 in 1947, 43.7 points above the 39.6 percent average concentration of all 158 industries in 1947. We expect average concentration, then, to decline by 4.5 percentage points. It actually declined by 4.1 percentage points to 79.2.[37] Concentration increased more than 2 percentage points in a substantial portion of this group (29 percent).

Examining the changes in four-firm concentration for twenty-two concentrated industries for which 1947 and 1972 data are available, a stronger case appears, by the declining market share test, for the Stigler collusion hypothesis. For this period, thirteen industries showed appreciable (more than 6 percentage points) declines in contrast to the 9 in Kamerschen's twenty-two for 1947–63. (Four showed appreciable increases, as did five in Kamerschen's sample, and five had no appreciable change in comparison with eight in Kamerschen's group.)

Again, however, this is due to the regression phenomenon, which calls for industries located at the extremes to move, on the average, toward the mean. The longer the period chosen for analysis, the greater the expected regression. In the industry samples used here, as the period lengthens, the expected decline in average concentration increases from 3.9 points to 4.5 to 6.9 to 8.2 (see Table 10-5). The average concentration in 1947 of the twenty-two highly concentrated industries is 83.3. We can expect, with average experience, that concentration would drop 8.2 percentage points. The actual drop was greater, 8.6 points to 74.7.[38] In this group, five industries' concentration increased by 4 percentage points or more. Behavior in this and in the larger groups of concentrated industries discussed above is much too heterogeneous to

TABLE 10–5

Average Actual and Predicted Concentration of Industries
in Later Years, That Were 75 Percent Concentrated or More
in 1947 and Their 1947 Average

Terminal Year	*Four-Firm Concentration Percentage*				
			1947	*158 industries*[a]	
	Actual	*Predicted*	*Average of Terminal Year Group*	*Average Concentration*	*Standard Deviation*
1947	83.8(43)	—	83.8(43)	39.6	23.6
1958	80.5(39)	79.2	83.1(39)	39.2	23.6
1963	79.2(25)	78.8	83.3(25)	40.9	23.6
1967	77.7(24)	76.4	83.3(22)	39.8	21.6
1972	74.7(22)	75.1	83.3(22)	41.2	21.6

Source: U.S., Bureau of the Census, CENSUS OF MANUFACTURERS, 1972, SPECIAL REPORT SERIES: CONCENTRATION RATIOS IN MANUFACTURING, MC72 (SR)-2 (1975). Number of industries 75 percent concentrated or more in 1947 for which terminal year data were available shown in parentheses.

[a] Industries for which concentration and number of firms data are available in each manufacturing census year. This includes eighteen of the forty-three industries that were 75 percent or more concentrated in 1947.

treat them all as per se violators of a law simply on the basis of their concentration exceeding an arbitrary standard.

The Expanding Number of Firms Test

In addition to examining four-firm concentration trends as his test for determining whether major firms in concentrated industries characteristically collude to set supracompetitive prices, Kamerschen also examined trends in numbers of firms in concentrated industries. He cited Stigler's statement that "it may be more profitable to set higher prices and *gradually yield up part of the market to new rivals.*" Kamerschen contrasts this with Bain's limit price hypothesis that *"established sellers anticipate and, if it is profitable, forestall entry"* (emphasis is supplied by Kamerschen).[39]

If we couple the change in concentration test with the change in number of firms test, a paradox appears. Stigler predicts that if concentrated industries collude, market shares for the Big Four will decline and the number of firms will rise. Bain predicted collusive limit pricing with a stable market share for the Big Four and an unchanging number of firms. We find concentrated industries that fit neither of these patterns. Some of the concentrated industries show substantially rising market shares for the Big Four and a declining population of companies. While this fits neither hypothesis, the negative correlation between concentration and number of firms is not surprising. It is simply the opposite of the pattern expected by Stigler for industries with colluding firms and refutes Stigler's expectation (in his earlier writing) that firms in concentrated industries would collude and maintain supra-competitive prices and that this would invite entry and cause declining concentration and a rising number of firms. This is a reasonable hypothesis in the case of collusion, as the case of the Gunpowder Trade Association described in Chapter 4 shows. It happens, however, not to fit the case of concentrated industries.

What is surprising is that in a large number of concentrated industries, both concentration and company population rise. For example, in industrial gases (SIC 2813) concentration rose from 83 to 84 percent and the number of firms from sixty-nine to 101 between 1947 and 1954 (see Table 10-6). Another surprise is the simultaneous decline in both concentration and company population in other industries. For example, in distilled liquor (SIC 2085) concentration fell from 75 to 64 percent despite a decline in the number of firms from 144 to ninety-eight between 1947 and 1954 (see Table 10-7). A declining number of firms would lead to an expectation of rising concentration. These phenomena must be understood and their frequency determined to arrive at a judgment of whether concentrated industries are to be suspected of colluding and to move from that to the view that a law should be passed putting concentration on the same footing with express conspiracy as a per se violation of antitrust laws.

Using trends in firm population as a test for collusive behavior is likely to be considerably more troublesome even than using concentration trends. The level of concentration is already determined by a variety of factors that have nothing to do with collusion. It may decline in a concentrated industry because scale economies shift adversely as technology changes, markets become diffuse (both unlikely in view of increasing population concentration and increasing labor cost relative to capital cost trends), su-

TABLE 10-6
Concentrated Industries with Increasing Concentration and Number of Firms
(Concentration Ratio, Number of Firms, and Coverage)

Industry SIC Number[b]	1947 CR(N)CV[a]	1954 CR(N)CV	1958 CR(N)CV	1963 CR(N)CV	1967 CR(N)CV	1972 CR(N)CV
2043	—(—)—	—(—)—	83(34)81	86(35)86	88(30)82	—(—)—
2066	—(—)—	—(—)—	—(—)—	75(24)82	77(27)75	90(34)84
2111	—(—)—	—(—)—	—(—)—	80(7)100	81(8)100	84(13)100
2271	—(—)—	—(—)—	—(—)—	—(—)—	76(55)84	78(64)85
2813	83(69)84	84(101)84	—(—)—	—(—)—	—(—)—	—(—)—
(2841)	79(223)81	85(267)84	—(—)—	—(—)—	—(—)—	—(—)—
(2862)	—(—)—	88(22)98	89(76)NA	—(—)—	—(—)—	—(—)—
2895	—(—)—	70(12)98	73(13)98	—(—)—	—(—)—	—(—)—
2895	—(—)—	—(—)—	—(—)—	72(8)D	72(11)100	74(11)95
(2898)	81(25)98	86(28)97	—(—)—	—(—)—	—(—)—	—(—)—
3011	—(—)—	—(—)—	—(—)—	70(105)99	70(119)99	73(136)99
3275	85(33)98	90(48)98	—(—)—	—(—)—	—(—)—	—(—)—
3313	—(—)—	—(—)—	73(19)76	79(20)77	—(—)—	—(—)—
3411	78(102)99	80(109)99	—(—)—	—(—)—	—(—)—	—(—)—
(3492)	—(—)—	90(25)97	91(31)97	—(—)—	—(—)—	—(—)—
3511	—(—)—	—(—)—	—(—)—	—(—)—	76(20)78	90(59)90
3571	69(50)94	74(73)93	77(122)91	—(—)—	—(—)—	—(—)—

TABLE 10-6 (Cont)
Concentrated Industries with Increasing Concentration and Number of Firms
(Concentration Ratio, Number of Firms, and Coverage)

Industry SIC Number[b]	1947 CR(N)CV[a]	1954 CR(N)CV	1958 CR(N)CV	1963 CR(N)CV	1967 CR(N)CV	1972 CR(N)CV
(3572)	—(—)—	—(—)—	—(—)—	76(17)99	81(20)99	—(—)—
3612	73(134)91	78(152)94	—(—)—	—(—)—	—(—)—	—(—)—
3624	—(—)—	—(—)—	—(—)—	83(40)96	86(49)96	—(—)—
3636	77(69)94	81(78)94	D(80)94	D(83)96	81(83)96	—(—)—
3692	—(—)—	78(20)98	84(24)98	89(26)91	—(—)—	—(—)—
3711	—(—)—	—(—)—	—(—)—	—(—)—	92(107)99	93(165)100
(3723)	—(—)—	91(16)87	97(17)95	—(—)—	—(—)—	—(—)—
3932	78(27)70	81(30)74	—(—)—	—(—)—	—(—)—	—(—)—
3933	71(34)82	76(37)88	—(—)—	—(—)—	—(—)—	—(—)—
3996	—(—)—	—(—)—	83(11)NA	87(15)98	89(18)97	91(18)99

Sources: U.S., Bureau of the Census, CENSUS OF MANUFACTURERS, 1972, SPECIAL REPORT SERIES: CONCENTRATION RATIOS IN MANUFACTURING, MC72 (SR)-2 (1975); U.S. Bureau of the Census, CONCENTRATION RATIOS IN MANUFACTURING INDUSTRY, 1958 (1962).

[a] First two-digit figure in each column is the four-firm industry concentration ratio (CR). Figure in parentheses is the number of firms (N) with establishments whose primary product is classified in the industry. Where the number of firms might have increased because of increased coverage, it is italicized. Following next is the coverage ratio (CV), that is, the percentage of the total shipments of the industry's products from all U.S. establishments that is produced in the establishments classified in the industry.

[b] All SIC numbers from the 1972 Standard Industrial Classification Code except those shown in parentheses. Where the SIC number is italicized, a change in definition of the industry occurred in 1958.

TABLE 10–7

Concentrated Industries with Decreasing Concentration and Number of Firms
(Concentration Ratio, Number of Firms, and Coverage)

Industry SIC Number[b]	1947 CR(N)CV[a]	1954 CR(N)CV	1958 CR(N)CV	1963 CR(N)CV	1967 CR(N)CV	1972 CR(N)CV
2043	—(—)—	88(37) 80	83(34) 81	—(—)—	—(—)—	—(—)—
2046	—(—)—	75(54) 96	73(53) 96	71(49) 93	68(32)96	63(26)97
2067	—(—)—	—(—)—	—(—)—	90(20) 96	86(19)95	—(—)—
2085	75(144) 99	64(98)100	60(88)100	58(70) 99	54(70)98	—(—)—
(2091)	83(39) D	80(32) 90	—(—)—	—(—)—	—(—)—	—(—)—
2111	90(19)100	82(12)100	79(12)100	—(—)—	—(—)—	—(—)—
2141	88(93) 98	79(92) 99	73(64)100	70(59)100	63(54)99	—(—)—
(2282)	76(45) 97	73(32) 96	70(23)NA	—(—)—	—(—)—	—(—)—
2813	—(—)—	—(—)—	79(111)84	72(104) 87	67(113)98	65(105)92
2813	—(—)—	—(—)—	—(—)—	—(—)—	—(—)—	—(—)—
(2825)	—(—)—	80(20)99	78(17)99	—(—)—	—(—)—	—(—)—
2892	—(—)—	—(—)—	77(45)96	72(41)94	67(37)93	—(—)—
(2882)	—(—)—	85(8)90	81(7)NA	—(—)—	—(—)—	—(—)—
2895	78(13)97	70(12)98	—(—)—	—(—)—	—(—)—	—(—)—
(2898)	—(—)—	86(28)97	81(27)NA	—(—)—	—(—)—	—(—)—
3021	81(20)99	72(19)85	—(—)—	—(—)—	—(—)—	—(—)—

TABLE 10-7 (Cont)
Concentrated Industries with Decreasing Concentration and Number of Firms
(Concentration Ratio, Number of Firms, and Coverage)

Industry SIC Number[b]	1947 CR(N)CV[a]	1954 CR(N)CV	1958 CR(N)CV	1963 CR(N)CV	1967 CR(N)CV	1972 CR(N)CV
3275	—( )—	—( )—	88(72)98	84(60)98	80(55)98	80(44)99
3331	—( )—	—( )—	—( )—	—( )—	77(15)NA	72(11)NA
3411	78(102)99	74(28)93	—( )—	74(99) 98	73(96)98	—( )—
(3424)	92(34)93	78(25)60	—( )—	—( )—	—( )—	—( )—
3568	—( )—	—( )—	67(19)46	—( )—	—( )—	—( )—
3574	—( )—	—( )—	—( )—	—( )—	83(132)84	73(74)86
3612	—( )—	78(152)94	71(153)93	68(144)94	—( )—	—( )—
3672	—( )—	—( )—	—( )—	91(148)90	84(95)98	83(69)98
(3983)	83(18)100	74(14)98	—( )—	—( )—	—( )—	—( )—

Sources: U.S., Bureau of the Census, Census of Manufacturers, 1972, Special Report Series: Concentration Ratios in Manufacturing, MC72 (SR)-2 (1975); U.S. Bureau of the Census, Concentration Ratios in Manufacturing Industry, 1958 (1962).

[a] First two-digit figure in each column is the four-firm industry concentration ratio (CR). Figure in parentheses is the number of firms (N) with establishments whose primary product is classified in the industry. Where the number of firms might have decreased because of decreased coverage, it is italicized. Following next is the coverage ratio (CV), that is, the percentage of the total shipments of the industry's products from all U.S. establishments that is produced in the establishments classified in the industry.

[b] All SIC numbers from the 1972 Standard Industrial Classification Code except those shown in parentheses.

perior management fails to maintain its superiority, or changing demands for various types of product design and for variety shift with technology, income, and size of market. And, of course, rapid market growth relative to the economic scale of operation may decrease concentration. A rise in transportation cost or a change in the ubiquity of input (raw materials) locations can also cause declines in concentration.

In addition to these influences operating on both the number of companies and on concentration, the number of firms will respond to the profitability of the industry. A highly profitable, concentrated industry will attract more firms and concentration will ultimately decline.[40] This, of course, is equally true in less concentrated industries. Gort found that ranking industries by profitability, those in the highest 20 percent by profitability rank attracted new entrants and that leading firms in this group suffered marked declines in market share from 1947 to 1954.[41] The rise in firm population (and decline in market shares of leading firms) was strongly related to profitability and not to concentration. *A rising number of firms is an index of profitability of an industry*, not of collusion.[42] Profitability is, itself, negatively related to collusion according to Asch and Seneca.[43] This could mean that collusion and a declining firm population could be correlated because collusion occurs in unprofitable circumstances where a rise in profitability or price resulting from collusion does not reach a level which makes the industry attractive.[44]

With these provisos, let us examine firm population trends in concentrated industries for what light they can shed on the Stigler and Bain hypotheses. Kamerschen and Shepherd's twenty-six concentrated industries split equally between rising and declining number of companies between 1947 and 1958.[45] This occurred again between 1958 and 1963 in Kamerschen's twenty-two industry sample. Enlarging the 1947–58 sample to forty-three industries, the result remains unchanged.[46] There is an even split of industries between increasing and decreasing population (nineteen each) with five showing no change. The same experience is repeated in 1958–63 with thirty industries using members of the previous sample for which data are available and adding any industries 75 percent or more concentrated in 1958 not in the previous sample. Of the thirty, the number of firms decreased in fourteen industries, increased in fifteen, and remained unchanged in one. Neither the Stigler nor the Bain hypothesis receives sup-

301

port as a universal characterization of behavior in concentrated industries. This is simply the same random behavior found in less concentrated industries. The direction of trend in number of firms in an industry cannot be predicted simply by knowing that it is a concentrated industry.

On these grounds, no case can be made for Stigler's hypothesis (since retracted)[47] that the major firms in concentrated industries are likely to collude, that they price supracompetitively, holding a price umbrella, and that they yield market share to new entrants attracted by supracompetitive prices. Neither does the data support the hypothesis that leading firms are likely to price at a level that avoids attracting entry and that maintains shares, i.e., that they practice limit pricing. Perhaps it can be argued that the circumstances of some concentrated industries result in behavior of the sort suggested by Stigler, circumstances in others result in limit pricing, and in still others in competitive behavior, assuming there is any difference between limit pricing and competitive behavior. (After all, every competitive industry in long-run equilibrium is limit pricing.) Competitive behavior can be taken as characteristic of at least those industries that display rising concentration and declining numbers of firms since these trends fit neither the Stigler nor the Bain hypothesis.

Also, the seeming paradox of both declining concentration and a declining number of companies shown at one time or another in twenty-four concentrated industries (see Table 10-7) cannot be called Stiglerian except in another sense described in Stigler's *Economies of Scale*.[48] Efficient firms compete, survive, thrive, and, in this instance, are those not in the top four. They are in the middle to upper echelons below the top four. Perhaps the top four in industries with declining concentration and firm population are yielding market share to those below by holding an umbrella but are not holding the umbrella high enough to shelter firms smaller than the Big Ten or Big Twenty since economies of scale prevent smaller firms from surviving under a low umbrella. Perhaps we should characterize this as Worcesterian[49] behavior, which results in firms approaching a similar size. The Big Four decline and the next four, eight, or dozen grow with a decreased inequality in size distribution resulting. Whether that is a result of Stiglerian survival of efficient size or Worcesterian dominant firm (oligopoly) behavior cannot be tested without data on the volatility of demand, the cost of speedy conversion of capacity to alternative uses,[50] and the penalties for using less specialized equipment.

Conclusion

With the results of these tests, the one thing that seems to characterize the behavior of concentrated industries is their failure to conform to any single image of oligopoly. To treat them all as in need of some remedy or control simply because they are concentrated is to force them into a mold unsuited for efficiency. Different industries find themselves in a wide variety of circumstances. Technology, resource supplies, demand stability, stage of development, and the amount of product variety demanded differ across industries. These factors dictate industry structures. Restrictions on their structure would curtail the adaptability needed when circumstances change. Very little persuasive evidence has been advanced that challenges the view that concentrated industries are as competitive as it is possible to make them. If that is true, then any attempt to remake them in an image different than that dictated by the market will impose costs with no benefits, or perhaps too little benefit to cover those costs.

We should add that the existence of the regression phenomenon should not be interpreted as a prediction that the concentration level in all industries will ultimately become equal to the average concentration level. Unusually tall or short parents have offspring who are closer to the average height of all people without changing the distribution of heights in subsequent generations. Likewise, the "offspring" of industries with unusually high or low concentration levels will be closer to the average value without changing the distribution. Groups of industries with unusually low or high concentration will more frequently be populated by a few that are "accidentally" in those groups. Their movement back toward their equilibrium levels will give rise to the regression phenomenon. But many members of each group are "naturally" concentrated or unconcentrated, and their subsequent movements may be in either direction depending on "accidents" and economic and technological forces.

Notes

1. *F.T.C. v. Kellogg, et al.,* Docket No. 8883; *F.T.C. v. Exxon Corporation, et al.,* Docket No. 8934.
2. W. J. Liebeler, *Bureau of Competition Litigation: Antitrust Activities,* in K. W. Clarkson and T. M. Maris (eds.), THE FEDERAL TRADE COMMISSION SINCE 1970: ECONOMIC REGULATION AND BUREAUCRATIC BEHAVIOR (1981).
3. Judge Wyzanski's decision in the United Shoe Machinery case follows in Hand's footsteps, condemning United for monopolizing by "honestly industrial" practices.
4. D. F. Turner, *The Scope of Antitrust and Other Economic Regulatory Policies,* 82 HARVARD LAW REVIEW 1218 (Apr. 1969).
5. Harold Fleming, TEN THOUSAND COMMANDMENTS: A STORY OF THE ANTITRUST LAWS 57 (1951).
6. See Turner quotation in text at note 4.
7. Aaron Director and Edward Levi, *Law and the Future: Trade Regulation,* 51 NORTHWESTERN LAW REVIEW 286 (May 1956).
8. "These practices of proliferating brands, differentiating similar products and promoting trademarks through intensive advertising result in high barriers to entry into the RTE cereal market." Complaint, *F.T.C. v. Kellogg, et al.,* Docket No. 8883.
9. Richard Schmalensee views the behavior of the four major RTE cereal firms in this way, but his analysis is vitiated by his use of a one-attribute model of cereal qualities with localized competition as a consequence. Also, he fails to incorporate consumer demands for variety in his model. *Entry Deterrence in the RTE Cereal Industry,* working paper WP961–77 MIT (Dec. 1977).
10. R. D. Buzzell and R. E. Nourse, PRODUCT INNOVATION, THE PRODUCT LIFE CYCLE, AND COMPETITIVE BEHAVIOR IN SELECTED FOOD PROCESSING INDUSTRIES, 1947–1964 105 (1966).
11. "... defendant has ... induced officials of municipally-owned transit systems to adopt bus specifications for use in obtaining so-called competitive bids which prevented other bus manufacturers from competing." *United States of America v. General Motors Corporation,* Civil Action No. 15-816, U.S. District Court for Eastern Michigan.
12. Bell later retreated from recommending the use of blanket legislation to proposing that the Congress hold hearings on individual industries. "There, he claims, quite lax rules of evidence can prevail and data can be presented in summary." Frank Vogl, *Broad Hints from Bell on Antitrust Reform Plans,* 1 FINANCIER 15 (Oct. 1977).
13. John McGee, IN DEFENSE OF INDUSTRIAL CONCENTRATION (1971); Harold Demsetz, THE MARKET CONCENTRATION DOCTRINE (1975); Y. Brozen, *The Concentration-Collusion Doctrine,* 46 ANTITRUST LAW JOURNAL 826 (Summer 1977); Stephen Hymer and Peter Pashigian, *Firm Size and Rate of Growth,* 70 JOURNAL OF POLITICAL ECONOMY 556 (Feb. 1962); *1976 Budget Overview* (1974) *supra* note 14, Chapter 6; B. Bock, *Rediscovering Economic Realism in Defining Competition,* CONFERENCE BOARD RECORD 6 (June 1974); Paul McCracken and Thomas

Moore, Competition and Market Concentration in the American Economy (1973); R. Bork and W. Bowman, *The Goals of Antitrust*, 65 Columbia Law Review 363 (Mar. 1965); George J. Stigler, *A Theory of Oligopoly*, 72 Journal of Political Economy 44 (Feb. 1964); The Theory of Price 219–20 (1966); *The Economic Effects of the Antitrust Laws*, 9 Journal of Law & Economics (Oct. 1966).

14. Richard A. Posner, Antitrust Laws: An Economic Perspective 54 (1976). He does not indicate whether these are all necessary conditions, whether a smaller number is sufficient, or whether all or some are sufficient without high concentration.

15. The eleven conditions are (1) no fringe of small sellers, (2) inelastic demand at competitive price, (3) entry takes a long time, (4) many customers, (5) standard product, (6) the principal firms sell at the same level in the chain of distribution, (7) price competition is more important than other forms of competition, (8) high rate of fixed to variable costs, (9) demand static or declining over time, (10) sealed bidding, (11) the industry's antitrust "record." See *id.* at 55–62.

16. See *id.* at 62.

17. See *id.* at 62–71. Posner dismisses profitability as an appropriate criterion for inferring collusion except in a few cases. Persistent high profitability may be a result of accounting biases (measurement error) or superior efficiency; and "the absence of abnormally high profits need not imply the absence of collusion" (*id.* at 69). The usual studies inferring collusion in concentrated industries from a correlation of the profitability of major firms and concentration are stood on their heads by Posner when he says "that at the initial formation of a cartel, the profits of the *smaller* firms will increase by a greater proportion than the profits of the larger firms" (emphasis supplied).

   Posner warns that "A long-term decline in the market shares of leading firms . . . is a symptom of price fixing, *though an ambiguous one* since it may attributable to other factors." *Id.* at 68 (emphasis supplied).

18. David R. Kamerschen, *An Empirical Test of Oligopoly Theories*, 76 Journal of Political Economy 615 (Jul.-Aug. 1968); William G. Shepherd, *Trends of Concentration in American Manufacturing Industries, 1947–58*, 46 Review of Economics & Statistics 200 (May 1964).

19. See Kamerschen *id.* at 616.

20. See Posner *supra* note 14, at 68.

21. Stigler himself discarded the hypothesis before Shepherd questioned it and well before Kamerschen came to its support. See *A Theory of Oligopoly*, and *The Economic Effects of the Antitrust Laws, supra* note 13. In the latter, he states, "When the event we wish to study is clandestine, we cannot rely upon direct observation. I believe my theory of oligopoly is a useful tool for this study, precisely because it seeks to isolate the determinants and forms of successful collusion—or rather the determinants of successful cheating and hence unsuccessful collusion. The argument turns on the problem of getting reliable information on the observance of collusive agreements; invoices and sellers and buyers, and even physical shipments, may lie. *And where an agreement cannot be enforced, it will not be obeyed.*" (emphasis supplied).

22. It has been suggested that concentration remains stable or rises in any concentrated industry whose firms produce differentiated products. L. Weiss, *Factors in Changing Concentration*, 45 Review of Economics

AND STATISTICS 70 (Feb. 1963); M. Gort, *Analysis of Stability and Change in Market Shares*, 71 JOURNAL OF POLITICAL ECONOMY 58 (Feb. 1963) finds that the rank of firms by market share tends to be stable more frequently in industries subjectively classified as producing differentiated products, a view disputed for a later time period than that tested by Gort, at least in terms of stability of market shares, by N. Schneider, *Product Differentiation, Oligopoly, and the Stability of Market Shares*, 5 WESTERN ECONOMIC JOURNAL 58 (Dec. 1966).

23. Sam Peltzman, *The Gains and Losses from Industrial Concentration*, 20 JOURNAL OF LAW & ECONOMICS 229 (Oct. 1977).

24. See Demsetz *supra* note 13, at 23–25; *More on Collusion and Advertising: A Reply*, 19 JOURNAL OF LAW & ECONOMICS Table 2 at 207 (Apr. 1976). This table shows no correlation of rates of return in the largest firms and concentration, which is inconsistent with the concentration-collusion hypothesis.

25. ". . . an attempt to deconcentrate industries will redistribute output away from the more efficient firms to the less efficient firms." Demsetz *id.* at 24. For an analysis of this alternative, see John S. McGee *supra* note 13, at 76–79, reprinted in Y. Brozen, THE COMPETITIVE ECONOMY 40–42 (1975). Also, see McGee *supra* note 13, at 84.

26. Paul McCracken and Thomas Moore, COMPETITION AND MARKET CONCENTRATION IN THE AMERICAN ECONOMY (1973), find that "the second-largest firm does unusually poorly in concentrated industries. This is consistent with scale innovation or superior management as the cause of concentration (and as the source of profits in concentrated industries) and with the passing on to buyers of some of the gains in efficiency.

27. Yale Brozen, *Concentration and Structural and Market Disequilibria*, 16 ANTITRUST BULLETIN 241 (Summer 1971).

28. Kamerschen and Shepherd omitted industries 2091, 2821, 2862, 2882, 2895, 3313, 3352, 3492, 3511, 3723, 3932, and 3982, all of which had concentration ratios greater than 75 percent in 1947. Shepherd explains three of the omissions as being industries with a patent barrier and the rest as not having employment data available. Kamerschen also omitted industries 2066, 2067, 3571, 3633, and 3717, which became 75 percent or more concentrated in the 1947–63 period because they were not at this level in 1947. We include these latter to provide tests in subsequent years. (Of the industries that were less than 75 percent concentrated in 1947, Kamerschen mentions only 2066 and 3633 as becoming 75 percent or more concentrated. See Kamerschen *supra* note 18, at 619).

29. See Shepherd *supra* note 18, at 210. Tires are a poor choice as an exhibitor of steady decline since concentration rose from 77 percent in 1947 to 79 in 1954 before declining to 74 in 1958. This industry fits better into Shepherd's "erratic" category. Also, see Lloyd Reynolds, *Competition in the Rubber Tire Industry*, 28 AMERICAN ECONOMIC REVIEW 459 (Sept. 1938).

30. See Shepherd *supra* note 18, at 210.

31. George J. Stigler, THE THEORY OF PRICE 230 (1952). In the 1966 edition of this work at 219 Stigler shifts emphasis from "the likelihood of collusion" to the unlikelihood of successful collusion.

> A collusive system encounters two main problems. First, agreement is difficult to reach if the transaction[s] in which the firms deal are highly heterogeneous. . . . But heterogeneity is typical. . . .

> Second, an agreement must be policed. Even a whole-hearted colluder—and few are whole-hearted—cannot control all of his salesmen. Since there are many indirect ways of cutting prices, there will usually be some chiseling—as it is fondly termed— indeed the difficulty of detecting chiseling makes it sensible for each firm to engage in some chiseling in the realistic assumption that his rivals are doing it.

32. See Posner *supra* note 14, at 59–60.
33. U.S., Department of Commerce, Bureau of the Census, CONCENTRATION RATIOS IN MANUFACTURING INDUSTRY, 1958, Part II, Table 21 at 469– 72 (1962). If we substitute distilled liquors for tires as a more appropriate exhibitor of steady decline, we have another industry in which the ranks of the four leading firms changed between 1947 and 1958.
34. Stigler did not expect all, or perhaps even most, concentrated industries to fit his hypothesis. See the discussion noted at *supra* note 31.
35. D. W. Gaskins, Jr., *Dynamic Limit Pricing: Optimal Pricing Under Threat of Entry*, 3 JOURNAL OF ECONOMIC THEORY 306 (Sept. 1971) suggests that a larger proportion of concentrated industries than of the unconcentrated have concentration levels above the equilibrium level. Similarly, it may be expected that a larger proportion of low concentration industries have concentration ratios below the equilibrium level in their industries. As it happens, this is a simple way of stating in an economic context what the regression phenomenon in fact is. A common textbook example used to explain it is the relationship between the heights of fathers and the heights of sons. Unusually tall or unusually short men will have male offspring who are closer to the average height, although the distribution of heights may remain the same. Likewise, the "offspring" of industries with unusually high or low concentration will be closer to the average value.
36. The regression phenomenon may appear to be inconsistent with Simon and Bonini's findings that firm growth rates are unrelated to size of firm and Hymer and Pashigian's findings that firm growth rates are unrelated to quartiles of firms grouped by selected two-digit industries. [S. Hymer and P. Pashigian, *Firm Size and Rate of Growth,* 70 JOURNAL OF POLITI- CAL ECONOMY 556 (Dec. 1962)]. Simon and Bonini limited their sample to the largest firms for 1954–56, however, and Hymer and Pashigian studied the 1,000 largest manufacturing firms in the decade between 1946 and 1955. The Hymer and Pashigian finding of "equal average growth rates for different size classes" used class sizes ranging from ten to thirty-four firms with an average size group of 22 firms. Since concentration ratio trends depend upon the relative growth rates of a smaller group of firms within more finely divided industries, the four largest within each four-digit industry, and upon the relative growth rates of firms not included in the 1,000 largest manufacturing firms (or the 500 largest firms used by Simon and Bonini), regression is not inconsistent with these findings.
37. The only control used by Kamerschen to determine the expected change in concentration in his twenty-two industries used for 1947–63 is the mean change of $+2.4$ "for all 177 industries in the 1947–63 sample . . . while the corresponding figure for the twenty-two 'oligopolies' is -4.4." He concludes that "the factors which cause concentration changes for the CR 'oligopolies' seem to be quite different than those for the entire population of industries." See Kamerschen *supra* note 18, at 619.

38. Using industries 75 percent concentrated or more in 1954, a similar, but weaker, regression phenomenon occurs. The decline in average concentration to 1963, 1967, and 1972 is 1.9, 2.9, and 3.6 percentage points from 83.5, 83.2, and 81.6 average concentration ratios in 1954. The predicted declines are 0.8, 2.1, and 3.0. In this case, actual declines slightly exceeded those predicted for 1963 and 1967 in contrast to the experience with changes in concentration from 1947.

The sample of industries used is confined to those that retained their definitions and their 4-digit classification from 1947 to 1972. Six of the 1947 4-digit industries more than 74 percent concentrated in 1947 continued with a shift to 5-digit status and one had an almost imperceptible change in its definition. Using all industries from 1947 falling in the more-than-74-percent-concentrated stratum, which can be tracked through the various censuses, twenty-eight industries can be traced to 1972 plus two as far as 1970. Concentration in eleven out of these thirty (37 percent) increased by more than 2 percentage points, two had no appreciable change, and concentration in seventeen (57 percent) fell by more than 2 percentage points.

39. See Kamerschen *supra* note 18, at 618.
40. Lester G. Telser, *Some Determinants of the Returns in Manufacturing Industries,* COMPETITION, COLLUSION, AND GAME THEORY 332–33 (1972); also, see the discussion in Chapter 1 at note 21.
41. Michael Gort, *Analysis of Stability and Change in Market Shares,* 71 JOURNAL OF POLITICAL ECONOMY 60 (Feb. 1963).
42. See Tables 1–5 and 1–6 and discussion preceding the tables.
43. Peter Asch and J. J. Seneca, *Is Collusion Profitable?* 58 REVIEW OF ECONOMICS AND STATISTICS 1 (Feb. 1976).
44. For a notable exception, see Kenneth G. Elzinga, *Predatory Pricing: The Case of the Gunpowder Trust,* 13 JOURNAL OF LAW & ECONOMICS 223 (Apr. 1970), reprinted in Brozen *supra* note 25, at 405.
45. See Kamerschen *supra* note 18, Table 3 at 622.
46. The number of companies data for both 1947 and 1958 is available for a larger number of industries 75 percent or more concentrated in 1947 than is the concentration data.
47. See Stigler *supra* note 31, and Chapter 15.
48. G. J. Stigler, *The Economies of Scale,* 1 JOURNAL OF LAW & ECONOMICS 54 (Oct. 1958), reprinted in Stigler, THE ORGANIZATION OF INDUSTRY 71 (1968).
49. Dean Worcester, MONOPOLY, BIG BUSINESS, AND WELFARE IN THE POST-WAR UNITED STATES 101–105 (1967).
50. W. W. Sharkey, *A Study of Markets Involving Increasing Returns and Uncertain Demands* (dissertation, University of Chicago, 1973).

11

Aggregate Concentration:
A Phenomenon in Search
of Significance

ADOLF A. BERLE, JR., and Gardiner Means, in their 1932 book on *The Modern Corporation and Private Property,* first gave us the number 200 designating the group of leading corporations that would engulf the wealth of the nation. They told us that the 200 were "growing between two and three times as fast as all other non-financial corporations." They added that it would take only to 1969, at the 1909–29 growth rate of the 200, "for all corporate activity and practically all industrial activity to be absorbed by 200 giant companies."

Berle and Means described this century as a period in which "American industrial property, through the corporate device, was being thrown into a collective hopper wherein the individual owner was steadily being lost in the creation of a series of huge industrial oligarchies."[1] With the economic concerns of that day, more copies of the book were sold than the ghost stories of Washington Irving. The tract went through ten printings by 1936.

The threat of a takeover by the 200 periodically resurfaces in Congressional hearings, in speeches by attorneys general, and in studies by government agencies and commissions of "megacorporations" and trends in "aggregate concentration." "Aggregate concentration," as used in many recent discussions, refers to the share of total manufactured *output* produced by leading manufacturing companies or the share of the nation's manufacturing *assets* owned by its leading manufacturing corporations. Less frequently, these days, it refers to the share of all nonfinancial corporate assets owned by leading nonfinancial corporations. When the declining trend in the 200's share of all nonfinancial corporate assets became well established (see Table 11-1), this aggregation was dropped from the debate and attention was directed to the manufacturing sector.

TABLE 11–1
Leading Nonfinancial Corporations' Shares
of All Nonfinancial Corporate Assets

Year	Percentage Share of All Nonfinancial Corporate Assets	
	Leading 50 Corporations	Leading 200 Corporations
1929	—	49.4
1933	—	57.0
1958	24.4	41.1
1967	24.5	41.2
1975	23.3	39.5

Sources: National Resources Committee, THE STRUCTURE OF THE AMERICAN ECONOMY: Part I (June 1939) at 290; William Comanor, Prepared Statement for the Subcommittee on Antitrust, Monopoly and Business Rights, MERGERS AND ECONOMIC CONCENTRATION (1979).

Typically the data focus on the top 50 or 100 or 200 firms. The choice of the number of corporations to aggregate is arbitrary. There is no accusation of any specific number acting collusively or even of similar interests among the top 50 or 100. But the intimation is that there is something sinister about 50 or 100 firms turning out a sizeable share of the country's product.

Occasional discussions of "interests" also crop up. The Rockefeller or Mellon "interests" are alleged to wield enormous power over the economy simply through their investments in half a dozen among several hundred large corporations. At other times attention is paid to corporate directors who sit on more than one board.[2]

Concern about these issues is expressed for the most part on what must be termed ideological grounds. Economic analysis offers no case against the growth of aggregate concentration in either manufacturing or in all nonfinancial corporate activity. Few legislative initiatives have been directed against aggregate concentration. The Public Utility Holding Company Act of 1935 is a major exception. In a recent interview, however, John Shenefield, then chief of the Antitrust Division, recommended legislation to block the acquisition of any other firm by a company with $2 billion or more of sales or assets. His reason:

> From the late 1940s until the early 1970s the fraction of manufacturing assets controlled by the 200 largest companies increased from 46 percent to more than 60 percent. He would not want to see the trend continue.[3]

This approach departs radically from our tradition of judging mergers on the basis of their effect on competition and efficiency in the use of resources. Occasionally measures of aggregate concentration have been interpreted as indexes of "concentration of economic power." But as Professor Carl Kaysen pointed out in Congressional testimony, such an interpretation

> . . . draws its validity from the association of overall measures with measures of concentration in particular markets, and cannot be given significance as an indicator of the distribution of economic power without consideration of concentration in particular markets.
> "Concentration of economic power" indicates some notion of a disproportionate distribution of influence on economic decisions. If [aggregate] concentration . . . is to be a measure of this, there must be a direct connection between the size of a firm or group of firms in relation to the whole economy . . . and the range and consequence of its . . . choices. Consideration of what determines the range of choice over which a firm exercises decisionmaking power shows that there is no such direct relation. The degree of competition in a *market* [limits] . . . the range of a firm's economic choice.
> . . . Some fairly high degree of [market] concentration is a necessary condition for a significant and persistent departure of a market from competitive behavior; it is not a sufficient condition, however, and markets characterized by the dominance in a statistical sense of a few large firms in terms of market share may behave competitively.[4]

Is Aggregate Concentration Increasing?

Whether rising aggregate concentration portends evil or good is an open question. But there is doubt as to whether such a trend exists. William Comanor, chief of the FTC Bureau of Economics, testifying in 1979, reported that

> In 1958, the 50 largest nonfinancial corporations controlled approximately 24.4 percent of all nonfinancial corporate assets; this figure declined slightly to 23.4 percent in 1972 and 23.3 percent by 1975. . . . Similar results appear for the aggregate concentration ratios of the top 200 firms. Concentration declined from 41.1 percent in 1958 to 39.9 percent in 1972 and 39.5 percent in 1975.
>
> . . . The 50 largest nonfinancial corporations accounted for 46.2 percent of corporate after-tax profits in 1958, 36.5 percent in 1972 and 24 percent in 1975. For the 200 largest firms, the corresponding ratios were 73.9 percent in 1958, 55.8 percent in 1972 and 39.2 percent in 1975.[5]

Berle and Means reported that "200 big companies [in 1929] controlled 49.2 percent or nearly half of all non-banking corporate wealth."[6] It would appear from these numbers that Shenefield had his trend on backward (see Table 11-1). Shenefield, however, referred to corporate manufacturing assets, which are only a quarter of all corporate assets, not to the larger group of nonfinancial corporations, which include merchandising, utility, mining, construction, and services corporations as well as manufacturing. In any case, assets are an inappropriate measure of ability to make discretionary decisions as to prices, quality of a product, or wage rates. Share of sales or production of a specific product in the hands of the leading two or four firms is regarded by economists as a far more appropriate measure, and many of them are doubtful even about the usefulness of that measure.

The Bureau of Census data on domestic manufacturing production show a *decline* in the share of the 50 largest manufacturing corporations from 28 percent in 1937 to 25 percent in 1977 (see Table 11-2). The 200 largest show a rise from 41 percent in 1937 to 45 percent in 1977. The fact that the shipments share of the fifty largest firms declined while that of the 200 rose manifests increasing equality of size. This, if size has any significance, reduced the power of the largest firms.

We should also take account of the fact that U.S. manufacturers compete with foreign producers as well as domestic rivals. Michael Gort suggests that "In view of increased imports, if we were measuring the proportion of U.S. *sales* rather than *production* of manufactured goods accounted for by the largest 200 firms, the

TABLE 11-2

Shares of Manufacturing Value-Added and Shipments of the Largest Manufacturing Companies of 1947 and of Each Census Year, 1937–77

Year	50 Largest Manufacturing Companies			100 Largest Manufacturing Companies			200 Largest Manufacturing Companies	
	1947	Largest in Census Year		1947	Largest in Census Year		Largest in Census Year	
	Percentage Share of Manufacturing							
	Value-Added	Value-Added	Shipments	Value-Added	Value-Added	Shipments	Value-Added	Shipments
1937	—	20[a]	28	—	26[a]	34	32[a]	41
1947	17	17	23	23	23	—	30	—
1954	21	23	25	27	30	—	37	—
1958	20	23	..	27	30		38	
1963	21	25	25	28	33	34	41	42
1967	20	25	25	27	33	33	42	43
1972	17	25	24	24	33	32	43	43
1977	19	24	25	25	33	35	44	45

Sources: Bureau of the Census, CONCENTRATION RATIOS IN MANUFACTURING (May 1981), Tables 1 and 2 at 9-7 and Table 4 at 9-9; CONCENTRATION RATIOS IN MANUFACTURING INDUSTRY 1963 (1966), Table 1B at 2, W. F. Crowder, A. G. Abramson, and E. W. Staudt, *The Product Structure of Large Corporations*, in Temporary National Economic Committee, THE STRUCTURE OF INDUSTRY (1941), Tables 1 at 583 and 1C at 715; R. L. Nelson, infra n. a at 90; National Resources Committee, THE STRUCTURE OF THE AMERICAN ECONOMY at 272, Table III.
[a] This is a low estimate since it is the value-added share of the largest companies *ranked by value of product shipments.* R. L. Nelson, CONCENTRATION IN THE MANUFACTURING INDUSTRIES OF THE UNITED STATES (1963), n. 2 at 90.

percentage may well have declined."[7] In 1960, we imported goods and services equal to 4.6 percent of total production in the United States. By 1980, imports increased to 12.1 percent of total U.S. production. Since many of these increased imports, such as automobiles, radios, calculators, typewriters, copiers, trucks, and petroleum products were the same goods as those produced by the 200 leading manufacturers, the effect on their share of *sales* in the United States may well have been the decline suggested as a possibility by Professor Gort.

Professor Jesse Markham, commenting on the views that are held on aggregate concentration and on the effect of the conglomerate merger wave that crested in the late 1960s, observed that

> One of the most popular views on the American economy is that it is dominated by a relatively small number of giant corporations, and this dominance increases with each passing year—largely through merger. This view is uncritically accepted and widely disseminated by authors of the nonprofessional literature on the subject. FTC reports on mergers and industrial concentration often draw this conclusion.[8]

Even if the leading 200 industrials were actually to use 60 percent of the corporate assets employed in *domestic* manufacturing, their share of the tangible assets of the nation would be about 3 percent. Corporate manufacturing assets are approximately one quarter of all *business* assets and one twentieth of all material assets. The other nineteen twentieths of *all* assets, excluding human capital (accumulated investments in education and training) whose total dwarfs all tangible assets, are held by mining and construction firms, public utilities, farmers, transportation, communication, forestry, fishery, wholesaling, retailing, and real estate firms, philanthropic institutions, governments, and individuals.[9] The assets held by the federal government (excluding military assets) amount to more than the total for the leading 200 industrials.

Some Causes of the Aggregate Manufacturing Concentration Trend

If we aggregate the assets of the 200 leading manufacturing corporations, the resulting figure cannot be compared to all manufacturing assets in the United States. An important portion of the assets of the 200 are not in the United States; it consists of investments in foreign subsidiaries. These are a larger part of the assets of leading corporations than of other manufacturers. Part of the upward trend that alarmed the Antitrust Division head was the result of growing investment abroad. This did not increase the leaders' shares of domestic assets or their alleged "control" of the domestic economy.

In addition, if RCA acquires a car rental firm or General Electric acquires a mining company (a major part of whose assets are located in other countries), these are counted as a growth in manufacturing assets held by the 200 because GE and RCA are classified as manufacturing companies. Since 24.7 percent of the employees of the largest 200 manufacturing firms worked in nonmanufacturing establishments (mines, public warehouses, wholesale, retail, and service establishments) in 1963, it is probable that over 20 percent of their assets were outside the manufacturing industries.[10] General Telephone and Electronics, classed by the FTC as a manufacturing corporation in its compilation of the assets of the leading 200 manufacturers, had $5 billion of assets in the telephone industry. GATX, also classed as a manufacturing corporation among the leading 200 corporations by the FTC, has assets consisting largely of railroad cars, which it leases to the railroad industry. It also owns a bank. Its manufacturing assets would not place it among the top 200 firms.[11]

If *nonmanufacturing* and *foreign* assets of all firms were stripped from corporate manufacturing asset data, and a fraction with a consistent numerator and denominator computed, the proportion of domestic manufacturing assets held by the largest corporation would look very different. Professor Scherer calculated that the largest 100 manufacturing firms had 36 percent of domestic manufacturing assets in 1963.[12] The FTC figure for that year without this correction is 46.5 percent.[13]

We get a more accurate picture of aggregate concentration trends in manufacturing by using domestically manufactured shipments of leading firms as a proportion of all domestically manufactured shipments. First, this uses consistent definitions and is not susceptible to the criticisms mentioned above. Second, leading firms are more captial intensive than other firms, using more assets per dollar of sales or dollar of value-added (see Table 11-3). The use of asset figures overstates the relative position of the products of these firms in the nation's markets.

The shipments share of leading firms dropped from the mid-

TABLE 11–3
Assets/Sales Ratio for the Largest and for
All Manufacturing Corporations, 1947–67

Assets/Sales Ratio[a]	50 Largest	100 Largest	200 Largest	All Corporations
Ratio in absolute terms				
For largest corpora-				
tions in terms of				
assets in each year				
1947	.88	.86	.82	.60
1958	1.04	1.01	.96	.74
1967	1.02	.96	.92	.76
For largest corpora-				
tions in terms of				
sales in each year				
1947	.80	.78	.76	.60
1958	.87	.89	.87	.74
1967	.89	.93	.89	.76

Source: Betty Bock and Jack Farkas, RELATIVE GROWTH OF THE "LARGEST" MANU-
FACTURING CORPORATIONS, 1947–1971 (1972) at 13. Copyright by The Conference
Board. Reprinted by permission of the publisher.
[a] The figures in this table are for the 50, 100, and 200 largest manufacturing corporations ranked in terms of total assets and in terms of sales, respectively, in each
specified year.

thirties to 1947, then rose from 1947 to 1954. The trend has been
flat since 1954. The leading 50 firms produced 28 percent of manufactured goods in 1937, dropped to 23 percent in 1947, rose to 25
percent in 1954, and remained at that level in the twenty-three
following years (Table 11-2), although the composition of the Big
Fifty has changed considerably. The only thing alarming about
this behavior of the share of manufactured output of the largest
fifty firms is its *failure to rise* since the largest firms use labor
more productively than smaller firms.

The share of the 100 largest industrials was the same in 1937
and 1963 and has increased by one point since 1963. The 200
largest share of domestic manufacturing shipments increased by
one percentage point between 1937 and 1963, another percentage
point between 1963 and 1967, and by two points since 1967. *These
data present a picture of industrial structure trends that is at
odds with the views presented in the 1970s by the officials of the
antitrust agencies.* They are the relevant data for understanding
the place of large firms in domestic manufacturing. The frequently used mixture of foreign and domestic manufacturing and
nonmanufacturing assets is irrelevant and misleading.

Even the character of the data on domestic shipments must be closely analyzed to understand what any trend in shares means. Changes in the relative position of various industries occupied by leading firms, for reasons having little to do with their own activities, cause fluctuations in their share of total manufacturing activity. The automobile firms, which ranked number 1, 3, 10, and 110 in 1977, occupy a cyclical industry. Since a small recession occurred in 1967, and since 1972 marked the second year of a recovery, their sales were lower in those years relative to total sales than they were in 1977, the third year of recovery from a recession. Also, eighteen petroleum refiners are among the 50 leaders. The rise in their raw material costs stemming from the restrictive activities of the Organization of Petroleum Exporting Countries (OPEC) and the consequent rise in the prices of petroleum products caused a large rise in the revenues of these companies (but not in their relative profitability[14]). This increased the shipments share of the top 50 firms between 1972 and 1977 even as their value-added share declined. The disproportionately heavy representation of automobile, metal, and appliance firms among the top corporations has a cyclical impact on their share, and the large contingent of oil companies causes events in that industry to be given a major influence in the measurement of shipment shares.

The trend in shares of value-added for the leading 50, 100, and 200 domestic manufacturing firms shows a stronger rise from 1947, which was a low point, than share of shipments data. But value-added too tends to mislead as much as to enlighten. The domestic value-added share of leading firms dropped from 1937 to 1947. It then rose strongly from 1947 to 1954. There was a much slighter rise from 1954 to 1963 with a flat trend since 1963 for the leading 50 and 100 firms. The second 100 added one percentage point to their share from 1963 to 1967 and two more from 1967 to 1977. The smaller firms among the top 200 grew faster than the larger firms.

After the 1937 to 1947 drop in leading firm share of value-added, the majority of the subsequent upward trend resulted from increasing fabrication of product by leading corporations (an increase in the ratio of value-added to shipments), not from an increasing proportion of manufacturing shipments. The value-added share rise resulted, in part, from the ratio rising in the thirty-five companies of 1947 that remained in the top 50 in 1954. (Their ratio of value-added to shipments rose from 0.35 to 0.40). It was also a *result of the replacement by 1954 of fifteen companies*

317

in the 1947 top 50 by companies whose ratio of value-added to shipments was much higher (0.48 versus 0.29).[15]

The rise in the ratio of value-added to shipments in the largest 50, 100, and 200 industrials, which played a major role in their early increases in share of manufacturing value-added, can be ascribed in part to decreasing amounts of material used per dollar's worth of product. With improving technology, fabrication increasingly replaced raw material. By this means materials were conserved. As transistors replaced vacuum tubes and integrated circuits replaced transistors and wired circuits, for example, the material required for any given output of electronic equipment dropped. The ratio of value-added to the value of materials increased, as did the ratio of value-added to the value of shipments. Also, the relatively greater growth of more vertically integrated firms, which displaced some of the original top firms, played a role in the increase in value-added relative to shipments. Assembly operations formerly fed by purchased parts began using internally produced sub-assemblies. Parts suppliers began using the parts they fabricated to make their own final products. Chrysler purchased Briggs Manufacturing, its supplier of bodies, and oil refiners began processing the raw materials they produced into chemicals.

This trend was simply a move toward the average degree of internal fabrication found among other firms. In 1937, the largest 50 firms produced only 20 percent of value-added in all manufacturing although they shipped 28 percent of all manufactured product. They did less fabricating work on the products they shipped than the average manufacturing firm. By 1972, the largest 50 were more like other manufacturers in their vertical integration. Value-added and shipment proportions became more nearly equal. A rise in their share of value-added and a *drop* in their share of product shipped (Table 11-2) brought about the equality.

The effect of mergers on aggregate concentration has been minuscule. Professor Markham examined the trend in aggregate share between 1963 and 1970 of the largest 50 and 100 industrials. This was the period in which some emerging conglomerates, such as Ling-Temco-Voight and Gulf & Western, moved into the top 50. He concluded that, "Since no increase in concentration occurred in the period of the conglomerate merger wave, the large volume of acquisitions in the 1960s appears to have left the overall structure of the manufacturing economy unaltered."[16] To this,

Professors Lorie and Halpern, writing in late 1969, add the following comment:

> Between 1960 and 1968, 909 firms in manufacturing and mining acquired other firms with assets of more than $10 million. The aggregate value of the assets acquired was $40.6 billion, an amount equal to the market value of the common stock of International Business Machines Corporation on September 22, 1969.[17]

The 50 or 100 largest industrial companies is not an unchanging group, each fixed in its position with enduring ties to the rest. Of the 50 largest manufacturing firms in 1947, only twenty-four remained in the top 50 in 1977. Seventeen of the 50 largest in 1977 came from outside the ranks of the 100 largest in 1947. Thirteen of the 50 largest in 1947 no longer appear among the top 100.

The reasons for such changes are straightforward. Each leading firm must work hard constantly to improve its products, keep its prices attractive, raise its productivity, adapt itself to the changing desires of American consumers, and compete effectively for labor, materials, and capital in order to stay solvent. If its major products become obsolete, it will have to change industries or join United States Leather (no. 7 in 1909) or American Woolen Co. (no. 21 in 1909) in the corporate graveyard. The only real power that large firms have lies in their ability to produce products at a low enough cost to offer wage rates and profits that are attractive to workers and suppliers of capital, and attractive products at prices low enough to entice buyers to choose their goods rather than those of their competitors. Essentially, any member of the top 50 is there because it uses the resources it employs more productively than other companies can use those resources. If it did not, they would be bid away by other firms.

That the top 50 employ people more productively than smaller firms is shown by the fact that they produced 24 percent of all value-added by manufacture and 25 percent of all product shipped in 1977 with only 17 percent of the workers employed in manufacturing. The wage paid per worker in the top 50 averaged 53 percent more than the wage paid in other manufacturing firms (see Table 11-4). Those who would stop the relative growth of the largest industrials seek, in effect, to foreclose growth in the opportunity for high wage employment. They would slow growth in productivity and speed the relative decline of the United States in the world economy.

How Powerful Is One of the Top 200?

Aggregate, or macro-, concentration cuts across individual product markets and depends upon the relative size of the largest firms. Macro-concentration is a meaningless concept in economic terms. A firm's ranking among the top 50 or 200 does not mean that it can exercise control over its product markets; nor does the ranking mean that the firm can depress the price of some inputs that it uses. Exxon, for example, which produces and sells worldwide, receives 73 percent of its revenues from its production and sales abroad. It has been ranked first or second in size by assets or sales among all *American* manufacturing firms for many years, yet its place is small in the domestic petroleum products industry. It has no market power in refined petroleum products nor can it control the prices of its raw materials. Its share of American manufacturing sales or assets is usually overstated by including its foreign sales or assets in the numerator of the ratio. It would not be at the top of the list if companies were ranked by domestic assets or revenues.

Nor is Exxon a very large firm in the U.S. market relative to other leading oil refiners operating in the United States. It produces only 8 percent of all domestically refined petroleum products. While that makes it the leading firm in its industry, even the market-concentration doctrine implies that such a small share leaves it bereft of any power. If it were to restrict output and attempt to raise its price relative to costs, its position in the market would fade quickly. Any supply vacuum would be filled by the dozens of other refiners (seventeen of whom are among the 50 leading industrial firms) eager for more business and by importers of petroleum products, assuming government controls would not prevent this. If Exxon even failed to increase its productivity constantly, it would find itself unable to pay wages high enough to hold its workers or offer returns attractive enough to obtain the capital needed to maintain its position in the industry. Its power to do anything—even to produce—depends on its ability to serve consumers well at competitive prices. It moved into first place in the retail gasoline market in the United States in late 1979 only

TABLE 11-4

Shares of Manufacturing Employment and Earnings Provided by the Largest Manufacturing Companies, 1937–77

Year	50 Largest Manufacturing Companies			100 Largest Manufacturing Companies			200 Largest Manufacturing Companies		
	Percentage Share of Manufacturing Production Worker Employment	Percentage Share of Manufacturing Payroll	Ratio of Payroll per Production Worker in 50 Largest to Rest of Manufacturing	Percentage Share of Manufacturing Production Worker Employment	Percentage Share of Manufacturing Payroll	Ratio of Payroll per Production Worker in 100 Largest to Rest of Manufacturing	Percentage Share of Manufacturing Production Worker Employment	Percentage Share of Manufacturing Payroll	Ratio of Payroll per Production Worker in 200 Largest to Rest of Manufacturing
1937	16.2	21.3	1.40	20.8	26.6	1.38	26.3	32.9	1.37
1963	17.2	21.9	1.35	23.1	28.8	1.35	28.9	35.6	1.36
1967	17.9	22.5	1.33	23.6	29.2	1.34	30.7	36.8	1.31
1972	17.9	23.6	1.42	24.0	30.5	1.39	32.5	39.6	1.36
1977	16.8	23.6	1.53	23.6	31.4	1.48	31.8	40.4	1.45

Sources: Bureau of the Census, CONCENTRATION RATIOS IN MANUFACTURING (May 1981), Table 4 at 9-9; CONCENTRATION RATIOS IN MANUFACTURING INDUSTRY 1963 (1966), Table 1B at 2; W. F. Crowder, A. G. Abramson, and E. W. Staudt, The Product Structure of Large Corporation, in Temporary National Economic Committee, THE STRUCTURE OF INDUSTRY (1941), Tables 1 at 583 and IC at 715.

because it received crude oil from Saudi Arabia priced about $5.00 per barrel below world market levels. That enabled it to offer gasoline at attractive prices and in larger amounts relative to the supplies available from other refiners.

The 1927 shutdown of the Ford Motor Company dramatically illustrates how little influence a "megacorporation" has even when it is large relative to its own industry. Ford was one of the giant firms of the 1920s (and is still America's sixth largest industrial firm although no longer number one in the automobile industry). It produced 60 percent of all automobiles turned out in the United States in 1921. From 1921 to 1925 it supplied as many automobiles as all other companies combined. Ford was a dominant firm. In 1927, it completely shut off its supply to the market for nearly the entire year. It closed down in January to retool for the change from the Model T to the Model A, resuming sales in December. If supplying a majority or near majority of a market gives a firm any power to control supply and price, then the complete withdrawal of that firm's supply would certainly cause a rise in price. Yet despite its "dominant" producer position, automobile prices failed to rise when Ford shut down. Other manufacturers quickly increased their output. As a result, prices not only failed to rise— they *fell* by mid-1927 despite the complete withdrawal of Ford from the new car market.[18]

The story of the American Sugar Refining Company was told above. It was one of the very largest industrial enterprises in the United States in the 1890s, and was still the eighth largest in 1901. At the end of 1891 it encompassed by merger 98 percent of its industry's capacity east of the Rockies. Yet what power it acquired disappeared after it raised prices in 1892 and 1893. By 1894, prices returned to their 1891 level. Similarly, American Can was a leader in size among all industrial and mining firms in 1901 and was still the twentieth largest in 1909 after losing one third of its market share. It too found its dominant position withered when it attempted to raise prices relative to costs.

If American Sugar or American Can could not long influence prices starting from positions with 98 and 90 percent of their industry's capacity, it matters little that they ranked among the 50 leading industrial firms at the time of their attempts. It matters even less that Exxon ranks number one among all manufacturing firms since its market position is vastly less important in its industry than was that of Ford, American Sugar, or American Can. The fact that Chrysler was the tenth largest among all industrial corporations in the United States did not keep it from being a troubled company. Only the most naive observer could possibly tell its president that he controls his output, produces what he pleases, names his price, and compels his customers to buy with advertising. Such news—if it were true—would certainly be welcome at Chrysler Corporation.

Bigness and Political Power

The final argument of those who are concerned about aggregate concentration is that bigness is a threat to democracy because of the political power of the giant corporation.[19] Since there are no systematic studies of the political power possessed by "megacorporations," we have only a few observations to report.

Professor Edward Banfield investigated business power in the city of Chicago. He concluded that business had essentially no power "except by main force of being right."[20] Professor Edward Epstein suggests that corporations are too reticent in the political process and should press their legitimate interests more vigorously than they do.[21]

Among the ten largest industrial corporations in America are six international oil companies. If firms among the largest 50 or 100 or 200 possess any political power, then the six international oil companies in the top ten must have overwhelming "clout." Yet they were the losers from 1960 to 1973 under the mandatory oil import quota program (see Table 11-5). They were losers again after 1973 under the oil "entitlements" and allocation programs. Douglas Bohi and Milton Russell, discussing the "interests" served by U.S. oil import policy, report that:

> The major large group which *paid* for the benefits of the greater energy security achieved under oil import controls was the undifferentiated portion of the consuming public. With one possible exception, other identifiable functional groups were either unaffected, or actually made better off.
>
> The "possible exception" is the international operations of major oil companies . . . The overall restriction on imports lowered their potential market, and its administration forced them to share the already limited market with newcomers. The special provisions further eroded their position. The sliding scale [which provided smaller re-

TABLE 11–5
Import Quotas of Refineries as Percent
of Daily Input of Petroleum
(Districts I–IV, July 1, 1959–Dec. 31, 1959)

Size of Refinery (Thousands of Barrels)	Percent Quota
0–10	11.4
10–20	10.4
20–30	9.5
30–60	8.5
60–100	7.6
100–150	6.6
150–200	5.7
200–300	4.7
300 and over	3.8

Source: Hearing, Select Committee on Small Business, U.S., Congress. 88th Cong., 2nd Sess., Aug. 10 and 11, 1964, [12] p. 121.

finers with special quota allocations and a relatively larger share of import "tickets"], the petrochemical quota, the Islands program, the resid program, and the overriding fact that traditional importers were required to share the quota with inland refiners all reduced the advantage of [having developed] overseas production. Virtually every controversy was resolved against the best interests of the original major company importers, a fact with important implications when the political economy of oil is examined. The political power of oil may be great, but based on the record of the mandatory quota program, the *power is not found in the international giants of the industry.*[22]

Professor George Stigler, generalizing from the nation's experience with regulation in many industries, concluded that

... the distribution of control of the industry among the firms in the industry is changed [by regulation]. In an unregulated industry each firm's influence upon price and output is proportional to its share of industry output (at least in a simple arithmetic sense of direct capacity to change output). ... [P]olitical decisions take account ... of the political strength of the various firms, so small firms have a larger influence than they would possess in an unregulated industry. Thus, when quotas are given to firms, the small firms will almost always receive larger quotas than cost-minimizing practices would allow. The original quotas under the oil import quota system ... illustrate this practice (Table 11-5). The smallest refiners were given a quota of 11.4 percent of their daily consumption of oil, and the percentage dropped as refinery size rose. The pattern of regressive benefits is characteristic of public controls in industries with numerous firms.[23]

Among the 200 largest industrial firms are eight pharmaceutical companies. It is enlightening to compare their political power with that of the owners of drugstores. When the Kefauver Committee investigated the pricing of drugs, the pharmaceutical corporations were treated harshly. Since the prices received by pharmaceutical manufacturers are only 48 percent of the retail prices paid by consumers, it was suggested that the Committee investigate the other 52 percent. Within a few hours after the investigation was contemplated, the suggestion was dropped. Reliable sources indicate that the force behind this was the far greater power of the National Druggists Association and the American Pharmacists Association. They had far more political power than the eight members of the 200 club.

Professor Richard Posner, examining special interest legislation, concluded that large corporations have no more influence in the political process, actually probably less, than small firms.

> The fact that a great deal of legislation appears to be designed to protect firms against competition . . . provides the basis for a serious criticism of our political system and, perhaps, more broadly, of the role which we allow "interest groups" to play in shaping public policy. It does not suggest a basis for a criticism of large corporations as such. The subordination of consumer to producer interests in the production of legislation seems quite independent of the size of the individual firms involved. We observe as much protective legislation in small business industries, such as agriculture, textiles, and trucking, as in large—perhaps more. We observe much protective legislation in industries where production is carried on by individuals rather than by firms—unionized trades [barbering, plumbing, pharmacy] and regulated professions such as medicine are important examples.[24]

The agricultural interests, labor unions, and environmentalists have more than held their own with the 200 in contests for political influence. Certainly the tax structure indicates a complete lack of political influence among the 200. There is, for example, heavier taxation of large corporations than of the small, a depletion allowance provided for the small oil producers but not for the majors, and double taxation of corporate earnings both as earnings and again as dividends or capital gains (the latter being largely fictitious as a result of inflation[25]) while noncorporate firms or small closely held corporations are taxed only once.

In contests with the National Highway Traffic Safety Administration, the three major automotive firms, who were among the ten largest industrial firms, and International Harvester, a major producer of trucks and number twenty-seven on the list of largest industrial companies, have lost along with their customers and the cause of highway safety. The lack of political power was demonstrated in their unsuccessful attempts to prevent the compulsory installation of antilock brakes on large trucks before they had been developed to the point where they would not be hazardous. Despite the "main force of being right," the four large truck manufacturers, who are among the top 50 industrials, did not prevail with the administration, although antilock brakes had been shown to reduce highway safety. Only the subsequent slaughter after the compulsory installation of these brakes finally led a federal court to order the cancellation of the requirement.

In contrast to the impotence of the biggest of the Big 200, the little firms that compose the nuts, bolts, and screws industry forced President Carter to reverse his position on tariff protection for the industry. As the *New York Times* put the matter, "The $1-billion-a-year industry . . . has powerful friends in Congress who protested when the President came down last February [1978] against a recommendation by the Government's International Trade Commission for protection."[26]

L. E. Birdzell has provided a succinct description of the power of the 200 largest industrial corporations.

> The argument that conglomerates represent a political power threat is . . . difficult to take seriously. A large concentration of wealth undoubtedly has a substantial political capability if it can lawfully be applied to political purposes, as illustrated by the successful political use of the Rockefeller and Kennedy fortunes. The fatal problem with similar political use of corporate concentrations of wealth is that they cannot lawfully be applied to political uses, even if stockholders could be induced to agree on common political objectives and the business organization could survive the necessary diversion of effort. Salaried corporate managers are probably not as rich a potential source of political contributions as oil lessors, owners of automobile dealerships, and other entrepreneurs with substantial personal fortunes. And corporate management is rarely able to deliver the votes even of corporate stockholders, let alone employees, dealers, or suppliers. The Automobile Dealers Day-in-Court Act is eloquent testimony to the comparative political power of some very large corporations on the one hand and a group of "small" businessmen on the other.[27]

And we can again turn to Professor Posner to add his observations of the political power possessed by large firms, whether large because they are the biggest in their industries and their industries are large or because they have operations in many different industries.

> That the condition of being a large firm is not itself sufficient to assure protective legislation is illustrated by the embattled condition of the conglomerate corporations. These very large firms were not able to ward off highly adverse accounting [requirements] and antitrust developments. . . .
>
> The conglomerates occupy much the same place in public rhetoric today over corporate abuse that the great monopolies of the turn of the century, such as Standard Oil, occupied in the muckraking journalism of their day. The political power of both groups proved to be weak, or at most transient. The trusts were dismembered, and the conglomerates have been buffeted from a variety of directions without obtaining any succor from the legislative branch. . . .
>
> . . . there appears to be an abiding public need to believe in the existence of invisible, global, omnipotent, indescribably sinister forces—Satan, Freemasonry, Papism, the Jews, and now the multinational corporations. The last satisfies the traditional requirements of a Sinister Force—worldwide in scope, mysterious in its modes of exerting influence, huge and monied. The multinational corporation, and its domestic cousin the conglomerate, have enabled the critics of business and the market economy to invoke and exploit the primitive emotional needs that unite us to our ancestors whom we deride for their superstitions.[28]

Conclusion

Politicians seldom pick on labor unions, which exercise monopoly power on a scale undreamed of by any corporation, or on farmers. These groups possess political power that not only makes them nearly invulnerable to attack, but also enables them to manipulate the political process in ways and to an extent that would make Thomas Jefferson shudder. Yet it is large corporations that are accused of threatening any Jeffersonian character left in our democracy.[29] The fact that they are so frequently picked on by politicians demonstrates what little political power they have.

The crusade against the growth of the top 100 or 200 industrial firms and against conglomerate acquisitions is bottomed on specious fears and a nonexistent trend in aggregate concentration. They provide convenient targets on which to vent anger over rising prices of petroleum products or inflation. If this were simply a harmless and entertaining political game, there would be no need for concern—but it is not.

If we continue to obstruct the growth of large firms and to thwart acquisitions by large conglomerates, we will be foreclosing opportunities to workers for higher paying employment, to stock-holders for rescue by acquisition from the dissipation of their assets by inept managements, and to the country for enhanced productivity that large firms can bring about. The United States is falling behind the rest of the industrial world in its productivity growth, although it once led—in the period in which the growth of U.S. corporations created some of the world's largest firms. It is time to renounce public policies based on superstition and igno-rance and to address the concrete economic issues this nation faces.

Notes

1. Adolf A. Berle, Jr., and Gardiner C. Means, THE MODERN CORPORATION AND PRIVATE PROPERTY v, 40 (1932). Adolf Berle was not alarmed at the trend. He wrote in his preface that "this development seemed in many ways a thoroughly logical and intelligent trend." He did add that, "Equally, it seemed fraught with dangers as well as with advantages." *Id.* at v.
2. U.S., National Resources Committee, STRUCTURE OF THE AMERICAN ECONOMY Part I at 298–317 (1939).
3. Edward Cowan, *Law for Size Limits on Mergers Sought,* NEW YORK TIMES 26 (Dec. 30, 1978).
4. Statement of Dr. Carl Kaysen, ECONOMIC CONCENTRATION PART 2, MERGERS AND OTHER FACTORS AFFECTING INDUSTRY CONCENTRATION 541, 543 (1965). Emphasis supplied.
5. W. S. Comanor, *Prepared Statement for the Subcommittee on Antitrust, Monopoly, and Business Rights,* MERGERS AND ECONOMIC CONCENTRA-TION 18 (1979).
6. See Berle and Means *supra* note 1, at 28.
7. Michael Gort, *The Consequences of Large Conglomerate Mergers* 4 (working paper, University of Buffalo, 1979).
8. Jesse Markham, CONGLOMERATE ENTERPRISE AND PUBLIC POLICY 114 (1973).
9. U.S., Department of Commerce, Bureau of the Census, HISTORICAL STATISTICS OF THE UNITED STATES, COLONIAL TIMES TO 1970 252–261 (1975).
10. U.S., Department of Commerce, Bureau of the Census, CONCENTRATION RATIOS IN MANUFACTURING INDUSTRY 1963, Part II (1967), Table 24 at 309.
11. Jules Backman, *An Analysis of the Economic Report on Corporate Merg-ers* in U.S., Congress, Senate, Committee on the Judiciary, Subcommit-

tee on Antitrust and Monopoly Hearings, THE CONGLOMERATE MERGER PROBLEM, PART 8 4718 (1970).

12. F. M. Scherer, INDUSTRIAL MARKET STRUCTURE AND ECONOMIC PERFORMANCE 40 (1970).

13. U.S., Federal Trade Commission, ECONOMIC REPORT ON CORPORATE MERGERS 173 (1969).

14. The Citibank compilation of return on equity of more than 2,000 leading corporations shows petroleum companies earning 15.6 percent on beginning-of-year equity in 1973 as compared to a 14.8 percent accounting rate of return of all leading manufacturing firms. In 1977, petroleum refiners earned 14.3 percent as compared to 15.9 percent for all leading manufacturers. See Table 8-2 for 1979 data.

15. Ralph L. Nelson, CONCENTRATION IN THE MANUFACTURING INDUSTRIES OF THE UNITED STATES 94 (1963).

16. See Markham *supra* note 8, at 119.

17. James H. Lorie and Paul Halpern, *Conglomerates: The Rhetoric and the Evidence,* 13 JOURNAL OF LAW & ECONOMICS 157 (Apr. 1970).

18. U.S., Federal Trade Commission, REPORT ON MOTOR VEHICLE INDUSTRY (1939).

19. See statements by John Shenefield and by William Comanor in Comanor *supra* note 5.

20. Edward C. Banfield, POLITICAL INFLUENCE (1961).

21. Edwin Epstein, THE CORPORATION IN AMERICAN POLITICS (1969).

22. Douglas R. Bohi and Milton Russell, LIMITING OIL IMPORTS: AN ECONOMIC HISTORY AND ANALYSIS (1978).

23. George J. Stigler, *The Theory of Economic Regulation,* 2 BELL JOURNAL OF ECONOMICS AND MANAGEMENT SCIENCE 7 (Spring 1971).

24. Richard Posner, *Power in America: The Role of the Large Corporation* in J. F. Weston (ed.), LARGE CORPORATIONS IN A CHANGING SOCIETY 99 (1975).

25. Martin Feldstein and Joel Slemrod, *How Inflation Distorts the Taxation of Capital Gains,* 53 HARVARD BUSINESS REVIEW 99 (Sept. 1975).

26. NEW YORK TIMES D1 (Dec. 27, 1978).

27. L. E. Birdzell, *The Conglomerates: A Neighbor's View,* 44 ST. JOHN'S LAW REVIEW 314 (1970).

28. See Posner *supra* note 24, at 100, 103.

29. See Comanor, MERGERS AND ECONOMIC CONCENTRATION *supra* note 5.

12

Mergers and Conglomerate Power

SOME recent arrivals on the 50 largest list, such as Gulf & Western, International Telephone, and Tenneco, got there by acquiring
dozens of diverse firms and divisions sold by other firms. They are
conglomerates—or, as they prefer to call themselves, multi-industry or multi-market companies.[1] Harmful effects purportedly stem
from their size. Sinister motives are said to underlie their diversification. Fears that conglomerates will engage in reciprocal arrangements—transactions in which the conglomerate says to a
seller, "I will buy your product if you buy mine"—are raised. It is
also suggested that these multi-marketers use cross-subsidization
to grow larger and to dominate markets in which their divisions
operate. Presumably, they subsidize predatory activity by some
divisions with the profits of other divisions.

The desire to present the conglomerate corporation as a destruc-
tive or exploitive economic organism often leads to a Jekyll and
Hyde caricature in which the pitiless competitive instincts of one
minute are replaced by the collusive, parasitic impulses of the
next. Conglomerates *might* entrench their acquisitions in their
markets by predatory cross-subsidization or they might profit from
mutual competitive forbearance.

Potential Predatory Pricing

The cross-subsidization argument is another version of the predatory pricing fear. That is, it assumes that one of the divisions of a

330

conglomerate *might* price below cost, financing this money-losing endeavor with profits earned in other divisions, to drive out competitors. Once it drives competitors from the field, the division could, it is asserted, raise its price to monopoly levels, recouping its losses with interest and more.

Although this possibility has gained adherents in Washington and in the courts—despite the fact that antitrust laws can be applied by the government and that injured competitors can sue for treble damages in such cases—hardly an economist specializing in industrial organization believes that this strategy is feasible or profitable.[2] Professors Lorie and Halpern observe that, "In the long run, and in the absence of effective barriers to entry, it seems impossible to maintain an effective monopoly by a temporarily superior capacity to lose money."[3] Professor David Kamerschen tells us that

> I think there is something of a consensus among industrial organization economists that true predation is very unusual, probably illogical, and not a serious social problem in the U.S. The following quotations from respected scholars in this area should suffice to illustrate this consensus: (1) Elzinga . . . "Predatory price cutting, given its unlikely occurrence and visual similarity to healthy business rivalry, should be well down the priority list of the antitrust authorities"; (2) Dewey . . . "From the foregoing remarks, it also follows that predatory price-cutting constitutes a minor threat to competition"; (3) Scherer . . . "Distinguishing price cutting with predatory intent from price cutting in good faith to meet tough local competition is singularly difficult . . . It is fair to say that the predatory pricing doctrine is one of shakiest pillars of existing antimerger law. Its absence would not be mourned by lovers of competition and/or logic."; and (4) Scherer . . . "in actual situations the line between meeting competition and destroying it is seldom sharp, since a great deal depends upon intent, which is hard to pin down." The legal profession seems equally outspoken as how threatening a "clog on competition" is predation, arguing that the dangers of predation are few in principle, unlikely in occurrence, and speculative in demonstration.[4]

Speaking directly on the issue of the likelihood of predatory pricing as a consequence of conglomerate mergers, Professor Donald Turner, a former head of the Antitrust Division, notes that

> . . . the belief that predatory pricing is a likely consequence of conglomerate size, and hence of conglomerate merger, is wholly unverified by any careful studies; research and analysis suggest that in all likelihood this belief is just wrong.

> To sum up predatory pricing seems so improbable a consequence of conglomerate acquisitions that it deserves little weight in formulating antimerger rules based on prospective effects.[5]

Even the Federal Trade Commission's Bureau of Economics treated the prospect of cross-subsidized, predatory activity by conglomerates with undisguised skepticism after engaging in a detailed study of conglomerate behavior and performance. In its report on its survey of nine large conglomerates, it states that it found no evidence of predatory behavior nor could it find "any rational incentive for them to do so." It says

> It should be noted that in calculating the returns from a predatory pricing strategy, a time discount factor would have to be applied to the expected monopoly return. The "deep pocket" losses would occur in the present, whereas the monopoly returns would begin at some distant point in the future, perhaps ten years hence. Only when the losses were small or of short duration, or the monopoly profits very large, would such a strategy be economically rational for a conglomerate. In addition, a predatory strategy presumes that there are significant entry barriers in the market where the conglomerate is attempting to eliminate smaller rivals. Otherwise, new firms would enter after prices were raised and the conglomerate would not be able to reap monopoly profits.[6]

Similarly, the President's Task Force on Productivity and Competition states that

> There is now an impressive body of literature arguing the improbability that a profit maximizing seller, even one with monopoly power, would or could use below-cost selling to monopolize additional markets. Yet . . . the alleged danger of predatory pricing remains a principal prop of [the FTC] vertical and conglomerate antimerger cases.[7]

The unlikelihood of predatory pricing was cogently demonstrated by L. E. Birdzell. The considerations he lists that would have to be taken into account in preparing a business plan for taking over an industry via predatory pricing show that such a plan would be extraordinarily expensive.[8] The improbability of predatory pricing is confirmed by its rarity.[9]

The direct evidence on the market share trends of conglomerate acquisitions after merger demonstrates that neither entrenchment nor predatory pricing is a common tactic (or else conglomerates were remarkably inept in their use of predatory pricing).

[The] post-acquisition changes in market positions acquired by conglomerates from 1963 to 1969 were predominantly decreases. . . . After the massive merger activity of the 1960s, the market share of the conglomerate firm in 1969 was less than 5 percent in 82.4 percent of the five-digit product classes in which they operated.[10]

Potential Reciprocity

Reciprocity is an even weaker pillar of antitrust than predatory pricing. Professor Wesley Liebeler suggests that any cartel laying down rules to prevent secret, difficult-to-detect price cuts that cheat on the cartel's price policy would forbid purchases by any member of the cartel from its customers. If such purchases could be made and were allowed, it would be simple for any member to overpay a customer for supplies bought from the customer as a way of secretly shading the cartel price to obtain business.[11]

The lower price would not appear on any invoice and inspection of the cartel member's books would show no violation of the cartel agreement. Professor Liebeler goes on to suggest that if the Antitrust Division had stumbled across a reciprocity ban by a price colluding group, it would have become antitrust doctrine to forbid the *prevention* of reciprocal purchases. As matters stand, however, the Antitrust Division forbids reciprocal dealing, behaving as an enforcer of cartel arrangements.

Reciprocal dealing is either a procompetitive[12] or innocent practice.[13] In one instance, it was a method of exporting profits from a division where they would be subject to renegotiation on defense contracts to a division where they would be sheltered. There is no case, to our knowledge, where reciprocity has been an anti-competitive device. It was most extensively used by railroads unable to compete for business by offering a lower rate because of the price *floors* set by the Interstate Commerce Commission. Given the restrictions on methods of competing, railroads commonly resorted to offering to buy supplies from potential customers if they would purchase the railroad's services.[14] Similarly, other firms wishing to cut prices secretly have engaged in reciprocal deals to disguise a price cut.

Instead of being imposed as a condition for purchase, as usually argued by the antitrust agencies, reciprocal dealing is ordinarily a sales device in which the seller offers to buy from his prospective buyer to persuade him to purchase. It has the same competitive effect as an offer of generous credit terms, quick delivery, payment of transportation charges, provision of display or shelf stocking service, et cetera.

Secret, discriminatory price cutting works to undermine collusion.[15] It provides a method of competing when the explicit price is fixed. Also, it helps move a competitive industry to a new, long-run, lower-price equilibrium more quickly.[16] Since reciprocal dealing is a way of granting price concessions that would not be granted if such concessions had to be offered openly, it would seem that we should welcome additional possibilities for reciprocal dealing. While this might be a reason for favoring conglomerate mergers, rather than disapproving of them, it turns out that conglomeration evidently does not increase the amount of reciprocal dealing.[17] Modern methods of managing multi-industry firms, with division managers judged by division profit performance, militate against the use of reciprocal dealing by conglomerates to any greater extent than by single industry firms.[18]

Entrenchment and Potential Mutual Forbearance

The "entrenchment" argument against conglomerate acquisitions, used recently by the Antitrust Division in its attempt to stop the merger of Occidental and Mead, is the opposite of the "competitive forbearance" argument. Corwin Edwards argued that when large firms face each other in many markets, "there is an incentive to live and let live, to cultivate a cooperative spirit, and to recognize priorities of interest in the hope of reciprocal recognition."[19] Yet the Division argued against Occidental Petroleum's acquisition of Mead on the ground that Occidental would entrench Mead's position in the paper industry by expanding its business. Apparently, entrenchment was used in this case as another name for the "deep pockets" argument. Occidental would, said the Division, provide Mead with additional capacity for increasing business with current customers and for winning additional customers.[20] This hardly smacks of competitive forbearance.[21] If expansion of capacity and trade is what entrenching means, then let us have more entrenching. The antitrust laws are aimed at restraints on trade, not at the expansion of trade.

Implicitly, the entrenchment argument suggests that there are advantages to size that will automatically accrue to any large-size company moving into a market. It will acquire an ever-increasing share of that market by taking business from existing firms. If there are such important advantages of size, we should capitalize on these advantages to the fullest extent by moving large-size corporations into every industry. We should encourage conglomerate mergers.

The evidence does not suggest such uniform and automatic advantages in every industry, however. Professor Michael Gort's study of 111 diversified firms showed that these firms continued to occupy only a minor share of most markets many years after entry.[22] The FTC's Bureau of Economics detailed study of nine conglomerates came to the same conclusion. In the language of the report

> Looking at leading positions—market shares over 10 percent—increases and decreases after acquisition were evenly matched. The conclusion to be drawn . . . is that there is no systematic tendency for market shares either to increase or decrease after acquisition. This is true both for "toehold" and for leading positions.[23]

Decline in Number of Potential Entrants

One of the arguments advanced against allowing large conglomerates to grow larger by acquisitions does not concern itself primarily with size or aggregate concentration. Instead the issue is the desirability of atomistic market structures—a turn back to the arguments against market concentration. The antitrust authorities are concerned that a conglomerate making an acquisition ceases being a *potential* competitor when it becomes an actual competitor by acquisition. Their hope, apparently, is that foreclosing diversification by acquisition will lead the would-be acquirer to undertake de novo entry into the same industry by internal expansion (or if by acquisition, then by no more than a "toehold" acquisition). They seem to believe that the motive for conglomerate mergers is a desire for diversification into specific lines of business.

335

The use of this argument simply demonstrates that the antitrust authorities do not know why conglomerate acquisitions occur. Chief among the many reasons for conglomerate mergers—and the best substantiated hypothesis—is that conglomerates take advantage of opportunities to acquire poorly managed assets. On these, they earn as much as they would be able to make on any other investment. They succeed in making a competitive return on what they invest by managing the assets well. The FTC's Bureau of Economics examined the earnings record of eighty-five large firms acquired by nine major conglomerates in the 1960s. It found that

> . . . on the average, the manufacturing firms acquired by the survey firms were significantly less profitable than the average for their industries. . . . The median relative profit rate was 76.5 percent. Thus, the median acquired manufacturing firm was about three-fourths as profitable as the average of other firms in its industry.[24]

The conglomerate acquisition record demonstrates that poorly managed firms predominate among those acquired by merger. Stockholders of the average New York Stock Exchange (NYSE) listed firm acquired in the postwar years lost 14 percent on their investment in the four years preceding the news of the acquisitoin bid as compared to the returns to stockholders of the average NYSE listed firm (see Figure 12-1). Acquirers paid a competitive price (the value of the firm in competent hands) for their acquisitions (which provided a premium on the price of the stock of the acquired firms that more than made the stockholders of the acquisitions whole). The acquirers earned a competitive return on their acquisitions (see Figure 12-2), demonstrating that (1) they managed them better than they were previously managed, and (2) conglomerate takeovers are rational, competitive economic occurrences.[25] Making better use of formerly badly managed assets is a social service. It raises productivity, moderates inflation, and should be allowed to proceed instead of being restricted.

This evidence suggests that the motive for conglomerate acquisition does not usually rise out of a desire to enter a specific industry.[26] The opportunity to acquire poorly managed assets, judging by Professor Paul Asquith's findings in his examination of mergers in the post–World-War-II years, provides the motive for the spe-

FIGURE 12-1

Earnings of Stockholders of Acquired Firms Relative to Average Stockholder
Earnings in the Four Years Preceding Acquisition Announcement

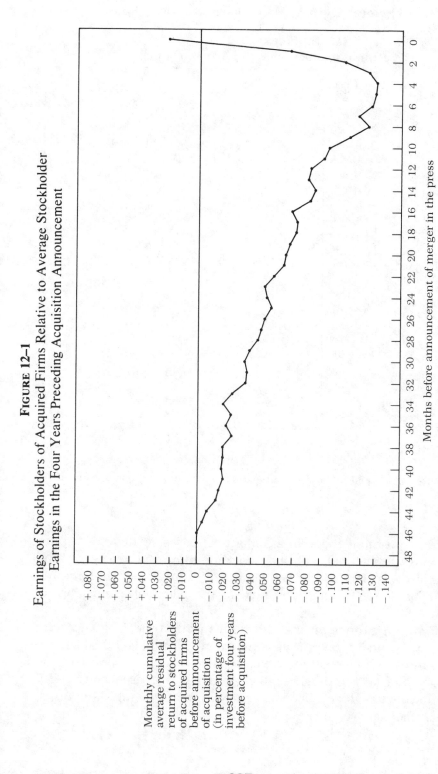

Source: Paul Asquith, *Mergers and the Market for Acquisitions* (mimeographed, January 1979).

FIGURE 12–2
Returns to Stockholders of Acquiring Firms

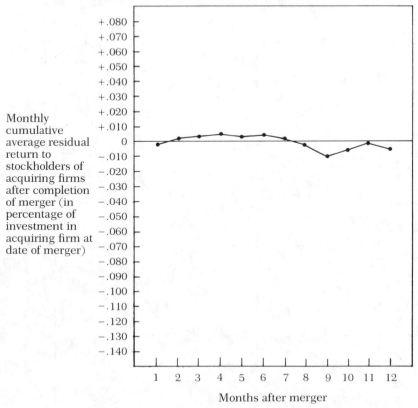

Monthly cumulative average residual return to stockholders of acquiring firms after completion of merger (in percentage of investment in acquiring firm at date of merger)

Months after merger

Source: Paul Asquith, *Mergers and the Market for Acquisitions* (mimeographed, January 1979).

cific acquisitions made in a majority of cases.[27] The antitrust authorities' "potential entrant" doctrine, however, rests on the premise that foreclosing conglomerate acquisitions will force the conglomerator to enter the field of the potential acquisition de novo.

Conceding the premises of the antitrust doctrine, it still does not follow that mergers by large conglomerate firms should be barred. It can be argued that entry will be decreased by such a bar. The prohibition will be a barrier to entry rather than an encourager of de novo entry. It will decrease entry by conglomerates and it will decrease do novo entry.

Decreased Entry by Conglomerates If Acquisitions Are Foreclosed

If a major portion of specific conglomerate acquisitions occurs because poor management of assets causes their price to be below their value if well managed, preventing the acquisition of these assets will simply decrease the interest of conglomerates in entering the industries where the assets are employed. Stockholders in 72 percent of the acquired firms had inferior returns relative to an average holder of NYSE stocks in the period from four years to six months before the announcement of the merger bid. Sixty-two percent of all acquired firms suffered relative losses of more than 10 percent. The majority of acquisitions evidently consists of poorly managed firms.[28]

If the earnings experience of acquired firms' stockholders is, in part, the consequence of the maturation of the industries in which the firms carry on their business, the industry will not be an attractive one to enter de novo. With sufficient capacity already in place to depress earnings to a level where a firm earning less than the average in its industry suffers relative to the average of firms in all industries, de novo entry would be a misuse of resources. In this case, it would not be attractive since additional capacity placed in such industries would not earn as much, on average, as alternative investments. It is unrealistic to believe that a conglomerate will crash its way into an industry, which is unfamiliar territory and which has sufficient capacity already in place, with new capacity.

Some of the firms whose stockholders suffered losses may be in industries in which earnings are attractive, but this is likely to be only a small proportion of such firms. For them to produce relative losses for their stockholders, their managements have to be grossly inadequate. In such a case, the argument for allowing their acquisition by other firms is even more compelling, even at the price of precluding a de novo entry.

The inefficiency of the former management of an acquired firm does not necessarily lie in how well or poorly it managed production or marketing or employee relations. It may simply have consisted of not knowing enough to stop throwing good money after bad. If a firm's industry was mature or had begun to decline, continuing to invest in such an industry wasted resources. Borrowings from stockholders in the form of retained earnings or depreciation did not earn enough to maintain the value of the firm's assets and caused the value of the shareholders' assets to decline. Nor was this a service to buyers in general, who obviously preferred the product of alternative investments. Their unwillingness to buy the products of the firm at a price that would yield as good a return as the product of alternative projects demonstrated this.

In fact, it is on exactly this point that those directing conglomerates have displayed good management. Examining a sample of firms that engaged in multiple mergers in the 1960s, Professors Weston and Mansinghka found that these firms raised the ratio of earnings before interest and taxes to total assets from 8.7 percent in 1958 (as compared to 16.7 percent in a control sample) to 15.1 percent in 1968 (as compared to 15.6 percent in the control group).[29] These multiple-merger firms obviously were based in over-expanded industries. Instead of throwing good money after bad, they proceeded to allocate resources to more productive uses than could be found in their home industries. Professor Michael Gort's work analyzing the sources of growth for the period 1967 to 1977 in the 100 largest non-oil companies confirms the slower growth of the home industries of these firms. If they had not been or become conglomerates and simply grown at the same rates as their home two-digit industries, their share of manufacturing sales and assets would have been below what they actually attained.[30]

A portion of the acquisitions of conglomerates consists of firms whose stockholders have suffered no losses. These cannot be categorized as having been inefficiently managed. It could be argued that there is, in this case, an intent to enter a specific industry or to acquire the facilities of a particular firm. But does it follow that barring the acquisition route would result in de novo entry?

If a potential entrant interested in a specific industry chooses to enter by acquiring an established firm, it will have to offer a price for the firm greater than the present value of the returns expected by the sellers if they retain ownership of the firm. It will offer such a price if it believes that it can manage the acquired assets more efficiently and profitably than they are being managed. There may be management efficiencies as a result of integration or benefits from new or additional management to pursue overlooked or neglected opportunities. Alternatively, the acquiring firm finds it cheaper to enter the industry in this way than by building new assets, a new organization, a new set of business connections, acquiring know-how, and seeking to replicate the locational and resource advantages of the existing firm. If management efficiencies are possible, and such acquisitions are barred, improvements in efficiency are thereby barred. If cheap entry is the reason for the acquisition, blockage of acquisitions may block entry. More expensive methods of entry may mean that the industry will not be worth entering. Professor Jesse Markham found, in his extensive survey of acquiring firms, that "companies seldom regard entry by new investment as a feasible alternative to entry by acquisition in particular industries."[31]

In either case, prohibiting entry by acquisition *to a firm that might be a potential entrant* is likely to block the expansion of capacity that would be undertaken by such a firm or permit the greater decline of capacity likely to occur in a poorly managed firm. Entry consists of expansion of capacity or maintenance of capacity that would otherwise contract. *It is irrelevant whether the expansion is by an acquired existing firm or a firm new to an industry.* In the case where acquisition is motivated by the opportunity to acquire poorly managed assets, an improvement of efficiency will lower long-run marginal costs and lead to greater output than would otherwise occur. If the entrant is motivated by a desire to enter the industry and is choosing the cheapest method of entry, the would-be entrant evidently sees opportunities for expansion or for improvements in profit not recognized by the acquired firm. It is for this reason that it is willing to offer a price exceeding the value of the firm to its owners.

Decreased Innovation If Acquisitions Are Foreclosed

Where a potential entrant sees an opportunity in an industry— perhaps an opportunity to offer a new product or to apply a new technique—it may prefer acquisition of an established firm with a producing organization or established dealer body in order to move the new product into the market or apply its new technique quickly. If it must struggle to build a viable producing and marketing organization from the ground up at the same time that it is trying to develop and establish an innovation, it will find the speed with which it can move its innovation into use slowed.[32] The consequent slower growth may make the payoff too small and too distant to make the investment in a new product or technique worth the cost. Established competitors will also have a longer time in which to develop competitive new products.

It appears that an organization growing more rapidly than 10 percent a year (as measured by asset growth) finds itself faced with problems that increase costs markedly. This limits the rate of entry (expansion of capacity) and confines the de novo entrant with an innovation to a much lower rate of entry than if it enters by means of an acquisition. The result of foreclosing entry by acquisition could be a slower rate of adoption of innovations and less incentive to innovate.

Mergers Increase Entry

Preventing acquisition by major firms because they are potential entrants de novo may reduce the number of de novo entrants, expectations of the Antitrust Division and the FTC notwithstanding. Barring firms from selling their assets to leading firms will limit the marketability of those assets. De novo entrance into a field will be diminished by this reduced marketability. The incentive for entrepreneurs to establish new firms will be reduced and it will be more difficult to obtain financial resources. Reduced marketability of firms increases the risks to those who might provide financial resources for the establishment of such firms and reduces as well the prospective returns to entrepreneurs. Professor Donald Turner points out that

> . . . to forbid [a category of] mergers . . . would narrow . . . the category of acceptable mergers, thereby drastically weakening the market for capital assets and seriously depreciating the price entrepreneurs could get for their businesses when they wish to liquidate. Such a policy . . . might have adverse effects on entry and growth of small business . . . [33]

The recent "theater of the absurd" performance by the FTC in the proposed Lancaster Colony acquisition of Federal Glass provides a dramatic example of the losses that can be forced on a firm's stockholders and employees by forbidding the sale of a firm or a division to specific would-be acquirers. Lancaster offered $40 million for the Federal Glass division of the Federal Company in 1977. The FTC acted to stop the acquisition although the Federal Company informed it that the glass division was failing and would be out of business unless Lancaster acquired and operated it. The FTC replied that it should find a more acceptable purchaser although its investment banker had solicited offers from eighty firms with no takers. Lancaster indicated to the Federal Company that FTC opposition had cooled its interest, and it withdrew its offer. On February 14, 1978, Federal Company dismissed its 1,500 glass division employees, told its customers it would no longer supply them, shut down the operation, and called in liquidators to dispose of its plant, equipment, and inventories. The FTC eliminated the competitive influence of the company's capacity in the glass tableware market in the name of maintaining competition.[34]

The fate of Federal Glass and the losses caused by FTC's antimerger policy illustrate what led Professor Turner to conclude that decreasing the demand for companies by forbidding some class of acquisitions will decrease the birthrate and growth of companies. The usual response to a decrease in the demand for anything, of course, is a decrease in the rate of supply. Forbidding acquisitions by a class of firms in the name of encouraging de novo entrance, or for any other reason, will decrease the amount of de novo entrance. The number of new firms founded and the number of firms supplied with additional capital to grow to middle size will decrease with the decreased demand for firms. As Commissioner Robert Pitofsky pointed out in the Pillsbury-Fox Deluxe Foods merger decision,

> Long-term competitive considerations require preservation of ease of entry and opportunity for businessmen to take entrepreneurial risks. The other side of that coin is a largely unarticulated policy, a clear corollary to the first, which would preserve exit opportunities where significant anticompetitive results do not occur. It is essential that the owners of very small businesses with slight competitive potential have some reasonable flexibility to sell out.[35]

The record of the American economy in the 1960s, the period of the "giant" conglomerate merger wave, demonstrates that we need have no fears about the top 100 or 200 encompassing the whole of U.S. industry, as some alarmists would have us believe will be the consequence of allowing conglomerate mergers to go unchecked. What is notable about the actual change in the U.S.

industrial structure in the 1960s, in contrast to the hypothetical fears, is that the number of corporations did not decline in the face of the great number of mergers and acquisitions in that period. The number actually rose from 1,100,000 active corporations in 1960 to 1,600,000 in 1970 (see Table 12-1). There was an increase of more than 40 percent. There was increasing diversity in American business during the 1960s merger wave.

TABLE 12–1

Corporation, Business Enterprise, and Entrepreneurial
Populations of the United States, 1945–75

Year	Active Corporations Returns Filed (Thousands)	Business Enterprises Number Operating (Thousands)	Entrepreneurs Individuals With Self-Employment Income (Thousands)
1945	454	NA	7,377
1950	629	7,494 [a]	8,988
1955	807	9,046 [a]	10,200
1960	1,141	11,172	10,518
1965	1,424	11,416	10,751
1970	1,665	12,001	11,178
1975	2,024	13,979	13,003

Source: STATISTICAL ABSTRACT OF THE UNITED STATES 1978 at 561.
[a] Does not include partnerships. Figure not available.

Even if we confine our view to only the corporations in manufacturing and mining with over $10 million in assets, the same results emerge. There was roughly a 40 percent increase in their number, along with 1,199 acquisitions of firms in this size class, during the decade.

The increasing number of corporations and the increasing diversity of American business are both actually encouraged by mergers rather than damped by them. When mergers and acquisitions can be consummated without much interference, there is a market-place for firms, both healthy and failing, which offers owners of firms a fair price for their equities. It is encouraging to a potential investor that, no matter what the course of his business, he can get a fair price for it at any time, instead of having to go through the costly and time consuming process of liquidating assets and paying off debts.[36] Hence a strong market in mergers and acquisitions acts as a stimulant to entrepreneurship, new investment, and business innovation. Also, because there is a good market for firms, those who are trying to establish new businesses or expand their firms find capital available and on more convenient terms than would be the case if there were not an active market for businesses.

When *potential* providers of capital know that there is an active market for firms, they are more willing to become *actual* providers. Their opportunity for gain is greater and the risk of loss is less in an economy that has an active market for businesses.[37] If a firm seeks capital to take advantage of an expanding opportunity, it will find that capital is easier to obtain in these circumstances. If it grows to a size with which its current officers have little experience, the stockholders are not stuck with a management that cannot handle this problem. The firm can be sold to some corporation that has management accustomed to such a scale of operation. That is one of the reasons that small- and middle-size companies find capital easier to obtain than if there were a less active market for companies. Because a sellout to a larger firm is possible, potential stockholders and lenders know that they will be able to bail out of an investment that turns sour because of managerial error. Also, the possibility of profiting more quickly in the early development of a product, technology, or market, once its promise is demonstrated, makes investment in innovating activities more attractive. If this route were not open and active, there would be greater reluctance to invest in such companies. These firms would find it difficult to grow, and the rate of increase in the number of corporations and in the number of middle-size firms would decline.

Conclusion

When Senator Metzenbaum claimed that the growth of conglomerate mergers was accompanied by "the disappearance of independent firms and the steady increase in control by fewer and fewer firms,"[38] he simply disregarded history. During the rise of the merger wave in the 1960s and again in the 1970s, the number of firms continually increased. "Fewer and fewer firms" was not the direction of the trend in number of non-farm businesses.

The claim that aggregate concentration is increasing as a consequence of conglomerate mergers is equally specious. The usual trend figures cited are those for the share of 200 leading corporations in a sector of the economy whose share is itself shrinking. Aggregating all nonfinancial corporations shows a very different trend in the share of leading corporations. But whatever the trend, conglomerate mergers have had such an insignificant influence on aggregate concentration that the effect is hardly detectable. All the mergers of the 1960s do not add to the equal of one IBM, and all those mergers were not with the leading 200.

And the evidence that conglomerate mergers are anti-competitive does not exist. To suppose that conglomerates might engage in predatory pricing, reciprocal dealing, or mutual forbearance is not evidence.

The argument that the number of potential entrants into an industry is reduced or the threat of potential entry removed when a large firm acquires another outside its own field with a consequent lessening of the discipline imposed by possible entry disregards the common experience that any attractive investment opportunity has always been a *magnet* for many entrepreneurs. If anything, "the buildups in potential competition implicit in the growth of the free-ranging multi-product firm would appear to have pro-competitive effects of a general scope and importance completely offscale in relation to the rather finicky case made for the anti-competitive effects of particular conglomerate mergers."[39] An anti-acquisition policy would serve only to protect slothful management of existing firms from either a takeover or from entry and competition by a newcomer who is likely to disregard any anti-competitive folkways of the trade.

Notes

1. Practically all the 200 largest manufacturing corporations of 1968 were widely diversified. Those not labeled conglomerates differed from those that were only because they had not been heavily engaged in merger or acquisition activity in the postwar period. Also, they generally had a much larger share, frequently more than 50 percent, of their business concentrated in one industry. Only sixteen of the 200 operated in fewer than six four-digit industries, and only three produced in fewer than six five-digit product classes. Nearly three quarters (146) of the 200 operated in eleven or more four-digit industries and 90 percent (181) produced in eleven or more five-digit product classes. U.S., Federal Trade Commission, Bureau of Economics, ECONOMIC REPORT ON CORPORATE MERGERS 233 (1969).

   Conglomerates are simply spectacular examples of diversification. Not only are "most large firms diversified to some extent; the degree of diversification has increased significantly from 1950 to 1968. Thus, the conglomerates are not unique, but are merely extreme examples of a trend that has occurred in manufacturing generally." Staff Report to the Federal Trade Commission, CONGLOMERATE MERGER PRFORMANCE: AN EMPIRICAL ANALYSIS OF NINE CORPORATIONS 85 (Nov. 1972).

2. John S. McGee, *Predatory Price Cutting: The Standard Oil (N.J.) Case,* 1 JOURNAL OF LAW & ECONOMICS 137 (Oct. 1958); Roland H. Kolier II, *The Myth of Predatory Pricing: An Empirical Study* in Y. Brozen, THE COMPETITIVE ECONOMY 418 (1975); W. A. Leeman, *The Limitations of Local Price-Cutting as a Barrier to Entry,* 64 JOURNAL OF POLITICAL ECONOMY 329 (Aug. 1965); Bjarke Fog, INDUSTRIAL PRICING POLICIES 147–51 (1960); M. A. Adelman, A&P: A STUDY IN PRICE-COST BEHAVIOR AND PUBLIC POLICY 14 (1959).
3. James H. Lorie and Paul Halpern, *Conglomerates: The Rhetoric and the Evidence,* 13 JOURNAL OF LAW & ECONOMICS 156 (Apr. 1970).
4. D. R. Kamerschen, *Predatory Pricing, Vertical Integration, and Market Foreclosure: The Case of Ready Mix Concrete in Memphis,* 2 INDUSTRIAL ORGANIZATION REVIEW 144, n. 12, citing K. Elzinga, *Predatory Pricing: The Case of the Gunpower Trust,* 13 JOURNAL OF LAW & ECONOMICS 240 (April 1970); D. Dewey, *Competitive Policy and National Goals: The Doubtful Relevance of Antitrust* in A. Phillips (ed.), PERSPECTIVES ON ANTITRUST POLICY 81 (1965); F. Scherer INDUSTRIAL MARKET PERFORMANCE AND ECONOMIC STRUCTURE 484, 202 (1970).
5. Donald F. Turner, *Conglomerate Mergers and Section 7 of the Clayton Act,* 78 HARVARD LAW REVIEW 1339–40, 1346 (May 1965).
6. U.S., Federal Trade Commission *supra* note 1, at 4.
7. 2 ANTITRUST LAW & ECONOMICS REVIEW 35 (Spring 1969).
8. L. E. Birdzell, *The Conglomerates: A Neighbor's View,* 44 ST. JOHN'S LAW REVIEW 306–8 (Spring 1970).
9. Joel Davidow, *Conglomerate Concentration and Section Seven: The Limitations of the Antimerger Act,* 68 COLUMBIA LAW REVIEW 1256 (Nov. 1968). Also, see Turner *supra* note 5, at 1340, 1346.
10. J. F. Weston, *The FTC Staff's Economic Report on Conglomerate Merger Performance,* 4 THE BELL JOURNAL OF ECONOMICS AND MANAGEMENT SCIENCE 685 (Autumn 1973).
11. W. J. Liebeler, Remarks at the Conference on Antitrust at the Center for Law & Economics, University of Miami, December 1, 1978.
12. "If this interpretation of *Consolidated Foods* is correct, reciprocity appears to have had a profoundly pro-competitive effect." W. J. Liebeler, *The Emperor's New Clothes: Why is Reciprocity Anticompetitive?,* 44 ST. JOHN'S LAW REVIEW 558 (Spring 1970).
13. ". . . reciprocal buying . . . might, of course, lead to greater efficiency (for example by reducing marketing costs) or it might lead to inefficiency. If this practice leads to inefficiency, there is no reason why the conglomerate should adopt it (since it would reduce its overall profits)." Ronald Coase, *Working Paper II: The Conglomerate Merger* (for the President's Task Force on Productivity and Competition), 2 ANTITRUST LAW & ECONOMICS REVIEW 45 (Spring 1969).
14. ". . . the most striking reciprocity cases go back to the 1930s and arise out of efforts to break legally regulated monopoly prices . . ." See Birdzell *supra* note 8, at 312.
15. George Stigler, *A Theory of Oligopoly,* 72 JOURNAL OF POLITICAL ECON-

omy 44 (Feb. 1964), reprinted in George Stigler, The Organization of Industry 39 (1968); John S. McGee, *Price Discrimination and Competitive Effects: The Standard Oil of Indiana Case,* 23 University of Chicago Law Review 401 (Spring 1956).

16. See Y. Brozen *supra* note 2, at 379.

17. "Nor is the reciprocity argument supported by the data. Among the functions analyzed [to determine the extent to which their administration in an acquired firm was changed after acquisition], the least number of changes was observed in purchasing—about 4 percent of the acquisitions covered." See Weston *supra* note 10, at 686.

18. Jesse Markham, Conglomerate Enterprise and Public Policy (1973). Also, Jules Backman, *Conglomerate Mergers and Competition,* 44 St. John's Law Review 99–100 (Spring 1970).

19. *Conglomerate Bigness as A Source of Power* in National Bureau of Economic Research, Business Concentration and Price Policy 335 (1955).

20. *Government Widens Trust Suit Opposing Occidental Petroleum Bid for Mead Corp.,* Wall Street Journal (Oct. 26, 1978).

21. Weston points out that the evidence on the post-acquisition fate of market positions acquired by conglomerates does not square with the competitive forbearance hypothesis. "In 98 percent of the acquisitions, a change in market position took place—either an increase or decrease. This high frequency of changes in market share positions does not support the mutual forbearance theory." *Supra* note 10, at 686.

22. Michael Gort, Diversification and Integration in American Industry (1963).

23. See U.S., Federal Trade Commission *supra* note 6 at 84.

24. See U.S., Federal Trade Commission *supra* note 6, at 28.

25. K. Paul Asquith, *Mergers and the Market for Acquisitions* (mimeographed, Industrial Organization Workshop, University of Chicago 1979). The data provided in Lorie and Halpern, *supra* note 3, also substantiate this point, although they do not discuss this inference.

26. There are exceptions of course. The recent acquisition of Reliance Electric by Exxon was, according to Exxon statements, a result of a desire to enter the electric motor industry.

27. It has been argued that the poor performance of the average stock in the average acquisition is not necessarily an indication of poor management, but may be the result of inefficiency in the capital markets in valuing the company. This undervaluation argument is used by Professor F. M. Scherer, for example, who says, "The stock market is myopic, and the information that drives it is often flimsy. As a result, some companies tend at any moment in time to be undervalued . . ." Industrial Market Structure and Economic Performance 131 (1980). But Asquith finds evidence indicating that the firms whose acquisition was attempted were not temporarily undervalued. When merger bids failed, the stockholders of the target firms suffered a loss on average of 8 percent. *Supra* note 25.

28. See Asquith *supra* note 25. Professor Asquith examined all NYSE firms, other than railroads, acquired by other NYSE firms between 1955 and 1976. Of the 286 mergers in his universe, forty-three were horizontal and twenty-two vertical. The rest were conglomerate. Since the horizontal and vertical acquisitions did not display poor performance on average, segregation of conglomerate acquisitions would have produced a much

larger percentage showing inferior performance. The loss to stockholders would be found to be greater than 14 percent in the firms acquired
in conglomerate mergers.

29. J. F. Weston and S. K. Mansinghka, *Tests of the Efficiency Performance
of Conglomerate Firms,* 26 JOURNAL OF FINANCE 919 (Sept. 1971).
30. *Prepared Statement of Michael Gort* in U.S., Congress, MERGERS AND
ECONOMIC CONCENTRATION: HEARINGS BEFORE THE SUBCOMMITTEE ON
ANTITRUST, MONOPOLY, AND BUSINESS RIGHTS OF THE COMMITTEE ON
THE JUDICIARY, UNITED STATES SENATE, Serial no. 96–2, Part I at
461–63 (1979).
31. J. Markham, CONGLOMERATE ENTERPRISE AND PUBLIC POLICY 16
(1973).
32. See Markham *supra* note 8, at 16.
33. Turner *supra* note 5 at 1326.
34. A. F. Ehrbar. *The Needless Death of Federal Glass,* 100 FORTUNE 58
(July 2, 1979).
35. U.S., Federal Trade Commission, *FTC Permits Pillsbury Acquisition of
Small Pizza Producer,* FTC NEWS SUMMARY 3 (July 6, 1979).
36. Professor Asquith, note 23, presents evidence that the loss to stockholders of acquired firms would have averaged more than the 14 percent loss
actually suffered if potential acquisition were not a prospect. Evidently,
the likelihood that a firm will be acquired maintains the value of its
stock. In those cases where a merger or tender offer was a complete
surprise, the acquired firms had suffered an average loss of 33 percent.
The prospect of acquisition minimizes losses to stockholders who must
sell before a merger offer materializes.
37. Prepared Statement of Dennis C. Mueller, U.S., Congress *supra* note
30.
38. Opening Statement of Senator Metzenbaum in U.S., Congress, *supra,*
note 30 at 8.
39. L. E. Birdzell, *supra,* note 8 at 313.

13

Conglomerate Mergers and Efficiency

I<small>N</small> 1979, when Senator Howard Metzenbaum opened the hearings on S. 600, a bill designed to stop conglomerate mergers by corporations with assets or sales exceeding $350 million, he said,

> . . . it's hard to make a convincing case that putting cigarettes, Hawaiian punch and offshore oil and gas under one corporate umbrella will have any startling effects on the efficiency with which our economy operates. There is of course some argument about capital allocation, managerial skills, and so forth. But the consensus . . . among industrial or organizational economists, is that most large conglomerate mergers, are at best neutral, with respect to efficiency, and actually may have adverse effects in many instances.[1]

Neither Metzenbaum nor any witness at these hearings provided any evidence that conglomerate mergers do not improve efficiency. Professor Dennis Mueller thought he provided such evidence by citing a survey of the research on the profitability of investing in the acquisition of companies. He testified that the survey showed that "no one who has undertaken a major empirical study of mergers has concluded that mergers are profitable, i.e., profitable in the sense of being 'more profitable' than alternative forms of investment." Mueller concluded "that mergers neither increase nor decrease economic efficiency on average."[2]

Evidence Showing Mergers Improved Efficiency

That acquiring companies, on the average, earned only normal returns on their investments in acquisitions should not be surprising. The average return on *all* investments is equal to the normal return. Any class of investments on which above average returns can be earned does not long remain in that position unless knowledge of such investments is a secret. Once such investments become known, investors bid their prices to the level where only normal returns are earned. If the market for acquisitions is competitive, then acquirers can be expected to earn only as much, on average, as they would earn in "alternative forms of investment."

Acquirers of New York Exchange listed firms in the postwar years have paid substantial premiums for their acquisitions. The premiums averaged 25 percent from 1955 through 1976 on the value prevailing before each merger or tender offer announcement.[3] Even these pre-offer values were influenced by the expectation that a bid would be forthcoming. They would have been lower but for that expectation. For the acquired firms where there was no expectation that someone would offer to buy them (the merger offer came as a complete surprise), the premiums averaged more than 50 percent.[4] In recent years, premiums have trended upward, reaching 50 percent in 1979.

The fact that premiums have been paid suggests that the acquirers expected they would employ the acquired assets more efficiently than they were previously employed. Premiums would be offered only if the buying firms expected to produce returns of greater value to their stockholders than the value to acquired firm's stockholders of the expected returns under the old managements. Since the acquirers' stockholders enjoyed returns following the mergers roughly equal to those of all NYSE firms (see Figure 12-2), the expectations were accurate. A marked improvement in the value of the returns must have occurred subsequent to the acquisition. Otherwise, the premiums paid would have produced losses in the acquiring companies. They would have suffered below normal returns with a consequent loss to their stockholders if the premiums had not been subsequently justified and their value sustained by efficiency improvements.

Professor Paul Asquith points out that findings in his study of postwar mergers show that

> [M]ergers cause a change in real activity, and this change produces a real gain for the combined firm. That is, the firms are worth more when they are combined than when they are alone. . . .
>
> Furthermore, the results suggest that the resource which is being acquired in a merger is . . . [an] inefficient[ly] manage[d] . . . target firm.[5]

Other Evidence of Conglomerate Efficiency

That conglomerates are more efficient, or at least use their labor more productively, than single-industry enterprises was demonstrated by Professor Victor Fuchs in his examination of the Company Statistics portion of the 1954 Census of Manufactures. Fuchs found that value-added per employee in conglomerates exceeded that in single-establishment companies by 28 percent. It exceeded that in multi-unit, single-industry companies by 11 percent. Also, conglomerates paid their employees 9 percent more than single-unit firms and 4 percent more than multi-unit, single-industry firms.[6] On average, conglomerates produced 22 percent more with each worker than single-industry firms and paid their workers 7 percent more in 1954 (see Table 13-1).

An analysis of the 1963 Census of Manufactures enterprise statistics shows even greater productivity and pay rates in conglomerates, relative to single-unit and multi-unit, single-industry companies, than in 1954. The amount by which value-added per employee in conglomerates exceeded value-added in single-unit firms rose from 28 percent in 1954 to 38 percent in 1963. Conglomerate value-added per employee rose from 11 percent to 15 percent more than multi-unit, single-industry firms between 1954 and 1963. Pay rates in conglomerates rose from 9 percent more than single-unit firms in 1954 to 13 percent more in 1963. Wage rates in conglomerates rose from 7 percent more than single-industry firms in 1954 to 11 percent more in 1963 (see Table 13-1).

This disequilibrium in 1963 may have been one of the more important reasons for the conglomerate merger wave of the 1960s. Why the increase in the disequilibrium occurred, we do not know. Whatever the reason, the rise in conglomeration in the 1960s

Conglomerate Mergers and Efficiency

TABLE 13–1

Comparisons of Value-Added and Wages per Employee in
Conglomerate Firms and Single-Industry Firms

Ratio of Conglomerate Firm Employee Productivity (or Wage) to Single-Industry Firm Employee Productivity (or Wage)	Number of Enterprise Industries in Each Range of Ratios of Conglomerate Firm Employee Productivity to Single-Industry Firm Employee Productivity			Number of Enterprise Industries in Each Range of Ratios of Conglomerate Firm Wage Rate to Single-Industry Firm Wage Rate		
	1954	1963	1972	1954	1963	1972
2 and over	1	4	1	—	—	—
1.90–1.99	2	3	1	—	—	—
1.80–1.89	0	2	0	—	—	—
1.70–1.79	1	3	3	—	—	—
1.60–1.69	3	2	2	—	—	—
1.50–1.59	1	5	1	—	—	1
1.40–1.49	6	6	6	1	3	2
1.30–1.39	7	13	7	0	3	5
1.20–1.29	14	14	12	8	13	8
1.10–1.19	19	31	23	22	38	28
1.00–1.09	13	16	11	27	36	32
.90– .99	7	6	14	18	14	14
.80– .89	4	2	8	2	--	1
.70– .79	—	0	2	—	—	—
Total number of industries	78	107	91	78	107	91
Median	1.15	1.19	1.13	1.07	1.10	1.09
Mean	1.22	1.30	1.17	1.07	1.11	1.10

Sources: U.S., Bureau of the Census, ENTERPRISE STATISTICS: 1963, Part 1, GENERAL REPORT ON INDUSTRIAL ORGANIZATION (1968), Table 5A; ENTERPRISE STATISTICS (1977), Table 2.

brought the economy back toward a structural equilibrium between 1963 and 1972. Value-added per employee fell from 30 percent greater in conglomerates in 1963 than in single-industry firms to 17 percent greater in 1972 (measured by arithmetic means) as a result of the reallocation of resources from single-industry to multi-industry firms (see Table 13-1). This suggests that it was the less efficient single-industry firms that conglomerates acquired. It was in these that conglomerates could bring about the improvements in output per employee. In this, the conglomerate merger wave of the 1960s may have been similar to the horizontal mergers of the 1930s and 1940s. Most of the firms acquired in those horizontal mergers had sub-optimal capacity.[7]

353

Combining their assets by merger formed firms with a larger, more economic scale of operation. These mergers achieved efficiencies without driving some less than optimum-sized firms into bankruptcy or voluntary liquidation—a more costly process for increasing productivity.

Sources of Conglomerate Efficiency

The sources of the greater productivity of employees of conglomerates have not been determined. Perhaps conglomerates are quicker to take action when performance in a division lags. Perhaps conglomerates move more rapidly to discontinue inefficient or unproductive operations than single-industry companies and to move their employees and capital into more productive uses. Perhaps they do not throw good money after bad. Perhaps their ability to raise capital at less cost than smaller or less diversified firms enables them to use more capital-intensive technology. Perhaps the internal capital markets of conglomerates in a day of shortened product life cycles work more efficiently than impersonal capital markets.[8]

The opportunity to use an internal capital market rather than going to external sources can be crucial when financing is necessary in order to make use of proprietary information. A firm seeking capital from outside the company to apply new technology developed in its research department may have to disclose some of the information on its new development in order to obtain funds less expensively. But disclosing the information may dissipate some of its value since competitors may, as a consequence, come into the market more quickly.

> The subsidiaries of a conglomerate can disclose proprietary information to corporate headquarters, and thus the corporation can allocate its capital based on a full information set. . . . This is . . . why the internal capital market of a large firm may be a more efficient allocator of capital than the external capital market.[9]

Professor Richard Nelson, in his analysis of *The Simple Economics of Basic Scientific Research,* concluded that conglomerate firms obtain a better return on their investments in research and development because they "have their fingers in many pies." Their interests in many fields enable them to produce and market a larger proportion of the unexpected inventions that occur in their research efforts, and they make more use of basic research. According to Nelson

> A broad technological base insures that, whatever direction the path of research may take, the results are likely to be of value to the sponsoring firm. . . . It is not just the size of the companies that makes it worthwhile for them to engage in basic research. Rather it is their broad technological base, the wide range of products they produce or will be willing to produce if their research efforts open possibilities. . . . Strangely enough, economists have tended to see little economic justification for giant firms not built on economies of scale. Yet it is the many-product giants, not the single-product giants, which have been most technologically dynamic. . . .[10]

Conglomerates, by increasing their size through their acquisitions, may also economize in staff functions. A study by Professor Peter Pashigian of the 284 respondents (most of whom were conglomerates) to a questionnaire on legal costs sent to the leading 500 industrial firms, found a strong inverse relationship between legal costs per million dollars of sales and size (see Table 13-2). If the average cost of other staff functions per dollar of sales drops anywhere near as rapidly as legal costs, these economies may be a factor in the willingness of conglomerates to pay substantial premiums for their acquisitions. These economies make it possible to earn a normal return on these investments despite the large premiums paid.

TABLE 13–2
Legal Costs per Million Dollars of Sales by Firm Size

Approximate Average Sales Size of Firms ($ Millions)	Average Legal Costs per $1 Million of Sales
$ 300	$2,227
750	1,527
1,000	1,085
Over 2,000	440

Source: B. Peter Pashigian, *The Legal Costs of Firms: Prevention versus Legal Defense* (presentation before the Law and Economics Workshop, University of Chicago, May 20, 1980).

Perhaps, as Harold Geneen, former president of International Telephone and Telegraph explained, a conglomerate "has numerous individual specialists and experienced managers in many fields, and . . . the very untraditional outlook such a company brings to an industry is the key to innovation and new progress."[11] When Mobil acquired Montgomery Ward, it placed its own credit management specialists in Ward's troubled credit operation. Also, it loaned real estate experts and location specialists from its filling station location group to Ward's store location group. In addition, it applied its retailing expertise and its purchasing know-how to Ward's operation. The superior management and staff of a firm may enable it to improve operations in other firms lacking such management and such staffs.[12]

Conclusion

Whether conglomerates increase the efficiency of the American economy is a question that has baffled many observers. How can putting cigarettes and Hawaiian Punch under one corporate umbrella have any startling effects on efficiency? Whether or not the answer is apparent to the naked eye is irrelevant. No doubt, there have been and will continue to be instances in which it is clear, after the fact, that a merger was a mistake. But it should be even clearer that to prevent mistakes government would have to prevent people from making decisions. If our capital, labor, material, and product markets function competitively, they will accord rewards to those that are efficient and losses to those that are not.

Some acquisitions were mistakes. Some conglomerates overreached themselves. Some large firms overexpanded in times past. But the market cured this. Would-be conglomerates that failed to manage acquired assets as competently as others could, as apparently was the case at Whittaker Corporation and Ling-Temco-Vought, were forced to disgorge some of their acquisitions and reorganize their operations to stay alive. American Brands, W. R. Grace, and other conglomerates have sold portions of their acquisitions to finance their activities and to confine their operations to what they can manage well. Professor W. G. Shepherd found that

Many mergers are divestitures rather than a combination of two free-standing companies. Such selling off of branches rose in 1975 to 54

356

percent of all acquisitions (by number), up from 11 percent in 1967 and 39 percent in 1973.[13]

What is surprising is that evidence of greater relative efficiency in conglomerates shows so strongly in the data (Table 13-1). It would not if the economy were in a long-run, static, structural equilibrium. With full adjustment to tastes, resources, and technology, wage rates and productivity would be no higher in multi-industry firms than in single-industry firms. Only to the extent that capital is less expensive to conglomerates would we see higher output per labor hour in conglomerates when the economy is at or near a secular equilibrium. In this situation, we would also see lower rates of return in the multi-industry firms.

The data showing larger than normal disparities in value-added per employee hour in different enterprises, as in 1963, indicate a disequilibrium, which could be expected to produce the structural rearrangements of the sort seen in the latter 1960s. A disequilibrium means that resources are not being allocated to their most productive uses. Conglomerates, by moving employees and capital from less productive to more productive applications (perhaps by simply improving the management of those resources in their current use), contributed to growth and improvements in the level of living.

On average, acquirers improved asset management, provided stockholders of poorly managed firms with an improvement in the value of their holdings, reallocated capital and labor from less productive to more productive uses, and improved the economic health of the country. They brought us closer to a long-run, efficient equilibrium in the allocation of resources, despite the continuing movement of the equilibrium position. And democratic political processes did not suffer except to the extent that a new minority—those who happen to own the stocks of large corporations or of potential acquisitions—was made the focus of primitive and uncomprehending jealousies that some politicians attempted to exploit.

Notes

1. U.S., Congress, Mergers and Economic Concentration: Hearings Before the Subcommittee on Antitrust, Monopoly, and Business

RIGHTS OF THE COMMITTEE ON THE JUDICIARY, UNITED STATES SEN-
ATE, Serial no. 96-2, Part 1 at 8–9 (1979).

2. *Prepared Statement of Professor Dennis C. Mueller* in U.S., Congress, *supra* note 1, at 304.

3. Paul Asquith, A TWO-EVENT STUDY OF MERGER BIDS, MARKET UNCER-
TAINTY, AND STOCKHOLDER RETURNS (dissertation, University of Chicago, 1980), Tables 6 and 12, at 26 and 35.

4. See *id.*, Table 27 at 52. For all takeovers in the United Kingdom from
1957 to 1969 the average premium was 64.9 percent. D. A. Kuehn,
TAKEOVERS AND THE THEORY OF THE FIRM (1975).

5. See Asquith *supra* note 3, at 2–3.

6. Victor R. Fuchs, *Integration, Concentration, and Profits in Manufacturing Industries,* QUARTERLY JOURNAL OF ECONOMICS 281 (May
1961). According to data provided in Thorp and Crowder, THE STRUC-
TURE OF INDUSTRY 161, 211 (1941), multi-industry firms paid annual
wages 23.8 percent higher than single-industry firms in 1937.

7. L. Weiss, *An Evaluation of Mergers in Six Industries,* 47 REVIEW OF
ECONOMICS AND STATISTICS 172 (May 1965).

8. For a discussion of managerial techniques in financial, managerial, and
concentric conglomerates, see J. Fred Weston, INDUSTRIAL CONCENTRA-
TION, MERGERS, AND GROWTH II-9-14 (presented before U.S. Department of Commerce Workshop on Mergers and Economic Efficiency,
1980).

9. Jay R. Ritter, *Innovation and Communication: Signaling With Partial
Disclosure* (presentation before the Workshop in Applied Price Theory,
University of Chicago, March 4, 1980).

10. R. R. Nelson, *The Simple Economics of Basic Research,* 67 JOURNAL OF
POLITICAL ECONOMY 302–3 Jun. 1959).

11. Harold S. Geneen, *Conglomerates: A Businessman's View,* 44 ST. JOHN'S
LAW REVIEW 723 (Spring 1970).

12. Although companies needing management assistance may call on con-
sultants, anyone providing consulting services can relate many stories of
how often advice suggesting obviously productive possible improvements is disregarded. The ability to enforce the adoption of advice is
necessary as well as the advice itself.

13. W. G. Shepherd, THE ECONOMICS OF INDUSTRIAL ORGANIZATION 163
(1979).

14

Policies Toward Concentration:
An International Comparison

THE loose and cavalier use of the term "economic concentration" in criticisms of Western industrial structure confuses two issues and two sets of arguments. In one meaning, "economic concentration" refers to the fraction of a product's output, say automobile tires, supplied by the leading producers in an industry. Although market concentration is often considered to be an index of monopoly power, its usefulness as such, as we have seen, is in doubt.[1] In its other sense, "economic concentration" refers to aggregate concentration: the share of a country's economic production that its largest firms turn out.

Since dominant firms in small industries are small while giant corporations in a very large industry may have only a small share of the industry,[2] aggregate and market concentration are not necessarily related. And while economic theory and research give a modicum of support to the uneasiness some people feel when they discover that x percent of the widgets made in the United States are produced by one firm, there is no support for those who are concerned about aggregate concentration except prattle about industrial infrastructures and countervailing powers. It comes as no surprise, then, to discover that economic policy in industrialized countries occasionally has concerned itself with market concentration and the problems said to stem from it, but never with aggregate concentration.[3]

The chief difference between public policy toward market and aggregate concentration in foreign countries and that in the United States is the lively sense displayed abroad of the economic gains that size confers. Europe's post–World-War-II economic policies, for example, deliberately aim at producing an economic structure comparable to the one the United States acquired by accident and the operation of market forces. In particular, the European Economic Community (EEC) was intended to provide a market large enough to support firms as big as those in the United States. "The EEC's industrial policy is to encourage size," writes *The Economist,* Britain's prestigious weekly.[4] The policies followed in individual countries are consistent with this approach. Particularly in France,[5] but to varying degrees in other countries as well, mergers are encouraged or tolerated as a way of setting the units of the national economy on a level equal to that of competitor nations. The active concern of policy makers in Europe is not the prevalence of industrial concentration but rather the handicap of inefficient, undersized industrial units.

In cases where firms are not merged, official policy often encourages agreements that allow several firms to collaborate. Research by a number of companies in such sophisticated technology as aviation or nuclear energy is often orchestrated by government. In Japan, and to a lesser extent in France and Italy, the organization of production is influenced by government through informal channels. Whether correct or not, they believe that concerted action is often necessary, especially in an economic downturn. The bias in favor of cartel arrangements is partly attributable to the inferences that were drawn from the economic troubles of the 1930s. "Rationalization" of production was seen as the proper antidote to the run-amok competition widely believed to have brought on the Great Depression.[6] It also reflects the belief that certain forms of collective action among firms, such as establishing uniform standards for parts or combining marketing activities, have a productive function.

The concentration policies of America's competitor nations appear to allow, and often promote, the growth of their firms to the size of the larger U.S. firms. European and Japanese firms are now approaching, and in some cases have surpassed, their American rivals in size and in their capacity for innovation. In industry after industry, the fraction of world output attributable to American producers has declined.

Table 14-1 shows the world's leading fifty industrial firms ranked by sales in 1980 along with their 1967 ratings. Note that foreign firms are moving into the top fifty spots. In 1967, twelve of the fifty were foreign; today twenty-seven are. Foreign firms in the top fifty more than doubled in number in the past decade. The increased representation of European and Japanese chemical, electrical, and automobile firms is particularly noteworthy. Matsushita rose in world rank from eighty-first to forty-fifth and Hoechst from fifty-third to twenty-ninth. In contrast Western Electric, operating under the restraints of an antitrust decree that forbids its competing for certain classes of customers, dropped from thirteenth to forty-ninth and du Pont from fifteenth to thirty-eighth.

In diverse industries, U.S. firms are losing ground to their foreign competitors. In banking, for example, six of the eight leading banks of the world were, in 1960, U.S. firms. Now only two of the eight leading banks are domiciled in the United States. In metal manufacturing, seven of the eight leading firms were based in the United States in 1960. Now only three are. While some of this change is due to economic factors that are independent of national concentration policies, it should be noted that new firms created through mergers have taken some of the top positions (Nippon Steel, Peugeot-Citroen, and Elf Aquitaine). Similar mergers in the United States are prohibited.

The growth of many foreign firms came from their deliberate copying of U.S. organizational features and from the ability of the EEC to foster a home market similar in size to that of the United States. Public policy in this country, on the other hand, is hostile to increases in firm size. While foreign policy makers consider American industrial structure worth copying, the Federal Trade Commission and others in government prefer to see it altered. Yet rising standards of living and productivity in Europe and Japan suggest that the foreign appreciation of size may be more advantageous than the American aversion to it.

The somewhat more favorable attitude abroad toward mergers and increases in firm size augments the factors that work to the benefit of many overseas firms. This does not, to be sure, provide a justification for adopting wholesale the industrial policies of overseas competitor nations. Many factors besides government policies govern the changes in the size and commercial success of firms. It should also be cautioned that the policies that promote

361

TABLE 14–1

The World's Leading Industrial Firms
(Ranked by 1980 Sales)

Company	Rank 1967	Rank 1980	Sales ($ Billions) 1980	Net Income ($ Millions) 1980
Exxon (USA)	2	1	103.1	5,650
Royal Dutch/Shell Group (Netherlands/UK)	4	2	77.1	5,174
Mobil (USA)	7	3	59.5	3,272
General Motors (USA)	1	4	57.7	(762)
Texaco (USA)	10	5	51.2	2,643
British Petroleum (UK)	17	6	48.0	3,337
Standard Oil of California (USA)	14	7	40.5	2,401
Ford Motor (USA)	3	8	37.1	(1,543)
ENI (Italy)	80	9	27.2	98
Gulf Oil (USA)	11	10	26.5	1,407
International Business Machines (USA)	9	11	26.2	3,562
Standard Oil (Ind.) (USA)	19	12	26.1	1,915
Fiat (Italy)	45	13	25.2	NA
General Electric (USA)	5	14	25.0	1,514
Française des Petroles (France)	75	15	23.9	947
Atlantic Richfield (USA)	82	16	23.7	1,651
Unilever (Netherlands/UK)	8	17	23.6	659
Shell Oil (USA)	16	18	19.8	1,542
Renault (France)	60	19	19.0	160
Petróleos de Venezuela (Venezuela)	—	20	18.8	3,451
International Telephone & Tel. (USA)	23	21	18.5	894
Elf Aquitaine (France)	133	22	18.4	1,378
Phillips' Gloeilampenfabrieken (Netherlands)	33	23	18.4	165
Volkswagenwerk (Germany)	36	24	18.3	171
Conoco (USA)	42	25	18.3	1,026

362

Siemens (Germany)	43	18.0	26	332
Daimler-Benz (Germany)	61	17.1	27	605
Peugeot (France)	141	16.8	28	(348)
Hoechst (Germany)	53	16.5	29	252
Bayer (Germany)	65	15.9	30	356
BASF (Germany)	88	15.3	31	198
Thyssen (Germany)	54	15.2	32	62
Petrobras (Brazil)	284	14.8	33	767
PEMEX (Mexico)	173	14.8	34	17
Nestle (Switzerland)	48	14.6	35	409
Toyota Motor (Japan)	90	14.2	36	616
Nissan Motor (Japan)	85	13.9	37	462
E. I. du Pont de Nemours (USA)	15	13.7	38	716
Phillips Petroleum (USA)	44	13.4	39	1,070
Imperial Chemical Industries (UK)	24	13.3	40	(46)
Tenneco (USA)	49	13.2	41	726
Nippon Steel (Japan)	71	13.1	42	496
Sun (USA)	97	12.9	43	723
Hitachi (Japan)	50	12.9	44	503
Matsushita Electric Industrial (Japan)	81	12.7	45	542
U.S. Steel (USA)	12	12.5	46	505
Occidental Petroleum (USA)	162	12.5	47	711
United Technologies	39	12.3	48	393
Western Electric (USA)	13	12.0	49	693
Standard Oil (Ohio) (USA)	231	11.0	50	1,811

Sources: FORTUNE 204 (Aug. 10, 1981); J. H. Dunning and R. B. Pearce, PROFITABILITY AND PERFORMANCE OF THE WORLD'S LARGEST INDUSTRIAL COMPANIES (1975) at 144–47.

363

size abroad often do so at the expense of efficiency and by converting what ought to be economic decisions into political ones. Subsidization and nationalization of firms have had unhappy consequences. The current difficulties of the British Steel Corporation are illustrative. It can be argued, however, that a good deal of the more productive aspects of European policy are aimed at remedying the economic fragmentation of Europe. This appears to be sound policy, just as it would be sound policy for the United States to remove internal restrictions (such as those on branch banking at the state level and across state lines) and pursue an essentially neutral policy toward both aggregate and market concentration.

U.S. Policy

Although legal scholars are divided on the issue of whether such an interpretation is correct, the Supreme Court held in several instances that certain structural features together with the "intent" to obtain a monopoly constitute a violation of U.S. antitrust laws. The attempt to "monopolize" was declared illegal in the Sherman Act of 1890, the aim apparently being to outlaw the nineteenth-century cartels; such at least was the interpretation initially upheld by the courts.[7] The Court in 1895 allowed the mergers to stand that created the American Sugar Refining Company with 95 percent of its industry's capacity, but then reversed itself in the Northern Securities case. Merger to monopoly could no longer occur, but increases in concentration were still allowed. Subsequently, however, amendments to the Sherman Act, the Federal Trade Commission Act of 1914, and further interpretations by the Supreme Court made market structure an issue.[8]

Section 7 of the Clayton Act prohibited stock acquisitions whose effect "may be substantially to lessen competition, or to tend to create a monopoly." This had little effect in stemming horizontal mergers that did not create a dominant firm. The 1950 Celler-Kefauver amendment, however, expanded Section 7 to cover mergers by purchase of assets. This brought horizontal mergers of more than a de minimus effect to a halt, but did not outlaw existing large market shares.

The Supreme Court's interpretation of Celler-Kefauver, at least up to the time of its *General Dynamics* decision, has been that no compelling evidence is required. To be outlawed, a merger *may* only *potentially* lessen competition. In practice, the courts relied on market shares of the merged firms and trends in market concentration in evaluating whether a merger might tend to lessen competition. They did this, in part, because the economic aspects of such cases are difficult to evaluate. Vertical as well as horizontal mergers are covered, although on what grounds vertical mergers are included is not clear (despite the enunciation of a "foreclosure" doctrine).[9]

An example of what has come to be taken as the Supreme Court's general view on structure is provided by Judge Learned Hand's opinion in the *Alcoa* case.

> It is no excuse for "monopolizing" a market that the monopoly has not been used to extract from the consumer more than a "fair" profit. The Act has wider purposes. Indeed, even though we disregard all but economic considerations, it would by no means follow that such concentration of producing power is to be desired, when it has not been used extortionately.[10]

This case is generally regarded as holding a firm liable for conduct otherwise lawful, but which the defendant knew would maintain its position as the sole domestic producer of virgin aluminum. As the court itself noted, the offense was anticipating market developments. "We can think of no more effective exclusion than progressively to embrace each new opportunity as it opened."[11] The argument advanced in *Alcoa* and in *United Shoe Machinery*[12] is that, although a firm's relative size is not an issue in itself, it becomes an issue when accompanied by behavior that in the courts' view is designed to preserve a large market share. In the *United Shoe Machinery* case, for example, the primary behavioral offense was that the firm leased rather than sold its equipment and provided maintenance services to keep its machines operable. This was interpreted as the means used to keep a large share of the market. Ten-year leases with rentals dependent on usage were regarded as offensive to antitrust laws when used by a firm with a large market share while perpetual leases with all rentals paid in advance, which is what a sale is, would not have been.

Just how effective the legal doctrine in this area has been in altering industrial structure is difficult to ascertain.[13] It is not enough merely to point to cases where antitrust violations were found. The courts can misinterpret evidence concerning firm behavior, especially when suspicion is aroused by large market shares. Large firms may, as a result, be under considerable anti-trust pressure even if their practices are innocent. Firms may have refrained from aggressively expanding for fear of coming under antitrust attack.[14] For the law to have a chilling effect it need only be applied sporadically.

While the courts do not, in their own view, consider competition itself an offense, the Justice Department and the courts display considerable ingenuity in their interpretation of what constitutes a culpable business practice. Richard Posner points out, for example, that Alcoa was treated more harshly for charging low prices for virgin aluminum (of which it was the sole domestic producer until World War II) than U.S. Steel was for charging high prices for steel (of which it had only a 50 percent share).[15] Faced with a difficult analytic question, the Court may very well have fallen back on market shares in these cases. The *Alcoa* decision put firms on notice, in effect, that sound and fair business practices were unlawful if they lead to or preserve a large market share. The FTC complaint in the titanium dioxide case is the latest in a long series of warnings against acquiring a large market share. Deliberate mismanagement or charging a higher than competitive price are, then, the only sure ways of avoiding antitrust action.[16]

The merger prohibition of the Celler-Kefauver amendment to Section 7 of the Clayton Act is generally considered to have had the intended effect on mergers. It need not, however, have a last-ing effect on industrial structure. The curious aspect of this issue is that if technological or market changes dictate an increase in firm size, a less efficient alternative route (than merger) must often be taken by the industry to achieve its least-cost structure. If, for purposes of argument, we take the output of an industry to be fixed over time, then more efficient, large-scale production will have to be reached by running some firms into the ground. Posner makes this point in his comment on *Brown Shoe:*

> If an integrated firm like Brown has lower costs than nonintegrated retailers, it will expand its share of the retail shoe market whether or not it acquires Kinney. The principal effect of a very strict rule against horizontal mergers is not to retard economic progress; it is to reduce the sale value of small firms.[17]

The brewing industry provides a vivid example of Posner's point. The industry's increasing concentration is a result of internal expansion rather than acquisition.[18] The internal growth route has been used as "a result of very strict antitrust enforcement by the Justice Department."[19] The Department blocked acquisitions by Anheuser, forcing it to divest itself of its 1958 purchase of Blatz. Justice compelled Schlitz to rid itself of its 1961 Burgermeister acquisition and its 39 percent stock interest in Labatt. It also prevented smaller brewers such as Lucky Lager and Heileman from retaining companies they had acquired and prevented Pittsburgh Brewing from completing a tender offer for Duquesne Brewing. The net result was that the efficient leading firms built large new breweries, excess capacity mounted, reaching 40 percent of total capacity, and small firms exited. Despite the closing of many breweries, capacity still exceeded sales by 23 percent in 1976. The Federal Trade Commission's Bureau of Economics staff concluded that the industry would be *less* concentrated if mergers had not been foreclosed by the Justice Department's enforcement of the Celler-Kefauver Section 7 amendment.[20]

European Community Policy

European concentration policy is carried out at two levels of jurisdiction. In each country the national laws apply, although European antitrust usually consists only of restrictions on abusive practices and merger registration requirements. In some states, notably Britain and West Germany, mergers can be prohibited, but less severe standards than in the United States are used and considerable discretion is allowed to the authorities to promote scale economies. Among EEC members, commercial activity with effects across national boundaries is also subject to the provisions of the Treaty of Rome as well as the earlier European Coal and Steel Community (ECSC) treaty. The latter's somewhat more stringent provisions with regard to mergers applies, of course, only to the coal and steel industries.

Although the ECSC and the EEC can be viewed in part as an attempt to achieve certain political ends, the economic arguments used to muster support for them were the most immediate and clear-cut. Among the architects of the two agreements, and among contemporary commentators as well, there was explicit recognition that the aim was to create a free trade zone allowing firms to operate on an "American scale." The belief was that countries party to such agreements could share in the benefits of large firm size and lowered tariff barriers.

Community Coal and Steel Policy

Article 66 of the ECSC Treaty of Paris addresses the issue of industrial concentration in two ways. First, it requires that mergers subject to its regulations be approved by the ECSC High Authority (now incorporated into the EEC Commission). A merger must be allowed if it is found that it will not give a firm power over output or input markets. As such it provides for a different allocation of the burden of proof than U.S. anti-merger law. In practice, however, coal and steel mergers have been quite frequent. Second, the High Authority is empowered to direct "dominant firms" to alter their prices and output if anti-competitive behavior is found. No power is given, however, to split up enterprises that achieve a large market share by natural growth, regardless of market behavior. ECSC directs its policy at conduct and extensive regulation encompasses price discrimination, joint buying and selling, and "abuse" of dominant position.

The concentration of European steel has proceeded in a relatively unhindered fashion. The view of the High Authority has been that with new technological developments and stiff competition from outside the EEC, European steel firms should be allowed to increase in size. The favorable attitude in this area contrasts with U.S. policy, which prevented the Bethlehem-Youngstown merger in the 1950s. A similar merger, that between Phoenix-Rheinrohr and August Thyssen Hütte, was permitted in 1963. By 1977, the sales of Thyssen passed those of Bethlehem. Thyssen now ranks among the world's leading fifty industrials while Bethlehem does not even appear on the list.

European governments are so convinced of the gains that a concentrated steel industry can bring that they have undertaken efforts to increase firm size themselves. British Steel Corporation, an amalgam produced by the nationalization effort of the 1960s, ranked among the world's top three producers when it was formed. It is not a startling commercial success, however, and its size is now being trimmed.

A subtler approach has been used in France, where the two largest steel firms, Usinor and Sacilor, plus a third firm are now government owned, although not, according to the government, "nationalized." The aim of the government, whose policies will be carried out by the executives it appoints, is to "return the industry to health through mergers and groupings, the closing of obsolete plants and improved productivity."[21] The French steel industry was in sad shape—largely, some contend, as a result of government controls—and the aim of the program is to trim the industry to a profitable size. The French President called the action "part of the government's effort to adapt the country's industrial potential to the demands of international competition."[22]

The effectiveness of the Community's coal and steel policy, including its merger policy, can to some extent be gauged by the change in market shares of EEC producers relative to that of other producers. The figures in Table 14-2 show that over the period

TABLE 14–2
Shares of World Iron
and Steel Sales, 1962, 1972, and 1979

Nation or Region	Sales of Largest 46 Steel Firms in 1962	Sales of Largest 38 Steel Firms in 1972	Crude Steel Production of Largest 49 Steel Firms in 1979[a]
	Percentage		
United States	48.6	36.2	27.0 (9)
Europe (EEC)	38.6 (29.2)	37.5 (28.3)	34.4 (22) (30.7) (18)
Japan	7.8	18.3	24.0 (6)
Other	5.1	8.0	14.6 (12)
Total	100	100	100

Sources: John H. Dunning and R. B. Pearce, PROFITABILITY AND PERFORMANCE OF THE WORLD'S LARGEST INDUSTRIAL COMPANIES (1975) at 42; American Metal Market, METAL STATISTICS (1980) at 191.

[a] Number of firms shown in parentheses. The smallest firm produced 1.2 million metric tons. Although the Ford Motor Company is the ninth largest producer of steel in the United States, it is not included in any year in the computation.

1962–79 the percentage share increases of Japanese and "other" producers (chiefly Canada, India, and Australia) came mainly at the expense of the U.S. market share. In view of the many aspects of ECSC competition policy that appear to work against the expansion of trade by the firms under its jurisdiction, the absence of severe restraints on the natural tendencies toward consolidation seem to have been beneficial. Yet, given the parlous state of the steel industry in Europe, it can hardly be said that the ECSC policy has been a great success.

The Treaty of Rome

The Common Market's antitrust provisions are set out in Articles 85 and 86 of the Treaty of Rome. Article 85 prohibits certain practices such as price-fixing, market-sharing, and agreements to limit production.[23] Exceptions are allowed if such practices help "to improve the production or distribution of goods or to promote technical or economic progress." Article 86 prohibits the abuse of a "dominant position" in particular through such practices as those cited in Article 85. A comparison of these statutes with the U.S. court opinions in *Alcoa* and *United Shoe Machinery* leads most observers to stress that EEC law follows an abuse standard while U.S. law follows a market structure standard. While the U.S. approach prohibits mergers between corporations and has in several instances found "monopolization" if a large market share was merely obtained "deliberately," though not otherwise in violation of the law, EEC policy encourages mergers and condemns only certain practices of firms in monopoly industries.

One seemingly contradictory case deserves mention. The American firm Continental Can sought to acquire a Dutch container producer when it already owned the firm that supplied most of the German market. Continental won the case, but the European Court held that the EEC can in fact stop mergers with Article 86 under the "abuse" proviso. Yet the general opinion seems to be that this is a strained interpretation of the Article. If it were intended as an anti-merger regulation, critics say, the framers would have said so. Subsequent mergers have not been challenged under these or other EEC regulations. Moreover, the interpretation of the court was that a firm must already have a "dominant position" in the market before the mergers it undertakes can be considered an "abuse."

The EEC policy bias in favor of size is especially evident in the case of transnational mergers such as those which formed Agfa-Gevaert and Dunlop-Pirelli. These are viewed as promoting industrial development and as supporting the main mission of the EEC, namely the establishment of a large integrated European market.[24]

National Policies

Canada

The Combines Investigation Act preceded the American's Sherman Act by one year. It is directed chiefly against practices, such as price discrimination and resale price maintenance, held to operate against the public interest. Although mergers are subject to a public interest criterion, the prohibition is narrowly defined by the courts.[25] Reliance is on a conduct rather than a structural approach.

Recently the government set itself the task of reviewing and updating Canada's antitrust laws. They had come under attack as being too lax and detrimental to the nation's welfare. Attempts had been made, for example, to introduce concentration ratios into amendments of the Combine Investigation Act. As a result of interest in such measures, the Prime Minister appointed a Royal Commission on Corporate Concentration. The Commission's 1978 report, to the disappointment of some, renounced deconcentration of Canadian industry as a productive policy alternative.

> Firms in most industries in Canada are still too small to compete internationally. Canada's problem is not in decreasing the size of existing firms, but in ensuring that the large firms necessary to compete efficiently actually realize economies of scale and that they pass lower costs on to the consumer.[26]

The Commission also pointed out, as have U.S. critics of deconcentration policies, that enormous legal and organizational problems would accompany any sizeable deconcentration effort.

Federal Republic of Germany

The basis for antitrust law in Germany is the 1957 Act against Restraints of Competition, which addresses certain practices and agreements among firms. The Act also stipulates that mergers involving firms above a threshold size must be reported. The Act's 1973 amendment provides for the prohibition of mergers deemed anti-competitive. Although the Federal Cartel Office decides in the

371

first instance if a merger would be anti-competitive, the Federal Minister of Economic Affairs may override the Cartel Office's decision. A large market share is not prohibited. Concern centers on the *abuse* of a market-dominating position.[27]

The history of antitrust activity in West Germany is interesting for the light it sheds on the economic forces at work, and how direct the connection between economics and politics can be when a country has a sizeable foreign trade. Following World War II, the leading industrial concerns were dissolved. The large chemical firm I. G. Farben, for example, was broken up into BASF, Hoechst, and Bayer. They have since grown to be the three largest chemical corporations in the world—suggesting that technical conditions determine firm size. The large banks were also broken up, but they later regrouped. And although the steel industry was deconcentrated, the Thyssen group as well as the number two and three German steel firms have expanded to a size that would look ominous to those who advocated deconcentration in the first place. The size of German firms is in fact a notable aspect of European industrial life. In 1976, fifteen of continental Europe's largest thirty firms were German. Yet the German approach is considered, among European approaches, as the one most based on advocacy of a competitive market order. The debate leading to the competition law of 1957 is said to have strongly influenced Articles 85 and 86 of the Rome Treaty. In fact, it is the neoliberal economic school of Röpke and Erhard that is generally credited with providing the intellectual argument in favor of a market economy, as the basis for the EEC as well as for German industrial policy. It might seem paradoxical then that the reconcentration of German industry took place under the auspices of this neoliberal school. Yet the tolerance and even encouragement offered concentration (especially in the case of transnational mergers) is not inconsistent with an emphasis on competition if both competition and concentration are viewed as promoting the efficient use of scarce resources and if the level of concentration is not an appropriate index for the measurement of the degree of monopoly.[28]

France

French policy makers in particular hold the view that their firms are too small. Various governmental agencies such as the Ministère du Développement Industriel et Scientifique, the Commissariat au Plan, and the Ministries of Finance and Industry exercise control over industrial policy. The primary antitrust legislation takes the form of various restrictions on pricing practices. Official policy, far from taking a critical view of mergers, actively promotes concentration. The aim of the government is to promote industrialization and to create French firms as large and as competitive as those of other EEC members and those of the United States. Mergers are encouraged through tax policies and by means of a Bureau des Fusions set up in 1967. Policies also exist to encourage cooperation in specific phases of production and for certain projects.

In major industries particularly, active government involvement is brought to bear in favor of concentration. In the 1960s, the state made an agreement with the French steel industry in which easy credit was advanced in return for the formation of two major steel groupings. In the automobile industry, when Peugeot-Citroën bought Chrysler's European holdings, it became Europe's largest automobile manufacturer and number three in the world after General Motors and Ford.

French policy aims in the automobile industry also include bringing together the manufacturers of automobile parts to form an internationally competitive entity like Germany's Bosch. To this end, the French government prohibited the sale in 1978 of Ducellier to the British Lucas Industries.[29]

Italy

The state in Italy plays a large economic role through the Instituto per la Ricostruzione Industriale (IRI), a state holding company. IRI's sales, exclusive of its banking operations, were $15.7 billion in 1977, making it Europe's fourth largest firm. It has reorganized the Italian steel, aircraft, construction, and food industries, among others. Its subsidiaries include shipbuilding operations, RAI-TV, Alitalia, and Alfa Romeo.

Italian law places only the mildest restrictions on commercial agreements. There is no legal concern with concentration or mergers—only EEC rules apply in this area.

Japan

Following World War II, the Allied Command undertook the deconcentration of Japanese industry.[30] The large corporations

373

were widely believed to have contributed to Japanese political developments and to be fundamentally incompatible with Western-style democracy. Economic realism on the part of the Japanese and the Americans, however, spurred by international political events, led to a modification of the policy, which allowed Mitsui, Mitsubishi, and Sumitomo, the three major prewar conglomerates, to reform. Similarly, the components of Nippon Steel were first joined in informal cartels, then merged in 1968 once the law in this area was sufficiently eroded (and the resistance to the merger by the directors of the two major component companies ended).

Although fragments of the 1947 antitrust law remain on the books, major antitrust action is rare. The Japanese Fair Trade Commission (FTC) works at cross purposes with other government agencies, in particular the powerful Ministry of International Trade and Industry (MITI).

Although a clear delineation of the various influences at work is made difficult by the inexplicit nature of MITI's role, it is generally agreed that MITI and the large corporations engage in consensus management of large parts of Japanese economic life (from which the "Japan, Inc." image springs). "Predictions" and "advice" of government officials are interpreted as goals by industry. (The consultive nature of policy has its parallel in the way individual firms solicit opinions from employees in arriving at decisions.) "The fascinating problem of the study of modern Japanese government," one authority notes, "is the fact that the formal and overt aspects of its institutions *are* misleading as guides to how society actually works."[31]

In the matter of market concentration, Japanese law makes it illegal to seek a monopoly but not to possess one. That is, the emphasis is on conduct, which, as in some U.S. Supreme Court interpretations, is not necessarily unlawful unless it leads to a large market share. In practice, however, few cases involving "monopolization" are taken up by the FTC. Emphasis is placed on prosecuting specific practices rather than intent. Mergers can be prohibited if the effect would be to reduce competition substantially. However, in the only merger case brought before the Fair Trade Commission (involving two of Japan's largest steel firms), approval to merge was granted.[32] Other restrictions (the prohibition of holding companies, for example) also exist and reflect in large part the attempt to prevent the formation of a prewar conglomerate industrial structure. While cartels are prohibited, the law in this area is riddled with exceptions. Rationalization and depression cartels, for example, can be formed.[33]

MITI policy is to promote firm size while remaining indifferent to the effects of this policy on market structure. The belief is that economies of scale are important and that to brace the Japanese economy against foreign competition firms must be as large as those in the United States. MITI gets its way through its ability to influence where easy credit goes, and its role as intermediary and protector in cartel arrangements. Until the mid-1960s, MITI had authority over foreign exchange allocations and used this authority as well to bring firms into line. In the bureaucratic skirmishes between MITI and the Fair Trade Commission, MITI is the consistent winner.

United Kingdom

Until 1948, Britain relied on the common law to control anticompetitive business practices. The Monopolies and Restrictive Practices Act passed that year permitted the government to take remedial actions when the practices of large firms were held to operate against the public interest. The Monopolies and Mergers Commission, as it is now called, has instances of possible monopoly practices referred to it and issues an assessment of the situation. This assessment may, however, be ignored by the Secretary of State for Prices and Consumer Protection. Very often the decision is made to negotiate with firms although the Secretary of State can proceed by statutory order. In contrast with United States policy, remedies do not include dissolution.

Since 1965, mergers are subject to a public interest test. Mergers that would result in a greater than 25 percent share of the market may be investigated. Recommendations made by the Mergers Panel are also only advisory, and take into account a number of factors. Regional policy, efficiency criteria, and balance of payments effects are considered in addition to the effect on market concentration. Between 1965 and 1974 the Mergers Panel issued twelve reports on horizontal mergers; in six the finding was unfavorable and the merger was abandoned.[34]

The British approach leaves considerable power of discretion with the authorities, and swings in their sentiments have been claimed. The general policy on industrial structure is favorable to the growth of firm size. Until 1971, the Industrial Reorganization Corporation actively promoted mergers in the name of efficiency and international competitiveness. Especially since the United Kingdom joined the Common Market, the feeling is that British firms, to be competitive, should be larger.[35]

Policy and Concentration

An industry-by-industry analysis reveals that U.S. firms have lost ground to foreign firms. Dunning and Pearce concluded in their study of the world's industrial giants that

> (i) Concentration among the largest 500 or so industrial companies appears to have diminished over the decade 1962–72, both overall and for most individual industries. An important contribution to this appears to be a decline in U.S. firms' dominance due to increased competition from the faster growing firms of other countries, e.g., Japan and Germany.

> (ii) At the same time concentration has diminished within the U.S. sample itself, indeed more notably than within the non-U.S. sample.

> (iii) At the top of each industry there has been considerable shuffling of firms, with, in particular, Japanese and European enterprises moving into this bracket supplanting U.S. enterprises.[36]

A few examples serve to illustrate this trend. Table 14-3 shows the percentage increase in sales from 1962 to 1972 and from 1972 to 1978 for the top firms in several important industries. In steel, the rate of growth, from 1962 to 1972, for the two large American firms is less than one third that of the German firm, and one sixth that of the Japanese. By the 1970s, moreover, Nippon Steel replaced U.S. Steel as number one in terms of steel tonnage. U.S. Steel's growth is in other industries such as chemicals.

A similar pattern exists in chemicals and pharmaceuticals. Again U.S. firms are distinguished by their slower growth rates. Hoechst with annual sales in 1978 of $12.1 billion, Bayer with $11.4 billion, and BASF with $10.7 billion have displaced du Pont with $10.6 billion from number one to number four. Among the top five paper products companies, the U.S. firms Crown Zeller-

376

TABLE 14–3

1962 Sales Rank and Percentage Increase in Sales, 1962–78

Leading Companies in Selected Industries	World Sales Rank 1962[a]	Percentage Increase in Sales	
		1962–72	1972–78
Aircraft, aerospace and components			
United Technologies (USA)	49, 392	74	209
Rockwell International (USA)	{ 30, 293, 439, 401	45	147
Boeing (USA)	27	34	130
McDonnell Douglas (USA)	216, 94	139	52
Lockheed (USA)	28	41	41
Chemicals and pharmaceuticals			
Hoechst (Germany)	76	371	196
Bayer (Germany)	62	230	244
BASF (Germany)	97	421	189
E. I. du Pont (USA)	14	79	143
ICI (UK)	32	161	105
Motor vehicles			
General Motors (USA)	1	108	108
Ford Motor (USA)	3	150	112
Chrysler (USA)	15	310	67
Volkswagenwerk (Germany)	34	214	165
Toyota Motor (Japan)	177	803	205
Rubber products			
Goodyear Tire and Rubber (USA)	35	156	84
Dunlop-Pirelli (UK/Italy)	92, 124	106	84
Firestone (USA)	39	111	81
Michelin (France)	196	285	182
B. F. Goodrich (USA)	82	86	72
Electronics and appliances			
General Electric (USA)	5	114	92
Philips (Netherlands)	36, 408	306	144
Siemens (Germany)	37	249	194
Matsushita (Japan)	115	470	192
Western Electric (USA)	11	137	45
Tobacco			
B.A.T. Industries (UK)	72	191	202
Philip Morris (USA)	234	290	253
R. J. Reynolds (USA)	71	130	139
Imperial Tobacco Group (UK)	212	445	90
American Brands (USA)	110, 412	165	90

TABLE 14–3 (Cont.)
1962 Sales Rank and Percentage Increase in Sales, 1962–78

Leading Companies in Selected Industries	World Sales Rank 1962[a]	Perceage Increase in Sales	
		1962–72	1972–78
Iron and Steel			
U.S. Steel (USA)	8	56	105
Nippon Steel (Japan)	103, 171	360	78
August Thyssen-Hutte (Germany)	59	197	200
Bethlehem Steel (USA)	18	50	99
British Steel (UK)		NA	56
Food products and beverages			
Nestle (Switzerland)	25, 303	128	166
Beatrice Foods (USA)	147	343	165
Esmark (USA)	12	30	80
Kraft (USA)	26	176	77
General Foods (USA)	43	104	122
Paper products			
International Paper (USA)	50	91	98
Bowater (UK)	198	252	102
Reed International (UK)	334	465	99
Crown Zellerbach (USA)	119	89	121
Mead (USA)	189	142	120
Textiles			
Courtauld (UK)	155	268	49
Burlington Industries (USA)	60	80	33
Kanebo (Japan)	431	428	92
J. P. Stevens (USA)	123	63	72
Toyoba (Japan)	414	343	53

Source: John H. Dunning and R. B. Pearce, PROFITABILITY AND PERFORMANCE OF THE WORLD'S LARGEST INDUSTRIAL COMPANIES (1975) at 50–53, 144–57, FORTUNE (Aug. 4, 1979).

[a] Where several ranks are shown, they are for firms merged to form the current corporation. Firms are listed within each category by order of 1978 dollar sales.

bach and St. Regis Paper Co. lost the number two and three spots to the British firms Bowater and Reed International. In rubber products, Michelin of France displaced slow-growing B. F. Goodrich from the fourth position and Dunlop supplanted Firestone from its number two rank by 1972. And the world's leading food products manufacturer is Nestlé, ahead even of the fast-growing

Beatrice Foods that held the number one spot in the United States in 1978.

Table 14-4 tells a similar story. The output of the world's largest firms has increasingly shifted away from U.S. and toward Japanese and European firms.

Certain caveats are in order in interpreting such evidence. First U.S. firms maintained their position in some industries, aircraft and packaging, for example. Second, the faster growth of European incomes made economies of scale possible in some industries. And third, lowering tariff barriers and enlarging the Common Market also contributed to the growth of firm size and to economies of scale.

Yet the inference is unavoidable that U.S. antitrust policy, in its attitude toward a large market share even in the absence of compelling evidence about misbehavior (witness the FTC cases against the major ready-to-eat cereal producers, the attempt to get ReaLemon for its 70 percent market share, and recent action against du Pont for its 40 percent share of domestic titanium dioxide production) restricts the size of U.S. firms and their positions in various world markets. One can be sure of this in the case of the steel industry where the 1950 amendment to the Clayton Act caused several firms to cancel plans to merge.[37] Similarly, when the cellophane case was brought against du Pont, the firm canceled plans to build additional capacity. Of the twenty-three U.S. firms left among the world's top fifty firms (Table 14-1), at least eighteen have been taken to the courts in major antitrust cases. Among the nine non-oil firms in the group, at least eight have been involved in such cases.[38] If nothing else, these cases consume company resources, which might otherwise have gone into growth, plus imposing costs, which reduce profitability and, consequently, reduce the attractiveness of investment in these companies.

A final point is that broad industrial categories such as those in Tables 14-3 and 14-4 are unsuitable for picking up the effects that restrictions on more narrowly defined product markets may have. The Supreme Court came very close, in fact, to considering cellophane a monopolized product. Firms in the United States have often taken exaggerated and costly steps to ensure that their production of an item cannot be viewed as a monopolization of it, regardless of their position in the more broadly defined product.

TABLE 14-4

Distribution of Sales of the World's Largest Firms,
by Industry and Geographical Area, 1962 and 1972[a]

Nation or Continent	Aircraft Aerospace and Components		Chemicals and Pharmaceuticals		Electronics and Electrical Engineering		Mechanical Engineering		Motor Vehicle		Rubber Products	
	1962	1972	1962	1972	1962	1972	1962	1972	1962	1972	1962	1972
					Percentage							
United States	97.2	84.0	71.9	57.0	68.2	62.0	71.4	62.5	72.8	61.1	70.0	61.3
Europe (EEC)	2.8 (2.8)	16.0 (13.7)	26.7 (13.5)	35.0 (22.9)	21.5 (12.7)	22.7 (15.8)	24.8 (8.3)	22.0 (10.5)	23.7 (17.3)	26.7 (21.5)	30.0 (18.6)	31.3 (13.6)
Japan	—	—	1.4	8.0	9.6	14.9	1.0	13.8	4.0	12.2	—	4.4
Other	—	—	—	—	0.7	0.5	2.8	1.7	—	—	—	2.7
Total	100	100	100	100	100	100	100	100	100	100	100	100

Nation or Continent	Tobacco		Paper Products		Food and Beverages		Packing Product and Containers		Textile Clothing and Footwear		Nonferrous Metals	
	1962	1972	1962	1972	1962	1972	1962	1972	1962	1972	1962	1972
					Percentage							
United States	59.7	50.8	68.2	57.5	75.7	64.9	92.9	92.6	70.8	65.0	82.9	54.8
Europe (EEC)	40.3 4.7	43.2 (5.3)	26.8 (4.7)	21.9 (3.2)	17.8	23.9 (1.1)	7.1 (7.1)	7.4 (7.4)	21.3 (5.6)	23.4 (4.8)	2.9 (2.9)	18.2 (5.6)
Japan	—	—	—	13.3	1.4	6.5	—	—	7.9	11.6	—	10.
Other	—	5.9	5.0	7.4	5.1	4.7	—	—	—	—	14.2	16.
Total	100	100	100	100	100	100	100	100	100	100	100	100

Source: Dunning and Pearce, PROFITABILITY AND PERFORMANCE OF THE WORLD'S LARGEST INDUSTRIAL COMPANIES, pp. 40–43.
[a] The sample of firms used is the world's 499 largest firms for 1962 and the 642 largest for 1972. "EEC" refers to the six original members.

The Aims of U.S. Industrial Policy

The purpose in comparisons of firm size is not to tally points in some senseless game in which the country with the largest or fastest growing firms wins. The case for large firms has to be made independently and has been made in fact by numerous researchers who have shown the resource savings produced by large firms. The reason large firms are formed is similar to that that motivates almost every other regularity in commercial behavior—the incentive for efficiency.

The uniformly more favorable attitude toward economic concentration in other industrialized countries indicates that they would like to take advantage of these efficiencies. Countries with large export sectors are particularly concerned with the competitiveness of their industries. Philips, Royal Dutch Petroleum, and Unilever, firms with sales in excess of $18 billion per year, are Dutch or Dutch-British firms. Nestlé, the world's largest food concern, is Swiss.

An argument often advanced in favor of large firms in the export sector is that they possess monopoly power, and that governments encourage industrial consolidation so that their firms will earn monopoly returns. But in which industry can this be said to be the case? Although France has only two major automobile producers, Peugeot-Citroën and Renault, do the French face anything but a competitive world automobile market? Can any of the major European steel producers, each with a world market share of less than 6 percent, hope to exploit world markets?

In the end, the policies of countries such as France, Germany, and Japan with regard to industrial structure must be seen in large part as efforts to lower costs and gain customers. The telling evidence on this issue is that success in world markets is usually accompanied by accusations of dumping and predatory practices (instances of which are rarer than inefficient producers like to imagine). The Japanese and the U.S. multinationals are regarded as economic powers because of their low prices. When a French minister complained about the U.S. "monopoly" in aircraft, he complained that the low prices charged by the U.S. aircraft companies and the high quality of their product made it difficult for French aircraft to compete.

Where, in fact, could a vigorous policy of deconcentration in the United States begin without inviting ridicule? In the context of a competitive world market the timeworn arguments about dominant position and barriers to entry have even less force than they once had. The Europeans and Japanese, faced with the problem of what to do about a thriving economic competitor, decided to promote large, modern enterprises. Now that the fundamental wisdom of such an approach has been demonstrated, a policy of deconcentration could only be undertaken in flagrant disregard of the economic grounds for our own successes as well as theirs.

Notes

1. Harold Demsetz, *Why Regulate Utilities?*, 11 JOURNAL OF LAW & ECONOMICS 55 (Apr. 1968); John S. McGee, *"Competition" and the Number of Firms*, IN DEFENSE OF INDUSTRIAL CONCENTRATION (1971); Eugene F. Fama and Arthur B. Laffer, *The Number of Firms and Competition*, 62 AMERICAN ECONOMIC REVIEW 670 (Sept. 1972); G. C. Archibald, *"Large" and "Small" Numbers in the Theory of the Firm*, 27 THE MANCHESTER SCHOOL OF ECONOMICS AND SOCIAL STUDIES 104 (Jan. 1959); Edward Chadwick, *Results of Different Principles of Legislation and Administration in Europe; of Competition for the Field, as Compared with the Competition within the Field of Service*, 22 JOURNAL OF THE ROYAL STATISTICAL SOCIETY 381 (Sept. 1859); Joan Bodoff, *Monopoly and Price Revisited* in Y. Brozen (ed.), THE COMPETITIVE ECONOMY: SELECTED READINGS 175 (1975); R. A. Posner, *Oligopoly and the Antitrust Laws: A Suggested Approach*, 21 STANFORD LAW REVIEW 1562 (Jun. 1969); P. Asch and J. J. Seneca, *Is Collusion Profitable?*, 58 REVIEW OF ECONOMICS AND STATISTICS 1 (Feb. 1976).
2. P. G. Porter and H. E. Livesay, *Oligopoly in Small Manufacturing Industries*, 7 EXPLORATIONS IN ECONOMIC HISTORY 371 (Spring 1970).
3. Deconcentration was imposed on Germany and Japan after World War II by their conquerors. It was not a voluntary choice. In Japan "The share of the 100 largest corporations in total paid in corporate capital for all industries decreased from 37.0 percent in 1937 to 30.4 in 1949." Masu Uekusa, *Effects of the Deconcentration Measures in Japan*, 22 ANTITRUST BULLETIN 696 (Fall 1977).
4. *Europe's Trustbearers*, THE ECONOMIST 52 (Aug. 31, 1974).
5. F. Jenny and A. P. Weber, *French Antitrust Legislation: An Exercise in Futility* in A. P. Jacquemin and H. W. de Jong (eds.), WELFARE ASPECTS OF INDUSTRIAL MARKETS (1977).
6. The U.S. Supreme Court briefly held the same views. In 1933, it upheld the use of a common selling agency for coal in *Appalachian Coals, Inc. v. United States*, 288 U.S. 344 (1933).
7. R. A. Posner, ECONOMIC ANALYSIS OF LAW 212 (1977).
8. *United States v. Aluminum Co. of America*, 148 F.2d 416 (1945); *United States v. Aluminum Co. of America*, 377 U.S. 271 (1964); *United States v. Von's Grocery Co.*, 384 U.S. 270 (1966); *United States v. Pabst Brew-*

ing Co., 384 U.S. 546 (1966); *United States v. Philadelphia Nat'l. Bank,* 374 U.S. 321 (1963); *Brown Shoe Co. v. United States,* 370 U.S. 294 (1962).

9. J. S. McGee and L. Bassett, *Vertical Integration Revisited,* 19 JOURNAL OF LAW & ECONOMICS 17 (Apr. 1976); W. J. Liebeler, *Integration and Competition* in E. Mitchell (ed.), VERTICAL INTEGRATION IN THE OIL INDUSTRY 5 (1976); R. Bork, *Vertical Integration and the Sherman Act: The Legal History of an Economic Misconception,* 22 UNIVERSITY OF CHICAGO LAW REVIEW 157 (Autumn 1954); W. J. Liebeler, *Towards a Consumer's Antitrust Law: The Federal Trade Commission and Vertical Mergers in the Cement Industry,* 15 UCLA LAW REVIEW 1153 (Jun. 1968); R. Bork, *Vertical Mergers,* THE ANTITRUST PARADOX: A POLICY AT WAR WITH ITSELF 225 (1978).

10. *United States v. Aluminum Co. of America,* 148 F. 2d 416 (2d Cir. 1945).

11. See *id.*

12. *United States v. United Shoe Machinery Corp.,* 110 F. Supp. 295 (D. Mass.), Affirmed, 347 U.S. 521 (1953).

13. George Stigler, after marshalling data on trends in concentration in the United States and England, "in which there is no public policy against concentration of control," concluded "that the Sherman Act was a modest deterrent to high concentration" and "that the 1950 anti-merger act has been a powerful discouragement to horizontal mergers," *The Economic Effects of the Antitrust Laws,* 9 JOURNAL OF LAW & ECONOMICS 232 (Oct. 1966).

14. Safeway Stores, Inc., the nation's largest retailer of groceries, was described by George Quint, a company analyst at Merrill Lynch, as being so large "they were always looking over their shoulder for the FTC. They were so careful to avoid being accused of predatory pricing that it seemed they bent over backwards not to be competitive." P. G. Hollie, *Safeway Flirts with Innovation,* NEW YORK TIMES D1 (Aug. 4, 1980).

15. R. Posner, ANTITRUST LAW: AN ECONOMIC PERSPECTIVE 206–7 (1976).

16. The du Pont Company canceled plans to build additional cellophane production capacity when a complaint was brought against it in 1947. Brozen, *Antitrust Out of Hand,* 11 CONFERENCE BOARD RECORD 14 (March 1974).

17. See Posner *supra* note 15, at 105.

18. K. Elzinga, *The Restructuring of the U.S. Brewing Industry,* 1 INDUSTRIAL ORGANIZATION REVIEW 108 (No. 2, 1973).

19. U.S., Federal Trade Commission, Bureau of Economics, THE BREWING INDUSTRY 64 (Dec. 1978).

20. See *id.* at 65.

21. *France Sets Plans to Rescue Steel Industry that Involves State Control, It's Indicated,* THE WALL STREET JOURNAL (Sept. 18, 1978).

22. *France Discloses Details of Its Legislation to Save the Debt-Plagued Steel Industry,* THE WALL STREET JOURNAL (Sept. 21, 1978) (WSJ's paraphrase of the French President's remarks). See also *Giscard Steels Himself for Nationalisation,* THE ECONOMIST 95 (Sept. 23, 1978).

23. The European Community's commissioners have come into conflict recently over this provision. "EC Industry Commissioner Etienne Davignon encouraged textile producers to reach a market-sharing agreement. The intent was to prevent the Italian industry, with its excess capacity, from starting a price war, by guaranteeing it a greater share of northern European markets. But Competition Commissioner Raymond

Vouel objected that the agreement is a flagrant breach of the treaty of
Rome. So last month, just in time to prevent Vouel from hauling them
before the European Court of Justice, Europe's eleven leading synthetic-
fiber producers announced they had abandoned the cartel, for which
they would substitute a series of 'gentleman's agreements.' An existing
agreement governing capacity cutbacks, which have improved the sector's immediate financial picture, will remain." *Textiles: Europe Reels
from the U.S. Onslaught,* 3 FINANCIAL TIMES WORLD BUSINESS
WEEKLY 9 (Feb. 4, 1980).

24. The case for transnational mergers, as well as for the argument that
Europe needs American-sized firms, received its most widely acclaimed
support in Jean-Jacques Servan-Schreiber, THE AMERICAN CHALLENGE
(1968). The topic of transnationals is again taken up in Christopher
Layton, CROSS FRONTIER MERGERS IN EUROPE (1971); and Renato Mas-
solini, EUROPEAN TRANSNATIONAL CONCENTRATION (1974).

25. G. B. Reschenthaler and W. T. Stanbury, *A Clarification of Canadian
Merger Policy,* 22 ANTITRUST BULLETIN 673 (Fall 1977).

26. Great Britain, REPORT OF THE ROYAL COMMISSION ON CORPORATE CON-
CENTRATION 98 (1978).

27. John Cable, *Merger Development and Policy in West Germany Since
1958,* WARWICK ECONOMIC RESEARCH PAPERS No. 150 (June 1979).

28. In the pre-1930s community of economists in the United States, it was
frequently argued that a market with two strong firms would be more
competitive than one with many weak firms.

29. *Nach Chrysler-Simca wird auch Ducellier wieder franzosisch,* FRANK-
FURTER ALLGEMEINE ZEITUNG (Sept. 30, 1978).

30. See Uekusa *supra* note 3, at 687.

31. Chalmers Johnson, JAPAN'S PUBLIC POLICY COMPANIES 9 (1978).

32. Charles Stevenson, *Japan: Competition Policy and Practices* in T. D.
MacDonald *et al.,* STUDIES IN FOREIGN COMPETITION POLICY AND PRAC-
TICE 287–89 (1975).

33. Richard E. Caves and Masu Uekusa, INDUSTRIAL ORGANIZATION IN
JAPAN 142 (1976).

34. J. P. Cairns, *United Kingdom: Competition Policy and Practices* in T. D.
MacDonald *et al. supra* note 32, at 348.

35. *You Can Be Big, Provided You Behave,* THE ECONOMIST (Nov. 6, 1971).

36. John H. Dunning and R. B. Pearce, PROFITABILITY AND PERFORMANCE
OF THE WORLD'S LARGEST INDUSTRIAL COMPANIES 47 (1975).

37. Jack W. Aarts, ANTITRUST POLICY VERSUS ECONOMIC POWER 328
(1975). Also, see Carl Eis, *The 1919–1930 Merger Movement in American Industry,* 12 JOURNAL OF LAW & ECONOMICS 267 (Oct. 1969), for
the effect of the 1920 antitrust case on merger activity by U.S. Steel.
One cannot, of course, generalize from the case of one industry or a few
anecdotes. Certainly, up to the time of the enforcement of the 1950
Celler-Kefauver Amendment to the Clayton Act, there was little restraint
on horizontal mergers in most industries. Since the 1950s, horizontal
mergers by sizeable firms have almost completely stopped. Now, any
expansion in scale of operations in a slowly growing industry must drive
some firms under.

38. Richard A. Posner, ANTITRUST: CASES, ECONOMIC NOTES, AND OTHER
MATERIALS (1975); Jerold G. Van Cise, THE FEDERAL ANTITRUST LAWS
(1975); and Aarts *supra* note 37.

15

Second Thoughts of Deconcentration Advocates

REPLICATIONS and extensions of the old studies of concentration using more complete and accurate data as well as other studies of recent vintage, some of which were described above, had a strong impact on the views of the "bust-'em-up" school. Many of its prominent members recanted. They no longer propose dissolution of leading firms in concentrated industries.

Turner and Kaysen

Professors Donald Turner and Carl Kaysen, who "recommended" a deconcentration program in *Antitrust Policy,* published in 1959, specifically retracted their recommendation in testimony before the Senate Subcommittee on Antitrust and Monopoly: Kaysen in 1965 and Turner in 1973.

Testifying in 1965, Professor Kaysen said, "Now the context in which the proposal . . . was placed in this volume was a discussion of possible alternatives to or expansion of the Sherman Act. And let me say we were writing in an academic or speculative fashion. We were not trying to draft a statute. . . ."[1]

Earlier in his testimony, Professor Kaysen said, ". . . if you want to look at a particular industry, then you cannot answer the question of how competitive is that industry merely by looking at the concentration figures."[2] At a later point he argued that "it would be undesirable public policy . . . to accept the argument . . . that concentration itself gives rise to the presumption of illegality. . . . [I]t doesn't seem to me . . . that it is a good idea."

Testifying in 1973 on the subject of a proposed Industrial Reorganization Act, Professor Turner indicated uneasiness about the use of market shares as a presumptive test of monopoly power, both as proposed in the bill and in his book jointly authored with Professor Kaysen. He told the Senate Subcommittee on Antitrust and Monopoly that

> In my view, the presumption suggested in the bill—presuming monopoly power if any four or fewer corporations account for 50 percent or more of sales in any year out of the 3 most recent years preceding the filing of the complaint—is not supportable.
>
> I do not believe economic evidence would support the proposition that such an industry structure will normally or even frequently produce substantial departures from competitive performance.
>
> And I am not sure about the presumptions suggested by Professor Kaysen and I in our book written some 14 years ago. Indeed, we were not sure then—namely, a conclusive presumption of market power where one company has accounted for 50 percent or more of the annual sales, or four or fewer companies have accounted for 80 percent of sales.[3]

Professor Richard Posner, in his paper on "The Chicago School of Antitrust Analysis," contrasts the view on deconcentration expressed in the 1959 Kaysen-Turner book with the view displayed in a book jointly authored by Turner with Phillip Areeda in 1978: *Antitrust Law*. Posner first points out that

> The [big firm in a concentrated industry] is by hypothesis charging a supracompetitive price as a result of the interdependence or collusion fostered by the concentrated market structure in which it finds itself. That price will attract new firms . . . and the oligopolist will either have to cut price or surrender market share. In the former case, profits will fall and in the latter, concentration will decrease.

He then goes on to say

> Deconcentration policy, then, is critically dependent upon belief in the existence of substantial barriers to entry in many industries. . . . To Kaysen and Turner they are numerous and include economies of scale, capital requirements, scarce know-how and inputs, and product

differentiation. No rigorous definition of barrier to entry is offered; nor do the authors deduce the concept of barriers to entry from the assumption that business firms act as rational profit maximizers. The important point, however, is that, believing barriers to entry to be numerous and prevalent, the authors have a rational basis for wanting to deconcentrate concentrated markets. Areeda and Turner greatly pare down the list of barriers to entry. . . . [T]hey . . . exclude economies of scale entirely. The related size-of-capital barrier is discarded also and product differentiation is discounted . . . The only barriers that remain are: (1) the Williamson risk-premium version of the capital barrier and (2) control of scarce input.* Thus, Areeda and Turner largely discard the concept of barrier to entry, finding some of the barriers theoretically invalid and others empirically unimportant. . . . And although Areeda and Turner do not expressly discuss the dependence of deconcentration theory on the belief in the existence of high and pervasive barriers to entry, they do draw quite different policy implications concerning persistent high concentration from Kaysen and Turner. Whereas the earlier book recommended a policy of deconcentration, the latter book recommends remedial action . . . only where there is proof of non-competitive performance.[4]

Members of the Task Force on Antitrust Policy

Of special interest are the members of the White House Task Force on Antitrust Policy (Neal Task Force). In 1968, the Task Force drafted a Concentrated Industries Act, a Merger Act, revisions of Section 2(a), (b), and (f) of the Robinson-Patman Act, and new patent legislation. The proposed Concentrated Industries Act would break up all firms with more than 15 percent of any market larger than $500,000,000 (in 1968 dollars) where four leading

* As Posner commented in a footnote: "Legal barriers to entry such as patents are quite properly ignored as beyond the reach of antitrust policy. As a detail, I think Areeda and Turner are wrong to treat control of a scarce input as a barrier to entry into the output market. To treat it so is a version of the leverage fallacy. If a seller of widgets controls an indispensable input into widget production, call it manganium, he will have little incentive to restrict entry into the widget market. His control of manganium will engage him to extract all of the economic rents obtainable in the widget market without selling any widgets, let alone trying to control the widget market. (To be sure, I am ignoring considerations of input substitution, in the variable proportions case, and of price discrimination, but these are second-order considerations and are in any event not the basis on which Areeda and Turner deem control of a key input a barrier to entry.) Alternatively, if the scarce input is not a good but, say, the services of an extraordinarily skilled manager, he will presumably extract all (or more realistically most) of the benefits that his services confer on the firm, in the form of a rent; consequently, the firm's costs may be little lower than those of other firms in the market, or of prospective entrants."

firms sell more than 70 percent of the product and in which the concentrated structure is not dictated by economies of scale or by regulation.

Professor Robert Bork, a member of the Task Force, dissented. He argued that the "recommendations . . . rest on erroneous analysis and inadequate empirical investigations. Their net effect seems more likely to injure consumers than to aid them."[5] A year later, the Presidential Task Force on Productivity and Competition agreed that "existing knowledge" did not provide grounds for the recommendations. Richard Sherwood, another member of the Neal Task Force, was also firm in refusing to endorse the proposals. He said that ". . . in the present state of economic and legal knowledge the sweeping condemnation which the Task Force has accorded [corporate concentration, conglomerate mergers, and patent licensing] appears to be rooted in dogmas which I do not share."[6]

Others, however, came to this view more slowly. Professor Paul MacAvoy weakly endorsed the Concentrated Industries Act proposal at the time, saying, "more work remains to be done to establish that oligopolies of four or five firms can be expected to restrict output and raise price under most or all market conditions, but the evidence presently available is strong enough to provide rationale for this legislation."[7] He refused to endorse the proposed Merger Act, designed to restrict conglomerate mergers. Since the publication of the Report, he has publicly retracted his endorsement of the Concentrated Industries Act (in testimony in the Federal District Court in Northern Ohio in 1977).

Professor William Baxter, who endorsed the Antitrust Task Force proposals at the time, has also retracted his endorsement. Speaking at the Spring 1977 meeting of the Antitrust Section of the American Bar Association, he said, "As one of the original drafters of the Deconcentration Act, which first appeared in the Neal Task Force Report of 1968, it seems particularly appropriate that I *recant*. The state of the economic art has changed somewhat since 1968."[8]

Schwartzman, Weiss, and Simons

Professor David Schwartzman is another economist who has changed his mind on the concentration issue. He had done a study of industries that were concentrated in Canada but not in the United States. He concluded that the comparison demonstrated that the effect of concentration was to raise prices by 8 percent.[9]

When a later Canadian census made data available on a larger number of industries, Professor Schwartzman supervised a replication of his earlier study by a doctoral student, Joan Bodoff. With a larger sample and a more substantial body of data, she found concentration did *not* increase prices.[10] As Professor Schwartzman testified in the 1973 Hearings of the Subcommittee on Antitrust and Monopoly, her study, and others, led him to conclude "that the concentration ratio is a poor measure of monopoly power,"[11] a reversal of his earlier position.

Even Professor Leonard Weiss, at one time a proponent of a strong anti-merger policy "whenever significant concentration is present or in prospect," has partially retracted his earlier view.[12] He now says ". . . evidence on the relationship between concentration and the extent of suboptimal capacity has led me to reconsider my views on merger policy. . . . It now appears that increased concentration creates social gains in the form of less suboptimal capacity . . ."[13]

One of the earliest economist proponents of deconcentration recanted very shortly after publishing his proposal. Professor Henry Simons, in a 1934 publication, proposed "A limitation upon the total amount of property which any single corporation may own designed to preclude the existence in any industry of a single company large enough to dominate the industry."[14] Within two years, he reversed his position, saying that "I am, indeed not much distressed about private monopoly power. . . . Serious exploitation could be prevented by suppression of lawless violence. . . . The ways of competition are devious, and its vengeance—government intervention apart—will generally be adequate and admirable."[15]

Stigler

Perhaps the most prominent member of the group that once believed that high concentration and collusion are synonymous is Professor George Stigler. He bluntly stated his position in 1952, asserting then, "When a small number of firms control most or all of the output of an industry, they can individually and collectively profit more by cooperation than by competition. . . . These few companies, therefore, will usually cooperate."[16]

The evolution of Stigler's thinking about concentration from this position to one where he expressed unwillingness to endorse a deconcentration proposal has produced an interesting track. His own research evidently demonstrated to him the inaccuracy of his 1952 observation. In a 1956 paper testing Schumpeter's hypothesis that monopoly leads to more rapid progress than an atomistic structure, Stigler drew a dividing line between "high" and "low" four-firm concentration at the 45 percent level.[17]

In *Capital and Rates of Return in Manufacturing Industries* (1963), Professor Stigler classified industries in the following way:

> Unconcentrated industries meet one of two conditions: (1) the market is national, and the concentration ratio is less than 50 percent; (2) the market is regional, and the [national] ratio is less than 20 percent. Concentrated industries are simply those in which the four leading firms produce 60 percent or more of the value added, and for which the market is national. Industries falling in neither of these categories are labeled ambiguous. . . . Readers . . . hardly need be told that a concentrated industry need not be monopolistic. High elasticity of demand for the industry's product, or ease of entry by new firms, or the extent of independent rivalry among firms may make the concentrated industry (in this definition) differ in, at most, trifling respects from a fully competitive industry.[18]

In *A Theory of Oligopoly* (1964) he examined some evidence on the relationship of the number of firms to prices and concluded "that the level of prices is not very responsive to the actual number of rivals."[19] He examined the difficulties of detecting cheating in a collusive arrangement and found that with more than two firms in an industry, collusion was unlikely to succeed (or as likely to succeed with many firms as with few). He then examined profitability and concentration and concluded, "In general the data suggest that there is no relationship between profitability and concentration if H [Herfindahl index] is less than 0.250 or the share of the four largest firms is less than about 80 percent."[20]

In 1969, when Stigler was called to testify before the House Special Subcommittee on Small Business, he gave no support to his 1952 assertion. He stated,

> I personally have serious misgivings about the Neal proposals for deconcentration. I worry about the fact that where we have substan-

tial large economies of scale, deconcentration puts burdens on us. Where the economies are not large, private rivals have a tendency to enter and eliminate (excess) profits themselves. . . . There was a time when I was younger and perhaps wiser when I was enthusiastic for that scheme. I no longer am.[21]

Conclusion

The overturning of earlier studies by those of the last decade has led proponents of deconcentration measures to reconsider their positions. The correlations of concentration and profitability, which were in 1968 thought by the majority of the Neal Task Force to provide adequate support for its deconcentration recommendation, were specifically criticized only a year later by the Presidential Task Force on Productivity and Competition. It said

> Concern with oligopoly has led to proposals to use the antitrust laws (perhaps amended) to deconcentrate highly oligopolistic industries by dissolving their leading firms. We cannot endorse these proposals on the basis of existing knowledge. As indicated, the correlation between concentration and profitability is weak, and many factors besides the number of firms in a market appear to be relevant to the competitiveness of their behavior.[22]

Professor John McGee's destruction of the enduring myth of the pre-dissolution Standard Oil Company's use of predatory pricing helped to begin the return to a more realistic view of the market power of the large corporation with a major share of a market.[23] He, and other students and colleagues of Professor Aaron Director (Professors Ward Bowman, Robert Bork, and Lester Telser, for example), who stimulated the application of the hard core of economic theory to antitrust cases, led the way from the incantations and "colorful characterizations" invoked in antitrust trials (leverage, foreclosure, predation, reciprocity, deep pockets, barriers to entry, differentiation, proliferation, dominance, concentration) to "the careful definitions and parsimonious logical structure of economic theory."[24]

The view of the pre-1930 economists who lived with and saw the successes and failures of the notorious trusts is once again becoming respected. The 1901 advice of J. B. Clark, who suggested that "We certainly need to know more than that in its natural appearance, a trust resembles an octopus," has been applied. It turns out that this fearsome-appearing beast is a friendly creature working hard, in most cases, under the guidance of the "invisible hand" to benefit mankind. Now that this is recognized, economists are now befriending the creature, with due caution, and are ending their attempts to exterminate this endangered species.

Notes

1. U.S., Congress, Senate, Commitee on the Judiciary, Subcommittee on Antitrust and Monopoly, HEARINGS ON ECONOMIC CONCENTRATION, Part 4, 89th Congress, 1st session, Sept. 1965, at 554.
2. See *id.* at 552.
3. U.S., Congress, Senate, Committee on the Judiciary, Subcommittee on Antitrust and Monopoly, Hearings, THE INDUSTRIAL REORGANIZATION ACT, Part 1, 93rd Congress, 1st session, March 1973, at 278.
4. Richard Posner, *The Chicago School of Antitrust Analysis,* 127 UNIVERSITY OF PENNSYLVANIA LAW REVIEW 946–47 (Apr. 1979).
5. See *Separate Statement of Robert Bork,* 2 ANTITRUST LAW & ECONOMIC REVIEW 54 (Winter 1968–69).
6. See *Separate Statement of Richard E. Sherwood,* 2 ANTITRUST LAW & ECONOMIC REVIEW 61 (Winter 1968–69).
7. See *Separate Statement of Paul W. MacAvoy,* 2 ANTITRUST LAW & ECONOMIC REVIEW 57 (Winter 1968–69).
8. William Baxter, *How Government Cases Get Selected—Comments from Academe,* 46 ANTITRUST LAW JOURNAL 588 (1977) (emphasis supplied).
9. David Schwartzman, *The Effect of Monopoly on Price,* 67 JOURNAL OF POLITICAL ECONOMY 352 (1959).
10. Joan Bodoff, *Monopoly and Price Revisited* in Y. Brozen, THE COMPETITIVE ECONOMY: SELECTED READINGS 175 (1975).
11. See U.S., Congress, Senate, Committee on the Judiciary, Subcommittee on Antitrust and Monopoly, *supra* note 3, at 455.
12. L. Weiss, *The Concentration-Profits Relationship and Antitrust* in H. J. Goldschmid, H. M. Mann, and J. F. Weston (eds.), INDUSTRIAL CONCENTRATION: THE NEW LEARNING 232 (1974).
13. L. Weiss, *The Structure-Conduct-Performance Paradigm and Antitrust,* 127 UNIVERSITY OF PENNSYLVANIA LAW REVIEW 1117 (Apr. 1979).
14. Henry C. Simons, A POSITIVE PROGRAM FOR LAISSEZ-FAIRE 20 (1934).
15. Henry C. Simons, *The Requisites of Free Competition,* 26 AMERICAN ECONOMIC REVIEW, Supp. at 68 (Mar. 1936).
16. George J. Stigler, *The Case Against Big Business,* 45 FORTUNE 123, May 1952.
17. John S. McGee, IN DEFENSE OF INDUSTRIAL CONCENTRATION (1971).
18. G. Stigler, CAPITAL AND RATES OF RETURN IN MANUFACTURING INDUSTRIES 57, N. 4 and 67.
19. JOURNAL OF POLITICAL ECONOMY (1964), reprinted in G. Stigler, THE ORGANIZATION OF INDUSTRY (1968).
20. See *id.*

21. U.S., Congress, House of Representatives, Committee on Small Business, Special Subcommittee on Small Business and the Robinson-Patman Act, p. 145, 91st Congress, 1st session, 1969.
22. U.S., 1969 Presidential Task Force Report on Productivity and Competition, 115 CONGRESSIONAL RECORD 6475 (June 16, 1979).
23. John S. McGee, *Predatory Price Cutting: The Standard Oil (N.J.) Case,* 1 JOURNAL OF LAW & ECONOMICS 137 (Apr. 1958), reprinted in Brozen *supra* note 11, at 380.
24. See Posner *supra* note 5, at 929.

16

Public Policy and Concentration

THE legislators who wrote the antitrust laws aimed at removing restraints on output. They did not design them to preserve inefficient firms, whether large or small. They outlawed "every contract, combination, or conspiracy in *restraint of trade*." They outlawed the use of unfair tactics, which might drive efficient firms from the market.

Should Antitrust Aim at Reducing Concentration?

Early court decisions were based on this legislative intent. Standard Oil and American Tobacco were not broken up by antitrust decrees in 1911 because they were big or "dominant." The court ruled that they had been built by a very large number of mergers to monopolistic proportions with wrongful intent and had then engaged in "acts and dealings wholly inconsistent with the theory that they were made with the single conception of advancing the development of business . . . by usual methods. . . ." The defendants failed to show that the intent underlying their mergers and their unusual methods were the normal one of efficiency and expansion of trade—they failed to show "countervailing circumstances" in Justice White's phrase. They were, therefore, subjected to antitrust remedies. The remedies were not applied

395

because of their market shares. They were applied because Standard Oil and American Tobacco were, in the Court's view, formed and maintained by monopolizing acts and with monopolizing intent, that is, by a desire to gain control of the supply of a product and to use that control to restrain trade and charge a monopoly price.

It is abundantly clear from Senator George Hoar's explanation to the Senate of the Judiciary Committee's final draft of the Sherman Act that antitrust policy was not aimed at fragmenting industry nor at preventing occupancy of a major share of a market by one or a few firms. He declared that a man who "got the whole business because nobody could do it as well as he could" would not be in violation of the Sherman Act.

If the resources used by the few large firms in a concentrated industry produce less when scattered among several small firms, then deconcentration or the prevention of concentration would restrain trade. Prevention of concentration when concentration would reduce costs and expand trade violates the intent of those who drafted and enacted the Sherman Act.

The presence of a persistently dominant firm (or small group of dominant firms) or of an increasing concentration trend in an industry is evidence of competitive behavior, not of monopolization, monopoly, or collusion. To understand why this is so, we should ask, "How did a firm become dominant or an industry become concentrated? Having reached this position, how did the firm remain dominant or the industry remain concentrated?" In the words of Professor John McGee,

If the goal [of antitrust] is to serve consumer interests, it makes no sense to judge the competitiveness of any market in terms of structure—however concentrated—without first understanding why that structure evolved and what consequences it produced.

If railroads wipe out oxcarts it would be odd to say that this is not competition, on the grounds that a more concentrated "industry" competed with a less concentrated "industry" and won out. But that is the kind of nonsensical inference to which the structural theories lead us.

Similarly, it would be very strange to argue that, if supermarkets displace smaller butchers, fish-mongers, and green-grocers, that this is not competition. Or to argue that competition had declined because the growth of the successful, and superior, firms resulted in higher concentration. But that is the route on which the structural theories put many economists. What is worse, it is the itinerary that courts have been following.[1]

If firms grow to where their market shares concentrate an industry or make one firm dominant, it must be because of superior management, economies of scale, or the production of better products that satisfy a major portion of buyers at a lower cost to them. The growth must be not only the result of lower costs but also of competitive behavior. The benefits of lower costs, to make low-cost firms "dominant," must be passed on to buyers in sufficient amount to attract them to the low-cost firms. To maintain a large market share, the dominant firm or firms cannot restrict output to maintain price but must expand with the industry. Any attempt at monopolistic or collusive behavior requires restriction of output. Such attempts entail a consequent sacrifice of market share.

Professor Robert Bork, dissenting from the recommendations of the White House Task Force on Antitrust Policy, expressed the objections to deconcentration in cogent terms.

> In judging whether it is worthwhile to break up a concentrated industry structure it is necessary to estimate whether more will be gained through the predicted end to noncompetitive pricing or lost through the destruction of industrial efficiency. . . .
>
> The proposed statute . . . would have its impact almost entirely upon industries in which concentration had evolved through the growth of leading firms or through mergers that occurred years ago. . . .
>
> The dissolution of such firms would be a disservice to consumers and to national strength. When firms grow to sizes that create concentration or when such a structure is created by merger and persists for many years, there is a very strong prima facie case that the firms' sizes are related to efficiency. By efficiency I mean "competitive effectiveness" within the bounds of the law, and competitive effectiveness means service to consumers. If the leading firms in a concentrated industry are restricting their output in order to obtain prices above the competitive level, their efficiencies must be sufficiently superior to that of all actual and potential rivals to offset that behavior. Were this not so, rivals would be enabled to expand their market shares because of the abnormally high prices and would thus deconcentrate the industry. Market rivalry thus automatically weighs the respective influences of efficiency and output restriction and arrives at the firm size and industry structures that serve consumers best.[2]

While some attach significance to the four-firm market share as an index to the ease or cost of successful collusion and its consequent frequency, the evidence runs against this hypothesis. Tacit collusion is unworkable and explicit collusion is actionable. There is no need to fear that high concentration will produce undetected collusion and there is no need for a deconcentration policy. The market deconcentrates the industries in need of deconcentration.

Some observers fear that a large firm with a large market share will have a partial monopoly and will use its partial monopoly to hike prices. But supracompetitive pricing invites other firms to expand output. It encourages entry, which soon ends the dominance of the firm. Prices can be no higher with a dominant firm than with a decentralized industry. Higher prices would attract the entry of small-scale firms or less-well-managed firms that would exist comfortably in a decentralized industry.

The very fact that some studies conclude that the average profitability of concentrated industries, or at least of leading firms in those industries, exceeds the all-industry average is evidence in itself that collusion or partial monopoly behavior is not prevalent in such industries. Collusion is more likely in industries that have excess capacity and below average profits. In these, profits can be enhanced by collusion without attracting entry. Collusion is, therefore, potentially workable and durable in such industries. A study of collusion and profitability confirmed the link between low profits and collusion.

Other studies confirm the fact that some industries are concentrated because efficient and innovative firms have grown large or have become efficient by growing large. This resulted in greater efficiency and lower prices *in those industries*. Instead of concentration leading to collusion and higher prices, relatively greater efficiency in some firms led to concentration and lower prices. And the heads that wore the crowns of leadership in size did not rest easy. Concentration persisted only when the foremost firms routinized innovation in processes and products and maintained their greater relative efficiency in the face of rising efficiency in other firms. Any lapse provided would-be entrants lurking at the edge of every industry an opportunity to strike.

The implications drawn by the antitrust agencies and the courts from the structuralist findings in the Alcoa and the du Pont cellophane decisions have been unfortunate. They force firms to behave like monopolists or to mute their competition in order to avoid attack under the antitrust laws. Judge Hand, in effect, instructed firms to avoid expanding capacity and supply of a product sufficiently rapidly to prevent prices from rising to levels that would attract entry. This was reinforced by Justice Reed in the cellophane decision, in which he implicitly warned every business not to pass on the benefits of cost reduction in the form of quality improvements and price reductions to such an extent that they would "eliminate . . . other producers from the relevant market,"[3] although he did not find explicitly to that effect. Oddly enough, he construed the fact that du Pont had not priced other firms out of the market as a mitigating circumstance, which helped show that du Pont had not violated the Sherman Act. To his credit, he did remind the Antitrust Division that "Senator Hoar, in discussing section 2, pointed out that monopoly involved something more than extraordinary commercial success, 'that it involved something like the use of means which made it impossible for other persons to engage in fair competition.' "[4] The staffs of the antitrust agencies need reminding again of Justice Reed's instruction, a task on which the newly appointed heads of the agencies appear to have embarked.

Should Horizontal Mergers Always Be Restrained?

Preventing horizontal mergers does not prevent rising concentration when the equilibrium (efficient) structure of an industry shifts in that direction. It simply prevents the efficient use of the industry's existing capital stock. It causes a misallocation of our economy's capital by diverting it to the construction of redundant capacity. The postwar history of the brewing industry provides ample demonstration of the waste caused by a stringent anti-merger policy.

Permitting mergers does not result in persistent concentration where that is inefficient if firms are allowed to compete. The pre-1950 history of concentration in many industries where large-scale mergers occurred illustrate this fact (Tables 3-1 and 3-2). Permitting horizontal mergers does not even result in temporary concentration in most industries, a fact also demonstrated by pre-1950 history when merger policy was very permissive.

If dominance or concentration is created by industry-wide mergers, we know from history that monopoly or cartel behavior—any attempt to set prices higher than a competitive level—results in loss of market share. Therefore, when dominance or concentration persists following such mergers, it must be the result of low costs together with the offer of a sufficiently large supply to keep prices

399

at low enough levels that entry or expansion by small firms already in the industry is unattractive. As the receiver for the bankrupt Distilling and Cattle Feeding Company pointed out in his testimony in 1899 before the Industrial Commission, "The moment [trusts] reach out for more than a reasonable profit on the cost of production, that moment other plants will be created faster than any can buy them up."[5]

With such forces operating, the potentially anticompetitive effects of mergers should not be worrisome. The Presidential Task Force Report on Productivity and Competition points out that the present merger guidelines are too restrictive. "The Department of Justice Merger Guidelines are extraordinarily stringent and in some respects indefensible."[6]

There is an inordinate fear of allowing even a modest increase in concentration, whether market or aggregate. In no case has it been shown that a rise in industry concentration decreases competition as long as there are at least two competitors, or a few potential rivals, willing to bid for business. (Regardless of this lack of evidence, it should be noted, some economists not hostile to concentration are unwilling to settle for less than three or four competitors.)

Robert Stillman examined horizontal mergers and their effects using data from the financial markets. If horizontal mergers improve efficiency and benefit consumers, the value of competitors' assets should fall. If increased market shares in the hands of acquiring firms enable them to influence output and prices in ways adverse to consumers—holding a price umbrella, for example—then the wealth of the owners of competing firms can be expected to increase. With the dissolution of horizontal mergers, opposite effects would follow.

Stillman, in his dissertation at UCLA, investigated the effects of horizontal mergers and of dissolutions of horizontal mergers using this methodology. The central question that he asked was, "Do the antitrust enforcers tend to challenge price-increasing mergers?"[7] He concluded that, "The evidence is that there has been no such tendency." This followed from the fact that "the data on rivals' abnormal stock returns indicate that the proportion" of wealth increases for firms competing with merged firms does not appear any different from the proportion to be expected if there had been no mergers to benefit or hurt them. It might have been expected that the antitrust authorities would challenge selected mergers, that is, those that would produce some market impact. Evidently, antitrusters did no better than challenge a random selection of mergers in their dissolution complaints.

These data assembled by Stillman show neither favorable nor adverse effects on rivals of merged firms where the mergers were horizontal. It follows that horizontal mergers had neither the effect of facilitating tacit or explicit collusion nor of improving efficiency. Why, then, did they take place?

One possible answer is that horizontal mergers do result in efficiency gains but rivals do not suffer because the efficiency gains are not passed on to buyers. If there are efficiency gains, and no misallocation of resources as a consequence of price raising effects, then there is a clear social gain. Resources are released to add to the economy's total output—resources that otherwise would have been used in inefficient production. There is, then, a clear social loss from the harsh application of the Celler-Kefauver Amendment.

A sample of postwar horizontal mergers too small to yield statistically significant conclusions, analyzed by Professor Paul Asquith in unpublished work, points in this direction. Acquired firms showed *no* abnormal losses in the four years prior to acquisition and significant abnormal market gains shortly before and at the announcement of the proposed merger. Acquiring firms showed normal returns at the time of announcement and in the year following the horizontal mergers despite the payment of substantial premiums. Normal returns could have been earned in these circumstances (given Stillman's finding of no more than the usual proportion of abnormal gainers among rivals) only if efficiency was improved sufficiently to yield a return on the premiums.

Asquith's data point to another explanation of Stillman's findings. The fact that acquirers paid a premium for firms in the same business and then earned normal returns on those premiums indicates a gain in efficiency from the horizontal combination of firms. The mergers occurred when they did because some change in technology or markets made efficiency gains possible. The efficiency gains, which would hurt rivals if passed through to customers, did not cause abnormal losses to rivals because they became prospective acquisitions with the possibility of efficiency gains from new technology applied in larger firms. This prevented the abnormal losses to their stockholders that would otherwise have occurred.

It appears that the antitrust authorities wasted public resources in attacking horizontal mergers. They prevented the social gains that can come from increased efficiency. Antitrust activities would serve the nation better if they were devoted to more appropriate targets than a merger between Brown and Kinney creating a firm with a 5 percent market share or a Vons-Shopping Bag merger creating an 8.9 percent firm in a hotly competitive local market.

Non-Horizontal Mergers and Aggregate Concentration

A case can be made against horizontal mergers of industry-wide proportions when there are high entry barriers. A merger of firms holding competing process patents or patents on competing products with no close substitutes and few distant substitutes could achieve sufficient control over supply to yield monopoly rents (returns in excess of a normal return on their investments in developing their processes or products).[8] But there is no economic case against vertical or conglomerate mergers or for vertical or conglomerate divestitures. Yet, antitrust decrees have prevented some vertical and some conglomerate mergers and have decreed vertical and conglomerate dissolutions. The 1911 dissolution of American Tobacco split divisions and subsidiaries supplying licorice and tinfoil and retailing tobacco products from those manufacturing tobacco products. Standard Oil of New Jersey was divested of pipelines and of marketing companies in neighboring regions, which it had supplied from its refineries—a vertical divorce. It was also divested of regional refining and marketing subsidiaries, a conglomerate divestiture. No horizontal divestitures were required. The antitrust case itself seems to have slowed technological progress,[9] and it did nothing to make the market any more competitive than it already was in the static sense. The Standard Oil conglomerate and vertical dissolution probably did no great harm, given the rapid growth of the industry, except for the temporary loss of scale efficiency in refinery operations in a few areas and the loss of some transaction and financing efficiencies, but neither was any good accomplished.[10]

Vertical mergers produce no anticompetitive effects. Preventing them in the name of preventing "foreclosure" simply prevents the use of the cheapest method of obtaining the efficiencies of vertical integration. Hostility to such mergers may cause waste of the existing capital stock, redundant capacity, and the misallocation of current capital supplies as preventing horizontal mergers did in the brewing industry. Also, where a firm buys from a non-competitive set of suppliers with excess capacity, earning little because of the excess in spite of a non-competitive price, acquisition of a supplier will be cheaper than building new facilities and will avoid wasting the economy's limited supply of capital. Such an acquisition, by decreasing cost to the buyer, may then force competition into the supplying industry by the buyer's competition with others in his industry and their defensive reactions. Vertical mergers, in this case, are pro-competitive. They should be encouraged. The mergers between cement and ready-mix firms attacked by the FTC were probably of this character and the FTC did a great disservice to consumers of cement while protecting the non-competitive elements in the cement industry.[11]

As for conglomerate mergers, whether of the chain, product extension, or pure type, there is simply no economic case against permitting the reshuffling of assets into more efficient packages. As Professor Turner, FTC Commissioner Pitofsky, and Justice Harlan have pointed out, if the market for firms whose owners wish to exit, for whatever reason, is restricted, the result will be less entry. Decreasing the demand for firms will decrease the number of firms produced.

The charade played in applying anti-horizontal-merger strictures and language to conglomerate mergers should be recognized as such and ended. Market extension and product extension mergers are not mergers between competitors. Such artful leaps of logic do not promote potential or actual competition. As Justice Harlan remarked, in his concurring opinion in the Procter & Gamble Clorox case.

> The court, following the Commission, points out that this merger is not a pure "conglomerate" merger but may more aptly be labeled a "product-extension" merger. No explanation, however, is offered as to why this distinction has any significance . . .[12]

What effect have conglomerate mergers had on aggregate concentration? Fifty years of merger activity leaves us even further from all non-financial corporate assets being in the hands of 200 corporations than we were when Berle and Means warned that a continuation of the 1909–29 trends would place us in that position by 1969.

The present doctrine used in forbidding many conglomerate acquisitions is in complete contradicion to other antitrust doctrines. If the law is to have any consistency, the "potential competitor" doctrine should be dropped, and the Alcoa structural approach should be discarded. The Alcoa and cellophane doctrine instructs firms not to expand capacity and output rapidly enough to keep prices down or push them down to the competitive level. The court premises its decisions striking down conglomerate mergers, such as the Procter & Gamble acquisition of Clorox, on the maintenance of one potential competitor who *might* enter the industry of the would-be acquisition by building new capacity. The value of a potential competitor lies in the fact that by its threat to enter if prices rise to attractive levels, it compels firms to expand capacity and output sufficiently to supply as much as the market wants at a price that does not attract entry. Which does the court want— capacity expansion by firms in an industry to the level that avoids attracting entry, or a lag in expansion, as demanded by Judge Hand, which raises prices to entry-attracting levels?

In bringing merger dissolution cases, the Antitrust Division and the FTC seem to unerringly select the socially most beneficial mergers to attack. Their cases are brought against acquiring firms with the most able managements who are likely to make the most efficient use of acquired assets. The 279 firms against which proceedings were brought earned abnormal positive returns of 26 percent in the 100 months *before* the acquisition—which was attacked—was made. The 493 acquiring firms left undisturbed earned abnormal returns of only 18 percent before making an acquisition. In both instances, most of the abnormal return had been earned in the period preceding the forty-eight months before the acquisition. It was not, then, the prospect of the acquisition and "capitalization of monopoly rents" that generated the pre-merger abnormal gains.[13] That leaves only greater efficiency or luck to account for the greater than average returns to the stockholders of these acquisition prone firms.

The selection of firms ordered to divest among those against whom cases were brought was even more perverse. The 123 defendants ordered to divest their acquired assets provided abnormal returns of 30.8 percent to their stockholders in the 100 months prior to acquisition. The less effective managements whose stock provided only 11.9 percent abnormal returns were allowed to keep their acquired assets.[14]

The Proper Focus of Antitrust Efforts

The antitrust agencies attack the wrong targets when they ask for deconcentration and the prevention of conglomerate growth by acquisition. Persistent concentration or dominance demonstrates either superior performance or the continuing use of predatory or other improper exclusionary devices. If the former is the case, deconcentration will cause large costs. If the latter, then the use of such devices should be attacked and such tactics stopped. In the event of proof of the use of such devices, penalties will be large, through treble damage actions if nothing else.

The use of exclusionary devices such as predatory pricing is rare, in part because of the hostility of antitrust authorities to behavior that even *appears* exclusionary,[15] but also because it is generally unprofitable. Exclusionary practices impose costs on other firms without benefiting the user. Such tactics, by definition, neither reduce his cost nor do they provide valuable services to customers. Because there is confusion in present antitrust law as to what an exclusionary device is, the charge that such devices are used is more common than the actuality. Many an arrangement has been called exclusionary that is not.

> . . . [M]any of these so-called, exclusionary or predatory practices are, in fact, efficiency creating in nature. Others appear to be manifestations of competitive rivalry in real-world markets which do not ordinarily comport with the perfect competition model.[16]

Antitrust should focus its attention on improper exclusionary devices rather than on concentration or dominance per se. It should, however, not confuse nonstandard practices and vertical restrictions with trade restraints.[17] Secondly, it should seek out trade restraining, explicit collusion rather than concentration, the proxy used in economic studies that relied on assumption rather than proof about the genesis of collusion.

In searching for trade restraining, explicit collusion, it is not concentrated industries that should be the center of attention. Neither should it be high-profit industries. If leading firms in concentrated industries are using improper exclusionary devices, that is, if exclusion is the result of reasons other than the efficiency of these firms, the cost of those activities will result in low profits for these firms. Predatory pricing or advertising inflicts losses upon predators as well as on victims. And the losses to predators are greater than to the firms preyed upon. If the alleged predators are very profitable, that is a demonstration that they are efficient and that their competitors are objecting to their efficiency, not to predatory actions.

If firms in concentrated industries collude, concentration will decline. Collusion carries its own cure unless capacity is excessive and profits are low. If any concentrated industries deserve special attention, it is those with declining concentration despite slow growth and unchanging products, not the persistently concentrated industries. But on this argument special attention should be given to less concentrated industries with the same characteristics. There is no particular reason for focusing attention primarily on even a subset of concentrated industries. Any industry is a proper subject of antitrust attention if (1) firm market shares in each and every region do not vary over long periods, (2) each firm sells only in a specific territory different from those in which other firms sell, (3) all firms expand or contract capacity by the same proportionate amounts at the same time, (4) leading four-firm shares decline without mitigating circumstances, or (5) industry profits are persistently low and high-profit firms within the industry fail to expand.

To attack any firm at any time for expanding capacity stands antitrust on its head. To attack proposed conglomerate mergers on the ground that the capacity of the acquisition will be expanded by the acquiring firm is to attack the essence of what makes some conglomerate mergers desirable.[18] Such attacks restrain trade. They are, themselves, a violation of the spirit of the antitrust laws.

It is entry that destroys undetected collusion and polices entrepreneurial or managerial sloth. Entry barriers are the appropriate arena for antitrust action. The antitrust agencies are to be commended for beginning action in this arena in the last decade. Again, however, there is much confusion in the agencies and in the courts (and among economists) as to what constitutes a barrier.[19] The only significant barriers are those administered by regulatory agencies and licensing authorities. Praise is due the antitrust agencies for beginning to move on these.

It is time to remove dominance and concentration, whether industry or aggregate, from the center of the antitrust stage. Above and beyond the restrictions on national economic growth and productivity imposed by keeping these stage center, is the fact that Americans have voted with their dollars (by their purchases) for the concentration that exists and against it where it does not. They have voted with their feet for and against concentration by their selection of jobs and their investment of their savings. It is time that we stop quarreling with their vote.

Notes

1. John S. McGee, *Why Not "Deregulation" for Antitrust,* 46 ANTITRUST LAW JOURNAL 779 (Summer 1977).
2. Phil C. Neal et al., *Report of the White House Task Force on Antitrust Policy,* 2 ANTITRUST LAW AND ECONOMICS REVIEW 11 (Winter 1968–69).
3. *U.S. v. E. I. du Pont de Nemours & Co.* 351 U.S. 377 (1956).
4. See *id.*
5. PRELIMINARY REPORTS OF THE INDUSTRIAL COMMISSION AND TESTIMONY 217 (1900).
6. U.S., *1969 Presidential Task Force Report on Productivity and Competition,* 115 CONGRESSIONAL RECORD 6475 (June 16, 1969).
7. Robert Stillman, *Examining the Antitrust Case Against Horizontal Mergers* (dissertation, University of California, Los Angeles, 1979).
8. Ward Bowman, PATENT AND ANTITRUST LAW: A LEGAL AND ECONOMIC APPRAISAL (1973).
9. Paul Giddens, STANDARD OIL COMPANY (INDIANA), OIL PIONEER OF THE MIDDLE WEST 149 (1955).
10. However, for the opposite view, see S. M. Loescher, *A Sherman Act Precedent for the Application of Antitrust Legislation to Conglomerate Mergers: Standard Oil, 1911* in Jesse Markham and G. V. Papecek (eds.), INDUSTRIAL ORGANIZATION AND ECONOMIC DEVELOPMENT 154 (1970).
11. W. J. Liebeler, *Toward a Consumer's Antitrust Law: The Federal Trade Commission and Vertical Mergers in the Cement Industry,* 15 UCLA LAW REVIEW 1153 (Jun. 1968).
12. 386 U.S. 583 (1967).
13. James C. Ellert, *Mergers, Antitrust Law Enforcement, and Stockholder Returns,* 31 JOURNAL OF FINANCE 727 (May 1976).
14. See *id.* at 721.
15. See *supra* note 14, chapter 14, for an example of the avoidance even of hard competition because of the hostility.
16. Wesley J. Liebeler, *Market Power and Competitive Superiority in Concentrated Industries,* 25 UCLA LAW REVIEW 1238 (Aug. 1978).
17. Oliver Williamson, *Assessing Vertical Market Restrictions: Antitrust Ramifications of the Transaction Cost Approach,* 127 UNIVERSITY OF PENNSYLVANIA LAW REVIEW 959 (Apr. 1979).
18. Oliver Williamson, *Commentary on Political Economy of Antitrust* in Robert Tollison (ed.), POLITICAL ECONOMY OF ANTITRUST, discussion at n. 15 (1981).
19. Y. Brozen, *Competition, Efficiency, and Antitrust,* 3 JOURNAL OF WORLD TRADE LAW 659 (Nov. 1969). Reprinted in Brozen, THE COMPETITIVE ECONOMY: SELECTED READINGS 6 (1975).

Index

Index

A

Accounting bias, 229–30, 237–38
  in measured profit rates, 258ff.
Acquisitions, by conglomerates,
  336–38
Adams, Walter, quoted, 97, 219
Administered-price theory, 188–92
Advertising, 109, 117
  as a barrier to entry, 159–60
  charged with creating or
    contributing to monopoly
    power, 247–50
  collusion in, 254–55
  and concentration, 266–73
  and entry, 253–54, 261–65
  entry-barrier view of, 250–54
  and hazards associated with
    products, 249–50
  as an investment, 250
  as a low-cost means to an end,
    273–74
  misrepresentation in, 248–49
  new economics of, 247–50
  and number of firms in an
    industry, 38

  and prices, 265–66
  and profits, 254–60
  provision of information through,
    248–50
  and social purpose, 246–47
"Aggregate concentration," 12–14,
  309ff., 345, 359, 403
  attempts to picture, 315–19
  data on 50 and 100 largest
    corporations, 312–14
Agricultural Adjustment Act, 7
Airline industry, 168–69
Airline Pilots' Association, a
  monopoly, 225, 243, 245*n*.35
Alaska, effect on tax policies of, on
  oil production, 229
Alcoa, 29, 30, 46, 48, 365, 366, 404
  effect of decision in case of, 398
  Judge Hand's decision in case of,
    277, 278, 279
Allen, Bruce, 74
Aluminum, 46, 47
Aluminum industry, 29–30, 52,
  278
American Airlines, 169
American Brands, 356

411

American Can Company, 83–84, 119, 215, 322

American Motors, 227

American Pharmacists Association, 325

American Strawboard, 57, 216

American Sugar Refining Company 57, 214–15, 322, 364

American Telephone & Telegraph Company (ATT), 4, 19

American Tobacco Company, 19, 20, 215, 395–96

  dissolution of, 402

  v. United States, 177–79

American Woolen Company, 319

American Writing Paper Company, 216

Anheuser Busch, 367

Antitrust Division, 13

  merger dissolution cases of, 404

  proper focus of efforts of, 9–10, 405–407

Antitrust doctrines, 333, 334, 335–36, 338

conflict within present, 404

Antitrust laws

  of Canada, 371

  in France, 372–73

  in Germany, 371–72

  in Italy, 373

  in Japan, 373–75

  original aims of U.S., 395

  perversion of, by market concentration doctrine, 48

  Supreme Court interpretation of, 364–67

  in United Kingdom, 375–76

Archibald, G. C., quoted, 143n.1

Areeda, P., and Turner, D. F., quoted, 163

Argentina, 53, 170

Armour and Company, 41

Asch, P., and Marcus, M., quoted, 202

Asch, P., and Seneca, J. J., quoted, 152, 154, 207

Asquith, K. Paul, 336, 337, 348n.28, 352, 401

Assets, share of all material, held by 200 industrials, 314

Atack, Jeremy; Bateman, Fred; and Weiss, Thomas, profitability data of, 240–41

Automobile industry, 67, 69–70, 118, 162

  and measurement of market concentration, 52–53

  risk in, 123–24

Automobile manufactures, antitrust case against, 3–4

Avon Products, 258

Ayanian, Robert, 258

B

Bain, Joe S., 25, 193, 194, 197, 253, 262, 267, 295

  hypothesis of, 301

  quoted, 98

Balance of payments, U.S., 75–79

Banfield, Edward, quoted, 323

Banking industry, 164, 182n.9, 361

Barrier(s) to entry, 247, 259

  Kaysen and Turner on, 387–88

Baumol, William, quoted, 137

Baxter, William, 389

Beatrice Foods, 379

Beer industry, *see* Brewing industry

Bell, Attorney General Griffin, 283–84

Berle, A. A., Jr., and Means, Gardiner, 1, 22, 309, 312, 403

Bethlehem Steel, 368

Bigness, and political power, 323–27

Birdzell, L. E., 332

  quoted, 326, 346

Blair, John, quoted, 161, 162, 180

Bloch, Harry, 258–59

Bock, Betty, and Farkas, Jack, quoted, 70, 72, 73

Bodoff, Jean, 390

Bohi, Douglas R., and Russell, Milton, quoted, 323–24
Bombardier, Inc., 54
Bork, Robert, 140, 392
  objections of, to deconcentration, 397
  quoted, 19, 389
Bowater (British paper company), 378
Bowman, Ward, 392
Brand names, 247, 248
"Brand proliferation," 279, 283
Brewing industry, 39–40, 52, 92, 96, 101, 117, 118, 218–19, 366–67, 399
  concentration today in, 17
  tacit collusion charged to, 180–81
British Steel Corporation, 364, 368
Brown & Williamson, 4, 20
Budd Company, 54
Bureau of the Census, concentration measurements by, 48–50
Business Roundtable, 27
Business Week, quoted, 69
Buzzell, R. D., and Nourse, R. E., 279–80

C

Camel cigarettes, 20, 177
Canada, antitrust policies of, 371
Capital
  costs of raising, 82–83
  unrecorded intangible, 237–38
Capital formation, 14n.1
Capital intensity
  and concentration, 107, 109
  and number of firms in an industry, 38
Carrefour (French discount store chain), 69
Cartel(s)
  cheating and entry weaknesses of, 148
  European, 172–73

international, 169–73
OPEC, 228
restriction of industry output by, 182n.10
sugar, 170–72
unstudied, 243
U.S. government-sponsored, 225
Cartelization, 152–53, 228
Carter, John R., 203–204
Cavaleri, Marie, 80, 81
Celanese Corporation, 31
Cellophane, 47–48
Census Bureau, admission of inadequacy of classification system, 52
Centralization, in sugar refining industry, 38–39
Chamberlin, Edward, 251
  influence of, 174
  quoted, 135–36, 137, 252
Chesterfield cigarettes, 20, 177, 179
Chicago, 132
Chrysler Corporation, 69, 123, 226, 318, 323
Cigarette industry, 19–20, 21, 177–79
Civil Aeronautics Board (CAB), 132, 154, 168
Clark, J. B., quoted, 186, 392–93
Clark, J. B., and Clark, J. M., quoted, 186–87
Clark, J. M., quoted, 224n.56
Clarkson, Kenneth, 238
Clayton Anti-Trust Act, 96
  Celler–Kefauver Amendment to, 364–65, 385n.37
Clorox Company, divested from Procter & Gamble, 246
Collusion
  agreements for, 149
  alleged instances of, 177–80
  arguments supporting theory of tacit, 149–50
  assessment of efforts to substantiate charges of tacit, 181

Collusion (*cont.*)
"brand proliferation" and, 283
and concentration–profit correlation, 197–203
economic factors bearing on likelihood of, 150–63
economics of tacit, 173–77
essential ingredients in, 164
examples of explicit, 163–69
expected evidences of successful tacit, 151
experience abroad on, 169–73
Fellner's view on tacit and express, 175
horizontal mergers and, 401
parallel pricing and, 176
and profitability, 301, 398
proper antitrust target, 9–10
sanctioned by exemptions from antitrust law, 183*n*.35
tacit, 147–81, 277
tacit and explicit, 131–32, 135–36, 140, 141, 142
technological change and, 156–57
see also Price fixing
Comanor, William S., quoted, 312
Comanor, William S., and Wilson, Thomas A., 255
quoted, 272
Communications industries, 23
Competition, 101, 141, 204, 217, 366
clashing views on, 20–22
defined by Winston, 239
"dominant firm" and, 396–97
effect of, on concentration, 98–101, 131
not a function of the number of firms selling, 219
indicators of, in concentrated industries, 290
in manufacturing economy today, 242
and shifting equilibrium structure, 101–102
Winston's test of, applied, 240
Computers industry, 28–29

Concentrated industries, 242, 386
competition present in, 290
efficiency of leading firms the cause of, 204
fail to conform to any single image of oligopoly, 303
little evidence of lack of competition in, 303
market power of leading firms in, 186–219
and prices in inflation, 75
productivity and prices within 63–70
and profitability, 233
Stigler's 1963 classification of, 391
wage rates in, 60–63
Concentrated Industries Act, proposed, 388, 389
Concentration, 7, 8, 175, 290–95
advantages and benefits of, 56–86
and advertising, 266–73
antitrust aim at reducing, 395–99
became synonymous with collusion, 187–88
Bell's recommendation to outlaw high, 283–84
capital intensity and, 107, 109
as cause of shared monopoly, 277ff.
clashing views on, 21–22
cycle of, following innovation, 27–28
deconcentration as a U.S. policy examined, 382–83
degree of, in U.S. industry, 22–26
determinants of, 91–124
difficulties within Census Bureau's figures on, 52–53
of diffused industries, 38–41
"economic," two meanings of, 359
of economic power, 311
ECSC Treaty of Paris and, 368–69
effect of competition on, 98–101
effect of high industry profitability on, 105–10

effect of intra-industry profitability on, 102, 104–105
effects of reduced transport costs on, 42
efficiency leads to, 398
entry barriers as an influence on, 114–16
equivalence of collusion and high, examined, 284–87
European policy toward, 367–70
experience as factor leading to high, 80, 82
of 50 largest nonfinancial corporations, 312
foreign attitudes toward, 4–6
horizontal mergers and, 399–401
industry trends in, 26–27
and inflation, 75
influence of distribution on, 116–18
and international competitiveness, 75–79
Japanese law and, 374–75
market, 335, 359
meaning of declining, in some industries, 290–91
measurement of, 48–53, 54n.8
not to be confused with monopoly, 219
in other industrialized countries, 382
persistence of, 217, 399–400
poor measure of monopoly power, 273
primary reason for, 56–57
and productivity, 208
and profit cycle, 32–33
and profits, 192–208
public policy prescriptions for, 3–4
reasons for decline in, 296, 301
reasons for high, summarized, 118–19
risk and, 119–24
risk of loss of efficiency in preventing trend toward, 285
and R & D, 84–86

U.S. and foreign policies toward, 359–83
in U.S. industry, 19–43
views of Shepherd on, 92
and wage earners, 60–63
wage rates and, 110–14
wrong object of focus in antitrust activities, 405
see also Aggregate concentration
Concentration–collusion doctrine, 130–43
Concentration–collusion theory, 253
Concentration–monopoly hypothesis, 235
Concentration–profit correlation, 147
examined, 193–206
negative correlation, 206–208
Concentration ratios, 25, 26, 92, 110
centripetal tendency of, 96–98, 291, 293, 307n.35
determination of, 48–50
problems affecting, 51–54
Conglomerate mergers, 330–46
efficiency of, 354–56, 357
and entrenchment, 334–35
as examples of diversification, 346n.1
and foreclosure of acquisitions, 339–42
merger wave of, in 1960s, 352–54
motives behind acquisitions by, 336–38
and political power, 326–27
and predatory pricing, 330–32
and reciprocal dealings, 333–34
see also Mergers
Conspiracy, see Collusion
Consumer loyalties, 259
Consumers, advertising as supplier of information to, 248–50
Continental Can Company, 370
Cordage manufacturing industry, price-fixing conspiracy in, 167–68

Corporations
  growth in number of, 344, 345
  large, 3–6
  largest (50, 100, 200), trends in
    aggregate concentration of,
    314–20
  political power of giant, 323–27
  reason for forming large, 382
  restrictions imposed on growth of
    U.S., 379
  top 200, 343, 346n.1
  use of exclusionary devices by,
    405
Cotton Duck Manufacturers
    Association, 153
Cotton textile industry, 31–32
Cournot, Augustin, 133, 134
Crown Zellerbach, 376
Cuba, in sugar conspiracy, 170–71

D

Deconcentration, 86, 382–83, 396
  Bork's objections to, 397
  key argument for, 51
  revised opinions of earlier
    advocates of, 386–93
Delorean, John Z., 123
Demsetz, Harold, 80, 139, 158–59,
    203, 286
  quoted, 100–101, 124n.14, 164,
    202
  study of advertising-to-sales ratios
    by, 259–60
Denmark, cartels in, 172
Dewing, Arthur, quoted, 152–53,
    211
Diesel locomotive industry, 162
Director, Aaron, 392
Director, Aaron, and Levi, Edward,
    quoted, 279
Distribution, influence of, on
    concentration, 116–18
Diversification, geographic, 83–84
Domestic commercial aviation, 164
Dominant-firm doctrine, 209

Drug retailing, 69
Duke, James B., 19
Dunlop–Pirelli (British–Italian
    rubber company), 370, 378
Dunning, John H., and Pearce, R.
    B., quoted, 376
Duopoly theory, 133, 134
duPont, E. I. & Company, 30, 67,
    278, 279, 361, 376, 379
  cellophane antitrust suit of, 47–
    48
  cellophane case doctrine, 404
  effect of decision in case of, 398–
    99

E

Eads, George, quoted, 168–69
Eastman Kodak Company, 201
Economist, The, quoted, 360
Economy, "planned," of Galbraith,
    226–27
Edwards, Corwin, quoted, 334
Efficiency, 382, 401
  conglomerate mergers and, 350–
    57
  in drug retailing, 69
  leads to concentration, 398
  primary reason for concentration,
    56–57
  in profit-seeking enterprises, 65
  sources of conglomerate, 354–56
  and survival, 217
Electrical equipment industry,
    conspiracy of, 166–67
Ellert, James, 197
Elzinga, Kenneth, 164
Engels, Friedrich, 97
"Entrenchment" doctrine, 334–35
Entry
  as additional capacity, 221n.21
  advertising and, 261–65
  de novo, 335, 338, 339, 340–41,
    342
  effect on, of foreclosing
    acquisitions, 339–41

increased by mergers, 342–45
limitations on, 225
restricted, 164
Entry barrier(s), 131
advertising as an, 159–60
appropriate arena for antitrust action, 406
and concentration, 114–16
influence of, on collusion, 158–64
Epstein, Edward, 323
European Coal and Steel Community (ECSC), 367–70
Treaty of Paris of, 368–69
European Economic Community (EEC), 360, 367–70, 379
antitrust approach of, 370
market-sharing in, 370, 384n.23
Treaty of Rome of, 370
Experience, as factor leading to high concentration, 80, 82
Exxon, 320–21, 348n.26

protected noncompetitive elements in cement industry, 403
quoted on auto industry, 123
study by, of advertising and profitability, 258–59
Federal Trade Commission Act, 56
Fellner, William, quoted, 174–75
Ferguson, James M., 262, 269
Firestone Tire & Rubber Company, 378
Fisher, Franklin, 47
Fisher Body Company, 138
Fixed costs, as deterrent to entry, 155
Fog, Bjarke, quoted, 172–73
Ford, Henry, 67, 226
Ford Motor Company, 69, 123, 124, 226, 322
France, antitrust laws in, 372–73
Fuchs, Victor, conglomerate efficiency studies of, 352–53

F

Fairless, Benjamin, quoted, 9
Fama, Eugene F., and Laffer, Arthur B., quoted, 140
Farben, I. G. (German company), 372
Federal Glass Company, 342–43
Federal Trade Commission (FTC), 1, 3–4, 13, 14, 65–66, 130
actions of, regarding shared monopoly, 277ff.
aversion of, to firm size, 361
Bureau of Economics of, quoted, 332, 335, 336, 367
figures of, on domestic manufacturing assets, 315
and Procter & Gamble, 246
profit and concentration data of, 194–97
in proposed Lancaster Colony acquisition, 342–43

G

Galbraith, John Kenneth, 21, 230
planned economy views of, 226–27
Geneen, Harold, quoted, 356
General Artificial Silk Company, 30
General Electric, 138
General Motors Corporation, 15n.9, 69, 84, 119, 123, 124, 139, 161–62, 226
alleged monopolization of buses by, 283
General Telephone and Electronics, 315
George, K. D., 106
Germany, 76
antitrust laws in, 371–72
in sugar pricing conspiracy, 171
Goodrich, B. F., 378
Gort, Michael, 106, 340
quoted, 312, 314

Grace, W. R., Company, 356
Great Atlantic & Pacific Tea Co., 15*n*.9
Greer, Douglas, 269
quoted, 114
Growth, and restraints imposed on large firms, 13–14
Gulf & Western, 318
Gunpowder Trade Association, 98–99

H

Hall, Charles, 29
Hallinan, Charles T., quoted, 172
Hand, Judge Learned, 46, 47, 277, 278, 279, 365, 398
Harlin, Justice John Marshall, opinion of, in Clorox case, quoted, 403
Hawker Siddeley, Ltd., 54
Hoar, Senator George F., 56, 396
quoted, 399
Hoechst (German chemical company), 5, 361, 376
Hormel (food company), 41
Horowitz, Ann and Ira, quoted, 180
Household laundry equipment industry, 92, 117
Household vacuum cleaner industry, 50
Hunter, Alex, quoted, 208

I

Imports, 312, 314
Industrial Fibre Corporation, 31
Industries
concentrated, and profits, 10–11
concentration in diffused, 38–41
definition of, by Bureau of Census, 48–50
reasons for emergence of concentrated, 11–12
unconcentrated, 100–101, 105

Industry
aggregate concentration trends in, 26–27
concentration in American, 19–43
concentration ratios for U.S. manufacturing, 25, 50
criteria of oligopolistic, set by Neal's task force, 227
dynamism of U.S., 97
market structures of, 100–101
structure of, a cause not a result, 118–19
U.S. and foreign policies toward, 359–83
Inflation, 7
and concentration, 74
Inland Steel, 67
Innovation, effect on, if acquisitions are foreclosed, 341–42
Intercity transportation market, 48–49
International Business Machines (IBM), 4, 5, 28–29
International Harvester, 325
International Paper Company, 57, 216
International Sugar Agreement, 171
Interstate Commerce Commission (ICC), 131, 154, 164
rate floors of, 225
Inventory, 109
Iowa Beef Processors, 41
Italy, antitrust laws in, 373

J

Japan, 4–5, 76
antitrust laws in, 373–75
Fair Trade Commission in, 374, 375
Ministry of International Trade and Industry (MITI), 374, 375
public policy toward concentration, 360
in sugar-pricing collusion, 171
and world steel market, 176

Jet engine industry, 162
Jones, Eliot, quoted, 187

K

Kaiser Aluminum & Chemical
  Company, 30
Kaldor, Nicholas, 266
Kamerschen, David, 285, 286, 287,
  294, 295
  quoted, 331
Kaun, David, 111
Kaysen, Carl
  quoted, 311
  Senate hearing testimony of, 386–
  87
Kaysen, Carl, and Turner, Donald,
  Antitrust Policy, 386, 387–88
Kefauver Committee, 325
Keithahn, Charles, quoted, 218–19
Kettering, Charles, 138
Keynes, J. M., quoted, 181
Kwoka, John E., Jr., "price-cost"
  views of, examined, 204–206

L

Labor unions, 325, 327
Lancaster Colony, 342–43
Landon, J. H., 58
Lev, Baruch, quoted, 203
Lewis, Gregg, quoted, 133
Liebeler, Wesley, 333
  quoted, 160
Liggett & Myers, 19, 20, 177, 179
Ling–Temco–Voight, 318, 356
Liquor industry, advertising in,
  261–62
Livermore, Shaw, quoted, 212
Lockheed Aircraft, 120, 140
Locomotives industry, 28, 53–54
Lorie, James H., and Halpern, Paul,
  quoted, 319, 331
Lorillard, P. (tobacco company), 19,
  20

Lucky Strike cigarettes, 20, 177,
  179
Lumber production industry, 114
Lustgarten, Steven, 39, 57, 65, 74,
  85, 208
Lustgarten, Steven, and
  Mendelowitz, Alan, 188
Lynk, William, study of advertising
  by, 262–65

M

MacAvoy, Paul, 171, 389
Machlup, Fritz, 174
  quoted, 230
Mack Truck Company, 140
Mansfield, Edwin, 206
  quoted, 106, 114, 156–57
Marblehead Lime Company, 278
Market(s)
  ability of a business to control,
  227
  dynamics in an oligopoly, 139
  dynamism of U.S., 43
  rivalry within, 397
  simple structural test for
  categorizing, 227–28
  view of, by pre-1930s economists,
  6
  warns against attempts to
  monopolize, 219
Marketability, of firms, 342
Market concentration, and census
  concentration, 51–54
Market-concentration doctrine, 48,
  209
Market power, in concentrated
  industries, 186–219
Market share(s), 106, 107, 365
  concentration–collusion doctrine
  and, 131
  determination of, in courts, 46–48
Market structures, 159
Markham, Jesse, 166
  quoted, 16, 179, 314, 318, 341
Marx, Karl, 97

Matsushita Electric Industrial, 361
Maxwell Motor Company, 124
Mayer, Oscar (meat packing
    company), 41
McCloskey, Donald, quoted, 39
McCracken, Paul, and Moore,
    Thomas, quoted, 80
McDonnell Douglas, 140
McGee, John S., 392
    quoted, 70, 134–35, 182n.16,
    396
McKie, James W., quoted, 85, 141
Means, Gardiner, 220n.10
    "administered price" hypothesis
    of, examined, 188–92
Meat packing industry, 15n.9, 38,
    40–41, 96
Mergers, 76, 77, 330–46
    and aggregate concentration,
    345–46
    in Canada, 371
    conglomerate, 13, 403–404
    during 1890s, 209, 217
    effect on entry of, 342–45
    effects of restraints on horizontal,
    399–402
    and efficiency, 350–57
    European view of, 360
    focus of Antitrust Division and
    FTC regarding, 404
    horizontal, 399–402
    in Japan, 374–75
    motives behind conglomerate
    acquisitions, 336–38
    no economic case against, 402–
    403
    profitability of those of 1890s,
    212–14
    in United Kingdom, 375–76
    vertical, 402
    wave of, 1898–1901, 91, 119,
    239; in 1960s, 352–53
Metals industry, 361
    as treated by Bureau of Census,
    49
Metzenbaum, Senator Howard, 345
    quoted, 350

Michelin (French rubber company),
    378
Miller, Richard, quoted, 192
Misrepresentation, 248
Mobil Oil Company, 356
Monopolization, 211
    tests for, 229–30
Monopoly, 56, 101, 135, 225, 251,
    272, 278, 395–96, 399
    concentration of sales as evidence
    of, 48
    current discussions of, 225–26
    flaw in conventional theory of,
    139–40
    link with advertising assessed,
    274
    a neglected problem in non-
    manufacturing areas, 242–43
    not to be confused with
    concentration, 219
    partial, 398
    share of domestic production poor
    index to, 242–43
    "shared," 130, 277, 279
    tests for, 229–30
    of U.S. manufacturing markets,
    225–43
Monopoly pricing, 133, 134
Montgomery Ward, 226, 356
Motor vehicle industry, 26
Mueller, Dennis, quoted, 350
Mueller, Willard, 72, 73
    quoted, 114
Multinational corporations, and
    political power, 327

N

National Biscuit Company, excerpt
    from 1901 annual report of,
    217–18
National Druggists Association, 325
National Highway Traffic Safety
    Commission, 325
National Industrial Conference
    Board, 65

National Industrial Recovery Act, 7
Nationalization, of firms, 364
National Science Foundation, quoted, 84
National Steel, 67
Neal, Phil, 227; *see also* White House Task Force
Nelson, Ralph, quoted, 60
Nelson, Richard R., quoted, 354–55
Nestlé (Swiss food manufacturer), 378, 382
Nippon Steel, 5, 54, 361, 374, 376
Norfolk & Western Railroad, 138
Northern Securities, 364
North Sea oil, restraint on exploration in British sector of, 229
Nutter, Warren, 97

O

Occidental Petroleum, and Mead acquisition, 334
Oil industry
and cartels, 228–29
under mandatory import quota program, 323–24
Old Gold cigarettes, 20
Oligopolization, 239, 240
Oligopoly, 92, 102, 285, 392
concentrated industries fail to conform to images of, 303
criteria of, 227
dynamics in locomotive, 139
and successful explicit collusion, 131
in the U.S. economy, 21
Oligopoly theory(ies), 138, 206
classical, 174
contribution of, 132–35
digopoly model of, 135–37
postulates of, 284–87
speculative nature of, 142–43
Organization of Petroleum Exporting Countries (OPEC), success of, 228–29, 317

P

Pacific Southwest Air, 67, 69
Packard Motor Company, 124
Pagoulatos, E., and Sorenson, R., 79
Paper industry, 215–16
Pashigian, Richard, 355
Passenger transportation industries, 25
Pavitt, K., and Wald, S., 85–86
Peltzman, Sam, 57, 208, 286, quoted, 197
Petro, Sylvester, quoted, 13
Petroleum exploration industry, risk in, 20–23
Petroleum refining industry, 97–98, 187
Peugeot–Citroen, 361, 373, 382
Pharmaceutical industry, 325
high accounting return in, 238–39
Philip Morris (cigarette company), 20
Philips (Dutch electronics company), 382
Phlips, Louis, quoted, 63
Phonograph records industry, 96
Pillsbury–Fox Deluxe Foods, merger of, 343
Pitofsky, Robert, quoted, 343
Pittsburgh Reduction Company, 29, 30
Plummer, Alfred, 169
quoted, 170, 171
Political power, bigness and, 323–27
Posner, Richard A., 284, 366
on conditions favorable to collusion, 305n.15
on profits of smaller firms upon formation of a cartel, 305n.17
quoted, 48, 102, 285, 289, 325, 326–27, 387–88
Potential entrant doctrine, 335–41
Predatory pricing, 163, 330–32, 405

Presidential Task Force on
Productivity and Competition,
389, 392, 400
quoted, 332
Price fixing, 151–56, 164, 169
conspiracies of, 165–73
Price rigidity, in concentrated
industries, 188–92
Prices
advertising and, 265–66
in concentrated industries in
inflation, 75
lower, with higher profits, 65, 67,
69–70
Pricing
parallel, 176
predatory, 163
Primary Product Specialization
Ratio, 50
Procter & Gamble, 246
and its Clorox case, 403, 404
Product differentiation, 160–62
Production, multi-product and
multi-brand, 84
Productivity, 81
and concentrated industries, 72–
74
increases with increasing
concentration, 74–75
relation of, to concentration, 208
Profit
accounting rates of, unreliable
indices, 230
rate of, in major manufacturing
industries, 240–42
Profitability, 43, 116
above-average, sustained, 229–
30
concentration and, 391
effect of high industry
concentration on, 105–10
effect of intra-industry, 102, 104–
105
and greater concentration, 33
of monopolizing, 209–14
and number of firms in an
industry, 38

rising number of firms in an
industry an index of, 301
Profits
and advertising, 254–60
in concentrated industries, 10–11
and concentration, 192–208
as consequences of superior
performance, 192
higher, with lower prices, 65, 67,
69–70
return on net worth in leading
manufacturing corporations,
1948 and 1956, 231–32; 1966
and 1979, 234–35
shift on rate-of-return ranks, 231–
39
and theorizing about
concentration, 8–9
Profits–concentration correlation
examined, 193–206
negative correlation, 206–208
Pryor, F. L., 25
quoted, 44n.6
Public Utility Holding Company Act
of 1935, 311

Q

Qualls, David, 188, 237
quoted, 189

R

Railroad brotherhoods, 225
Railroad industry, 131, 164
Rayon fiber industry, 30–31
tacit collusion charged to, 179–80
Ready-to-eat cereal industry, 26,
130, 277, 279–83
Reciprocity, within conglomerates,
333–34
Reed, Justice Stanley F., 398–99
Reed International (British paper
company), 378
Regression, 290–95

Regulation, of industry, 324
Renault (French auto company), 382
Republic Iron & Steel, 211
Research and development, 84–86, 201, 238
Restraint of trade, 395
Reynolds, R. J. (tobacco company), 19, 20, 30, 177
Reynolds International Pen Company, 33
Reynolds Metals, 30
Risk
  in automobile industry, 123–24
  and concentration, 119–24
  in petroleum exploration, 120–23
Robinson, Joan, quoted, 251–52
Royal Commission on Corporate Concentration, quoted, 371
Royal Dutch Petroleum, 382
Russia, 170

S

Sanitary Potters' Association, 165–66
Sanborn Map Company, 227
Scherer, F. M., 125n.7, 315
  quoted, 5–6, 117
Schumpeter, Joseph, 15n.8, 138
Schwartzman, David, quoted, 136–37, 389–90
Scitovsky, Tibor, quoted, 253
Sears, Roebuck & Company, 226
Securities and Exchange Commission, study of costs of raising capital by, 82
Shenefield, John, 312
  quoted, 311
Shepherd, W. G., 285, 286, 287
  predictions of, in market power of dominant firms, 212–14
  quoted, 356–57
  views of, on concentration, 92
Shepherd–Kamerschen tests, replicated, 287–90

Sherman, Senator John, 56
Sherman Anti-Trust Act, 56, 183n.35, 187, 364
  and prevention of concentration, 396
Sherwood, Richard, quoted, 389
Shoe industry, 75
Simons, Henry, quoted, 390
Slater, John, 31
Smoot–Hawley Tariff of 1930, 7
Standard Industrial Classification Code (SIC), 23, 28
  problems of, 51–53
Standard Oil Company, 57, 214, 392, 395–96, 402
Steam locomotive industry, 138–39
Steel industry, 176, 379
  consolidation within, 211
  in Europe, 368–70
Steiner, Robert, 266
Stigler, George G., 105–106, 177, 193, 194, 208, 228, 229, 296
  collusive-price-umbrella hypothesis of, 287, 288, 289, 290, 301, 302
  evolution of thinking of, about concentration, 390–92
  quoted, 51, 53, 132, 134, 144n.10, 145n.23, 181, 187, 211–12, 232, 324
  on unlikelihood of successful collusion, 306n.31
Stigler, G. G., and Kendall, James, quoted, 189
Stillman, Robert, examination of horizontal mergers by, 400–401
Stock brokerage industry, 119
Stocking, G. W., and Watkins, M. W., quoted, 148
St. Regis Paper Company, 378
Structure–conduct–performance paradigm, 8
Sugar refining industry, 38–39, 51
  conspiracy in, 170–71
  International Sugar Agreement (1931), 171
Sullivan, T. G., 80, 81, 106

Sultan, Ralph G. M., 137
Supreme Court, duPont cellophane
    case decision of, 47–48
Swift & Company, 40

T

Tariffs, 225
Task Force on Antitrust Policy, *see*
    White House Task Force
Teamsters Union, a monopoly, 225
Television, and advertising, 262–65
Telser, Lester, 33, 73, 206, 207,
    237, 261, 262, 392
    quoted, 36, 128n.40, 144n.8,
    178–79
Tennant, Richard, 178
Tennessee Valley Authority (TVA),
    225
Textile industry, 75
Third World, 137, 138
Thyssen (German steel company),
    368, 372
Tobacco industry, 111
Transportation
    costs and collusion, 156–57
    effect of reduced costs of, 42
Trans World Airlines, 169
Trenton Potteries Company, 165
Tubize Artificial Silk, 31
Turner, Donald, 343
    quoted, 278, 331–32, 342
    Senate hearing testimony of, 386,
    387
Turner, Donald, and Areeda, Phillip,
    387, 388
Twentieth Century Fund, 58
Typewriter industry, 54

U

Unilever, 382
Union Bag Machine Company, 215
Union Paper Company, 216
United Airlines, 169

United Kingdom, antitrust laws in,
    375–76
United Shoe Machinery, 48, 99–
    100, 365
United States, public policy about
    corporate growth in, 13, 14
United States Leather (company),
    319
U.S. Bureau of Labor Statistics, 60
U.S. Postal Service, 225
U.S. Steel, 5, 16n.14, 91–92, 107–
    108, 202, 211, 212–14,
    222n.34, 376
Utility industries, 4

V

Vatter, Harold, quoted, 42
Vernon, J. M., and Nourse, R. E.,
    255–58
Viscose Company, 30, 31
Voigt, Fritz, 155, 173
Volkswagen, 162

W

Wage earners, in concentrated
    industries, 60–63
Wage rates, 70–72
    and concentration, 110–14
Wages, federal minimum, 111
Wallpaper manufacturing industry,
    216
Warren, Chief Justice Earl, dissent
    of, in duPont case, 47
Webbink, Douglas, 36
Weiss, Leonard W., 258
    change of views of, on
    concentration, 141–42
    quoted, 74, 206, 390
Western Electric, 15n.9, 361
Weston, J. Fred, 53, 208
    quoted, 77, 79
Weston, J. F., and Mansinghka, S.
    K., 340

Wheat Agreement of 1933, 169
White House Task Force on
    Antitrust Policy (Neal Task
    Force), 9, 193–94, 216–17,
    227, 228, 231, 388, 389, 392
Whitney, S., quoted, 215–16
Whittaker Corporation, 356

Wilcox, Clair, quoted, 22
Winston, Ambrose P., quoted, 40,
    239
Woodward Governor (company),
    227
Worcester, Dean, quoted, 137–38
Word processors, 33

About the Author

Yale Brozen, Professor of Business Economics in the Graduate School of Business of the University of Chicago, is an internationally known economist who has lectured and published in England, Canada, Japan, Belgium, Italy, Switzerland, Argentina, Brazil, Peru, and Venezuela. Scholarly articles by him have been reprinted frequently in collections, inserted in the *Congressional Record,* and translated into French, Italian, Spanish, Portuguese, and Japanese. He is the author of *Advertising and Society* (1974), *The Competitive Economy* 1975, and *Textbook for Economics* (1948).

Professor Brozen has served as a consultant to a number of major coporations, including General Motors, American Telephone and Telegraph, and the Kellogg Company; to various governmental agencies, including the Antitrust Division of the U.S. Department of Justice, the National Science Foundation, and the President's Materials Policy Commission; and to a number of trade associations and foundations. At the University of Chicago he directs the Program in Applied Economics. He is an Adjunct Scholar at the American Enterprise Institute for Public Policy Research.

PROGRAM FOR STUDIES OF
THE MODERN CORPORATION
Graduate School of Business, Columbia University

PUBLICATIONS

———

FRANCIS JOSEPH AGUILAR
  Scanning the Business Environment

MELVIN ANSHEN
  Corporate Strategies for Social Performance

MELVIN ANSHEN, *editor*
  Managing the Socially Responsible Corporation

HERMAN W. BEVIS
  Corporate Financial Reporting in a Competitive Economy

COURTNEY C. BROWN
  Beyond the Bottom Line

COURTNEY C. BROWN
  Putting the Corporate Board to Work

COURTNEY C. BROWN, *editor*
  World Business: Promise and Problems

YALE BROZEN
  Concentration, Mergers, and Public Policy

NEIL W. CHAMBERLAIN
  Social Strategy and Corporate Structure

CHARLES DE HOGHTON, *editor*
  The Company: Law, Structure, and Reform

RICHARD EELLS
  The Corporation and the Arts

RICHARD EELLS
  The Political Crisis of the Enterprise System

RICHARD EELLS, *editor*
  International Business Philanthropy

RICHARD EELLS and CLARENCE WALTON, *editors*
  Man in the City of the Future

JAMES C. EMERY
  Organizational Planning and Control Systems: Theory and Technology

ALBERT S. GLICKMAN, CLIFFORD P. HAHN, EDWIN A. FLEISHMAN, and BRENT BAXTER
Top Management Development and Succession: An Exploratory Study

NEIL H. JACOBY
Corporate Power and Social Responsibility

NEIL H. JACOBY
Multinational Oil: A Study in Industrial Dynamics

NEIL H. JACOBY, PETER NEHEMKIS, and RICHARD EELLS
Bribery and Extortion in World Business: A Study of Corporate Political Payments Abroad

JAY W. LORSCH
Product Innovation and Organization

IRA M. MILLSTEIN and SALEM M. KATSH
The Limits of Corporate Power: Existing Constraints on the Exercise of Corporate Discretion

KENNETH G. PATRICK
Perpetual Jeopardy—The Texas Gulf Sulphur Affair: A Chronicle of Achievement and Misadventure

KENNETH G. PATRICK and RICHARD EELLS
Education and the Business Dollar

IRVING PFEFFER, *editor*
The Financing of Small Business: A Current Assessment

STANLEY SALMEN
Duties of Administrators in Higher Education

GUNNAR K. SLETMO and ERNEST W. WILLIAMS, JR.
Liner Conferences in the Container Age: U.S. Policy at Sea

GEORGE A. STEINER
Top Management Planning

GEORGE A. STEINER and WILLIAM G. RYAN
Industrial Project Management

GEORGE A. STEINER and WARREN M. CANNON, *editors*
Multinational Corporate Planning

GUS TYLER
The Political Imperative: The Corporate Character of Unions

CLARENCE WALTON and RICHARD EELLS, *editors*
The Business System: Readings in Ideas and Concepts

The colophon for this book as for the other books of the Program for Studies of the Modern Corporation was created by Theodore Roszak.

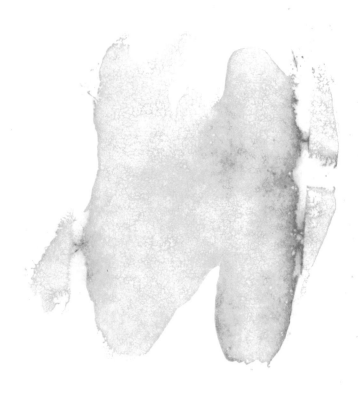